Back
from the Front

Back from the Front

Combat Trauma, Love, and the Family

Aphrodite Matsakis, Ph.D.

Sidran Institute Press
Baltimore, Maryland

Cover photo by Air Force Master Sgt. Patrick J. Cashin. Photo Courtesy of U.S. Army. Use of this photograph does not constitute approval or endorsement by the U.S. Army.

Parts of this book have been adapted from *Vietnam Wives: Facing the Challenges of Life with Veterans Suffering Post-Traumatic Stress,* 2nd Edition, by Aphrodite Matsakis (Baltimore: Sidran Institute Press, 1996).

13   12   11   10   09   08   07   2   3   4   5   6   7   8   9

ISBN: 1-886968-18-7
ISBN-13: 978-1-886968-18-9

LIBRARY OF CONGRESS CATALOGING-IN-PUBLICATION DATA
Matsakis, Aphrodite.
     Back from the front : combat trauma, love, and the family / Aphrodite Matsakis. — 1st ed.
         p. cm.
     Includes bibliographical references and index.
      ISBN 978-1-886968-18-9 (alk. paper)
     1. Veterans—Mental health.   2. Veterans—Family relationships.
3. Post-traumatic stress disorder.   4. War neuroses.   I. Title.
RC550.M38 2007
616.85'212—dc22

                2007001770

Contents

Acknowledgments

This book required the efforts of many gifted and dedicated persons. I am grateful for the creative labors of Mary Lou Kenney and Therese Boyd, whose careful editing of this book contributed greatly to its organization and clarity, and to Peter Valerio, M.A., L.C.P.C., for his many insights into the stresses borne by those who serve in combat zones and by their family members. I would also like to thank Esther Giller and the staff of Sidran Institute Press for their support and assistance, and Maria Christina Herdoiza, Rebecca Lee, K. Houston Matney, Maria Morel, Theodora Scarato, and Steve Steckler for their research and other contributions to this book.

I owe a special debt of gratitude to my psychotherapy clients, the men and women who work or have worked in the military, and to their family members. Without their willingness to share their struggles and pain with me, this book would not have been possible. They have served as models of inspiration in their efforts to bear what, for most people, would be unbearable emotional stress.

*Back
from the Front*

ELIZABETH'S STORY

All I want is even one day without the pain, without the hurt. Maybe I wasn't in the Army, but after being married to a combat veteran for eight years, I have paid my price.

I met my husband two years after he was discharged. Basically, Big Al is a kind and giving person, but there's another side to him, the angry side. But I didn't see this side until after we were married. Big Al had lots of anger, which was directed at everything and everybody, including me. Just a few weeks after the honeymoon, he started going out and not coming home, and he started drinking. He cared about me very deeply, yet he continually ran away from that caring.

I didn't understand what was going on—how he could switch from the good and kind Big Al to the angry one. When he put holes in the wall and had car accidents, I thought it was just the alcohol. But once when he ran into a pole, then went on to hit two or three more objects in the road, I realized that he had a death wish. Yet I never traced it to his combat duty because he never talked about it. We had many problems: sexual problems, economic problems, depression, and loneliness. My husband was a loner. He tended to lose friends easily because he'd refuse to forgive. He withdrew from his parents and began to do poorly at work. At this point, I was starting to become depressed and withdrawn, too. I got sick with migraines and was angry a lot. Yet not being able to count on my husband for very much gave me a drive to succeed at work. Even though I started out a GS-5 secretary in the government without a college degree, I've worked myself up to a supervisory mid-level position and have enjoyed one professional success after another.

I had to succeed at work because I had to pay all the bills. My husband had trouble keeping jobs, and there were always lawyer bills, fines, car wrecks, and other expenses. When Big Al would be out all night, I used to wonder if he was dead or in jail. I hate to admit it, but a part of me used to wish he was dead because we couldn't afford any more lawyer bills and court costs.

Even when he didn't come home at night, the next morning I'd go to work and function as if nothing had happened. I couldn't break, because if I did, where would I be? And what would happen to our three children?

I couldn't break, but I did internalize everything and began to withdraw even more. Besides, most of my friends couldn't cope with my problems. If I'd start talking about Big Al, they'd just tell me to leave him, not understanding that with three children, this is not easy. Also, I am a committed family woman. If Big Al had cancer, I wouldn't have left him. In my view, Big Al had a mental disease, not a physical one, and I was not going to abandon him.

Even when he would call me names, I knew a part of him didn't mean it—that it was somebody else being so nasty, not my Big Al. Besides, leaving Big Al would have felt like defeat and I was a fighter, just like he was. Deep inside, I knew Big Al was a good man and that the only reason he couldn't feel for me was because he couldn't feel for himself. Even when he'd get locked up in jail, he'd be as kind and good to me as could be.

Now when I see my husband not taking care of himself, I know that he has reached the point of depression, and I beg him to go for help. Therapy has helped my husband a great deal, but we still have problems. I have problems, too: mainly pent-up anger from years of always having to be strong and responsible. I'm afraid that if someone would put their arms around me, I would start crying and never stop.

Introduction

To write about the combat veteran is to write about fortitude, dedication, and selflessness and about experiences unfathomable to those who have never known the indescribable horrors of war. To write about you—the soldier's spouse or partner—is to write about another kind of loyalty and perseverance and yet another kind of pain and sadness.

Our culture is quick to laud the sacrifices of the troops—to whom we owe so much. Yet it is often difficult for the general public to fully comprehend, or accept, the emotional and physical toll involved in waging war. The stresses involved in loving someone who has served in a war zone are often minimized as well. Like your partner, you too may have often been misunderstood and insufficiently recognized; your many efforts to be supportive of your partner may have gone unappreciated and unacknowledged.

World War II veterans suffered from high rates of psychiatric breakdown, not only on the battlefield but also upon their return. Yet they were treated like heroes. In contrast, Vietnam veterans were shunned by society. Since they represented a painful episode in our history, they were often rejected. During the war they received bad press, and after the war they were victimized not only by a negative public attitude but also by job discrimination and few government benefits. Many mental health professionals, historians, and social commentators view the ways Vietnam veterans were treated after the war as a national disgrace.[1]

Perhaps our country learned an important lesson from the shameful treatment of Vietnam veterans: to separate the war from the warrior. Since Vietnam, numerous efforts have been made to support the troops, regardless of political positions, and to educate both military personnel and the general public on the possible psychological consequences of combat duty.[2] Nevertheless, the average American remains largely ignorant of how the brutal realties of war can scar even the most courageous soldier. Also, empathy for the soldier's postwar sufferings, when it exists, tends to be time limited. Soldiers generally are expected to "get over" their war experiences relatively quickly. If they can't, then they risk being viewed as morally or psychologically deficient.

Hence, despite the increased regard for combat veterans and increased recognition of combat trauma, the stigma of experiencing signs of combat trauma, such as depression, anxiety, fear, or post-traumatic stress, persists.[3] This stigma can be so strong that even when soldiers are actively encouraged to seek help for combat stress, many are too ashamed to do so. For example, a U.S. Army survey found that about two-thirds of combat soldiers in Iraq and Kuwait who were diagnosed with combat stress failed to seek help for fear of being seen as "weaklings," "mentally unbalanced," or "less competent."[4] Similarly, in 2004, over half of the combat troops in Afghanistan and Iraq who were diagnosed with a mental disorder did not seek help for fear of harming their career, being blamed for their symptoms, or being treated differently by or losing the confidence of their comrades.[5]

Those veterans and soldiers who do have the courage to seek help usually try to keep their help-seeking efforts a secret from all but a trusted few. Perhaps they wish to avoid incidents such as those experienced by John, a Marine with two Purple Hearts. Upon John's return from the Persian Gulf, some of his coworkers began calling him "Shelly Shell Shock" because he would startle easily when he heard a car backfire. Some snuck up behind him or played audiotapes of machine-gun fire. When John would duck for cover, they'd laugh and say things like: "You vets like to blow up buildings, don't you? Are you going to blow up the Empire State Building? If you are, I'll cancel my trip to New York."

On the job, John pretended that this abuse did not bother him, but in my office he wept and wondered how long he could tolerate such mistreatment. He was so terrified of the possibility of losing control of his anger and hurting someone that one day he just walked off the job.

John's wife, Susan, was relieved. She felt it was better that she take on additional work than have her husband land in jail. But John's father called him a "lazy bum," a "quitter," and "half a man" for leaving his job, and John's therapist accused John of being "full of self-pity" and "living in the past." The therapist also accused Susan of "sabotaging" John's therapy. In the therapist's view, most women partners of combat veterans consciously or unconsciously enjoy having control over their veteran. Therefore, John's wife, even if she didn't acknowledge it, wanted her husband to continue having symptoms so that she could feel superior to him and continue to control him.

At the same time, well-intentioned friends and therapists were telling Susan that staying with a veteran who suffered from combat stress meant that she was just as "sick" as he was. Based on pop psychology, they decided that Susan was either a "masochist" who liked to suffer, a "drama queen" with a pathological need to be needed, or a "codependent" who refused to grow up and be her own person.

Only two people seemed to be supportive of John and Susan: Cindy and Paul.

Cindy was active-duty military and, despite the long hours and unpredictable separations, her husband, Paul, was fully supportive of her career. Many of their friends and family members were also proud of Cindy. Yet some of them made snide remarks about Paul being "henpecked" by his "military wife." After Cindy was flown overseas for a combat mission, however, John heard comments such as "You're the man. You should be over there fighting, not her!" and "Listen, you wimp, there's a war going on over there. If Cindy is killed or raped, it'll be your fault for letting her go! If you couldn't stop her from going, you could have at least signed up and gone with her." Other comments were "Get ready, Paul. Cindy's going over there a woman, but she'll come home a man, hard as nails. But don't worry. If she ever beats you up for not having dinner ready on time, I promise not to tell the other guys."

The above examples may seem extreme. Unfortunately, in my experience, they are not uncommon. Just as your partner's agonies may have often been mistakenly seen as signs of personal failure, your dilemmas may have also often been misinterpreted as some form of weakness or psychological deficiency. Keep in mind that the same culture that assaults your partner with unrealistic images of heroes and heroines who can always figure out the "right thing to do" (even in the most impossible situations) and who can bear the heaviest of burdens (without a single complaint) also assaults you, a real person, with images of happy-face people who never age, never weep, and never feel overwhelmed or painfully alone.

In many circles in our society, long-term or severe suffering, no matter how legitimate, receives little respect. People who struggle with economic, medical, or psychological stresses are expected to remain cheerful and optimistic in the face of adversity and keep their despair to themselves. When they cannot make lemonade out of every single lemon life has handed them, often they are made to feel guilty and ashamed. This only further saps their spirits, making it even more difficult for them to recognize or act upon any options that might be available to them.

In contrast, some cultures have widespread acceptance of the fact that life entails not only goodness and joy but misfortune as well. For example, in cultures influenced by Buddhist and Hindu thought, suffering is not seen as a defect of character or a sign of mental illness, but rather as a normal part of life and even a pathway to wisdom and emotional and spiritual growth. People who aren't made to feel ashamed or guilty because they are hurting or unhappy have been found to develop fewer long-term scars from traumatic events. For example, one possible reason that many of the 2004 tsunami victims in Sri Lanka were able to resume functioning as quickly as they did was because of their Buddhist and Hindu philosophies.[6]

This book is about veterans suffering from some of the predictable, often involuntary, psychological and physiological consequences of war and about you, the veteran's spouse or partner—both of you people who have had the courage to bear the many scars that life can deal to people who have been deeply affected by prolonged or severe life stresses. To all of you spouses and partners who think your suffering is unique, I wish to reassure you. You are not alone.

Your suffering is real. And there is help. This book is my small contribution to helping you understand why your family is in such pain and to helping you see what you can do about it. Keep in mind that the turmoil you and your veteran are experiencing can lay the foundation for a stronger, more meaningful relationship and for an improved outlook on life.

As is well known by now, the trauma of war can affect not only the warriors but their spouses, partners, and children as well. In cases where the veteran suffers from extreme forms of combat trauma, he or she is often held together emotionally, socially, and, in some cases, financially by his or her spouse or partner. Often it is you, the veteran's partner or spouse, who helps sustain the veteran during his or her depressed, sad, or anxious times and, if your veteran suffers from posttraumatic stress, through his or her flashbacks and nightmares as well. Perhaps it is you alone who has maintained your veteran's will to live during his or her most anguished moments and who may serve as a buffer between him or her and the world. In some cases, it is also the partners of veterans who serve as scapegoats for the veterans' anger: their anger toward themselves and toward those whom they feel have treated them unjustly.

Typically combat veterans repress their grief and anger and experience these feelings as depression. Some may try to make these emotions and the combat memories that gave birth to these emotions disappear by drowning them in alcohol or drugs or by becoming workaholics. Yet even when taxed by their veterans' emotional turmoil, many partners remain loyal, not only from a sense of duty but from compassion, realizing that the vet's troublesome emotional states and behaviors are not solely due to his or her temperament, but due to the horrors of war. Intuitively, you may have sensed that underneath your vet's anxiety attacks, depression, irritability, or other difficulties lie enormous amounts of confusion, fear, guilt, and, in some cases, self-hate.

You have sacrificed much. Yet despite your many sacrifices you may have received insufficient acknowledgment of your pain, stress, and disappointments. Perhaps, like John's wife or Cindy's husband, you have been as misunderstood and unsupported by your family and community as your veteran. To the extent that your veteran has been perceived as "crazy" or "sick," you may have sometimes been perceived as "crazy" or "sick," too—for loving and trying to support a combat veteran.

Your veteran's problems—and yours—are compounded by the fact that our cultural ideal is often that of emotional coolness. In other societies, it is and has been perfectly permissible for warriors to openly grieve about having been in a war. However, in our society, and in our military system especially, to be emotional is considered a sign of weakness or mental instability. If one is "too happy," "too sad," or "too angry," he or she may be judged by others, even by some mental health professionals, as being "neurotic" or "abnormal." Yet in other cultures, emotional intensity is the norm.

In such cultures there is no such thing as loving "too much," grieving "too long," or suffering "too deeply." Depth of emotion is not only expected but applauded. Individuals are allowed to suffer without being accused of self-pity or of dwelling in the past. In the face of death or loss, they are permitted to rant and rave and wail loudly for as long as they need to. In contrast, in our society the appropriate response to loss is often a form of stoicism. One is expected to "get over it" as soon as possible. "Don't cry, don't feel, don't suffer, or, if you do, don't show it" is the message. Yet what here is disparagingly viewed as falling apart or going crazy may elsewhere be considered a normal emotional reaction.

As a result, your veteran may have felt that he or she had to stifle some emotions. Similarly, you may have felt that you have had to keep your feelings to yourself lest you be judged as weak or crazy. Your veteran's reactions to the trauma and horrors of war and your responses to these reactions are often entirely appropriate, even when judged by uninformed outsiders to be otherwise. In this sense, both of you can be seen as victims of our society's tendency to look down upon those who are in emotional pain and to view any form of emotional suffering as a mental illness.

Upon coming home from the war, your veteran underwent a readjustment period, as did you and your family. Today there is increased recognition that the emotional and other difficulties of this transition period are entirely normal. However, it is rarely recognized that the readjustment period can take months, if not years. When the readjustment difficulties do not disappear in a few days or weeks, as is often portrayed in the media, both you and your veteran may be blamed for your plight. You might be told that if only one or both of you were "stronger," your family wouldn't be having such readjustment difficulties. You may have been accused of impeding the readjustment process because you were "too supportive" or, alternatively, because you were "not supportive enough." The notion that both of you were abnormal may have undercut your self-esteem and possibly strained your relationships with your extended family, your neighbors, and other natural support systems. Although you may not be as socially isolated as your veteran, you too may be suffering from profound feelings of loneliness and alienation. While you may have many loving friends, outside of any support groups you may be attending you may have very few people in your life to whom you can open your heart and share your most important struggles.

Since Vietnam, to some limited degree societal understanding of combat stress has increased not only as the result of media references to combat stress, airline crashes, family violence, and criminal assault, but also as the result of terrorist attacks at home and abroad. Yet the image of the "crazy" veteran persists, supported by those few cases where veterans have expressed their emotional pain and frustrations by committing suicide or in violent episodes widely publicized by the media. For example, much was made of the fact that the serial sniper who terrorized Washington, D.C., in 2002 had military training. Criminals in contemporary crime television programs are often depicted as having had military training

More typically, however, veterans with untreated combat trauma internalize their pain and suffer alone. Some may express their dissatisfactions in the context of their families, yet when the partners of veterans seek understanding and help from others, they, like their veterans, may receive an unsympathetic response. Just as few people want to listen to veterans, few want to listen to their partners, who, in some cases, are made to feel inadequate as mates because they cannot wave a magic wand and produce a home life as happy as the Huxtables on *The Cosby Show*.

While this book describes some of the harmful effects of untreated combat trauma on family life, it also emphasizes some of the ways a veteran's war experiences can help strengthen individual family members and the family as a whole. For example, combat duty can increase a person's self-reliance, desire to help others, and appreciation for human life, especially for caring relationships.[7] Such benefits often spill over to family members who may also come to have more respect for fair play and more empathy for others who suffer.

A person can develop other strengths and virtues—such as self-discipline and self-sacrifice for the benefit of the greater good, whether one's country or one's family—from serving in a combat zone or from loving someone who has. Among those in our society who put material gain and personal satisfactions above the needs of their families, communities, or nation, such values often do not receive the respect they deserve. (See "What are some benefits of combat duty?" on page 61.)

The descriptions of some of the harmful effects of combat trauma on family relationships in this book are not meant to promote unfair negative stereotypes about combat veterans. Neither are they intended to imply that your veteran wants you or your children to suffer because of his or her war experiences. Rather they reflect the fact that your family is an integrated, interdependent system. One part of your family cannot suffer without that suffering affecting the entire unit. By the same token, if your veteran has grown emotionally, spiritually, or otherwise as the result of combat, his or her growth can influence and inspire you and other family members.

In writing this book, I reviewed the available research on veterans and their families and on trauma and its impact on family life. In general, much more research has been completed on Vietnam veterans and Persian Gulf veterans than on veterans of prior or subsequent wars. The literature on the children of veterans and on women veterans from any time period is relatively sparse, and on military couples it is almost nonexistent. Clearly, more research is needed to obtain better answers to the many questions surrounding how combat trauma can impact families in general and families of women veterans or of dual military couples in particular. Hopefully in the future other investigators with more refined research instruments will provide us with comprehensive information.

This book is based on some thirty years of clinical experience with male and female combat veterans and their spouses and partners and children, who, like you, were looking for help. There is reason to believe that the majority of the men and women seeking help for relationship problems are involved with veterans who endured more intense combat stress or who received less support than the average veteran. (See "Why are some veterans more affected by combat than others?" in chapter 2.)

I've worked with many couples, within the Veterans Administration and in private practice, where both partners were highly functioning in most areas of life, yet they found that the war intruded on their ability to communicate and enjoy their relationship. For example, Ken, who served both in Vietnam and the Persian Gulf, came to counseling not for help with combat trauma but in hopes of finding more ways to show his wife how much he loved her.

While the number of untreated veterans is in the tens of thousands, it is important to point out that numerous veterans and their families have made adequate psychological adjustments following combat duty. This book is written for those whose suffering is not yet over and who wish to start the healing.

The book contains my opinions, observations, and suggestions regarding psychological and family issues. These do not reflect any particular political or spiritual point of view. Neither do they necessarily reflect the opinions or policies of any of the mental health, educational, or correctional facilities in which I served as psychologist, such as the Veterans Administration Medical Centers Program or the Vietnam Veterans Readjustment Counseling Program. The case studies in this book are composites of actual counseling clients and client issues as described in published articles and books. All identifying details have been changed and any resemblance to any person, dead or alive, is coincidental save for those few instances where individuals granted written consent to relay their story.

I have written primarily from the point of view of the spouse or partner. However, there are no "good guys" and "bad guys" in this book. Instead I view the veteran and his or her partner as two suffering people who, after being wounded severely by external forces and stressed by life's demands, have, for a multitude of reasons, had difficulties connecting and, at times, wounded one another. In many cases, I have heard the veteran's side of the story as well as that of his or her spouse or partner, parents, siblings, and children. Throughout the book, the vet's pain and social predicament, as well as that of family members, are emphasized. In cases of physical battering and other forms of mistreatment, however, I view the abused person, male or female, veteran or family member, as the victim.

In this book I have attempted to describe the problems and issues facing you in a manner helpful to you. I have also attempted to dispel any negative stereotypes that exist about veterans and their families. Just as your veteran may feel painfully different and apart from others because of having seen war, you may feel different, too. You may think you are the only person in the world who is undergoing such struggles. Being in a spouses or partners group, where the effects of trauma on marital intimacy and family life are discussed, often helps dispel this burden of isolation. I hope this book will present the same possibility.

Despite the significant increase of women in the military, the majority of military personnel (some 85 percent) are men.[8] The proportion of men serving in combat zones is even higher. Hence this book is addressed to heterosexual women. However, most of the material in this book is relevant to both men and women, regardless of their sexual orientation.

How This Book Can Help You

One purpose of this book is to provide you with some basic information about combat trauma and its possible effects on intimate relationships and family life. Another is to increase your awareness of the stresses in your life as the result of loving a combat veteran, or being one yourself, and to help you appreciate your strengths.

This book provides some limited guidance in how you and your veteran can manage those difficult moments when his or her combat memories are triggered by a situation in the present. However, this book is not a self-help guide for healing from trauma, depression, and alcoholism or another addiction. If you or a family member is experiencing any of these problems, any other type of severe emotional distress, or physical or sexual abuse, the help of a qualified mental health and medical professional will be needed. (See appendix A, which provides resources that will assist you in finding help for these and other related concerns not covered in this book.)

It is important to note that a full discussion of the topic of severe injury is missing from this book. Space limitations did not permit an exploration of this important issue and its enormous impact on the entire family. Under the best of circumstances, which would include adequate financial coverage, superb medical care, and adequate home-care services, severe injury and disability can be a nightmare for everyone. Even relatively minor injuries can be the beginning of a long, complicated journey of medical procedures and time-consuming expensive home care. It is a gross disservice to those who have sacrificed their physical well-being for the public good to laud their ability to make the best of the situation without also acknowledging their often long-term physical and emotional suffering and the immense losses incurred not only by them but by all who love them.

Physical disabilities that are visible can be especially painful, particularly for women veterans. Any type of disfigurement can profoundly affect a woman's sexuality and her relationship to her body. This takes on enormous importance given that, in our culture, a woman's body and sexuality are central to her identity. No matter what a woman has achieved at home, in her military career, or in her community, in our society she is still frequently evaluated on the basis of her appearance. Even women veterans who adamantly reject the idea of women being rated according to their looks live in this society. This makes it hard for them to not be affected by these cultural standards. (See appendix A for information on disability benefits.)

How This Book Is Organized

The first three chapters of this book describe combat trauma and its possible effects on the veteran. The remaining chapters focus on some of the most common problems confronting veterans and their families, such as emotional distancing, sexual difficulties, anger, grief, guilt, and family violence. There are also chapters on suicide, children, women veterans, and military couples.

Appendix A, "Resources," provides a listing of helpful organizations and appendix B, "Suggested Readings," a listing of helpful books. Appendix C, "Guidelines for Effective Communication," provides suggestions on improving couples' communication, and appendix D is a list of "do's and don'ts" for partners of veterans suffering from combat trauma.

As you read this book, you may find that you do not share the views or the concerns of some of the men and women whose experiences contributed to this book. This is to be expected, given that this book is based on clinical experience with and the available research on veteran families from a wide variety of backgrounds. Feel free to skim over those parts of a chapter that don't apply to you or that conflict with your goals, values, or personality. Be careful, however, not to skim over certain sections because they touch upon issues that are so difficult and painful that you may naturally wish to avoid them. As is sometimes the case, we often resist what we need most.

Cautions

While you are reading this book, if you experience any of the following reactions, seek professional help immediately and do not continue reading this text without first consulting your physician or a licensed mental health counselor:

- Memory problems

- Feeling disoriented or out of touch with reality, even temporarily

- Suicidal or homicidal thoughts

- Self-destructive behavior, such as substance abuse or self-mutilation

- Hyperventilation

- Extreme nausea

- Hemorrhaging

- Uncontrollable shaking

- Irregular heartbeat

- Increased symptoms of a preexisting medical or psychiatric problem; or any intense, new, or unexplained pain

You can expect to feel sad, anxious, numb, angry, or confused as you read this book. At times, your emotions may even feel overwhelming. Do not become alarmed at having such strong emotions if they subside within a short time and if you regain enough emotional and mental balance so that you can function. However, if your emotions take a long time to subside or if they do not subside enough so that you can resume functioning, you must contact a mental health professional immediately or go to the emergency room of a local hospital.

Some of you may not only have a partner who is a combat veteran, but are combat veterans yourselves or have been in war zones as civilians. Some of you may never have set foot in a war zone but have been exposed to child abuse, sexual or physical assault, vehicular accidents, natural catastrophes, or other traumas. As a result, this book may stimulate thoughts and feelings about your own traumas, and reading it may be extremely difficult for you. If so, you are encouraged to read this book at your own pace, one chapter at a time. If you continue to feel overwhelmed and distressed and experience any of the symptoms mentioned in the bulleted list above, stop reading this book immediately and follow the instructions provided.

If you are currently being physically or sexually abused, you need professional, legal, and other types of assistance immediately. Consult appendix A for guidance in locating resources.

A Final Note

No book, regardless of its quality, is a substitute for individual, couples, or family counseling. During times of extreme stress or loss, you, your veteran, and other family members may need the assistance of a qualified medical or mental health professional and, if you wish, a spiritual adviser as well. As you work through this book, you may find that a particular suggestion is not suitable or helpful to you. This may reflect the unique aspects of your situation, as well as the fact that there are no simple solutions for the complex problems confronting you and your veteran. However, by increasing your understanding of combat trauma and ridding yourself (and hopefully your veteran as well) of shame- and guilt-producing views of your difficulties, you can lighten some of your burdens considerably.

My husband Joshua is a "half-breed," half one race and half another. But hardly anyone notices because he's so good-looking—and so funny. I've never met a more articulate man, or a more organized one. He was already efficient before Iraq, but the military made him even more efficient. Now his business is even more successful than ever.

Joshua joined the Air Force soon after 9/11 and flew about twenty bombing missions in Iraq. His air strikes killed people, but he doesn't feel guilty about it. "War is war and war is about killing," he always says. What bothers him is his feeling that most Americans don't really understand how ugly war can be or appreciate the hardships of the soldiers and civilians living in war zones. He faults the media for this, for giving the Americans such a sanitized view of war.

Last Thanksgiving the pastor read the names of those in our congregation who had died in Iraq. Yet during the coffee hour people seemed more upset about the Sunday school children having gobbled up most of the cookies than about the men and women who had died serving their country. Joshua almost blew a fuse. Good soldier that he is, he managed to control himself.

But he lost it at Thanksgiving dinner. My sister was serving dessert when the news came on, showing photographs of American soldiers who had been killed by roadside bombs that month. I squeezed John's hand and his mother looked at him with tears in her eyes. But everyone else kept on eating as if nothing important had really happened. Then, with a voice as cold as ice, Joshua said, "I can't believe it. Our boys are dying over there and all you people care about is what flavor ice cream you want on your pumpkin pie." Then he got up and went home.

Afterwards a few of my relatives apologized to Joshua for their insensitivity, but most of them felt Joshua had no right to ruin their Thanksgiving dinner. As for me, I'm caught in the middle—as usual. I understand how Joshua feels and I understand how they feel, too. But what I can't comprehend is how they decided that now Joshua is a walking time bomb. He's never been mean or violent to me, our sons, or anyone in the family, either before the war or afterwards. In fact, my family makes jokes about the fact that Joshua hates disagreements so much that he agrees with me, or them, about almost anything. Yet now they're saying they're afraid to talk to Joshua for fear he'll be offended and "go postal" on them.

Joshua doesn't drink or do drugs and, to the best of my knowledge, has never cheated on me. But our relationship is at a standstill because he cannot tolerate any discussions having to do with our relationship or having to do with feelings. He doesn't flare up at me: he just goes mute. He can't discuss matters pertaining to the home or children either. He says he can't take the pressure and shuts down. If there's a decision to be made, I have to make it. Yes, that gives me some power, but it also puts all the responsibility on me and if something goes wrong, then I'm to blame. I thought marriage was supposed to be a partnership, not a one-woman show.

Another problem is how Joshua flirts with death. He's gone flying on airplanes that he knew had mechanical problems. So I won't fly with him anymore and won't let our sons go either. Joshua thinks I'm "overreacting." So do our sons, and we argue about it all the time. Maybe because he survived a war, he thinks he's invulnerable now, but I know differently.

Joshua's shutting down when it comes to any conversations about feelings and our relationship and his need to dance with death are probably our only war-related problems, but they are big ones. Since he can't, or won't, talk to me about either of these issues, there's not much I can do about either one of them, and I don't know how to handle this. Since everything else between us is okay, sometimes I don't feel I have the right to complain. Yet something is missing in our marriage, something that was there before he went to Iraq. There's a whole side to him I don't know about. He won't let me in and that hurts.

Even though Joshua never talks about it, I know that the chasm between us hurts him too. In my view, it's the war that caused this distance between us, but this makes it difficult for me to be angry with him. How can I be angry at him for something he really can't help, especially since he already blames himself for the distance between us? He feels guilty enough as it is, *and if I complain about too much I might drive him into the ground and I don't want to do that. But don't I have a right to speak my mind? I think I do. In fact, I need to—desperately. But the situation is such that sometimes I find myself shutting down emotionally, just like Joshua does, and that scares me.*

I

"He doesn't talk much about the war"

The Reality of Combat Trauma

I don't know whether to hate the military or love it. Ed went over-seas a warm, outgoing person. He came back so happy to be alive and with me and the kids again, I was shocked by his bouts of depres-sion. Sometimes he's his old self, but sometimes he snaps at me and the kids—the ones he loves the most—over nothing. He always apologizes, but then he'll stay away from us. He says he needs time to chill. But I miss him. So do the kids.

Sometimes it's like I'm another person to him, a stranger, not the wife who has stood by him through thick and thin. It hurts deep, very deep.

—JESSICA, WIFE OF A COMBAT VET

Jessica met Ed just before he was sent overseas, first to the Persian Gulf, then to Iraq. They fell in love almost immediate-ly and she has been his faithful partner ever since. Upon his re-turn from Iraq, Ed found himself wishing he had died in battle. He was troubled by other thoughts totally alien to his personal-ity. Not until he sought help did he realize he was not alone: over one-fourth of the U.S. troops who have served in combat in Op-eration Iraqi Freedom (to date) have developed either physical or mental health problems requiring professional help.[1]

Jessica sought help, too. She joined a support group for the wives and girlfriends of soldiers and other military personnel who served in combat zones. All the women share Jessica's pain, fears, and confusion about how best to relate to the man they love.

"Ed is still one of the deepest-hearted people I know. The war didn't change his love for me either. In fact, he's probably more committed to our marriage than ever before," says Jessica. Yet there are times Jessica feels alone and abandoned. Her husband, it seems to Jessica, is involved with another woman. Many of the other women in the group have the same complaint: at times their men seem to be involved with another woman, too.

What is the name of the other woman? Vietnam, Cambodia, Grenada, Lebanon, Bosnia, Somalia, Kuwait, Afghanistan, El Salvador, Iraq, or another site of an armed conflict. This other woman, a ghost from the past, is ugly and battle scarred. But her power over their men is great.

This ghost crosses gender lines. Men whose wives or girlfriends have served in war zones express similar feelings. "I don't doubt my wife's loyalty or love for me one bit. But sometimes it feels like I'm sharing her with someone—or something—else," says John, the husband of a combat nurse.

From the beginning of time, warriors have come home only to find the war they left behind still raging in their hearts and minds. For some, the impact of combat begins on the battlefield or soon after coming home; for others, it manifests itself years or even decades later; for still others, it never surfaces in any recognizable form, yet it leaves an indelible stamp upon their lives and the lives of those who love them.

"The first week I was over there, an explosion put me into a coma," explains Alexander, a Korean War veteran. "My military records show I recovered and was sent back into the field, but I can't remember anything about the war after I was blown up. I can remember my life after I got home, but whatever happened in the war after that explosion is a blur to me." Alexander sought group therapy in hopes that listening to other combat veterans would spark his memory. But it didn't.

Alexander's life story reveals patterns common to veterans who suffer from combat trauma. He felt terribly alone in life, yet he repeatedly walked away from close relationships. He was struggling financially, yet he repeatedly abandoned good jobs because he feared he might lose his temper and harm someone. Whenever he had extra money, he'd give it away to homeless veterans and others in need, as if he didn't deserve to hold on to any good fortune. He had no idea why he felt this way.

For many men and women, the emotional aftermath of military duty in a combat zone (whether as a soldier, a medical or support worker, an intelligence or special operations officer) can make it difficult to feel emotionally close to the ones they love or to enjoy a fulfilling life. This can be excruciatingly painful, not only for their families, but for the veterans themselves. Discovering that their war experiences set them apart from others and create unwanted relationship tensions can hurt terribly. For veterans who came home with an increased appreciation of the importance of close personal ties, it can lead to a deep despair. For example, the first words that came out of David's mouth when he came for counseling were:

Tell me, Doc. Will I ever love again? Will I ever be able to let in the love my girlfriend has for me? I know I love her, but too many times I can't feel the love for her. I can't show it to her the way I want to either. Why am I afraid that she might die if she's with me?

Don't get me wrong. I'm not afraid of hurting her. After all the death I've seen, I don't even swat flies anymore. I'm just afraid that one day I'll get so relaxed with her that I'll blurt out some of the things I saw and did over there. Then she'll leave me for sure. But if I keep backing off from her or doing things to push her away, I'll probably lose her, too.

I'm not coming here for help with my nightmares and panic attacks. I can live with those, but I can't live with an empty heart.

David believes that anyone close to him will be harmed. As author and psychiatrist Jonathan Shay points out, veterans "see themselves as toxic because they expect to harm others with their knowledge of the hideousness of war—'if you knew what I know, it would fuck you up.'"[2] David's girlfriend, however, doesn't understand the reasons for David's wall of silence and experiences it as rejection. She also doesn't understand how David can want her love, then run from it. "We can be all cozy, then all of a sudden his guard goes up," she weeps. "But he never clams up like that with his buddies," she adds, her tears turning to anger.

David is like many veterans who, after having shared life-and-death experiences with certain comrades, forge an intense bond with them that excludes their intimate partner and anyone else who doesn't have firsthand knowledge of war. While partners may be glad that their veteran has supportive buddies, they can still feel left out of their camaraderie. Should some of these buddies be of the opposite sex, partners may also feel threatened or jealous.

What Is Trauma?

In life, we all face crises, large and small, ranging from the loss of a wallet to the death of a loved one. Yet these events, although stressful and often called traumatic, are not considered "trauma" according to the official psychiatric definition.[3] As of the writing of this book, *trauma,* in the technical sense of the word, refers only to events involving death and injury or the possibility of death and injury either to oneself or to other people standing nearby. These events evoke a state of such extreme horror, helplessness, and fear that they would overtax almost any human being's ability to cope: for example, man-made traumas (such as war, family violence, physical or sexual assault, technological disasters, and vehicular accidents) and natural catastrophes (such as fires, floods, earthquakes, and hurricanes). In addition, recent studies have shown that post-traumatic stress disorder (PTSD) can develop following the onset of a unexpected life-threatening illness where death is imminent.[4]

It is not just the events themselves but the experience of those events that makes them traumatic. Even if you or those about you are never harmed, you are in a traumatic situation when you feel that you (or others about you) may be injured or killed. For example, soldiers who anticipate enemy fire, even if they are never fired upon, are undergoing a traumatic experience because they have good reason to believe that at any moment harm can come their way.

In this sense trauma involves three elements: being afraid, feeling overwhelmed, and being or feeling helpless. Being afraid, but not feeling overwhelmed and being able to take decisive action on your own behalf may be very stressful, but it doesn't necessarily constitute trauma. Similarly, you may be in a situation where you are overwhelmed and feeling helpless, but if you are not afraid of possible death or injury to yourself or others about you, it is not considered trauma. For example, although the loss of a job or a parent (through natural causes) may change your life forever, these events are not considered traumas because they are expected life losses. However, if instead of losing one family member, you lost several family members or friends in an accident or natural disaster, you would be considered a trauma survivor. Such simultaneous multiple losses are clearly overwhelming.

Hence persons who witness trauma on a daily basis (such as military medical staff or those working in graves registrations) or who are subject to the nearly constant stress of making life-and-death decisions as a part of their job are also considered trauma survivors and suffer from traumatic reactions. This statement holds true even for individuals who are carefully screened for mental health problems prior to admission to their field such as medical and support staff in combat zones and civilian police officers, firefighters, rescue workers, and medical staff in burn units or emergency rooms.[5] Except for areas of the world suffering from high infant mortality rates due to poverty or war, the death of a child is considered a trauma because it is a reversal of the natural order of things.

Wounding as Trauma

Perhaps you have heard a doctor talk about head trauma, bone trauma, or trauma to some other part of the body. On a physical level, trauma has two meanings. The first is that some part or particular organ of the body has been suddenly damaged by a force so great that the body's natural protections (the skin, skull, and so on) were unable to prevent injury. The second meaning refers to injuries in which the body's natural healing ability is inadequate to mend the wound without medical assistance.

Just as the body can be traumatized, so can the psyche. On the psychological level, trauma refers to the wounding of your emotions, your spirit, your will to live, your beliefs about yourself and the world, your dignity, and your sense of security. The assault on your psyche can be so great that your normal ways of thinking and feeling and the usual ways you have handled stress in the past are now inadequate.

Being traumatized is not like being offended or rejected in a work or a love relationship. Such events can injure your emotions, your pride, and perhaps your sense of fairness, but they are not of the order of magnitude of trauma. During trauma, you touch your own death or the deaths of others. At the same time, you are helpless, or feel helpless, to prevent death or injury.

As human beings, we must all confront the fact of our mortality. We and our loved ones will die some day, no matter who we are or what we do. Usually this awareness becomes most powerful in our middle or later years, when we see parents and their contemporaries dying or when we ourselves acquire an illness. However, participating in a war, whether as a combatant or noncombatant, means confronting the existential reality of death sooner, and more vividly, than most.

Man-made Versus Natural Traumas

While negative reactions have been found among survivors of natural catastrophes, negative effects tend to be more prevalent, more long-term, and more intense among individuals involved in man-made traumas.[6] Because, it is argued, natural catastrophes can be explained away as "acts of God" or "nature" or "bad luck," natural catastrophe survivors are also less likely to lose their trust in other human beings and in society than are those subject to man-made catastrophes. Yet natural disasters often involve one or more significant human errors or betrayals, either by individuals or institutions. In some instances survivors may feel betrayed by rescue operations and other services and are not adequately compensated for their losses.

People involved in natural catastrophes are also less likely to be blamed for their own pain or for developing signs of traumatic stress. Those who develop stress reactions as the result of man-made traumas, such as war, are more likely to be seen by others, especially their all-important peers and superiors, as lacking in strength, caution, intelligence, or moral integrity.

Combat Trauma

Like all traumas, war involves an imminent threat of losing one's life, limb, or physical health. However, it involves much more than life threat; it involves numerous other traumas and stressors. Some of these are described below.

Deaths of Comrades

Not only do comrades die, but they die horrifically. Some may be blown to bits or burned beyond recognition, others skinned alive or tortured to death in other unimaginably cruel ways, In today's world of suicide bombings and guerrilla warfare, almost any place, from a restaurant to a place of worship, can become "the front line." Hence even military personnel whose primary duties do not involve combat (for example, military administrative staff, medical and mental health workers, mechanical and technical staff, and other support staff) may witness the deaths of their countrymen, resulting in trauma that should not be considered "minor" or inconsequential. Even people living in comfortable suburban homes have been found to develop long-term psychological problems following the violent death of a loved one, even if they did not witness the death directly.[7]

Ground troops depend heavily on one another and on support staff for survival. Similarly, support staff depend on other support staff and on ground troops to help keep them safe. Hence the death or injury of a ground soldier, combat support soldier, interrogator, medic, or other support staff worker represents a loss of protection and support for those who remain alive. If, in addition, the deceased was a special friend or someone who was highly respected, the fear generated by his or her loss is compounded by grief.

Although this grief may or may not be experienced at the time, it can be profound. In war zones military staff are so far away from home and depend on each other so much that they often come to view those in their unit or working group as "family." Hence on a symbolic level, the injury or loss of a fellow soldier or military coworker may be experienced as the loss or injury of an actual family member. For some, the death of a female soldier or military staff can feel like the death of their own mother, wife, or sister; the death of a male soldier or staff member like the loss of their own father, brother, or uncle.

Killing as Trauma

For some soldiers, the act of killing another human being is traumatizing in itself. Even civilians who kill in situations where there is little risk to their own lives have been found to develop traumatic stress reactions simply from the act of having taken a life. Soldiers often report that the first few "kills" are the most difficult but that over time, to one degree or another, they become numb to it and come to view killing as just a routine part of their job. Soldiers who develop this type of attitude are often judged as "inhumane," not only by others, but by themselves. However, distancing one's self from the killing is the only way a humane person can go on fighting without having a psychiatric breakdown.

"Friendly Fire"

Instances of friendly fire, where soldiers accidentally harm their own countrymen, have been a part of every war. If the act of killing can be traumatizing for some soldiers, imagine how much more traumatic it is for them to inadvertently kill or harm someone on their own side. On a rational level, soldiers may know that they are not responsible for the error in judgment or the technical or mechanical failure that caused the accident. On an emotional level, however, the guilt can be enormous, as can their anger toward whomever they perceive as responsible for the deadly mishap.

Similarly, on an intellectual level, soldiers wounded by friendly fire may fully understand the inevitability of such incidents in war. Perhaps they themselves were in situations where they unintentionally harmed fellow soldiers. On an emotional level, however, knowing that you were wounded by someone on your own side can add to the emotional pain of having been shot, burned, gassed or almost poisoned, drowned, or suffocated. Even soldiers who are not directly involved in friendly fire incidents can be deeply affected in that simply hearing about such instances makes it clear that friendly fire isn't just a remote theoretical possibility, but a real and perhaps eminent danger. This awareness usually results in increased fear for their own safety, as well as self-doubts and doubts about the competence of their commanders, fellow comrades, or whomever they view as the cause of the friendly fire.

Physical Stress

All too often it is forgotten that combat involves not only emotional but physical duress as well. The importance of this physical duress is reflected in the terms *combat fatigue* and *combat exhaustion*. In the past, these terms were used to describe the extreme state of physical depletion that leads to the diminished capacity, if not total inability, of soldiers to keep on fighting. A vivid example of combat fatigue comes from the 1727 diary of a soldier who describes how his comrades were so physically exhausted that they "would refuse to eat, drink, work, or fight in defense of the city, even though they would be repeatedly whipped for not doing so."[8]

There are many sources of physical strain on combat soldiers. At the same time that their bodies have increased nutritional needs, they may have little interest or opportunity to be concerned about proper nutrition. At times they may not have access to food, clean water, or a safe or reasonably comfortable place to sleep. During the Persian Gulf War, for example, soldiers reported having to drink water or eat food containing sewage, smoke, oil, and other contaminants.[9] Both ground troops and support staff are subject to sleep deprivation, long working hours, extreme temperatures, horrible smells, and unfamiliar and almost uninhabitable physical environments, sometimes for protracted periods of time.

Military staff on foreign soil can be exposed to parasites and illnesses for which they have no natural immunity. Even physical stresses that may not be life threatening (such as snake and insect bites, leeches, body lice, and extreme allergic reactions to nondangerous substances) can tax the immune system, thus making soldiers more vulnerable to more serious illnesses on the field or later in life.

Their immune systems can also be compromised if they fail to seek medical care for relatively minor injuries or medical problems. It is not unusual for a wound or a medical problem that is not incapacitating to be as viewed as "minor" compared to the need to complete a mission and remain with one's unit. For example, during the Battle of Hue in Vietnam, some Marines who sustained two or three wounds chose to stay and fight rather than leave their comrades. Some who were being forcibly evacuated due to the seriousness of their wounds even tried to escape and rejoin the fighting. Albert was among them. "We watched each other's back," he explains. "I told myself that until I got to the point where I couldn't pull the trigger, I was staying. If I leave, others have to pick up my load, which makes it harder for them to stay alive. I would rather be in pain than think that another Marine was wounded or killed because I wasn't there to help."

Some men and women may hesitate to seek or accept medical care for anything but the most serious problems for fear of being viewed as slackers, sissies, softies, or cowards; still others may think that they don't deserve it because others are experiencing greater suffering. For example, Rob injured his back jumping out of a burning helicopter. "I had a lot of pain, but I told the medic I was fine. I didn't feel I had the right to complain—not when others around me were dying."

Yet lack of immediate medical attention can sometimes result in long-term medical problems. For example, Don hid the fact that he had malaria as long as he could so he could go on fighting with his unit. Only when his feverish tremors became so extreme that he became a liability to his unit did he seek medical care. Don responded so well to treatment that he returned to the front lines. However, malaria can have lifelong effects. Today Don must contend not only with his psychological reactions to the war but also with the ongoing physical symptoms caused by malaria. If Don had sought medical care before he reached the point of being incoherent with malarial fever, the after-effects he is enduring today would probably be less severe.

Untreated medical problems, even if they are relatively minor, can also have serious psychological consequences. While someone with a safe job might be able to get by working with a low-grade fever or severe rash, being a soldier requires a high degree of alertness. On slow days, minor medical problems may not cause major difficulties. But under fire, combined with the other demands of combat, even relatively minor physical problems can impair a soldier's competency. This can lead to feelings of shame and inferiority that some soldiers carry with them all their lives. If, in addition, a soldier's error results in the death or injury of a fellow soldier or compromises the mission, the resulting guilt may cripple that soldier's life forever.

Multiple Traumas

There is no "hierarchy of suffering." It is both unfair and insensitive to compare one person's pain to that of another. Everyone's losses and sufferings need to be respected. However, researchers have found what common sense would indicate: that the extent of a person's traumatic stress reactions is related to the severity and numbers of traumas that person has experienced. For example, being raped once is traumatic; being raped multiple times can be even more traumatic. Similarly, seeing people die in a car accident, although traumatic, is generally not as traumatic as being in combat and seeing death and violence day in and day out.

Not only do soldiers experience multiple traumas, but often these traumas occur so close together in time that there is no opportunity to recuperate from one horror before being ambushed by another one. For example, a soldier may experience the trauma of being wounded at the same time that he or she is being traumatized by the sight of comrades being tortured or killed or of corpses being mutilated by people or being eaten by animals. As a result, combat military veterans usually require more time and more help for healing than those who have seen less death and destruction or who at least had a break between one trauma and the next. Combat veterans, whether male or female, who were subject to sexual or physical assault while on combat duty can also be expected to require more intensive help and a longer recovery period.

Catastrophic Traumas

Just as a distinction can be made between experiencing a single trauma as opposed to multiple traumas, a distinction can be made between traumas that involve harm to one or more persons but which preserve these individuals' community and those that also involve the almost total destruction of the social and economic fabric of an entire community or area. Traumas that result in the death, injury, or geographic relocation of a significant proportion of the population of an area or the destruction or severe crippling of its fundamental institutions (such as its educational, financial, cultural, and religious facilities) are often called *catastrophic traumas*. In catastrophic traumas, individuals may experience not only personal injury, material losses, and the loss or injury of loved ones but also the loss of much (if not all) of their social and economic supports and other aspects of their community that are important parts of their personal identity.

One example of catastrophic trauma is the 2004 tsunami disaster, which resulted in thousands of deaths, the elimination of entire villages, and serious, if not irreparable, damage to many more areas. Another example is Hurricane Katrina in 2005, which not only caused many deaths, but obliterated large sections of the city of New Orleans, destroyed most of the city's infrastructure, and forced the evacuation of thousands of people. If Katrina had caused a handful of deaths and destroyed a few homes and businesses, but had preserved the vast majority of the residences and almost all of the government offices, power plants, and business establishments, this hurricane would be considered a major trauma for New Orleans, but not necessarily a catastrophic one.

Soldiers are more likely to witness or be involved in catastrophic traumas than the general public or even than most civilian police, firefighters, or rescue workers. Hence soldiers, as well as medical staff, investigators, researchers, interrogators, and even journalists and peacekeepers, may be carrying the burden not only of the many stresses described thus far in this chapter but also the emotional and spiritual "bomb" of having witnessed the dissolution or near-dissolution of a group's way of life.

Reactions to Trauma

Depersonalization

During trauma you are subject to a process called *depersonalization.* Depersonalization refers to the stripping away of your personhood— your individuality and your humanity. At the moment of attack, whether the assailant is an enemy soldier, a land mine, or an attack dog, you do not feel like a valuable person with the right to safety, happiness, and health. At that moment, you feel more like a thing, a vulnerable object subject to the will of a power or force greater than yourself.[10] This is especially true in modern warfare where killing has become increasingly impersonal. Former Army Ranger and paratrooper Lt. Col. Dave Grossman notes that even the language used to describe war doesn't use the word "kill." "Most soldiers do not 'kill,' instead the enemy was knocked over, wasted, greased, taken out, and mopped up. The enemy is hosed, zapped, probed and fired on. The enemies' humanity is denied."[11]

In war it is common for soldiers to come to view their enemies as less than human, for example, as "Japs," "gooks," "slope eyes," or "towelheads" rather than as people like themselves. Yet the more soldiers deny the humanity of their enemies, the more likely they are to eventually deny their own humanity, thus intensifying the depersonalization process. This sense of being depersonalized or dehumanized is especially strong when injuries are sustained or when the injuries and death witnessed seem senseless.[12]

The sight of corpses can also evoke feelings of depersonalization, especially if they are mangled or mutilated. A veteran explains:

> *When I saw bodies stacked one on top of another or rotting on roadsides, I realized that one day that could be me. It hit me hard that I—someone with a name and parents and brothers and sisters—was really nothing but a disposable commodity, more like a used-up piece of equipment you'd throw in the trash and never think about again than a person.*

Self-Ideal Threat

Trauma survivors often feel guilty for not having lived up to their image of their ideal self. Perhaps they had imagined that in certain dangerous situations they would have acted more efficiently, wisely, lovingly, or bravely. Yet the more extreme the circumstances, the more difficult it is to act, think, or feel as one thinks is best or right.

War being one of the most extreme traumas imaginable, it is impossible not only for ground troops but for any military staff in a combat zone to always meet some of the high standards they have set for themselves. No one can react perfectly or be a hero every single time he or she is called to action. Often soldiers, like other trauma survivors, focus on their errors (perceived or real) and on other ways they did not live up to their ideal image of themselves. They might also fail to fully appreciate their contributions to their mission and the magnitude of the obstacles they encountered in trying to fulfill their difficult duties. The resulting sense of failure can be enormous.

Impulse Threat

War is a fertile breeding ground for the development of rage, homicidal and suicidal urges, and a guilt so intense it can generate a profound self-hate and insecurity. After life in a war zone, individuals who used to be (or viewed themselves as being) relatively self-confident, loving, peaceful, kind, and emotionally and socially well adjusted can find themselves afraid of losing emotional control. They may especially fear losing control of their aggressive impulses.

The self-doubts, shame, and guilt generated by fear of one's self-destructive or aggressive impulses are even more difficult to bear for soldiers who view these or other strong impulses as violations of certain religious or spiritual beliefs or as violations of the values of their family, friends, and other people who matter to them. On the other hand, the surge of physical energy and the sense of power that can stem from rage and aggressive impulses can be a welcome relief from any feelings of helplessness and powerlessness. But this can become yet another source of shame and guilt. In the words of one soldier: "What's happened to me? I went overseas as part of a conflict resolution team and came home wanting to hurt someone. Even worse, I enjoy the idea of hurting someone. How bad is that?"

At the same time some combat veterans might feel threatened by the opposite—the degree of their compassion and caring toward others, which they may view as signs of weakness or qualities that make them vulnerable to danger. For example, developing a deep compassion for an innocent civilian trapped in the war zone can be dangerous.

In situations of guerrilla warfare, it's often impossible to distinguish friend from foe. A toddler may be laced with grenades or explosives. A handicapped child asking for help may be used to lure soldiers into an ambush or a booby trap.

For some soldiers, the conflict between the impulses toward aggression and compassion, like any of the multitude of other inner conflicts that are so easily generated by war, can lead to an identity crisis of major proportions. Not only are these identity crises emotionally destabilizing, but they are also potentially life threatening. Soldiers under fire can't afford to be having an identity crisis. Their situation calls for immediate and decisive action. Any indecision on their part could put their lives and the lives of other soldiers at great risk.

Worldview Threat

Being in combat shocks your body, your emotions, and your view of yourself. Even worse, perhaps, is the way it rocks your basic beliefs about yourself, human nature, and the nature of the world. The challenge (or shattering) of these beliefs can greatly increase your psychological distress. Any anxiety, confusion, depression, or disequilibrium experienced after combat is heightened by such thoughts as: "Who or what should I trust now? After what happened, I don't know what to believe in anymore."

As psychology professor Ronnie Janoff-Bulman points out, persons who have endured a trauma often are forced to reconsider at least these three assumptions about themselves and the world: that they are personally invulnerable, that the world is orderly and meaningful, and that they are good and strong people.[13] Wars, like other situations of multiple traumas involving exposure to extensive human violence and human error, pose severe challenges to ideas such as: "You get what you deserve and you deserve what you get"; "The world is basically safe, orderly, and fair"; "If you strive to be careful, competent, and good, you can avoid harm to yourself and your loved ones." As a result, some combat veterans suffer from the profound despair that goes along with the idea that life is meaningless.[14]

The shattering of the veteran's assumptions can have profound effects on his or her family members' worldview. It can also become a source of conflict between the veteran and his partner. If the veteran entered the military with a pessimistic view of life, then his combat experiences may have only confirmed his negative outlook. But if he entered the military with an optimistic or semi-optimistic view of life, his combat experiences may have tarnished, if not almost eroded, his faith in life.

He may have lost his innocence all at once, in one shattering moment of personal horror. Or he may have lost it piece by piece, a little bit at a time. Along the way, his partner may have learned more than she ever wanted to know about the fragility of life or the dark side of human nature. Even if the veteran tried to protect her by not talking about combat, she probably has a sense of what her veteran encountered from the media or from other sources. For some partners, this knowledge may severely challenge certain long-cherished beliefs, such as that people are basically good. As a result, a partner can lose some, or much, of her innocence as well. If she retains her confidence in the goodness of life, her disillusioned veteran may view her as being childish, uninformed, or naive.

On the other hand, the veteran may have retained an optimistic view of life or altered this view only to a limited extent. Sometimes it is the veteran's partner, rather than the veteran, who becomes disillusioned, and the partner views her veteran's more positive outlook as naive or unrealistic. When a partner's worldview is vastly different from that of her vet, conflicts may result. Unfortunately, such disagreements become yet another source of psychological stress for both the vet and his partner.

It bears repeating that it is not only soldiers in the line of direct fire who are subject to changes in their worldview and the many other challenges and traumas described in this chapter, but any individual who works or lives in a war zone or who encounters the destructive powers of human aggression. For example, those who interrogate or supervise terrorists or other individuals who enjoy inflicting suffering on others can suffer the loss of their belief in a just and fair world and subsequently also can develop one of the traumatic reactions described in chapter 3.

Additional Stressors

In addition to the stressors described above, those who serve in combat zones face other pressures, such as the emotional, financial, and other practical stresses associated with deployment: separation from loved ones and concerns about the impact of deployment on loved ones, such as loneliness, sexual deprivation, changes in working hours for one's partner, in child-care arrangements, in health care, in finances, and in household and automobile maintenance. Leaving behind an elderly or ailing parent, a beloved pet, or certain community or church responsibilities can pose additional strains.

Even the most patriotic soldier may feel some guilt about the kind of burdens that being separated will impose on his or her family and even the most patriotic partner may have difficulties coping with deployment. According to a 2005 survey of over a thousand partners of active-duty Army soldiers who had been deployed at some point since September 11, 2001, the majority of respondents indicated they experienced increased pride and a sense of self-sufficiency as the result of their spouse's deployment. Approximately one-fourth indicated that coping with deployment was a "major problem"; one-half a "minor problem"; and the remainder "no problem at all." However, over three-fourths of the partners surveyed believed that there would be serious reenlistment problems precisely because of the strain of active duty on family life.[15]

Furthermore, 42 percent of partners reported feeling lonely "very often"; 36 percent "somewhat often"; and only 22 percent "not at all." The hardest hit were spouses of enlisted personnel (74 percent of whom reported experiencing some type of practical problem); spouses of those whose deployment had been extended (64 percent of whom reported feeling anxious "very often" and 41 percent "somewhat often"); and those who were relative newcomers in that their spouses had been in the Army four years or less (56 percent of whom reported feeling depressed "very often" and 37 percent "somewhat often").[16]

The stresses of deployment can be even greater for those in the National Guard or Reserves in that deployment often results in dramatic losses of income and numerous legal and family complications. In addition, unlike family members of active-duty military who often have available to them an established support system, family members of the Guard and Reservists must often create their own.

Summary

From ancient times until the present, warriors have come home to find themselves changed in ways they had never imagined possible—

ways they may find undesirable and difficult to manage, even with help. Such changes were born as the result of coming face to face with the destructive forces of human aggression (either in others or within themselves) or from witnessing or participating in situations that invalidate the cherished idea that the world is orderly, fair, and kind.

War is one of the most traumatic experiences known to humanity. Not only does it involve multiple traumas, but sometimes these traumas occur simultaneously or within such short periods of time that combat soldiers, medical or technical support staff, military investigators or interrogators, or other military staff do not have the chance to recuperate from one trauma before they are confronted with yet another overwhelming experience. Combat duty, whether it involves engaging in armed conflict, caring for the wounded, or performing support or intelligence work, also involves physical stresses that can have lifelong psychological as well as physical consequences.

2

Frequently Asked Questions about Combat Trauma

Q: *How many veterans really suffer from symptoms of combat trauma?*

Information about the prevalence of combat-related traumatic reactions among military personnel is sparse. Compared to other areas of psychological research, studies of combat trauma are relatively few in number. Furthermore, the results of these studies can often be confusing. For example, studies of veterans who served in Vietnam, the Persian Gulf, Afghanistan, and Iraq repeatedly have found that simply being deployed to a combat zone can result in rates of traumatic stress higher than those who remain stateside. Exposure to combat results in even higher rates. Yet some studies do not distinguish between troops who saw combat from those who do not, so the results can be misleading. For example, a 2004 U.S. Army study found that men and women returning from Iraq had higher rates of battlefield symptoms than those returning from Afghanistan. As the researchers point out, however, an important reason for this difference is that at the time the study was conducted the troops from Iraq were more likely to have seen combat than those sent to Afghanistan.[1]

Another difficulty in interpreting the available statistics about combat-related traumatic reactions is that the definitions of these reactions may vary from one study to the next. Some researchers check for the presence of symptoms of depression (or other problems) in a soldier, but not for whether or not he or she has a full-blown case of depression (or other disorder). So when we read that veterans from one war have higher rates of depression, for example, than those from another war, it is possible that the comparison is being made between veterans who have one or two symptoms of depression with those who have all of the symptoms of severe depression.

In addition, researchers gather information in different ways. Some use paper and pencil tests; some mail out surveys; some review medical records; some conduct telephone interviews; and some conduct face-to-face interviews which can vary in length from one study to the next. In many cases, the method used influences the results. For example, not all veterans reply to surveys sent through the mail. If a substantial number of veterans do not reply because they are so busy leading productive lives that they don't have time to answer surveys, the rates of traumatic stress found in the study may be higher than the actual rates. In contrast, if the majority of veterans do not reply because they are so depressed they don't have the energy to answer their mail or are so mistrustful of anything official they're afraid to reply, then the rates of traumatic stress found in the study may be lower than the actual rates.

Statistics based on reviewing medical records tend to underreport the prevalence of combat-related traumatic reactions because symptoms of these reactions may not be recorded in medical records. In some cases, the soldier may have failed to report them; in others, the doctor may have failed to ask about them or failed to record them or been more concerned about the soldier's physical injuries than his or her state of mind. The rates of traumatic stress may also be underreported in studies that do not include wounded soldiers, who tend to have higher rates of traumatic stress reactions than noninjured soldiers or soldiers already discharged for mental health reasons.[2]

In addition, some studies examine soldiers for traumatic reactions while they are still in country or immediately or soon after discharge. Yet for some soldiers, symptoms do not appear until years later. On the other hand, for some soldiers the symptoms dissipate after a few years. While some studies examine the rates of traumatic stress at different periods of time in a veteran's life, not all veterans who participate in the first survey are available for the second or third.[3]

The rates of battlefield symptoms have also been found to be influenced by society's view of these symptoms.[4*] Hence, as

*See "What effect can the atmosphere at home have on veterans?" on pages 44–46.

you read the statistics offered here and throughout this book, keep in mind that they may offer an incomplete or oversimplified picture of the prevalence of traumatic reactions.

Combat Trauma through Modern Times

War is seldom good for people. Even the ancient Greeks commented on the negative effects of war on man's psyche, as did Shakespeare and other writers. Indeed, the Department of Veterans Affairs had its beginning in concerns for Civil War veterans from both sides who were found staring into space for hours with vacuous looks in their eyes or who were found wandering aimlessly on city streets or in the countryside, unable to adapt to civilian life. Civil War soldiers were considered to be suffering from "soldier's heart." For decades, mental health professionals have noted the psychiatric effects of war and talked about "war neurosis," "combat fatigue," and "combat exhaustion."

World War I, World War II, and the Korean War Veterans

Among American troops, symptoms of battle fatigue caused the evacuation of some 10 percent of enlisted men during World War I and, at various points, of 30 percent more during World War II. The psychiatric casualty rate was high during World War II despite elaborate psychological screening procedures that supposedly weeded out weak men prone to mental collapse. After World War II, however, military experts concluded that the trauma of war was often enough to impair even men deemed to be among the "strongest" and "toughest."[5]

World War I and World War II veterans who suffered from symptoms of combat trauma often kept their problems to themselves or drowned them in alcohol. If it is not acceptable for soldiers to admit that they have inner turmoil today, it was even less so in the past. Yet even today surviving World War II and Korean War veterans are being treated by the Department of Veterans Affairs for nightmares and other symptoms of battle fatigue.

The psychological stress of war was first recognized by mental health professionals during World War I. During the Great War, the "idea developed that the high air pressure of the exploding shells caused actual physiological damage," which in turn led to numerous psychological symptoms that were later named "shell shock." By the end of the war, the malady that seemed to afflict so many survivors was called "war neurosis."[6]

During the Korean War, the military, now aware of "war neurosis," provided immediate, on-site help to afflicted servicemen. Such assistance reduced the percentage of evacuations for psychiatric reasons from 23 percent during World War II to 6 percent during the Korean conflict.[7] During the Vietnam War, in an attempt to further reduce the psychiatric casualty rate, the one-year tour of duty was adopted. The military reasoned that if men were subject to combat for only a year, they would be less susceptible to psychological breakdown. However, as the mental health statistics on Vietnam veterans presented below will attest, this reasoning was inaccurate. It was exposure to combat, regardless of the length of that exposure, which set the stage for post-traumatic reactions.

The symptoms of combat trauma in those who served in Vietnam, the Persian Gulf, Afghanistan, and Iraq are almost identical to those suffered by World War II and Korean War vets.[8] These symptoms also have been found among British soldiers who served in the Persian Gulf, among Australian troops who served in Vietnam and in the Gulf, and among Israeli soldiers both during and after the Lebanon war.[9]

Vietnam Veterans

The National Vietnam Veteran Readjustment Survey, the largest study to date of Vietnam theater veterans (that is, veterans who actually served in Vietnam proper, not veterans who served during the Vietnam era but did not actually go to Vietnam), found that approximately 15.2 percent of all male Vietnam theater veterans (or about 479,000 men) and about 8.5 percent of female theater veterans (or about 7,500 women) were suffering from PTSD at the time the study was conducted in 1988. However, the rates of PTSD rise to almost 136 percent among veterans exposed to heavy combat.[10]

Also excluded from these statistics are men and women who were in Cambodia, Laos, or elsewhere in Southeast Asia, but not in Vietnam proper. In some cases, these troops were on missions so secret that it is difficult, if not impossible, to find documentation of their whereabouts and activities. The 15.2 percent figure also does not include the 11.1 percent of male theater veterans and 7.8 percent of female theater veterans who suffer from partial PTSD or sufficient PTSD symptoms to cause emotional pain, but insufficient enough to qualify as having the full-blown disorder. Including men and women who suffer from partial PTSD adds another 350,000 persons to the list.

The study also found that about one-third of male theater veterans and one-fourth of females who served in country suffered from PTSD at some time in their life. While experts disagree on the true extent of PTSD among Vietnam veterans, in agreement with the Vietnam Readjustment study, most put the figure at close to 1 million.[11] Given that this figure does not include veterans who suffer from traumatic reactions other than PTSD, the actual number who bear emotional scars may be even larger.

Persian Gulf Veterans

Available statistics on rates of PTSD among veterans of the first Gulf War show rates of 2–10 percent among U.S. troops. For example, one study found that five years after the war, the rates of PTSD were 2 percent among active-duty sent overseas as opposed to 0.7 percent of those who were not deployed. Deployed troops were also more likely to report symptoms of two or more other medical or psychiatric problems. However, another study showed much higher rates of PTSD among Gulf veterans: 8 percent among active-duty veterans and 9.2 percent of Reserves sent to the Persian Gulf. A group of researchers who examined symptoms not only of PTSD but also of other disorders found rates of emotional distress such as 16–24 percent among the National Guard and Army Reserves deployed to war zones in the Persian Gulf. The rates were much lower for men and women in the National Guard or the Reserves who were activated, but not deployed, or who were deployed but had little exposure to combat. Among male Australian troops sent to the Gulf, approximately 31 percent were found to suffer from some type of full-blown psychiatric disorder. It is not clear, however, whether some of the troops already had symptoms of combat trauma from prior wars or traumas.[12]

Veterans of the Wars in Afghanistan and Iraq

Using strict definitions of PTSD, depression, and other mental disorders, a recent study conducted by the U.S. Army found significant increases in the rates of full-blown mental disorders after duty in Afghanistan and Iraq. The rates of PTSD and other traumatic reactions rose for troops after being deployed to Afghanistan or Iraq. More specifically, conservative estimates are that up to 9 percent of soldiers evidenced symptoms of mental distress before being deployed to either of these combat zones. Upon their return, approximately 11 to 17 percent were found to be at risk for PTSD or other forms of combat trauma, with higher rates of mental distress being found among those who had returned from Iraq.[13]

In truth, we do not actually know how many veterans suffer or suffered from some form of combat trauma. It was not until 1980 that PTSD was officially recognized as a "mental illness" by the American Psychiatric Association. Before that time, vets with PTSD were sometimes given psychiatric diagnoses that either excluded or minimized the role of the war on their psychological well-being.[14] Even today, given that PTSD is a relatively new diagnosis, not every mental health professional is familiar with it or other combat-related traumatic reactions. Furthermore, the diagnosis of combat-related stress reactions can be a very challenging task, for it can coexist with a host of other psychological problems—alcoholism, paranoia, and even schizophrenia.[15] Over time, as more and more mental health professionals become more knowledgeable about and better able to diagnose the effects of combat, the reported rates of combat trauma may change.

Another reason we do not know how many veterans suffer from some form of combat trauma is that some fail to seek help for fear of being labeled weak or unmanly. Some vets, especially those with relatives who boast that they made it through previous wars without any problems, feel it is shameful to seek counseling. Male veterans imbued with the masculine stereotype of the "real man" being one who is always strong and in control of his emotions, as well as female veterans who need to prove that they are just as "tough" as their male comrades, can find it difficult to admit that they have any psychological problems.[16] The 2004 Army study of veterans from Afghanistan and Iraq found that only 38 to 45 percent of the troops with symptoms of full-blown PTSD, depression, or generalized anxiety disorder showed any interest in obtaining help and that only 23 to 40 percent of those afflicted with one of these disorders had actually done so.[17]

"I was in denial for years," explains one vet. "I even pretended that I never went overseas. I thought if I ignored what the war did to me, it would go away." This denial serves as a major defense against feeling the extremely uncomfortable feelings that often go along with the combat experience: specifically, fear, guilt, grief, rage, and moral confusion.

Another reason it is difficult to measure the prevalence of combat trauma is that some stress reactions do not emerge until many years later. PTSD is, by definition, a delayed response to the war, and in many cases PTSD or PTSD-like symptoms only emerge years later. For example, a study of World War II POWs found that 22 percent had chronic PTSD, but 36 percent of these developed symptoms only after age forty. Of this 36 percent, about one-fourth had combat stress after the war but managed to contain it until midlife or old age.[18] A similar pattern has been found among veterans who served in Korea and Vietnam.[19] What problems will develop among veterans who served in the Persian Gulf, Afghanistan, and Iraq over time, especially as these veterans age, cannot be known at this time

Q: What effect does combat experience have on symptoms of combat trauma?

Study after study has shown that regardless of the nature of the war or differences in ethnic or socioeconomic background among soldiers, the greater their exposure to combat, the greater the likelihood that they will develop traumatic reactions either during or after combat duty. This has been found in studies of veterans from World War II, Korea, Vietnam, the Persian Gulf, Afghanistan, and Iraq and of veterans from Australia, Britain, Israel, and elsewhere.

In addition, PTSD and other disorders have been found to be prevalent among those who saw or participated in the abusive or random violence that is part of any war.[20] It is not clear whether more random violence occurred in Vietnam and in subsequent wars than in prior wars or whether, beginning with Vietnam, atrocities have been more publicized than in previous wars. Some argue that the reported atrocities are often exaggerations or outright lies perpetrated by the enemy; while others, especially enemy presses, argue that American violations of the Geneva Convention regarding treatment of prisoners and similar issues tend to be kept secret.

In truth, there is no way to measure the degree of brutality present in a war. Atrocities are committed in all wars, even during the Civil War in the United States, when in many cases brother fought brother. However, special factors are present in the type of guerrilla warfare that operated in Vietnam and elsewhere and which is currently in operation in Afghanistan and Iraq that can contribute to acts of random violence and abuse. In "Some Remarks on Slaughter," W. B. Gault, a psychiatrist who served in Vietnam, describes some of these psychological, social, and mechanical factors that can contribute to acts of random violence:

1. "The universality of the enemy": The fact that the enemy is or was everywhere;

2. "The cartoonization and dehumanization of the enemy": In Vietnam, Asians were not perceived as human, but as strange childlike creatures—"dinks"—who did not value human life anyway. In Afghanistan and Iraq, Muslims are often perceived as "towel-heads" and, given all the suicide bombers, as people who don't value human life either.

3. "The dilution of responsibility": The fact that entire squads simultaneously attacked or attack villages or crowds.

4. "The pressure to act": To prove that one is strong and patriotic or to execute revenge.

5. "The natural dominance of the psychopath": In certain combat situations, soldiers may follow the lead of the soldier who relishes the opportunity to kill, mutilate, or abuse.

6. "The ready availability of firepower."[21]

Many combat veterans are well aware that they are not the first soldiers in history to be unnecessarily cruel. Often they will say they would not have done some of the things they did had they not been under so much stress and seen atrocities committed by the enemy. Nevertheless, some vets feel that they were more animalistic and brutal than previous warriors. The resulting sense of shame and self-hate can be intense.

Some veterans experience this shame and self-hate on an unconscious level. They may not even be able to articulate any such feelings. If asked if they have a self-image problem, they may say "no." After all, shame, self-hate, and a negative self-image are not signs of soldierly strength. Yet veterans who are not able to acknowledge their shame or self-hate and deal with it in an open, constructive manner may act out these feelings destructively. For example, if on some level they view themselves as incompetent, evil, or bad, they might project these despised qualities onto their partners or children or some other family member. They may then accuse their partners or other family member of having these qualities or become overly critical of that person's behavior.

When veterans view themselves as murderers or sadists, their self-esteem plummets. Some vets may not wait for society, God, or the universe to punish them. They punish themselves with a relentless internal self-beating, often unconscious, often masked as boredom or depression. Or they abuse alcohol, food, or drugs; find themselves unwittingly making a series of mistakes on the job or at home; or find other ways to defeat themselves. Still others push away families and friends lest they inadvertently reveal their "secrets" to these significant others and thereby lose their love and respect.

For example, some vets are tormented by the fact that, after a certain amount of exposure to combat, or despite their moral scruples against killing, at times they actually enjoyed the fight and got "high" on blood. Other vets are troubled by the fact that in certain instances they were cowardly and that their cowardice may have caused the death or injury of a fellow soldier or an innocent civilian. Back home when a vet reflects on his or her past, he or she may wonder: "Was that really me? If it was, then what kind of person am I? How can I face myself, much less others? Would my partner continue to stay with me and my children continue to respect me if they found out what happened over there?" Sometimes when a veteran retreats into a shell or verbally puts down the people closest to him, he is just trying to temporarily shove them out of his life so that they will never guess that he has done things or experienced feelings that might be considered immoral or cowardly.

It bears repeating that PTSD and other traumatic reactions are not restricted to combat vets; these reactions can be found among those who experienced near-death or life-threatening situations or who were surrounded by death. Medics, nurses, doctors, therapists, as well as transporters, body-bag counters, embalmers, administrative officers, journalists, and other civilians who served in war zones have also developed serious symptoms, as have members of international peacekeeping forces.[22] Similarly, during World War II, war neurosis was found not only among combatants, for whom the "threat of annihilation and destruction . . . was very real and imminent," but also among soldiers in graves registration units and in Army Air Corps emergency fire squad units.[23]

Q: What effect can the atmosphere at home have on veterans?

In wars where returning veterans are greeted with gratitude and praise, soldiers may have felt guilty for killing, but their guilt was at least partially absolved because they were seen by friends, family, and society as "good warriors," that is, as heroes who killed as part of their duty. However, veterans who are viewed by significant segments of the American public as deranged, sadistic, cowardly, or inept lack the advantage of this societal absolution. Veterans who are greeted with hostility or—just as hurtful—apathy can be seen as suffering from two wounds: first, the wounds caused by war, and second, those caused by an unwelcome homecoming.[24]

World War II veterans escaped the disgraceful homecoming given to many Vietnam veterans. Whereas public opinion was heavily divided about the Vietnam War, there was almost universal support for World War II. Not only had our nation been attacked by an enemy at Pearl Harbor, but there was great fear of a land invasion. The enemy was clear-cut and the entire nation mobilized to support the war effort. Almost everyone felt the effects of the war due to the universal draft and due to rationing and other material deprivations. In contrast, during the Vietnam War, there was little fear of invasion, the draft was selective, and few civilians did without sugar, coffee, or other items because of the war.

Ever since the construction of the Wall (the Vietnam Veterans Memorial in Washington, D.C.), society has increasingly come to honor the contributions of Vietnam veterans. However, upon their return in the 1960s and '70s, many were treated like second-class citizens, or worse. Some of the Vietnam veterans I have worked with described how they refused to talk about the war or deliberately hid the fact that they had served in Vietnam, lest they be insulted or assaulted or be denied a job or promotion.

But it is not only Vietnam veterans who often received direct or indirect messages that they should not talk about their war experiences or their feelings about the war.[25] Combat veterans from all wars are often made to feel or determine themselves that such sharing would simply create too much anxiety and discomfort in their friends or family members. Veterans who served during World War II and in combat zones since, including Lebanon, Somalia, Afghanistan, and Iraq, have described how they have had to hide in closets or bathrooms to cry because their open expressions of grief are not tolerated by others. "You can't really help me. To me therapy is hogwash," a veteran told me. "The only reason I come here is because this is the only place I can cry without people telling me that I should stop thinking about the war and just be grateful I came home alive. Maybe they're right, but I still need to cry." Many other veterans have expressed similar sentiments.

Q: How can war affect a veteran spiritually and morally?

Even the best of men couldn't begin to realize what the war did to human beings. How it made good men bent and worse men blind.

—AN ARMY MEDIC IN VIETNAM[26]

For many veterans combat trauma is more than a psychological problem: it can be a spiritual and moral problem as well. Many religions teach "Thou shalt not kill." Yet, throughout history, governments and even certain religious groups have made exceptions to his general rule for purposes of defending the nation or the faith itself. For example, both Islam and Christianity prohibit killing, but Islam permits jihad, or "holy war," and the Catholic Church sanctioned the Crusades.

In situations where the killing is confined to a clearly defined enemy and where warriors kill for purposes they understand and in which they and most of their family and countrymen believe, warriors can sometimes kill and still consider themselves "good." However, in war zones where either the enemy or the goals are unclear, killing can create moral or spiritual confusion, if not despair. Some soldiers who enter a war zone with a firm belief in God or in the faith of their childhood can come to question God's existence or God's benevolence. How could God allow this war to happen? They may feel that their religious or spiritual beliefs have failed them or, the opposite, that they failed their faith, especially if they witnessed or participated in atrocities.* The few studies on changes in religious faith following combat have found that numerous veterans report that participation in the war greatly conflicted with the spiritual or religious values they once held.[27]

*See "What effect does combat experience have on symptoms of combat trauma?" on pages 42–44.

Those who went to war unsure about their religious beliefs may have emerged even more unsure. For atheists, the war may have confirmed their belief that there is no God, and for cynics, war may have confirmed their view of the world as unfair and cruel.

When vets who left the battlefield spiritually empty or in moral pain finally come home, they may reject their prior religion or spiritual beliefs. In some cases, this may make it difficult for partners and children to continue their normal religious practices. As a result, some partners withdraw from their religious or spiritual traditions. Others, however, increase their spiritual activities because they find that these activities provide them with the energy and strength to cope with a partner suffering from combat trauma.

On the other hand, for some veterans, the war intensified their faith with profound religious experiences on the battlefield. There are reports of being protected by guardian angels, feeling close to God, even "seeing the Lord." Some veterans who had near-death experiences reported "spiritual awakenings of great beauty."[28] If a veteran's partner is an atheist or agnostic, however, the veteran's spirituality or religious fervor may create yet another conflict in their relationship.

Veterans who happened to serve in a unit that developed a hedonistic lifestyle can have additional problems. In this unit it may have been "okay" to abuse alcohol and drugs and be sexually free, as it was to freely kill. Moral restrictions were ignored because the soldiers were far from home and because death was a constant threat. Yet many young soldiers often had conscious or unconscious ambivalence about these experiences.[29]

The veteran's unresolved conflicts about religious or spiritual beliefs or participation in some of these hedonistic activities may contribute to withdrawal from partner and family and from the faith he or she once held. The veteran may feel too "contaminated" or too much of a "sinner" to go back to his or her synagogue, church, temple, or other religious establishment or to participate fully in family activities surrounding religious holidays. Baptisms, bar mitzvahs, and similar events may be especially painful since they illustrate the contrast between how a veteran was when he or she went through those ceremonies as a child and what he or she has experienced since.

As a result, religious holidays, like patriotic ones, can be very difficult times for combat veterans and their families. Even when veterans force themselves to participate for the sake of the family, partners and children know that their veteran's heart isn't in it, which changes the entire tone and meaning of the event. Consequently, a religious or spiritual event, which could have brought the family closer, can end up driving the family further apart and creating more pain.

Unfortunately, some veterans are subjected to spiritual "blaming the victim" where others focus on the veteran's failure to live up to certain religious or spiritual ideals during or after combat. Sometimes a veteran's symptoms of combat trauma and even a veteran's physical pain and disability stemming from battle injuries are viewed as forms of "payback" for wrongdoings, such as killing (or not killing); indulging in alcohol, drugs, or sex in the war zone; or as forms of punishment for having had certain emotions during combat, such as being afraid or being glad at having survived even though others died.

Some veterans have been told that they can free themselves from the emotional scars of battle if they focus on their faith rather than their feelings. Yet others have been told the opposite: that their spirituality is an escape from their feelings and from taking responsibility for themselves and they need to focus more on their feelings than their faith. Veterans who seek help from more than one source—for example, from a mental health professional, a spiritual advisor, or a lay counselor from their church, from twelve-step programs, from various books, or from other veterans—may find that their helpers do not agree on what to put first: faith or feelings. This can lead not only to confusion but also to despair.

Q: Why are some veterans more affected by combat than others?

Some veterans, especially those who have succeeded in business or the professions, may appear to be relatively unaffected by having been in combat. Yet they may be suffering in ways that are not visible. For example, veterans with high-paying positions in banks or major companies could be having problems with emotional intimacy with their partners. Other veterans may achieve great fame in their field, yet in their private moments feel excruciatingly lonely because they have difficulty making and keeping friends.

Nevertheless, some troops are more severely affected by the negative aspects of war than others. Often this is the result of an imbalance between the number and severity of the burdens they carry (stresses and traumas they experienced or are currently experiencing) as compared to their supports (the amount of emotional, medical, financial, and social support and stability in their lives).[30] Some of the burdens and supports that have been shown to influence whether short-term symptoms of combat trauma develop into longer-term ones and the extent to which these symptoms disrupt or cripple a veteran's ability to sustain and find satisfaction in relationships and vocational, recreational, spiritual, and other pursuits are noted below.

Burdens

1. *The number and severity of traumatic stressors,* including degree of exposure to death and dying, to atrocities, to friendly fire, to toxic substances, and to other life-threatening experiences. The sections titled "What effect can combat experience have on symptoms of combat trauma?" and "How might war affect veterans spiritually and morally?" in this chapter describe the impact of combat on the development of traumatic reactions and low self-esteem. The effects of friendly fire, the deaths of comrades and civilians, and other traumas common to combat are described in chapter 1.

2. *Age and rank.* In general, the younger a person is when exposed to a trauma, whether it be sexual assault, combat, or a hurricane, the more that person is likely to suffer negative effects. Hence younger children are at higher risk for developing PTSD, depression, or other post traumatic reactions than are adolescents, teenagers more than young adults; and young adults more than older ones.[31]

According to experts on combat trauma, the age of a veteran when he or she enters the services can play a decisive role in the development of serious traumatic reactions.[32] Men and women who go to war in their late adolescence or early twenties are at a distinct disadvantage compared to older veterans. During late adolescence, the personality is not yet formed and the individual is more vulnerable to stress. Dr. John Wilson explains:

> [L]ate adolescence [is] the time of life when people put their identities together, their occupation, their sex role, their commitments, the normal developmental process that leads to a human identity. So if you take a nineteen-year-old soldier and subject him [or her] to tremendous war stress for a year . . . you end up with people who in their own words say, "I'm a different person," "I'm changed," "I don't fit in," "I'm twenty and feel like I came back fifty."[33]

Vietnam vets were sometimes called the "old young men" because they went to war at a significantly lower age than soldiers of previous wars, yet emerged "old men" with "aged hearts."[34] (The average age of the Vietnam veteran was nineteen; the average age of the World War II veteran was twenty-six.)

Yet it is not only Vietnam veterans who feel they lost their youth in a war zone. Veterans from subsequent wars also talk about not being able to relax and have fun like friends their age who didn't go to war. For many young soldiers, it is not only their first exposure to death but also their first time away from home and their first time in another country. A nineteen-year-old veteran explains: "This first time my unit pitched camp, I thought I was on a school camping trip. When it got dark, I started getting scared and wondered when my mother was going to come pick me up. When I finally realized that this was no camping trip, but a war, I started missing my mother, my dog, and all my friends back home so much I started vomiting."

In general, higher rates of post-traumatic symptoms have been found among younger veterans than older ones and among enlisted personnel than among officers.[35] Similarly, among Gulf War veterans, more psychological distress at exposure to stressful but not life-threatening events (such as false alarms about the use of chemical agents, being on board a ship or aircraft passing through hostile waters or airspace, or coming into contact with contaminated water) was reported by troops in the lower ranks than by officers who are generally older than troops in lower ranks.[36]

However these age and rank differences may reflect more than differences in age and rank. They also reflect differences in duties and living conditions. Younger troops tend to hold lower ranks than older soldiers and younger, lower-ranking soldiers are often exposed to more dangerous situations and more squalid living conditions than older, higher-ranking soldiers or officers.[37]

3. *The number and severity of nonlethal stresses.* As described in chapter 1, combat soldiers often encounter numerous stresses which, although not life threatening, can create considerable emotional and physical duress. Veterans who experience more of these such stresses can be expected to bear more scars from their combat experience than those who experience fewer of these stresses.

For example, deployment can create more hardships for military personnel who have a partner than for those who don't; for those who have children than for those who don't; for those who were ambivalent about serving in a war zone than for those who volunteered for combat duty. Deployed members of the National Guard and the Reserves can experience additional strains: loss of income, fear of losing their nonmilitary jobs, and the reality of fewer readily available support services for their families as compared to active-duty military families.

This is reflected in studies that show higher rates of emotional distress among non-active-duty military, such as those in the Reserves or the National Guard who are sent to war zones, than among active-duty military.[38] There is no information, however, on how symptoms among these particular groups have changed or are changing over time.

4. *Financial hardships and societal prejudices based on gender and ethnicity.* In general, symptoms of combat trauma tend to be more severe among veterans who are already burdened with financial hardships or with societal prejudices based on gender or ethnicity. This is not surprising given that minority status and financial difficulties often go hand in hand. Many, but not all, studies of combat stress reactions have found higher rates of PTSD among veterans with ethnic minority status or less education and among women veterans. Women have also evidenced higher rates of post-traumatic symptoms than men following traumas unrelated to combat, for example, vehicular accidents and criminal assault. Women also have higher rates of depression and various anxiety disorders than men in the general population. It is unknown, however, the extent to which these higher rates for women reflect the fact that women are more likely to admit to emotional distress than men because it is more socially acceptable for them to do so. In contrast, because of the shame involved in directly admitting to emotional suffering, men might express their psychological distresses indirectly, through substance abuse or violent behavior, for example, which occur at higher rates with men than with women.[39]

The higher rates of PTSD and depression among women may also reflect the fact that women are more likely than men to have experienced prior traumas such as sexual assault or partner abuse as well as sexual harassment and other gender-related stresses during their military or other careers. Current estimates are that perhaps one in every four females is a victim of sexual assault before she turns eighteen. The estimates for sexual assault for men are lower: one in six.[40] According to many experts, the actual rates are much higher since many victims, especially male victims, are too ashamed to admit or report being assaulted.

On the financial level, returning veterans who can find satisfactory employment tend to develop fewer long-term symptoms than those who struggle to find a job or who find that an employer who had promised to hold a job for them gave the job to someone else. Veterans also fare better when their employer permits flexible work hours so that they can attend any needed mental health or medical appointments or take leave if necessary during anniversary or particularly stressful times. Unfortunately, some veterans encounter harassment or discrimination (based on ethnicity, physical disability, veteran status, or some other reason) on the job. Even though the verbal insults and unfair practices associated with workplace harassment are not life threatening, when combat vets find themselves in situations where they are being attacked or feel they are being attacked, their combat-related traumatic reactions tend to persist or even worsen.

5. *Number and severity of injuries.* The more injuries a soldier sustains and the greater their severity, the greater the probability that he or she will develop PTSD and other traumatic reactions as compared to veterans who come home without a scratch.[41]

6. *Number and severity of noncombat-related negative events prior to and following combat duty.* In general, combat has a more negative impact on those men and women who were already coping with stressful situations prior to combat duty than on those who were relatively emotionally, financially, and socially secure prior to their war experience.[42] The same holds true regarding noncombat-related negative events upon return from war. Veterans who encounter positive events, such as their children receiving scholarships or a relative recovering from cancer, are likely to have fewer adjustment problems than those who encounter negative events, such as a death in the family or increased crime in the neighborhood.

In addition, for some veterans combat brings forth or intensifies memories of prior traumas, such as child abuse or gang violence. In one case, for example, a seasoned officer did not develop symptoms of PTSD until his third round of combat duty when he saw the corpse of a five-year-old girl lying on the side of a road. He had seen many dead children in his military career, but this body of this particular girl was in almost the identical position of his sister's body after she had been shot in a drive-by-shooting. Although this officer was only four when his sister died, he remembered her death. But he did not experience the full emotional impact of her death until he saw the dead girl by the roadside. This unleashed a flood of emotions, not only about his sister's death, but about all the deaths he had seen as a soldier.

7. *Substance abuse and other addictions.* Veterans who are addicted to

a substance such as alcohol, or to an activity such as gambling, may be trying to numb their emotions. Addictions can consume so many waking hours that a veteran doesn't have time to think about the human misery he or she witnessed during combat. An addiction can also be a form of self-medication for PTSD, depression, and anxiety attacks. Alcohol, certain drugs, and excess food, for example, have been found to help regulate sleep and suppress nightmares, reduce panic and anxiety attacks, and reduce despair and hopelessness, but only for a while.[43]

In the long run addictions have a rebound effect and symptoms worsen. Almost inevitably addictions lead to medical, financial, and relationship problems, which only aggravate any problems that already exist. Ironically, addictions can create the very problems they were intended to solve. Veterans who suffer from traumatic reactions as well as an addiction are coping with two sets of problems: those stemming from the war and those stemming from their addiction. Hence their readjustment process is usually longer, more complicated, and, unless they manage to control their addiction, impossible to complete. In addition, while they are actively practicing their addiction, they may suffer financial losses or alienate family members and others, which makes their recovery process even harder.

Supports

1. *Degree of support in the general population.* See the section titled "What effect can the atmosphere at home have on veterans?" starting on page 44, which describes another critical factor that affects the degree to which a veteran might suffer from combat trauma: the amount of support received from the general public.

2. *Degree of support from family and friends.* Also critical is the degree of social support and love and acceptance received from others, especially family members. Veterans who come home to families that embrace them with open arms and do not shame them for showing signs of combat trauma are much more likely to adjust to civilian life without long-term symptoms than veterans whose families berate or reject them for their reactions to having been in a war. It has been found, for example, that PTSD-afflicted combat vets who perceive support from their families have more hope than those who feel unsupported.[44]

Yolanda, a naval officer, explains:

When I first came home from Iraq and heard cars backfire, I'd nearly jump out of my skin and run for cover. I was so glad that my boyfriend said things like, "Wow, you must have been through hell." But my last boyfriend, the one I had when I came back from the Gulf, used to say things like, "Better get that sand out of your head or you'll end up just as crazy as the rest of those vets," or "I should have known better than to hook up with an Army brat like you. And I thought that you being a soldier-girl would be able to protect me. If I have to be your Mommy and baby you just because you went through some little ten-day war, this re-lationship is over." Comments like that made me worse. But my new boyfriend just tells me he loves me and asks me how he can help and that's made all the difference in the world. His caring has given me hope.

3. *Availability and quality of mental health and other services.* Veterans who do not have ready access to mental health and other services are at greater risk for developing longer-term symptoms than those who receive help early on or before the traumatic symptoms come to shape their lives or before they are tempted to turn to substance abuse or other addictions as forms of self-medication. The quality of the mental health treatment also plays a role. Veterans whose mental health prob-lems are ignored, minimized, or misdiagnosed or whose psychiatric medications are not sufficiently monitored for effectiveness must en-dure the stigma of being a "mental patient," as well as the potentially demoralizing effects of having sought help and experienced little or no improvement.

All too often veterans blame themselves for the persistence or wors-ening of their combat-related problems when, in fact, if appropriate, sufficient, and timely help had been available, their efforts to better man-age their combat trauma may have met with more success. The above holds true for medical and other services. Veterans who receive quality medical care and other services are more likely to recover from their combat experiences than those who experience delays or other prob-lems. Even the best mental health and medical care is of no avail, how-ever, if veterans do not use the services available to them in the military or in their communities.

Q: *How can war affect veterans physically?*

> *Paula took her two house cats to the vet. The first cat became so agitated at being locked up in a cat carrier and transported to a strange place that she hissed at the veterinarian and scratched anyone who came close to her. Even with the help of three trained assistants, the nine-pound cat's clawing and frantic movements could not be contained enough for the doctor to examine her.*
>
> *Paula's second cat went limp. From the moment he was placed in the cat box, he barely moved. He delighted the doctor because he was placid and easy to examine. But after his visit to the vet, the cat no longer delighted in life. He no longer purred when petted and was nonresponsive to any signs of affection from Paula that day and for days afterwards.*

The first cat's frantic fighting mode and the second cat's "shutdown" mode seem to be extreme opposites of each other. Yet they are part of the same phenomenon: the stimulation of the adrenal glands due to a perceived or real threat. For these two house cats, leaving the security of their safe place (home) and being put in unknown territory with strangers felt life threatening and dangerous. The first cat's adrenal glands were stimulated to produce adrenaline, which put the cat in a "fight" mode. The second cat's adrenal pumped out noradrenalin, which put the cat in a "freeze" or "numbing" mode.[45]

As the example of the cats illustrates, trauma can affect not only the emotions and the mind, but the physical self as well, specifically the central nervous system. When psychologist Abraham Kardiner studied the effects of war on veterans of World War I, he used the word *physioneurosis* to indicate that war had altered not only the thinking and feeling states of the warriors, but their physiology as well.[46] As a result, not only do some veterans continue "to live in the emotional environment of the traumatic event," but "[their] bodies . . . continue to be on the alert for a return of the trauma and tend to react to even minor stresses with physiological emergency responses."[47]

These emergency responses include the "three Fs": fight, flight, freeze. Under conditions of danger, the adrenal glands release either adrenaline or noradrenalin. Adrenaline enables the warrior to move quickly and powerfully, whether to fight with renewed strength or to run (flight) with increased speed. In the example of the cats above, the first cat became so empowered with adrenaline it fought off three human beings, which is like one human being combating three elephants. In contrast, the second cat had a noradrenalin surge. Unlike adrenaline, noradrenalin leads to numbing responses. Hence some warriors freeze in battle and find themselves unable to move. The freeze response can also be caused by the release of other calming neurohormones.

It is also possible for some veterans to be temporarily frozen (by noradrenalin), then empowered with adrenaline shortly thereafter, or vice versa. Some veterans have been puzzled by the fact that one minute they could barely move, but the next minute they found themselves fighting as if they were invincible. Upon reflection, they are angry at themselves for, on the one hand, being too "frozen" to kill and, on the other hand, being so energetic they killed "too much" or took foolish risks with their lives. Yet their fight, flight, freeze responses were, to one degree or another, out of their control. Their bodies automatically went into a fight, flight, or freeze reaction as a means of self-preservation.

The release of noradrenalin can lead to emotional, physical, and mental shutdown. In contrast, under the influence of increased adrenaline flow, heart rate, blood sugar level, muscle tension, and perspiration increase and pupils dilate. Some people may experience hyperventilation (rapid shallow breathing from the upper lung versus more normal, gentle breathing from the lower lung). Hyperventilation, in turn, can lead to irregular heart rate and dizziness, shortness of breath, choking sensations, lump in the throat, heartburn, chest pain, blurred vision, muscle pains or spasms, nausea, shaking, and numbness or tingling of mouth, hands, or feet. It can also generate mental confusion and difficulties with concentration.[48]

At first glance, an adrenaline surge may seem preferable to a noradrenalin response, especially in battle. However, adrenaline surges can be problematic because they cannot be turned off at will. Soldiers in battle whose adrenaline surges cause them to fight as powerfully as possible are easily tempted to discharge excess adrenaline through abusive violence, needless killings, or other acts of destruction. Or they may attempt to quiet the excess adrenaline by using alcohol or other drugs.

The adrenaline surge does not excuse excessive violence, but it plays an undeniable role in such incidents, not only in combat, but back home, when a veteran is triggered by an event that reminds him of war. When family members "walk on eggs," it is because they do not want to trigger their veteran into a rage reaction or a deep depression over which he or she may have little control. The veterans themselves also appreciate how powerful fight, flight, and freeze reactions can be and know that even the strongest warrior cannot successfully fight biology. Consequently, some veterans may avoid people, places, and events that may possibly make them agitated or severely depressed. Some have even left good jobs for fear of being triggered into an uncontrollable adrenaline-induced violent reaction on the job or a deep depression that might put them, or others, in harm's way. On the surface, it may appear to family members, friends, and coworkers that the veteran is standoffish, a loner, or severely disturbed because of his or her need to retreat. Yet the veteran's retreat may be highly socially motivated: he or she simply does not want to hurt anyone or drag loved ones down with his or her depression.

No matter how much they love their veteran, partners may find it difficult to cope with these symptoms. Unfortunately, they often mistakenly attribute the veteran's mood swings almost entirely to their own behavior, not realizing that one of the prime causes of these symptoms lies in the changes in the veteran's biochemistry due to the overuse of his emergency biological system.

There are many coping skills available that can help veterans (as well as others) calm themselves when they are in a "fight" or "flight" mode or help them regain their energy when they are in a "freeze" mode. (See appendix B, "Suggested Reading," for helpful books on coping skills.) Some medications, when properly administered and monitored, can also be helpful. When coping skills, medication, or a combination of both succeed in reducing the intensity of fight-flight-freeze reactions, veterans feel more in control and, consequently, may feel safer about interacting with others. However, while medication and coping skills can help control fight-flight-freeze reactions, they cannot eliminate these symptoms entirely unless, of course, the veteran becomes overmedicated and incapable of any kind of response, either negative or positive.

The subject of biological changes that occur when a person is exposed to repeated or prolonged trauma is complex, involving changes in the functioning of various neurotransmitters, neurohormones, and other biochemical changes. The freeze response, for example, can include biological changes other than the release of noradrenalin. A more complete discussion of the physiology of PTSD and other forms of combat trauma is beyond the scope of this book. Let it suffice here to state that veterans who suffer from some of these biochemical changes are vulnerable to clinical depression, mood swings, explosive outbursts, startle response, and overreacting to subsequent stress. The biochemistry of PTSD, depression, and other traumatic reactions is one of the new and promising areas of research in the field of traumatology.

Q: How can war affect the way veterans think?

Just as combat can change a soldier's biochemistry, it can change the way he or she thinks. For soldiers, after having been at war, the assumption that the world is a safe and loving place is destroyed. They feel vulnerable in ways and to a degree that they never felt vulnerable before. Afterwards, when new people or events come into their lives, they may tend to automatically view them as threats, or potential threats, instead of opportunities, or potential opportunities.

No matter how much ammunition they are carrying, at some point during combat soldiers come to realize how helpless they are in the face of enemy attacks and the many unpredictable dangers of war. Perhaps their greatest fear is being helpless again, and justifiably so. To protect themselves against that fear, they may approach new situations and people with mindsets learned in the war.

Three common war-related traumatic mindsets (ways of thinking) are all-or-nothing and now-or-never thinking; perfectionism or intolerance of mistakes in others or in oneself; and denial of personal difficulties. These and other mind-sets learned during combat as means of self-protection and survival may still be useful in some areas of life today. In other areas, however, they may distort perceptions and reactions and not serve a person well. These mind-sets can be found not only among combat veterans, but among victims of violence, natural catastrophes, and other traumas.

All-or-Nothing and Now-or-Never Thinking

Because so much is at stake during combat, issues tend to become black or white. Either someone is "with you" or "against you": there is no in-between. There is no such thing as trying to save your life "in moderation" or killing an enemy "just a little bit." In war, like other traumas, "moderate" and "medium" responses are not effective and often not even possible. In addition, during trauma, all that matters is the moment at hand. It doesn't matter what someone did in the past or will do in the future. All that matters is what he or she is doing now.

Therefore today, when the vet is thinking like a warrior, he might view someone in his present life the way he needed to view people in the combat zone: as friend or foe, as someone who would risk his life for him or someone who is trying to use him, someone who can be trusted with everything or someone who can be trusted with nothing.

The truth, however, may be somewhere in between: the other person may care for the vet, but not enough to die for him. Or that person may be confused about how he or she feels toward the vet. There is also the possibility that the individual may change his or her feelings in the future. Yet in his warrior mode, the vet views that individual in all-or-nothing terms, as bosom buddy or archenemy, with nothing in between. When thinking like a warrior, the vet will view another person based on what that person is doing at the moment or in the immediate past, rather than take into consideration other things he knows about that individual or all the other experiences he has had with him or her.

Perfectionism: Intolerance of Mistakes in Others/Self

In war, mistakes are intolerable. Even the tiniest mistake can result in death or injury to others or oneself. Most combat vets have seen how the mistakes of others caused needless deaths, injuries, and other losses. As a result, they may have developed a mind-set of "no mistakes allowed" and suffer from perfectionism in certain areas of their lives.

Perfectionism has sometimes been labeled a character defect, but for many veterans it hearkens back to the war zone, where being perfect or trying to be perfect in some areas of life was an absolute necessity. For example, in the military, keeping one's living area spotless and keeping one's weapons clean are requirements based on the need for soldiers to be constantly ready. In case of a surprise attack, there is no time to scramble through one's mess or clean a gun. Everything has to be ready to go!

Soldiers learn to equate neatness with dedication to the military and the country, with self-preservation, and with the preservation of one's unit. Often soldiers are punished severely for any form of untidiness or unreadiness. But what happens to soldiers when they become parents of messy children? "I go ballistic," says John, a former military officer. "My wife wants to know why I'm acting like it's the end of the world because the kids don't clean up their room. Because to me, a messy room is the end of the world . . . at least that's how it was when I was in the service."

Perfectionist standards impose a heavy weight on veterans and can affect their relationships in a number of ways.

1. Veterans may impose the same perfectionist standards they place on themselves onto others, thus making others feel incompetent or inadequate or angering or alienating them by their high standards.

2. The need to be perfect may stand in the way of developing relationships. For example, veterans may be spending so much time trying to meet their perfectionist standards that they don't have time for others. Veterans may have such high standards for how they are supposed to behave in a relationship that the minute they don't live up to their perfectionist standards, they conclude they are failures and withdraw from the relationship (either permanently or temporarily).

3. When someone else fails to meet the veteran's perfectionist standards, the vet might criticize that person or reject that person entirely. The vet may have an especially negative reaction to a family member, friend, or coworker if that individual's mistake or inability to meet a perfectionist standard reminds the veteran of a combat situation. Should a veteran become angry, for example, the family member or friend may be receiving some of the anger that belongs to those whom the veteran holds responsible for a deadly error committed in the war zone.

4. Vets also can become quickly frustrated, if not furious, when they encounter problems with an organizations, objects, or situations reminiscent of a combat experience. For example, many people become irritated and annoyed when they have to wait more than a half hour to see a doctor. However, a combat vet can become restless and annoyed much sooner, perhaps even after five or ten minutes. The vet's impatience with the delay may stem from memories of seeing wounded soldiers or civilians waiting for medical care in situations where even a few minutes' wait could spell the difference between life and death.

Denial of Personal Difficulties

Combat duty, like medicine, police work, and rescue work, emphasizes the necessity for solid thinking, quick action, and endurance, both physical and psychological. There is little tolerance for expression of emotion or personal weakness. Hence those who are involved in life-

and-death situations tend to keep their personal difficulties to themselves. These workers carry the legitimate fear that if they are emotionally open, they will be viewed as cowards, weaklings, incompetents, or unfit for duty.

Denial of personal difficulties is useful during life-and-death situations and when interacting with persons who are able to denigrate or harm you. However in intimate relationships, such denial is counterproductive and can lead to addictive behavior, psychosomatic problems, or worse.

Q: What are some of the benefits of combat duty?

This section presents some of the positive personality characteristics that can result from combat trauma. However, this section is not an attempt to sugarcoat combat experiences and make it seem as if "everything is fine." If someone has been in a war, everything isn't fine, but that doesn't mean that he or she may not have acquired certain strengths and insights as the result of combat duty.

The idea that a person can develop certain positive qualities and experience other benefits as the result of facing adversities is a common theme in many great works of literature, both in the West and the East. This idea can also be found in Christianity, Buddhism, and other religions. Yet it is only recently that mental health professions have begun to study the possible positive consequences of having undergone a trauma. For example, studies of combat veterans have found that combat can increase their desire to help others.[49] Survivors of other traumas, such as vehicular accidents, violent crime, child abuse, or sexual and physical assault, as well as cancer and heart-attack patients, have also reported improvements in their lives as the direct result of their life-threatening experiences.[50] Some of these positive outcomes include:

An increased desire to live each day to the fullest, including a reevaluation of one's life and a reordering of priorities;

Greater determination to achieve one's goals;

Increased self-reliance and confidence that one can cope with difficult situations;

An increase in self-understanding;

An increased ability to tolerate and manage uncertainty;

An increased ability to handle crises;

An increased awareness of the brevity and fragility of life;

Greater appreciation for close relationships, and a new closeness with family and community;

A stronger sense of belonging;

An increase in faith in people and compassion for others;

Greater tolerance of others;

Freedom from worrying about death;

Spiritual growth;

Respect for the power of emotions;

An increased ability to manage powerful emotions; and

Loyalty and commitment.[51]

This process whereby trauma leads to positive changes (sometimes called post-traumatic or adversarial growth) doesn't mean that a trauma survivor "gets back to normal"—that is, that he or she returns to the level of functioning he or she had prior to the trauma. Rather, it means that the trauma served as a "springboard that propels the survivor to a level of functioning higher than that which they held previously. . . . [It] reflects that something has been gained following the trauma, rather than that something was lost but recovered . . . or that nothing was lost despite the trauma."[52]

To say that some combat veterans have experienced some positive benefits because of their war experiences doesn't mean that they got back everything they lost as the result of their ordeals. They can never be the person they were before they went to war; some areas of their lives may be permanently scarred by their war experiences. In other areas of their lives, however, they may have achieved a degree of satisfaction, happiness, and emotional or spiritual growth that might have never been possible had they not seen war.[53]

According to the limited research available, it appears that positive traits and outcomes can develop whether or not a trauma survivor suffers from PTSD or other traumatic stress reactions.[54] For example, a study of altruism and empathy among Vietnam combat veterans found that there was no relationship between their level of PTSD and their degree of unselfish desire to help others.[55] In fact, a considerable degree of suffering seems to be a requirement for growth. Experts on adversarial growth agree that positive changes are more likely to occur among those trauma survivors who experience enough death and dying and enough emotional pain and material and other losses so as to propel them into a higher level of consciousness than among those survivors whose brush with death was relatively minimal and who suffered few or only temporary losses.[56]

Yet some traumas can create so many health, financial, family, and other problems that it is nearly impossible for positive qualities to develop. As Lars Weisaeth writes, there is "indisputable evidence" that concentration-camp survivors, prisoners of war, and others who experience "unpredictable, excessive, uncontrollable, and long lasting stress" are often devastated by their experiences.[57] In general, more psychological benefits have been found to result from "intermediate, rather than high or low" levels of trauma.[58]

Increased Appreciation for Life

Having come close to death, or seen death, some veterans can appreciate life in a way that those who ignore the reality of death cannot do. Veterans who have suffered much may also develop an empathy for others who suffer. Because veterans have been humbled by pain, they may have learned not to mock those who suffer or to feel superior to them. Some combat veterans find that their war experiences have isolated them or cut them off from people who are concerned with appearances or materialistic values, yet made them feel closer to the vast multitudes of human beings on this planet who struggle to keep their sanity and who go through their days with hearts full of grief and loss.

Hence combat duty can increase a person's ability to understand the parents who lost their children in a fire, the woman who is being beaten, the young man who is disfigured in a car accident, and the teenager who is raped and mugged.

Finding Meaning in Suffering

Viktor Frankl, a psychiatrist who survived the Nazi concentration camps, has written much about finding meaning in suffering.[59] If suffering is part of life, he says, it must have a purpose, one of which is that it binds us to the rest of humanity. In his philosophy of healing from war and other traumas, he stresses the need for finding meaning and purpose in life, often through helping others who are hurting or making a positive contribution to society.

History is full of examples of men and women who were traumatized but subsequently used their trauma–related energies and perspective to create empires, works of art, and major humanitarian efforts and institutions. Saint Francis of Assisi was a combat veteran, as were some of the ancient Greek playwrights. Peter the Great of Russia had PTSD. His high adrenaline levels caused him nightmares and seizures; they were also the basis of his numerous efforts to rebuild and Westernize what was then Czarist Russia. Beethoven, who suffered from depression, was a trauma survivor, too. His symphonies did not arise from a man who had a well-balanced middle-class life, but from a man who had known parental rejection and abuse. Presidents Harry Truman, Dwight Eisenhower, and John F. Kennedy were all combat veterans, as were Presidents George Washington and Ulysses S. Grant. Sargent Shriver, the first director of the Peace Corps, was a World War II veteran.

Today many veterans continue to contribute to society in medicine, education, religion, and politics. John McCain, who spent many years as a prisoner of war in Vietnam, later became a distinguished senator. Many veterans also have found great meaning and comfort in volunteer work or in helping veterans or other people who have suffered great losses.

Survivor Skills

As the result of combat, some men and women learn about the power of emotions. Having experienced intense fear, guilt, anger, and grief and the effects of these emotions on their lives, they may no longer be able to pretend that feelings are not important or that it's "easy" to acquire emotional stability. They know how powerful, and disruptive, feelings can be. If a veteran has ever been suicidal, homicidal, or severely depressed, he or she knows that feelings have the potential to kill. This respect for the power of emotions can help prepare some veterans for life, including future relationships, because they will never be naive enough to believe that they can "handle anything" or that they can disregard their feelings or the feelings of others.

Unlike others who have yet to be tested emotionally by trauma or hard times, combat veterans have experienced many uncomfortable feelings. Those veterans who have learned how to manage their emotions in constructive ways may have acquired an endurance to a wide range of human emotion. This is no mean feat. It's a source of strength.

This is an asset many veterans may fail to appreciate and others may fail to appreciate also until they are struck by tragedy. When family members and friends meet with undue hardships, often they turn to the combat veteran for advice and encouragement. When a brother's house burns down, when a neighbor is in a car wreck that leaves him paralyzed, when a coworker's mother commits suicide, when a nephew comes home from war, or when a cousin is raped, it is the combat veteran who knows something about what that feels like. Even veterans who were scorned or rejected by certain people because of their symptoms of combat trauma may now be sought after by some of these people because of the wisdom, insights, and perseverance they had to have had to get through both the combat and the psychological aftermath of combat trauma.

After the earthquakes, fires, and floods in our country in recent decades, Vietnam and other veterans' groups volunteered to help in rescue efforts and to help in counseling survivors. Many of these veterans had been rejected by their communities because of their psychological scars. Now they were being turned to as pillars of strength and sources of information on how to handle trauma.

Another quality that combat trauma can breed is loyalty. People who have gone through a war sometimes develop an intense loyalty to fellow soldiers, as well as to those who were helpful to them in their time of need. Just as combat veterans can never forget their war experiences and may never forget those who were callous or unhelpful, they may never forget those who showed them kindness and tried to be helpful. Veterans' loyalty to those people can be intense and long lasting. Because of their war experiences, some veterans have developed a capacity for loyalty—to a person, a job, or a religious, social, or political effort—which is enormous.

Mahatma Gandhi, known for his nonviolent approaches for social justice, had the utmost respect for soldiers. Even though Gandhi believed strongly in nonviolence, he felt that "soldiers were paragons of discipline and resolve, virtues often lacking in peacemakers who sometimes think that it is enough to stage antiwar marches and hold conferences to damn the military."[60]

I was eight months' pregnant and sick with the flu when for days on end all the local news seemed to focus on was a combat veteran who had barricaded himself and his family in his house and threatened to kill the first person in uniform who tried to enter the door. When our neighbor asked if my husband was a "weirdo," too, my eight-year-old quickly left the room. Later on I found him hiding under his bed crying, wondering how anyone could call his wonderful Daddy a "weirdo," and if his schoolmates were going to make fun of his father, too.

Meanwhile, my thirteen-year-old (from my former marriage) started yelling at me for marrying a "crazy veteran" who would some day ruin the family. "Divorce him, divorce him!" he shouted.

As the wife of a combat vet, I have lived through many crises. My husband has suffered from the usual symptoms—the flashbacks, the nightmares, the emotional numbing, and the rage reactions.

Every Fourth of July, Veterans Day, or anniversary date of the death of certain buddies, I can expect him to be irritable and to complain about things. I also expect that, sooner or later, I will be up all night holding him. For Dave, as for a lot of combat vets, anger and sorrow go hand in hand.

In between his "combat memory attacks," as I call them, however, he is a loving man. But he is scarred, emotionally and physically, and I blame his being in a war for this. After he got home, he broke off most of his friendships, and his family had no understanding of what he was going through. I was criticized, too. My family wanted to know why, after one bad marriage, I went and married a combat vet. Didn't I know that combat veterans were "all screwed up" and that I'd end up being his nursemaid all my life?

Over the years I've lost touch with my parents and brothers. I've also lost myself. I don't even know how I feel anymore. Maybe I'm depressed, maybe I'm not. All I know is that I must keep on functioning. My family depends on me. I'm constantly running, from one job to the next, one chore to the next. There's always some child who needs something, and of course, I never know when Dave is going to withdraw or act up again. I wish he would go get help, but he won't hear of it.

So I guess I'm Dave's therapist and most of my life is organized around arranging his life to be as comfortable and stress-free as possible. He simply can't handle too much pressure, and if he gets real depressed, I'll have yet another problem. I am the buffer between him and the world and, at times, his only link to sanity.

Sometimes he's with us 100 percent, but other times his intense need for peace and quiet makes me feel like a single parent. At times, he walls me out entirely. We can coexist for days, barely talking, never touching.

In the early years, I did my best to pierce his wall and enter his world. But he wouldn't let me in—because I was a woman, because I hadn't fought in a war and therefore could not understand. Now, after ten years of marriage, I have given up. Now when Dave withdraws, as long as he withdraws quietly, I don't care. It's a relief. It gives me time to get other things done.

Don't ask me what it means to be a woman anymore. My life is too hard, and I'm too bitter, and too afraid of the pain inside of me. I'm also afraid that someday my husband's depression will engulf him—that I will lose him entirely to that sad faraway look in his eyes.

3

"He's not the same"

Common Traumatic Reactions—Anxiety Disorders,
Dissociation, Depression, and Somatization

Common Traumatic Reactions

After undergoing any experience that is dangerous, frightening, or distressing, it is normal to experience shock, fear, confusion, helplessness, anxiety, and sadness. However the traumatic reactions described in this chapter—*depression, somatization,* and anxiety disorders such as *generalized anxiety disorder* and *post-traumatic stress disorder* (PTSD)—are something more. They include these emotions, but on a deeper, more complex, and more enduring level.

Not everyone who is exposed to combat develops obvious symptoms of distress. However, the incidence of emotional and physical distress among combat soldiers has been well documented since ancient times.[1] For some, the symptoms are temporary; for others, symptoms not only linger, but go on to create problems of their own, thus compounding the initial impact of combat. For many veterans, the main source of anguish is not so much their traumas, but the ways in which those traumas have resulted in any noticeable decrease in their ability to function, to enjoy life, and to feel good about themselves.[2] For example, vets with PTSD must struggle with unwanted increases and decreases in their emotional reactivity to situations and with involuntary biological responses to reminders of the war that can make them uncomfortably anxious or numb. Vets who become clinically depressed must contend with sleep and memory problems and a painful lack of enthusiasm for the activities that once brought them so much joy.

Even veterans who develop relatively serious or long-term symptoms do not necessarily suffer from each and every one of their symptoms to the same extent every day for the rest of their lives. A study of PTSD-afflicted Gulf War veterans found that some vets experienced an increase in PTSD symptoms over time, whereas others experienced a decrease. For still others, there was a variable course.[3]

Trauma survivors whose symptoms lift after a few days or weeks are usually those who have experienced a single-incident or short-term trauma, suffered relatively few or only temporary economic, physical, social, or spiritual losses, received ample medical and emotional support following their trauma, and did not encounter yet another trauma or hardship.[4] Military personnel deployed to combat zones usually experience multiple traumas, some of massive proportion.* Long-term psychological effects are to be expected, especially if quality and timely assistance is not available or not accepted. Furthermore, some men and women enter a combat zone already suffering from PTSD, depression, or another traumatic reaction as the result of an earlier combat experience or a trauma experienced prior to entering the military.[5]*

*See pages 22–29 for more on the types of combat trauma.

*See "Why are some veterans more affected by combat than others?" on pages 48–53.

A veteran's suffering may not always be obvious. Some soldiers go through several battles, or several wars, before developing symptoms. One particular traumatic event can bring forth memories of prior traumas, creating a "domino effect" and leading to the development of distressing symptoms.[6] For example, nurses on a military burn unit may not develop stress reactions after the first death on their ward but after the thirty-fifth, when they may be flooded with images not only of the thirty-fifth death, but of some of the previous deaths. Soldiers can return from years of heavy combat able to resume their premilitary careers or involvements and only develop severe traumatic reactions after they are confronted with a major financial or medical problem or some other setback or loss, such as a death in the family.

In addition to the traumatic reactions already mentioned, combat duty can trigger episodes of manic-depressive illness, paranoia, or other types of disorders, especially if there is a family history of such problems. It also can trigger dormant medical problems or worsen existing ones, which, in turn, can induce clinical depression.[7]

Many illnesses are known to be stress related, such as respiratory illnesses, including asthma and bronchitis, allergies, heart conditions, skin problems, and urinary or bladder infections. The degree to which stress contributes to these problems is not clear. However, repeated trauma and unrelenting stress do break down the immune system, leaving the veteran more vulnerable to illness.[8] If the stress continues, the veteran will have difficulty finding the rest and peace of mind necessary for either emotional or physical recovery. In addition, almost any medical problem can be aggravated by psychological or economic stress.

Note that although PTSD and depression are commonly viewed as emotional problems, they have a strong physiological component and hence are considered medical or biological problems by many medical and mental health professionals.[9] Recent studies have found that survivors of military combat, burn injuries, vehicular accidents, family violence, sexual assault, and other traumas suffer from more physical health problems than persons who have never been traumatized.[10]

Diagnosing Traumatic Reactions

The descriptions of traumatic reactions provided in this book are general in nature. Only a licensed mental health professional can determine if the symptoms you are concerned about constitute a genuine psychiatric disorder as defined by the American Psychiatric Association. Furthermore, mental health professionals (like compensation or Social Security review boards) may differ in their assessments of the severity of the impact of a person's symptoms on his or her social and occupational functioning.

As you read this chapter, keep in mind that the complex reactions people have to the horror of war cannot be reduced to a checklist of symptoms. No psychiatric diagnosis can fully capture the degree of suffering experienced by those who survive a war. For many, the pain is not only emotional, but also physical, spiritual, and mental.*

*See "How can war affect a veteran spiritually and morally?" and "How can war affect the way veterans think?" on pages 46–48 and page 58.

Furthermore, each veteran is unique. The symptoms of depression, for example, take different forms in different people, depending on their personality, their spiritual or religious beliefs, their cultural background, the amount and quality of their social support system, and the meaning they and their family ascribe to trauma and to emotional distress.

Furthermore, the symptoms of the various traumatic reactions often overlap. For example, headaches, fatigue, backaches, and gastrointestinal and other physical problems can signal any of the following: generalized anxiety disorder, PTSD, dissociation, depression, or some form of somatization. Similarly, the tremendous anxiety typical of PTSD is often difficult to distinguish from the anxiety symptoms of generalized anxiety disorder or panic disorder, and the numbing symptoms of PTSD from the emotional deadness, lack of motivation, physical fatigue, and other symptoms of depression or normal bereavement.

Another complication is that some veterans (or family members) suffer from more than one problem. For example, PTSD and depression, PTSD and substance abuse, and depression and substance abuse often go hand in hand among combat veterans.[11] Some symptoms that seem to be emotional in nature may be related to an undiagnosed medical problem, such as closed head injury. By their very nature, closed head injuries are difficult to diagnose and assess. However, such injuries have been found to lead to high anxiety, mood swings, and other symptoms and to contribute to the development of severe depression, post-traumatic stress, and other disorders. Soldiers and other military combat personnel are at particularly high risk for head injuries as the result of explosions, falls, beatings, or vehicular or other accidents. For example, researchers found that during the Vietnam conflict, 24 percent of troops hospitalized in-country needed medical care for head injuries. These researchers believe that most likely the percentage is considerably larger because troops with less severe injuries might not have sought, or might even have refused, medical care or may have been treated but not hospitalized.[12]

With certain exceptions, the traumatic reactions described here are normal reactions to an abnormal amount of stress, not necessarily signs of insanity or severe mental illness or mental retardation. Quite to the contrary, according to one combat vet, the traumatic stress reactions reflect the "sanity of those who fought in the war. Otherwise why be disturbed by the killing, by the stuff of war? . . . if some things don't make you crazy, then you aren't very sane to begin with."[13]

The traumatic reactions described in this chapter have developed among survivors of floods, tornadoes, hurricanes, and other catastrophes, many of whom had no previous significant psychological problems.[14] They have also been found among clergy, high-ranking military officers, physicians, and other medical and mental heath staff, as well as among highly trained men and women who were carefully screened prior to combat duty.[15] The few persons who don't develop some type of stress reaction to combat at some point in their lives are often sociopaths or self-absorbed persons with little conscience or capacity to care about others. Only when a veteran poses a threat to himself or herself or to others, or is out of control in some manner, should he or she be considered "insane." If some of the symptoms described in this chapter existed prior to combat duty, combat may have worsened them.

As a result of any of the traumatic reactions discussed below, whether PTSD, depression, dissociation, or somatization, veterans may also experience some memory loss or impairment or have trouble concentrating or remembering current information. They may forget not only therapy and doctor appointments but also where they have put money or when to pick up children from the babysitter's. Perhaps some veterans do lie about such matters, but for many, their forgetfulness may be the combined result of drinking or alcohol addiction and unacknowledged and untreated depression, PTSD, or other traumatic reactions. As Dr. Arthur Blank notes, such mental difficulties are clearly more than boredom, laziness, or lack of intellectual ability. They can represent a form of escape, a "distressful impairment of the capacity to appreciate" the experience at hand.[16]

Symptoms of combat trauma are not measures of personal worth, courage, patriotism, integrity, or physical or emotional strength. A common myth is that having symptoms of PTSD, depression, or somatization for more than three or four weeks means the veteran is a psychological wreck and can never be happy, rational, or productive again. Unfortunately, many veterans also believe this myth, which only adds to the distress caused by the symptoms themselves.

Severity of Symptoms

Veterans can suffer from any number of symptoms without those symptoms necessarily taking over their lives. For example, suppose you develop a rash from poison ivy. Your ability to continue with your normal activities will depend on the severity of the rash. Similarly, the crucial question in determining the severity of a veteran's symptoms is

"How much do the veteran's symptoms affect his or her ability to love, work, and play?"

Except for extreme cases, the answer to this question is highly subjective. Obviously vocational abilities can be considered impaired for those veterans who suffer from so many intrusive thoughts or so much sleep deprivation that they can't focus on the job at hand. Similarly, those veterans whose negative moods, cynical or critical attitudes, or other aftereffects of combat duty are so severe that they are unable to engage in or are uninterested in most, or all, human relationships can be considered to have sacrificed their personal life in the service of their country.

Usually the picture is more complex. Some veterans may have several symptoms that occasionally interfere with their functioning, but in general they may be productive on the job and enjoy some close personal ties. Other veterans can have very few symptoms, except around patriotic holidays or the anniversary dates of the death of a buddy, when they plunge into deep depressions or go on eating, gambling, or drinking binges, or seek chemical relief.

When to Be Concerned about Symptoms

In this chapter and throughout this book you will learn about some of the psychological stresses of having been in combat and about some of the psychiatric disorders that can result from such stresses. However, suffering from emotional stress is not necessarily the same as suffering from a severe mental illness. Do not assume that your partner (or you or another family member) has a mental disturbance just because one of you isn't happy most of the time or because one of you has one or two of the symptoms described in this book.

As a rule of thumb, you need to be concerned about symptoms when they result in self-harm, harming others, or destroying property; in delusion or hallucinations; or in an inability to meet responsibilities, to experience periods of contentment and joy, or to give and receive love. A single infrequent symptom that improves over time is not as much of a concern as having several symptoms, some of which seem to be worsening.

Nevertheless, it is highly recommended that you consult with a trained mental health or medical professional if your veteran or anyone in your family, including yourself, exhibits any of the symptoms described in the "Cautions" section of the introduction. Furthermore, the presence of more than three symptoms, one or two weeks of the same symptom with no sign of improvement, major decline in work performance, ongoing withdrawal from others or out-of-control behavior, frequent expressions of suicidal or homicidal thoughts or plans, or feelings of worthlessness or helplessness indicate that you need to seek help immediately. Even if you, your veteran, or anyone in your family is experiencing a symptom that is relatively infrequent or that appears to be causing very little damage to the ability to meet responsibilities and get along with others, if that symptom is causing mental or emotional pain inside, it deserves attention.

Anxiety Disorders

Combat trauma can lead to the development of one or more kinds of anxiety disorders. Although PTSD is the anxiety disorder most often mentioned in the media, many veterans develop somewhat less dramatic, but equally painful, kinds of anxiety disorders, such as generalized anxiety disorder, panic attacks, or panic disorder. Also, it is possible for a veteran to suffer not only from PTSD but from one or more of these other anxiety disorders as well.

Generalized Anxiety Disorder, Panic Attacks, and Panic Disorder

As described by the DSM-IV-TR (2000),* generalized anxiety disorder is "characterized by at least six months of persistent and excessive anxiety and worry" and by symptoms such as fatigue, muscle tension, irritability, and problems with sleep and concentration.[17] People with generalized anxiety disorder are anxious about a wide range of matters, not just one specific matter or situation, and find it difficult to control their worry. Sometimes generalized anxiety disorder is the result of medical problems, substance abuse, or withdrawal from an addictive substance.

*Diagnostic and Statistical Manual of Mental Disorders, Text Revision, 4th ed. (by the American Psychiatric Association)

In contrast to people with generalized anxiety disorder, people who suffer from panic attacks are not highly anxious almost all the time. Their panic attacks are distinct, time-limited episodes of intense fear accompanied by symptoms such as chills or hot flashes, numbing or tingling sensations, chest pain or discomfort, nausea or abdominal distress; feelings of choking, dizziness, light-headedness, or faintness; and fears of dying, losing control, or going crazy. After having one or two unexpected panic attacks, some people then develop panic disorder, a condition involving intense fear of having more panic attacks and worry about the damage these panic attacks would cause to their lives.[18]

Post-Traumatic Stress Disorder (PTSD)

Even when I'm happy, I'm sad. That war is like a permanent dent in my heart and mind. Tonight I was at a party with my wife. My favorite music was playing. I felt love for her and even for life itself. But this happiness only made me acutely aware of the pain of my past. As we did a fast dance, I found myself stomping the ground muttering, "Damn you, bitch. Damn you, bitch. You caused my buddy's death." When I started flashing, I knew it was time to leave. But, damn, where do I go to get away from my own head?

All I feel is anger and pain about what happened over there. Yet I'm sick and tired of thinking about it. Why can't I turn off the memories?

I saw a pregnant woman crossing the street yesterday proudly caressing her belly. I hated her for being happy and wanted to rip her belly open, like I saw overseas. Thank God, I never did anything like that, but I came close.

I want to be normal, like everyone else, and enjoy the good things in life. I have a wonderful wife, who has stood by me through all my depressions and explosions (not to mention my ten years of drinking) and a beautiful sixteen-year-old daughter, too. But am I happy? Hardly ever. I'm constantly worried that my daughter is going to be raped or in a car accident. Whenever her school bus is late, even two minutes, I break out into cold sweats, hyperventilate, and want to call the rescue squad. I keep thinking that God is going to punish me soon for things I did in 'Nam, or for things I was tempted to do by taking away my child.

I can't forget. In my dreams, dismembered bodies and teeth without the gold fillings float in the air and the people I killed come back to life—angry at me.

And then there's my cousin Ralph, Mr. Success. "You didn't have to enlist. But no, you had to go prove something. So don't cry now."

His old lady wears furs. Mine stands on her feet all day for minimum wage. My career was shot to hell by that war, but I don't care. Deep down, I hate myself—hate myself, hate myself, hate myself—for what I became over there, for things that weren't even my fault.

—A COMBAT VETERAN[19]

According to the official definition of PTSD (DSM-IV-TR, 2000), in order for a person to be considered as having PTSD he (or she) must:[20]

A. Have experienced a traumatic event or series of events (using the technical definition of trauma described above);

B. Relive the trauma repeatedly in some form of what are called re-experiencing or reliving experiences, which include the following: nightmares, flashbacks, and intrusive memories of the trauma; acting or feeling as if the trauma was occurring in the present; or hearing sounds or smelling smells associated with the trauma (this alternates with criterion C);

C. Experience a numbing of emotions and a reduced interest in others (which were not present prior to the trauma), as well as have difficulty remembering the event, and developing a tendency to avoid people, places, conversations, and other activities that arouse memories of the trauma (alternates with criterion B);

D. Experience signs of physical arousal (not present prior to the trauma), such as sleep disturbances, irritability and rage reactions, and problems with concentration, startle response, and hypervigilance (being constantly on the lookout for danger).

In addition:

E. Criteria B, C, and D must persist for at least one month after the traumatic event.

F. The traumatic event must cause significant distress or dysfunction in the individual's social, occupational, and family functioning or in other important areas of life.

Other symptoms of PTSD include feelings of impending doom, mood swings, and fears of mental instability, including fears of insanity. Associated with PTSD, but not part of the official definition of PTSD, are survivor guilt, substance abuse, a tendency to react under stress with survival tactics, fantasies of retaliation, alienation, negative self-image, cynical attitudes toward and problems with the government and authority figures, hypersensitivity to injustice, and a sense of being permanently damaged, inferior, or defiled. Like depression, PTSD is especially prevalent among men and women who are wounded or who blame themselves for the deaths or injuries of others.

It bears repeating that the symptoms described here vary in frequency, in intensity, and in their impact on a veteran's life. In order for a person to be officially diagnosed with PTSD, it is not enough to have symptoms. Criterion E must be met: that is, the symptoms must dehabilitate socially or occupationally or cause a serious inability to function in some important area of life.

One veteran describes his PTSD as an "inner agony that has no name, yet has many faces." Some vets run from their PTSD with drugs and alcohol. Others have dry heaves every morning and struggle to keep jobs where they feel they, or others, are being disrespected or mistreated. Some vets try to escape by overcontrolling others or by overcontrolling themselves with impossible to-do lists and other forms of workaholism. Some adopt a stance of extreme independence from others. Among those who insist that they don't really need or trust anyone (except perhaps a war buddy or two) are veterans who, in therapy, eventually admit how dependent they are on their partner or a special friend.

"I hate needing others," says Vanessa, an aircraft specialist who served six months in a war zone. "Yet, I don't know what I'd do without my boyfriend. We don't always get along, but I stay with him because I'm afraid that if I break up with him, I'll just hide out in my apartment, not answer the phone, and isolate myself from others, even my parents. Without him, my PTSD would probably take over and I might go off the deep end." Some veterans actually do withdraw from society altogether and live as virtual hermits in secluded parts of the country.[21]

The Biology of PTSD

Although we use separate words for them, the mind, emotions, and body are part of one whole. When trauma occurs, it affects the whole being—not just the mind or emotions but also the central nervous system and other aspects of human physiology. Hence many of the emotionally distressing symptoms of PTSD, dissociation, and depression have a biological basis.*

When human beings are faced with danger, their adrenal

*See "How can war affect veterans physically?" on pages 55–58.

glands flood their bodies either with adrenaline or noradrenalin. Adrenaline energizes the body into a fight or flight mode; noradrenalin creates a "freeze reaction," a numbing of the body and the emotions. This freeze reaction can also be caused by the endogenous opioid system, one of the body's natural calming systems, which reduces physical sensations and the intensity of emotional reactions.[22]

As a result of these involuntary reactions, during combat a soldier doesn't always have the power to decide whether he is going to fight, try to run (flight), or go limp (freeze). His adrenal glands and neurohormones do. The same holds true when he is exposed to a reminder of his war experiences or a trigger. Even in a safe situation, his body may respond as if he is being attacked. He is then subject to either a fight, flight, or freeze reaction, which can lead to anxiety, numbness, anger, and intrusive thoughts or flashbacks of war.[23] Experiencing any of these involuntary reactions if he is exposed to a trigger, such as media programs about violence, is to be expected. (See appendix B for helpful books on managing trigger reactions.)

Common signs of anxiety include nausea; sweating; rapid heartbeat; difficulties concentrating; rapid shallow breathing; rapid or slurred speech; racing or scattered thinking; hot and cold flashes, light-headedness or dizziness; tremors or shaking; fear of losing control, going crazy, or dying; and fatigue and body aches, especially stomachaches and headaches.

Signs of numbing, also called dissociation, include difficulties moving and speaking; dozing off or sleeping when not tired; disinterest in sex; frequent memory or concentration problems (such as forgetting appointments, what one or someone else just said, or details of the combat that usually are in the forefront of one's mind) not caused by depression, fatigue, head injury, medication, or substance abuse; confusion; feelings of unreality, floating in the air, or being in a trance or dream-like state; feeling like an observer rather than a participant in one's life; curling into a fetal position, covering oneself with a blanket, pillow, sheet, or even hands, sucking one's thumb or a blanket, or other childlike behaviors; and feeling detached from one's body, mind, or emotions, even to the point of feeling dead or like a robot.

Common triggers or reminders of war experiences include anniversary dates (of entering or being discharged from the military, an injury, the injury or death of a comrade, friendly-fire incidents or a particularly dangerous mission, major ruptures in relationships, suicide attempts, or the onset of a severe post-traumatic reaction); colors, smells, tastes, people, places (textures; landscape; shape, size, or structure of a room), things (food, furniture, or other items), or aspects of nature or time (weather, seasons, time of day) associated with the combat even if they were not part of the danger; people similar to those involved in the war in age, height, looks, tone of voice, or attitude; being or feeling confined or out of control in a situation; having to depend on others; being asked questions about the military, veterans, war, or other forms of violence; any strong emotion, even joy, but especially emotions similar to those experienced during combat; the sound of backfires, popping popcorn, or helicopters, the sight of plastic trashbags (reminiscent of body bags); encountering landscapes similar to those of the combat zone; sudden noises; any current stressor, such as financial, relationship, work, or medical problems; increased crime or other neighborhood problems; increased threats of terrorism, war, and pollution; witnessing or being involved in a current trauma (fire, crime); and even the slightest increase in everyday hassles.

Midlife brings additional triggers: the deaths of parents and other relatives and the premature death of veteran friends due to combat-related physical and emotional problems. Also potentially retraumatizing for PTSD-afflicted veterans is the departure of children from the home; the decision of sons or daughters to join, or not join, the military; and any aggravation of war injuries or psychological stress due to self-neglect, inadequate health care, or the aging process. Media coverage of current armed conflicts or documentaries about armed conflicts in Vietnam, the Persian Gulf, Somalia, or Chechnya, for example, or of the carnage in Bosnia and Rwanda and of other subsequent war zones are also powerful triggers.

Combat veterans usually respond to triggers with symptoms such as anxiety, panic, flashbacks, irritability, anger, feelings of helplessness and hopelessness, changes in sexual desire, social isolation, addiction and other forms of self-abuse, and memory and concentration problems. For example, every Veterans Day John dreams of the firefight that cost him his leg. He has repeatedly "ordered himself" not to have these nightmares, but to no avail. If a hundred years of research and many hundreds of scientific studies are correct, then John's recurring nightmares are likely based in the biology of trauma and are thus beyond his control.[24] In other words, PTSD symptoms are not in someone's "head," nor are they a play for attention. They are involuntary. They also have survival value.

Once soldiers have been traumatized by war, certain traumatic reactions are hard-wired into their brains because of their survival value. As much as veterans may loathe them, those adrenaline surges that make them so uncomfortably anxious or angry and/or those noradrenalin surges that dampen their life spirit are their friends, for these reactions helped them survive war.

For example, two common types of intrusive thoughts are (1) visions of events (which occurred just prior to the traumatic event), which, in retrospect, signaled the beginning of the traumatic event, or (2) visions of those particular moments during the traumatic event when the veteran realized the seriousness of the situation. Since these events were signals or cues of impending danger, having intrusive thoughts about them can be viewed as part of the human survival system.[25] If our prehistorical ancestors weren't reminded of the danger posed by large animals, we would not have survived as a species.

In another type of intrusive thought, veterans ruminate about why the traumatic event occurred or why they (or somebody else) acted, thought, or felt a certain way during that particular event. Examining the trauma in these ways can have survival value. If, by means of these intrusive thoughts, veterans can figure out why a trauma occurred and review their behavior during that trauma, then they may be able to anticipate the next trauma and behave more effectively.[26]

Intrusive thoughts (as well as flashbacks, nightmares, and other reliving symptoms) are typically viewed as abnormal and undesirable phenomena that ideally should be eliminated or reduced in frequency in order to improve mental health. However, as described in the previous paragraph, intrusive thoughts (like other reliving experiences) have survival value. They are ways of discharging the enormous amount of energy generated by the body during combat; they are ways of releasing traumatic memories; they are ways of mentally reviewing the past in hopes of figuring out how to avoid future dangers. Reliving symptoms can also be ways of commemorating the war. Since many aspects of a veteran's war experience are not known to others, symptoms serve to scream out: "It did happen. It mattered a lot then, and it matters a lot now."[27]

PTSD During Combat

Although PTSD is called *post*-traumatic stress disorder, many veterans and military staff developed PTSD *during* combat duty. For a variety of reasons, they may have tried to cover their symptoms with alcohol or drugs or suppressed them in other ways. Some feared being seen as weak or crazy, or feared being punished for not being able to fight or perform their duties. Others knew that their symptoms would only get them taken from their units. Loyalty to their comrades motivated them to hide their symptoms sufficiently so that they could fight to the finish. The same holds true for medical and other support staff. For many, their dedication to their work enabled them to push aside or hide their symptoms so they could go on supporting the troops.

Although post-traumatic symptoms often develop during combat, PTSD is, by definition, a delayed reaction to the war.[28] Symptoms may emerge one, two, even twenty or more years later. Symptoms of combat trauma may emerge after combat duty because it is only after returning to the relative safety of home that soldiers have the opportunity to realize the true extent of the dangers and horrors they have seen or to reflect on their behavior. During combat, they may have been so focused on accomplishing their mission or simply surviving that they had little opportunity to think about their circumstances. Among career military, symptoms of combat trauma may not emerge until after retirement or medical discharge. Being in a military environment surrounded by other soldiers provides a supportive environment for many career military. Hence it is only when they leave the military and lose the structure and sense of belonging that being in the military can provide that symptoms of combat trauma may emerge

Often stress in the present—economic difficulties, a death in the family, or the veteran's own midlife crisis—will bring out symptoms of combat trauma that the veteran had previously been able to control and force him or her to seek help. Tim, for example, had been working successfully as a dietician in a hospital for ten years following combat duty. His wife had noticed no signs of PTSD, except a tendency toward withdrawal, which she attributed to his family background. Also, he would sometimes drink too much. "But what man doesn't?" she reasoned.

However, last year, Tim had to deal with multiple stresses: the death of two nieces, a major car accident, and an overload at work. These combined pressures brought to the surface combat memories that he had previously suppressed. His drinking increased, as did his absences from home. While he was able to function at work, he found himself increasingly irritated with some of his patients, especially when they were rude to him. One day a patient was being particularly demanding and verbally abusive. Unable to contain himself any longer, Tim threw the man out of the bed. What frightened Tim was not that he attacked this man, but that he wanted to kill him. Tim feels he would have killed the patient had nurses and the hospital police not stopped him. Fear of his own rage sent Tim to a therapist for help.

Any situation in the present that reduces a veteran's physical strength and capacities, especially if it involves being dependent on others, can trigger symptoms. Having a serious illness or needing surgery, even a relatively routine procedure such as gum surgery, can make some veterans feel unsafe because they are less able to defend themselves against possible attacks. Hospitalization can feel especially threatening to veterans who felt they were betrayed by others whom they counted on for support or medical care during their combat days. Even if they trust their doctors and are surrounded by devoted family members and friends, on some level they may fear being abandoned as they were in the past. Hospitalization, especially in a veterans hospital, means being in an unfamiliar environment, as well as being exposed to wounded soldiers, a heart-wrenching reminder of combat day.

The PTSD Cycle

Since many PTSD symptoms overlap with symptoms of depression, panic disorder, and other disorders, how can one know if one is suffering from PTSD?

The unique feature of PTSD is the re-experiencing of the traumatic experiences (re-experiencing stage), followed by attempts to bury memories of the trauma and the feelings associated with the trauma (the numbing stage). This PTSD cycle sets PTSD apart from all other official psychiatric disorders. Usually the cycle is repeated in this sequence over and over.

The two parts of this cycle have no specific time frame. People may stay at the "numbing stage" for several hours, several weeks, or several years. Although they are unhappy and not really living, it is possible to be emotionally numb yet keep on functioning, at least on a minimal level.

People who are in the re-experiencing stages, with constant or nearly constant intrusive thoughts, nightmares, flashbacks, anxiety or panic attacks, usually find it almost impossible to function. Hence re-experiencing stages tend to be shorter than the numbing stages because there is a natural limit to how much anxiety and physiological arousal the human body can tolerate before it begins to shut down in exhaustion.[29] After a particularly intense period of anxiety attacks or flashbacks, vets usually experience a type of collapse where they feel fatigued and emotionally spent. The re-experiencing stage can also be cut short by an accident, a rage reaction, or some other out-of-control action, or by the veteran's conscious efforts to stop, or at least diminish, the intrusive thoughts and other re-experiencing symptoms. Gerald made himself stay awake all night in order to avoid the nightmares that came every December, a month of particularly heavy fighting for his unit. However, after four nights of no sleep, he slept for two days straight.

Some veterans curtail the re-experiencing stage with the help of coping techniques learned from individual or group therapy, from self-help groups, or from self-help books. Others find relief through spiritual practices, physical exercise, cultural or family traditions, work, or other activities requiring focused mental or physical energy. Those veterans who have not had the opportunity to learn constructive ways of managing their symptoms may try to do so with destructive means such as substance abuse or verbal or physical aggression toward themselves or others.

This cyclical recurrence of the re-experiencing stage followed by the numbing state is an essential characteristic of PTSD. As more than one wife, girlfriend, husband, or boyfriend has observed, his or her partner suddenly withdraws soon after intimate talks. Natasha says,

> I was so excited when Tom finally talked to me about the war. All these years, he hasn't said a word about it. Finally, maybe, I thought we could be close. But ever since he opened up, he's shut down more than ever. He won't even say what he wants for dinner and hasn't let me touch him for over a week.
>
> What did I do wrong? I didn't know exactly what to say when he told me about some of his firefights. I'm no psychologist, but I was sympathetic. Maybe I wasn't sympathetic enough. Did I turn him off somehow?

Natasha did not do anything wrong. She didn't turn off Tom either. Tom turned himself off. Like many partners, Natasha was shocked and dismayed at his withdrawal and assumed that she was responsible. But his withdrawal is not the result of her behavior—it is a predictable feature of the cyclical nature of PTSD. Tom, like many vets with untreated PTSD, is in a state of emotional numbing. He has shoved many of his emotions, especially those surrounding combat, out of his conscious awareness. But this does not mean that these feelings are not there or that they do not motivate him.

Feelings are real and powerful. Although we can't see or touch them, they can heavily influence our behavior, our mental outlook, and even our spiritual life. Like Tom, we can push our feelings down in an attempt to make them go away, pretend that they aren't there at all, or that they are relatively unimportant. But eventually the stifled emotions will surface and clamor for attention: "Here I am. Here I am. Deal with me. Deal with me."

Some PTSD-afflicted veterans are so absorbed with their combat traumas they have less psychic energy to devote to their jobs, their friends and family, and more important, to themselves in the present. This makes their lives much harder and is often the source of much shame and guilt. Almost every veteran I have ever counseled has expressed a heartfelt wish to be rid of intrusive thoughts and other re-experiencing symptoms so he or she could fully concentrate on life in the present. Joan, a naval officer, explains: "When I saw my husband in a hospital bed full of tubes, I started hyperventilating and had to be taken to the emergency room. Because of what I saw overseas, I can't be there for my husband when he's sick. Now how do you think that makes me feel?"

During a family crisis, some vets may find themselves shutting down emotionally, almost against their will.[30] Others may make conscious attempts to avoid the crisis because they fear it will aggravate combat memories and bring upon them the hell of nightmares, flashbacks, or other re-experiencing symptoms. On the other hand, it is also common for veterans to assume the leadership role during family or community crises. Having been in combat, they may be adept at handling crises and have the skills and willingness to take charge of almost all the practical and emotional aspects of the situation.

Reliving the War

Reliving or re-experiencing combat-related traumas may occur in the form of intrusive thoughts and images of the combat experience; dreams, nightmares, or night terrors; and flashbacks, both conscious and unconscious.

Dreams and Nightmares During dreams or nightmares, the veteran may "shake, shout, scream, and thrash about with considerable violence."[31] Although the dream may not be remembered upon awakening, the feelings of terror and fear contained in the dream may persist for quite some time. The insomnia that plagues some veterans can be viewed as a means of avoiding such dreams and nightmares. Some vets overindulge in alcohol, food, or drugs before they sleep, in hopes that these substances will obliterate the dreams. Others can only sleep with a weapon nearby or under their pillows.

Nightmares about combat-related experiences may be replays of real war events, scenes of probable or much-feared war events, or dreams that symbolize the conflicts and terrors experienced during war. Regardless of which kind of nightmare is experienced, it can easily create an inordinately high level of anxiety. Not only are these veterans forced to relive traumatic events, but the fears generated by nightmares can spill over into the next day and make them feel uneasy, disoriented, and unable to make decisions and enjoy whatever goodness the day may have to offer. Since traumatic memories tend to be stored as visual images, traumatic dreams often contain vivid images that can flash through the veteran's mind frequently through the following day or days. It does not take a psychologist to understand how being beset by traumatic images during the day can impede the veteran's daytime coping abilities.

The entire family's coping abilities may be impaired simply due to lack of sleep. Some families are awakened by the veteran's cries and screams. In other cases, veterans wake up their partners and children after nightmares to make sure they are still alive or to ask them for reassurance or for help in searching the home for enemy soldiers or other dangers.

Some veterans know themselves well enough to predict that certain situations, certain days or times of the year, or certain kinds of interactions with other people might result in more intrusive thoughts, nightmares, and other PTSD symptoms. For example, veterans who do public service work by speaking about their experiences to students or other groups do so knowing that afterwards they will probably have more intrusive thoughts or other PTSD symptoms. However, it isn't always possible to foresee when one's PTSD symptoms will flare up. When they do so unexpectedly, veterans feel as if they've been "ambushed" by their own minds.

Another disturbing element of these symptoms is that during their duration, they take over the veteran's mind, feelings, and behavior. Since the veteran cannot turn off the nightmares (or the intrusive thoughts or flashbacks) at will, he or she can come to fear that they might never stop, that they might consume his or her existence. Given the unpredictable nature of re-experiencing symptoms and their power to incapacitate and disorient the veteran, experiencing these symptoms can be traumatizing in itself.

PTSD nightmares are characterized by feelings of terror and helplessness. For example: "being trapped in a foxhole with enemy soldiers pulling at me and trying to drag me further down into the hole with them"; "suicide bombers sneaking up on me in my sleep and not being able to wake up in time"; "being wounded and put in a body bag and being carried to the cellar and I am screaming at people that I'm not dead, but they continue putting me there anyway"; "being chased by men with no faces through jungle and then I fall off a cliff"; "malfunctioning weapon"; and "four or five days per week I am being killed by a gun, knife, or an injection."[32]

For some veterans, the nightmares begin during combat, and for others, immediately afterwards. For still others, nightmares begin to emerge (or intensify) upon their becoming clean or sober or beginning a war recovery or another kind of healing program. As the therapy progresses, however, the nightmares may lessen in intensity or in frequency.

Yet even veterans who have been engaged in healing programs for quite some time may have a resurgence of nightmares at midlife or when exposed to new traumas or stresses. Andrew, for example, had struggled five years in group and individual therapy to cope with his recurring nightmares of the ghosts of dead Iraqis trying to kill him. Finally, the dreams became less frequent and horrifying to him. After his mother developed Alzheimer's, however, his nightmares returned in full force. "Just seeing my mother waste away brought back my nightmares about the hospitals in Iraq full of dying, crying people," Andrew states.

Veterans have also reported increases in nightmares and other PTSD symptoms in response to being in vehicular accidents, to being victimized by crime, or to seeing bodies of murder or accident victims, especially if the victims are young men or women. However, it is not necessary to have a dramatic or life-threatening incident occur for a nightmare or combat-related memory to be aroused. Even mildly stressful events can precipitate a mental tour of duty in the combat zone. When Larry's cat became ill with a mild case of respiratory infection, the veterinarian assured Larry that his cat would be well within days and showed Larry the X-rays and other medical tests to prove it. Larry went to bed assured that his cat would be fine, but that night he dreamt that his front lawn was covered with the disemboweled remains of dozens of cats and dogs. In dream analysis Larry related that once his unit had come upon a village where enemy soldiers had killed entire families. Next to the villagers' bodies were the disemboweled remains of cats, dogs, and other village animals. In his dream about the dead animals, Larry recreated this traumatic war experience.

Over time, some veterans may find that the subject matter of their nightmares isn't always related to combat experiences but rather to feared or actual life-threatening or highly stressful situations in the present. Even if these nightmares do not portray specific combat memories, they are considered forms of re-experiencing combat when they do so symbolically, by recreating the emotional impact of combat.

Monique, a combat nurse, had the same nightmare every night since her return from overseas. Her nightmare was a replay of an actual event where she witnessed bandits attack a convoy of wounded soldiers and civilians. She was then bound by the bandits and not permitted to help the wounded as they begged for her help. During her first two years of counseling, Monique continued to have the same dream, but she became less fearful of it. Eventually the convoy dream was replaced with dreams of her ten-year-old niece being run down by a drunk driver. In her dreams about her niece, Monique wasn't a prisoner and she was free to dash to her niece's side to offer assistance, but her niece was already dead. Although the content of Monique's nightmares differed, their theme is the same: feelings of helplessness and powerlessness in the face of injury and death.

Flashbacks Next to dreams, flashbacks are perhaps the most publicized forms of re-experiencing a trauma. Basically, a *flashback* is a sudden, vivid recollection of the traumatic event accompanied by strong emotion. Veterans do not black out or lose consciousness, but they do temporarily leave the present and feel as if they are back in combat. They may see the scenes of combat, smell the smells, and hear the sounds. They may or may not lose contact with present reality and they may or may not find themselves acting as if they are still in the war zone. Depending on the content of the flashback, veterans can sometimes confuse family members for the enemy. Partners report that sometimes their mates alternate between recognizing them as loved ones and seeing them as enemy soldiers, buddies, civilians, or others who were part of their combat experience.

Veterans may be reluctant to acknowledge that they are "flashing" for fear of sounding crazy. Yet their histories may reveal many instances of coming back with a memory of having once again been engaged in a war experience, such as going out on patrol or driving on a road in the jungle, desert, or mountain. While a few dramatic cases involving flashbacks have been well publicized in the media, most veterans who "flash" do so more quietly, in the privacy of their hearts and minds, without public commotion. "Flashing" is common among combat veterans and military personnel in combat zones. It has also been observed among survivors of Nazi concentration camps, in World War II aviation personnel, and among survivors of long-term sexual or physical abuse. In general people who have endured multiple traumas are more likely to experience flashbacks than those who experienced a single trauma.[33]

During *conscious* flashbacks, veterans experience vivid images of war events and can later report what they have seen, even if they had temporary amnesia during or after the flashback. During *unconscious* flashbacks, however, veterans may find themselves engaged in unusual behavior motivated by some memory of combat, but have no conscious awareness of any thoughts or emotions about combat, either during the time of the flashback or later. Upon examination during therapy, however, usually the episode will reveal itself to be a "repetition of some event(s) in the war."[34]

Flashbacks usually last anywhere from a few seconds to a few minutes. If they last more than an hour and the veteran finds himself or herself in a different place with no memory of how he or she got there, most likely more than a flashback is involved. He or she may have been under the influence of another psychological disorder or emotional force or under the influence of alcohol, illegal drugs, or prescribed medications in inappropriate doses or in unprescribed doses. The cumulative effect of years of substance abuse may also be involved.

Family members, including children, who are trying to help their veteran through an unconscious flashback usually show extraordinary coping abilities. Most report little fear for themselves. "Alexandra would never hurt me or the kids," says Gerald. "Even when she confuses me with the enemy, I can bring her out of it by caressing her face and telling her, 'It's me, Gerald, your fiancé. You're not in a war. You're home. You're safe. It's me, Gerald, your fiancé. I love you.'"

Even when Gerald fears that Alexandra might harm herself, he dares not call the county mental health team because the team includes at least one police officer and a registered nurse. The mere presence of a uniformed person, even a nurse, might drive Alexandra wild. He hesitates to call the neighbors for help, for fear that they would not understand and become alarmed and ostracize Alexandra and their family.

For the most part, the partners I have worked with do whatever their veteran asks of them: whether it be hiding under the bed to avoid enemy attack or making sure all the doors are locked. While younger children might think it's great fun to tiptoe around the living room with Mommy or Daddy at two in the morning with a flashlight, older children may be saddened, concerned, angered, or confused by their father or mother's behavior. Sometimes younger children imitate the behavior of their veteran mother or father. They may hide under the bed whenever a helicopter flies by or refuse foods associated with the geographical area where their parent served in the military.

Older children may not imitate their veteran parent as readily, but they may not understand their parent's problem either. They may be afraid to ask questions for fear of precipitating another flashback or family uproar. If the flashback has occurred in public or in front of friends, the child might be embarrassed and ashamed. If flashbacks are numerous, the child may resent the interruptions. Some children may feel helpless, yet at the same time take on adult responsibilities. Some may assist their nonveteran parent in "bringing Daddy [or Mommy] home." They may wipe their veteran parent's brow and whisper words of love and reassurance or regularly help to remove objects from the room with which their veteran parent could be hurt.*

*For more information on children and combat trauma, see chapter 11.

Some mental health professionals dismiss flashbacks as aberrations or signs of psychosis or severe mental illness. Others may become frightened when a client begins having flashbacks because they've received little or no training in how to handle this kind of extremely delicate situation.[35]

Flashbacks are usually visual, but they may contain voices and other sounds. Some combat veterans hear frightening or loud noises, sounds that indicate an upcoming attack danger, or the screams and moans of someone in distress. Sometimes they are the person in distress. Joe, for example, is afraid to be home alone because he never knows when the "voice" will call his name. When asked whose voice it may be, Joe says: "I wish I knew. It could be me, the old me, calling me back to my life now. Or it could be someone I served with who died and wants me to tell them how come they died and I didn't."

Joe rarely tells his doctors or therapists about the voice for fear they will think he is "schizo" and lock him up in a mental institution. In most instances, the difference between the visual and auditory flashbacks typical of PTSD and the hallucinations of schizophrenia is that flashbacks contain images and sounds that are clearly related to and solely related to combat-related traumas. It is highly unlikely that Joe, for example, is schizophrenic or psychotic because his auditory flashbacks began after combat duty, not before, and are only related to war experiences, not other events. In addition, he has no other signs of schizophrenia or another psychosis.

During olfactory flashbacks veterans smell odors associated with combat; during somatic flashbacks, the body re-experiences some or all of the pain or other physical sensations related to combat. For example, if a veteran's arm was bruised during an attack, at various times afterward it may ache as if it were still bruised. Veterans who experienced long periods of hunger may at various times feel ravenous, even though they just ate a huge meal.

Perhaps the most disturbing aspect of a flashback is not the flashback itself, but the destabilizing feelings that come with it. Flashbacks, like intrusive thoughts, are not just memories, but memories accompanied by strong emotions. Therefore when a veteran has an auditory, visual, or other type of flashback, he or she is likely to experience the horror and other emotions associated with combat.

With emotional flashbacks, veterans suddenly have certain painful or angry feelings that do not seem clearly related to any particular memory of combat or to any current, readily identifiable reminder of combat. These feelings may be seen as residues of the intense feelings aroused by combat. They may also indicate repressed emotions about combat. Often these feelings seem to descend upon a veteran out of nowhere. "Everything was okay, but then I just started screaming (crying or getting mad) for no reason," veterans often say. But there are plenty of good reasons for these reactions, as described in this book.

Withdrawal as Response Since re-experiencing the trauma can be so painful and possibly dangerous, veterans with PTSD may find themselves retreating mentally, socially, and physically. For example, one vet stopped going to shopping malls after flashing and falling to the ground in the middle of a department store. In working with veterans with PTSD I have observed a common pattern: A veteran will leave home temporarily, for a few hours up to several days, when he or she senses the onset of re-experiencing symptoms or begins having them.

Several men and women I have worked with have even separated permanently from partners they loved deeply after one or two instances of finding themselves mistaking their partner for an enemy in a flashback or reliving combat in their sleep. A few of these veterans actually struck their partner during flashbacks or nightmares. Most, however, never attacked their partner: they were just afraid that some day they would. For example, Bruce found himself sitting upright in the middle of the night looking around the room for enemy attackers. "What if I mistook my wife or kids for the enemy and caused them harm?" he wondered. On this basis, he divorced his wife and decided to live alone for the rest of his life. "I just can't take the chance of hurting anyone," he explained.

The preceding example may seem extreme and perhaps it is. Perhaps it is only those who drastically restrict their lives who seek help at counseling centers and clinics. There are no statistical studies to indicate how common such responses are to symptoms. We do know that avoidance of close ties is common among help-seeking veterans and that men and women seeking help as the result of physical or sexual abuse report an increase in re-experiencing symptoms when they become involved in intimate relationships. As a result of these symptoms, as well as the fears and general feelings of inadequacy stemming from their traumatic experiences, a proportion of these abuse survivors either refrain from developing close relationships or end them once they reach a certain level of intimacy.[36] The extent to which these patterns hold true for combat veterans is to date undetermined.

In sum, post-traumatic stress disorder occurs when veterans react to the trauma by experiencing extreme feelings of helplessness and terror, and then periods of emotional numbing, hyperalertness, and re-experiencing their trauma in the form of nightmares, flashbacks, intrusive thoughts, or other types of "reliving" experiences. Emotional numbing refers to a shutdown of emotions and to difficulties in feeling close to others. Hyperalertness refers to being constantly on guard, having difficulty sleeping or managing irritability and anger. Some symptoms of PTSD are similar to symptoms of other anxiety disorders, of depression or somatization, or of other forms of emotional distress. However, the unique feature of PTSD is the PTSD cycle where vets alternate between re-experiencing and avoiding re-experiencing the trauma.

Numbing or Dissociation

Numbing, or *dissociation,* is a form of blocking. The blocking can be partial or total, and physical, mental, or emotional, or some of all three. Numbing, commonly referred to as shutting down, "spacing out," "zoning out," or "going fuzzy," reflects not only the biological changes that occur during combat, but the wish that whatever is happening really wasn't happening. People in combat zones usually can't escape their traumatic circumstances. But they can flee mentally by dissociating. This helps them feel that what they are seeing, doing, or feeling isn't real and helps them preserve some identity and self-respect.

Each type of dissociation has its own unique characteristics. Regardless of the specific form it takes, dissociation often helps a person maintain emotional stability.[37] Through dissociation, soldiers can increase control over what seems to be uncontrollable shock, emotional and physical pain, anger, and suicidal feelings. Unless a medical or substance-abuse problem is causing the numbing, dissociation can be a much-needed defense against the unbearable emotions, sights, and physical discomforts associated with war.

Mental Dissociation Trauma-related dissociation can be mental (the blocking of information or memories), emotional (the numbing of the emotions associated with that information or those memories), or physical (the numbing of physical sensations such as physical pain or pleasure). Combat veterans who dissociate mentally may not recall all, most, or even part of their traumatic experiences, or may be confused or vague about the specifics of these experiences. I have found that some veterans remember the minute details of some incidents, but not all of them. Others can recall the names of the places where they served and little else; some remember some periods of time, but not others. For example, Steve can recall most of his experiences in Iraq up until the time he witnessed his first suicide bombing, after which, he states, "everything is a blur." Many veterans have difficulty remembering at least some of the details of what happened. It is also normal for a veteran to remember certain events at some times, but not others.

For veterans like Victor, the inability to remember can be of great concern. "I remember some things clear as a bell. But there are incidents listed in my after-action reports that I can barely recall. How did I act? Was I a hero or a coward? Did I hurt anyone by accident?" he asks, his eyes full of torment. "Except for two or three guys I was really close to, I can't remember the names of guys in my unit or much of what they did. Maybe that's for the best. But how do you think I feel when I run into their widows at reunions and they ask me about their husband's last days and my mind goes blank?"

Victor, who suffers from both PTSD and depression, is also troubled by the following recurring dream:

> I'm walking across a field when suddenly the ghosts of enemy dead and other people whom I can't recognize spring out of the earth. Then the ghosts—dozens of them—look at me and ask me how come I killed them, how come I buried them in a mass grave without any markers, and why I didn't feel anything as I did any of these things. When I wake up the bed sheets are soaked with sweat—beach towels full. For the next few days I'm so depressed I go into my room and tell the wife and kids not to bother me.
>
> But, Doc, the problem is, I'm not sure I did those things in the dream. I don't remember killing that many people, seeing that many dead bodies at one time, or digging any mass graves. Maybe I got that mass grave idea from reading books about war or from listening to the news. So maybe I'm feeling guilty about something I didn't even do. But maybe I did do it. If only I could remember.

But those veterans who do remember specific names, places, and events often wish they could forget.

Emotional Numbing

Although emotional numbing helps those in war zones function in the midst of fear and human misery, afterwards it can be the cause of considerable shame and guilt. For example, Roberta, a nurse who worked in a refugee camp with torture victims, was not sadistic by nature. Yet she poked fun at the refugees, took pictures of their grisly wounds, and laughed at the corpses. Today when she looks at the photos she asks herself: "Why haven't I thrown that scrapbook away? How come when I took those pictures those people meant nothing to me? In my mind they weren't even people, but things. So what does that make me? A human being with a heart or some kind of monster?"

Physical Numbing

Dissociation can help dull not only emotional pain but also physical pain, permitting people in war zones to continue functioning despite physical discomforts and injuries. For example, the soles of Suzanne's feet were beaten to the point where they bled. She also had a broken arm and two broken toes. Yet she was able to walk a long distance to safety because the pain was muted by dissociation. In other instances, veterans may remember the specifics of their experiences but have little recall of their physical state. Some realize they were wounded during a particular mission only after reading their after-action report.

When Dissociation Is Severe

Some degree of dissociation is normal. For example, everyone has times when they aren't paying attention because they are in their own world or times when they feel like they should be happy or upset about something but instead feel nothing. In milder forms and in the absence of other symptoms, dissociation may not present problems to veterans or their families. For example, to occasionally misplace one's keys is quite normal. However, misplacing them every second or third time is a sign of severe dissociation needing professional care.

Other forms of severe dissociation that require prompt attention include: frequent sleepwalking or travel away from home without remembering one's name or how one got to their present location; "losing time," that is, suddenly noticing that some time has passed and one can't remember what has occurred; feeling no emotion for long periods of time; not experiencing physical pain or extreme hot or cold when it would normally be expected; and any form of numbing that poses a potential danger to oneself or others.

Numbing that begins as a means of survival during combat can sometimes be continued back home. Depending on the circumstances and degree of numbing, it may or may not serve useful purposes. *

*See pages 141–50 for the potential effects of dissociation on intimate relationships, and pages 304–7 for the possible effects on children.

Depression

I want to write, to heal myself, but depression has immobilized me. Can I even move this pen? This morning I could barely get out of bed. Would I ever get up? Would I ever want to?

The world is cold and bleak. There's nothing to live for. I can't bear the deadness inside me any more.
—VICTOR, A COMBAT VET DIAGNOSED WITH PTSD AND DEPRESSION

What happens to a car that is driven cross-country many times without a tuneup, oil change, or tire rotation? What happens to a car that is well maintained but is driven coast to coast a thousand times? Would some parts start to wear out? Perhaps the car would eventually cease to function.

Clearly, people are not cars. However, what happens to a car because of overuse or inadequate care is similar to what happens to combat military or other people when they undergo repeated traumas or prolonged severe stress and do not have the time, money, ability, or opportunity to take care of themselves. Under such conditions, their emotional and physical reserves become taxed to the point where they develop clinical depression all too easily.

What Is Depression?

Everyone has "the blues" from time to time, and when it happens, we often say we're depressed. There is a difference, however, between these feelings and biochemical or clinical depression. The "blues" are temporary. In contrast, in clinical depression the sadness and other distressing feelings tend to grow over time. At some point the negative feelings become so overwhelming that they cause important problems in vocational, social, personal, and other areas of functioning. A clinically depressed person may not be able to make it to work, or it is a struggle to get there. He or she avoids socializing and may even stop going out altogether except when absolutely necessary. The smallest task seems like a monumental chore. It's too hard to concentrate enough to finish a newspaper article, much less a book, or to meet the most basic obligations to self and family. A clinically depressed person is plagued by indecision.

These decreasing abilities to function chip away at self-esteem. The lowered self-esteem, in turn, creates additional feelings of worthlessness because in our society self-confidence is valued. It isn't "popular" to have low self-esteem, so the person hides these difficulties from others. This pretending creates further stress and only increases his or her fatigue and sense of isolation from others.

Clinical depression can also impair reality testing, such as becoming hypersensitive to the reactions of others. Consequently, a person's views of how other people feel about them may be distorted. Or the depressed person may feel hopeless about situations in which there is, in fact, considerable hope.

The major symptoms of depression include feelings of worthlessness, hopelessness, and fatigue; depressed mood; eating and sleeping problems; irritability and anxiety; social withdrawal; memory and concentration problems; inability to experience pleasure; and thoughts of death or suicide. In some cases, these symptoms reflect the impact of a medical or substance-abuse problem, some type of medication, a psychotic disorder, or the normal grief reaction one would have to the death of a loved one.

Causes of Clinical Depression

Depression is by far the most common psychiatric problem in our country. Estimates are that one-third of adult women and one-tenth of adult men can expect to suffer from at least one bout of depression in their lifetime. Depression rates are higher among trauma survivors, such as combat military, and among those who are oppressed in some manner, for example, minority groups, women, the handicapped, and the poor.[38]

As previously noted, studies of combat veterans, including those from World War II, Korea, Vietnam, Grenada, Nicaragua, Iraq, and other armed conflicts, indicate that many veterans suffer from both PTSD and depression. This depression is frequently, but not necessarily, a result of war. But whether the depression predates the war or develops afterward, the effect is the same.[39]

There are many different explanations for what causes clinical depression as the following sections show. No one of these theories is 100 percent accurate in all cases, but they all have some validity in some instances. Clinical depression is caused by many factors, some of which are beyond individual control. Several of these causes can be directly related to combat trauma or to assuming a caretaker role toward a veteran who is physically disabled or who suffers from severe and long-term PTSD or depression. As you read these sections, keep in mind that causes for depression may vary over time—a given depressive episode may have an entirely different cause from the one preceding or following it. And the theory or theories that help explain one person's depression will not apply to another's.

Biological Theory

One way of looking at depression is as the result of disturbances in the neurotransmitter system, usually caused by a person having been subject to severe stress for a prolonged period of time.[40] A soldier's biochemistry can become so strained by the emotional and physical demands of combat that it may not be able to perform its functions as it did before going to war. It can also be strained by frequent indulgences in alcohol, drugs, or other unhealthy substances or by the wear and tear on the heart and other organs caused by the startle response and other hyperarousal symptoms of PTSD. Also at high risk for becoming depressed are the family members of veterans who suffer from unrelenting severe post-traumatic symptoms or who have long-term physical disabilities or medical problems. The ongoing emotional, and often physical, demands of living with a veteran who is in so much emotional or physical pain can deplete the physical and emotional resources of even the most loyal wife, husband, or child, especially if he or she has assumed a caretaker role in the family.

Breakdown of the neurotransmitter system in a veteran or in one of the veteran's family members can lead to low self-esteem, hopelessness, and other forms of negative thinking, and to difficulties with concentration, sleep, and decision making. It can also lead to irritability, anxiety, loss of the ability to experience pleasure, and hypersensitivity to the reactions of others—all of which are classic symptoms of depression.

Depression is also associated with physical illnesses, especially those of a chronic or severe nature, such as chronic pain due to battle injuries or certain infections and medical problems acquired overseas for which there are limited cures. In addition, depression can result from severe injury and permanent disability, or from the multiple medications that might be needed to treat these problems. Depression can also result from poor nutrition and inadequate sleep, conditions that can affect family members as well as the troubled veterans themselves.

Physical illness, disability, and medication tax the neurotransmitter system immensely. They also put a strain on other bodily functions. Physical injury or illness also often creates other problems—financial, social, sexual, and emotional. These stresses further disturb biochemical balances and negatively affect the central nervous system. If a man or woman was already ill or disabled before going to a war zone, or if he or she suffered from malnutrition or extreme sleep deprivation or was seriously injured during his or her tour of duty, that veteran is at special risk for depression. The risk is especially high if a part of the soldier's body essential to his or her work or interests was affected. For example, a military dentist who lost the use of his hand as the result of combat would lose not only the ability to function normally at home and in society but also his means of economic support—a double blow that would almost certainly lead to depression.

Loss and Grief Theory

A dentist's (or musician's) depression over the loss of his hand fits Freud's view of depression. He believed that depression was the result of grief over the loss of a loved one. However, the kind of grief he was referring to was grief mixed with anger and hostility toward the loved one. Freud also felt that the loved one need not be dead. The death or slow deterioration of the relationship with the loved one was sufficient to cause depression.

The concept of the loved one can be extended to include a cherished ideal, such as patriotism, certain spiritual values, or self-respect. Consequently, losing a long-held value or ideal or one's dignity can also lead to depression. If a soldier's dignity or self-respect were to be assaulted not only by certain combat experiences but also subsequently by others' reactions to those feelings, that soldier may be at a special risk for depression. Similarly, if a soldier's assumptions about the goodness and justice of the universe, or other values, were shattered by war, his subsequent grieving may also develop into a clinical depression. Family members can suffer a similar loss of innocence and despair as they learn about the brutal realities of war.

In all wars some soldiers (and sometimes family members) become disillusioned not only with life, but with the government or the military after observing hypocrisies, incompetence, and errors that resulted in needless deaths among their comrades. The resulting feeling among these soldiers (and some of their family members) was not only anger, but grief. They have lost the very ideals that caused them to join or support the military in the first place.

Behavioral Theory

The behavioral view of depression states that depression is the natural result of inadequate reinforcement, rewards, or recognition. Depression can easily develop among people who are inadequately rewarded or appreciated by others in their environment. Depression also results when people are unable to adequately appreciate, reward, or lovingly care for themselves.

Some popular self-help books on "how to love yourself" espouse or imply the idea that if you only can love and accept yourself, you don't need love and acceptance from others. In my experience, people need both. They need the recognition, love, and approval of at least a few other people as well as self-love and self-appreciation. Combat veterans are sometimes deprived of both; they lack reinforcement from others and self-reinforcement.

Vietnam veterans and many military service workers are prime examples of people who can suffer from depression caused by lack of reinforcement. In general, until recently, the Vietnam veteran was far from appreciated by our society. Instead of a Welcome Home parade such as greeted the Persian Gulf veterans, the Vietnam veteran was castigated and rejected for his sacrifices. There are still military staff who work long hours for relatively low pay or who receive little recognition for their many heroic efforts on behalf of others. Such situations are the breeding ground for depression. Military staff who were denigrated or not properly acknowledged for their efforts to survive or to help others survive, or who had to withstand long-term traumatic conditions where they received few rewards for their efforts, are at risk for depression.

Similarly, partners who invest considerable emotional energy in maintaining their relationship with their veteran, in promoting his or her physical and emotional well-being, and in taking care of domestic, financial, and other matters that he or she is unable to manage due to his or her traumatic reaction also tend to be unrecognized and unappreciated. Often they are criticized for giving "too much" or "too little" or for not supporting their veteran in some imaginary perfect manner. Obviously these critics have little understanding of how the combat experience can affect every aspect of a person's intimate relationship and family life; nor have they probably experienced the torture of seeing a loved one in an acute state of emotional suffering.

Learned Helplessness Theory

Part of learned helplessness is believing that you cannot exert control over the important events in your life. This feeling of helpless resignation or fatalism can lead to a clinical depression. Due to direct experience with powerlessness, and because of the biological changes that can occur during combat, combat military staff are especially susceptible to learned helplessness and, consequently, to depression.[41]

Family members of veterans with untreated or inadequately treated cases of substance abuse, depression, or any other traumatic reaction are also susceptible to learned helplessness. The wife of a former Army ranger explains: "I tried everything: being emotionally supportive, confronting him, ignoring him, leaving out books on combat stress, asking one of his buddies who had sought help to speak to him. I even got his ex-wife involved. But nothing I did worked. So now I'm starting to feel, like he does, that I don't have the power to make anything better, so I might as well give up."

Cognitive Theory

The cognitive view of depression is similar to the learned helplessness theory. However, cognitive theory states that depression is the result of problems with your thoughts and beliefs, rather than your feelings.[42] Once you think or believe you are helpless or ineffectual, then such thinking controls your behavior. Negative thinking can result in negative events, which further reinforce your negative thinking and view of life.

Cognitive theory further states that depressed people misinterpret life events, distorting their view of the world, themselves, and the future in a hopeless direction. Such distortions and misinterpretations are often directly related to traumas such as war, which in some cases teaches survivors that those in war zones are ineffectual, incompetent, or powerless.

Anger-Turned-Inward Theory

People who do not know how to express their anger, are afraid to express their anger, or feel they do not have the right to express it often turn that anger inward on themselves—resulting in depression. Turning anger inward is frequently a cause of depression in combat survivors who were in situations in which expressing anger could have led to physical abuse or other forms of punishment or even death (as is often the case with prisoners of war). Even when the captivity is over, the "habit" of suppressing anger can be difficult to unlearn.

Anger can often be turned inward in situations in which there is no clearly identifiable target for the anger: there is no one person or identifiable group to express anger toward (as is the case when a large bureaucracy or institution or a media presentation is nonresponsive to a veteran). For example, to whom do mistreated Vietnam and Korean War and World War II veterans direct their rage? In these cases, as one veteran stated, "Everyone was responsible, but nobody was responsible."

Individuals who were raised with the belief that anger is "bad" or immoral or that expressing anger is unacceptable, or who fear that expressing anger will alienate the people they love the most, may also find themselves turning their anger inward on themselves in the form of depression. Historically, women have been taught to suppress their anger, especially if they feel expressing their anger may harm a loved one. Wives, girlfriends, and daughters of combat veterans who deeply love their veteran and have empathy for his suffering often hesitate to speak up because they do not want to create even more stress for an obviously stressed partner or father. If, in addition, they feel that the veteran's problem behaviors are not his fault but the fault of the war and any negative experiences that followed, they may feel they don't have the right to tell him they are upset about something he said or did.

Other Theories

Depression can also be caused by events unrelated to combat. These include acute brain syndrome, some other organic mental disorder, or a psychiatric problem such as schizophrenia or paranoia. In some cases, depression is hereditary. If your veteran has a family history of clinical depression or manic-depressive illness, it does not automatically mean that he or she will develop that problem. However, the strain of combat can bring forth these and other latent genetically based psychiatric disorders. Similarly, if you have a family history of some type of psychiatric problem, that doesn't mean that you will automatically develop that problem. However, the strain of coping with an unhappy or emotionally turbulent mate or, if your partner is on active duty, the strain of coping with being separated and with fears about his or her safety may bring forth one of these or another latent genetically based psychiatric problem. Therefore, if you, your veteran, or another family member has a family history of depression or manic-depressive illness, watch carefully for symptoms of depression. If you observe some of these symptoms, seek help immediately (see appendix A for a list of resources). Depression is a highly treatable condition. There is no necessity for, or purpose in, continuing to suffer needlessly.

One final note about depression. Some depressed people tend to get "depressed about depression." They interpret their symptoms of depression as signs of personal inadequacy and failure and feel great shame and guilt over being depressed. Their feelings are reinforced by three factors: attitudes that blame people for their own pain; societal ignorance about depression; and cultural norms that view any person in emotional pain as "weak" or "deficient," even if that person has witnessed the horrors of war. These are the same attitudes that oppress veterans with PTSD or other traumatic reactions. These unsympathetic attitudes do not reflect reality; they reflect people's ignorance about mental health matters and their fears about themselves.

Somatization

Somatization, another possible response to trauma, occurs when the body carries or expresses the pain, anger, and other feelings associated with the trauma in the form of physical pain or impairment. Body memory, technically called somatic memory, is common among many kinds of trauma survivors, not just combat veterans. Somatization tends to occur more commonly in situations where speaking up is dangerous and may be punished or cause for social ostracism or rejection.[43] The type of physical symptom often reflects a soldier's cultural or religious background. Among some cultural groups, certain physical symptoms (such as falling down or burning sensations in the hands and feet) are acceptable ways of expressing distress.

Somatization does not mean that the sufferer is mentally deficient or a manipulator trying to "pull a fast one." The physical problem is genuine and involuntary. The pain is true bodily pain. At the same time, however, the body is also expressing the feelings and memories that cannot be easily or sufficiently put into words because, if expressed, they will put the individual into jeopardy. According to some scientists, there is a neurobiological explanation for somatization based on the instinct for self-preservation.[44]

Somatization can take various forms. Perhaps the most dramatic examples of somatization, often called "conversion reactions," occur where the eruption of a physical symptom (or the increase of a particular medical problem) is preceded by a traumatic event or by a seemingly unresolvable conflict within oneself or with important others. Under different names, conversion reactions have been documented by doctors, historians, and poets since the time of the ancient Greeks. For example, the historian Herodotus wrote that during the battle of Marathon in 490 BC an Athenian soldier who had suffered no wounds became permanently blind after witnessing the death of the soldier standing next to him.[45]

From ancient times to the present, soldiers have developed physical symptoms such as temporary blindness, deafness, joint pain, abdominal bloating, nausea, seizures, tremors, muscle spasms, loss of sensation in a particular part of the body, and various forms of physical pain in response to combat trauma.[46] These symptoms may be temporary or long-term. Even if they last but a few hours, they may return at some later point in time when a soldier is confronted with a person, place, or thing that reminds him or her of his or her combat experiences. Sometimes these symptoms are related to a known injury or illness but cannot be fully explained by that injury or illness or do not follow current understanding of body functioning. Despite the amazing advances of medical science, there are still many unknowns. Experts agree that some physical ailments that seem to have a psychological origin may have a physiological basis as well, one that has yet to be officially recognized or discovered.[47] Researchers who looked at the records for British veterans dating from 1872 to the Gulf War, for example, found many examples of unexplained medical symptoms. However, as medical science progressed, some of the symptoms that were "unexplainable" in the 1800s and early 1900s became medically understood.[48]

In combat veterans, somatization can take the form of an increase in the pain of war injuries. For example, Bill's arm was blown off on Thanksgiving Day. Around Thanksgiving each year, Bill has phantom pains in his shoulder. "I don't like to complain about not having an arm or about the fact that I still have to deal with infections, bleeding, and other problems because of that arm," says Bill. "But I guess the phantom pains do the complaining for me."

Somatization can also increase any physical pain and symptoms that were present before combat or would have developed after even if an individual had never seen combat. For example, ever since she was twelve years old Ramona had come down with strep throat once a year like clockwork, every September. After combat duty, however, she began having strep throat five or six times a year. She wasn't certain if she would have had this increase in strep throat even if she had never been in a war zone. However, after completing a recovery program, her incidence of strep throat reduced to two or three times, a major improvement that could possibly be credited to her having dealt with her combat experiences directly. Questions such as whether Ramona's health might have improved anyway, even if she hadn't persisted in counseling, are ultimately unanswerable. However, both psychological research and medical research have shown a correlation between emotional and physical well-being.

Symptoms of somatization may emerge not only during or after traumatic events, but years later should a veteran be retraumatized by a vehicular accident, criminal assault, natural catastrophe, family violence, or multiple personal losses, or if a family member or close friend is traumatized. Midlife can also retraumatize the veteran because the losses common to midlife can reactivate war issues. For example, if a partner or older relative dies, the veteran once again confronts one of the core issues of combat—that of one's own mortality and the loss of loved ones. Other midlife events that have the potential to be retraumatizing include children leaving home for school, marriage, or careers; a diminishment of sexual interest and other kinds of energies; or the loss of youthful appearance and vigor.

John, for example, never suffered from asthma until he was forty-two and his only child left home. At that time, John went into a state of psychological shock and mourning. Through this child, John had been able to feel young again. Even though John felt he buried his youth in Afghanistan, he was able to capture moments of his youth through his son. He delighted in his son's spontaneity, playfulness, and hope for the future, qualities he had lost but which he could vicariously enjoy by simply watching him.

When John's son left home, John was devastated. Beyond the normal feelings of loss parents can have as their children leave the nest, John was losing more than his son: he was losing his connection to some of the feelings that gave life meaning.

That same year, John was given a supervisor who acted very much like a commanding officer John had in Afghanistan. John had almost assaulted this C.O. because of his cruelty and incompetence. The absence of his son, combined with daily contact with what seemed to be a reincarnation of one of the most hated officers in John's unit, sent John back into the worst aspects of his combat experience. To make matters worse, the supervisor constantly berated John. Yet John felt he could not talk back, lest he lose his job.

In Afghanistan John couldn't talk back either. If he had talked back then, he would have been punished severely. For example, he might have been beaten or sent on the most dangerous missions. In Afghanistan John learned that his life depended on his not talking. Now his economic well-being seemed to depend on the very same survival tactic: silence. Within months, John developed a severe case of asthma.

At work, John sometimes literally held his breath to refrain from expressing his rage. At times he felt like he was suffocating from a lack of air. Emotionally, his pain and grief were suffocating him. In addition, he was trying to suffocate the anger this new supervisor triggered in him. On a psychological level, John's medical problem was doing the grieving, raging, and talking he dared not do openly.

Summary

Everyone who survives a war zone experience responds in his or her own unique way. While not all people develop a traumatic reaction, many do. Symptoms can emerge during or immediately after combat duty or even months or years later. The severity and duration of a traumatic reaction is influenced by many factors that are unrelated to a soldier's physical, emotional, or spiritual strength; his competence;

or his patriotism or dedication to the military. Some veterans develop an anxiety disorder, such as generalized anxiety disorder, panic disorder, or PTSD. Others develop a clinical depression, symptoms of dissociation, or various forms of somatization. Some veterans use alcohol, drugs, gambling, food, or other forms of addiction as a means of coping with these symptoms. Triggers, or situations that remind the veteran of war experiences, such as anniversary dates of the deaths of buddies, can intensify these symptoms or bring them forth in veterans who have become almost symptom-free or whose symptoms are relatively infrequent or mild.

Partners and family members often mistakenly take responsibility for their veteran's symptom or trigger reactions or misinterpret them as signs of rejection. If so, family members can then develop feelings of helplessness, loneliness, frustration, irritability, and resentment toward their veteran, which can lead to family conflicts, which only exacerbate the emotional pain, confusion, and feelings of powerlessness and hopelessness of each member of the family (including the veteran).

4

"All of a sudden his guard goes up"

Emotional Distancing

He loves you, but he doesn't trust you and he wants to run away from you—that's the double message you get from a combat vet. Looking back on the early years of my marriage, I don't know what was harder for me—Jim's anger or his depressions and his numbing. That numbing—it was, and is, one of the biggest problems we have. Sometimes I can't get through to him no matter what I do.

At first I tried to pierce his wall gently. No success. So then I tried rejection and anger. Maybe if I rebuffed and scorned him, he would come around. That worked—sometimes. But if his wall was really up, I could throw a first-class temper tantrum and he'd just shrug his shoulders and walk out the door.

I soon discovered that pressuring Jim for a response, whether I used loving tactics or not, was self-defeating. Either way, I'd usually drive him further away from me.

But he would always come back. He loves me. I know he loves me. And he's a good man, an honest man, who is only hurting himself. But in hurting himself, he hurts all of us—me and the kids.

"Why doesn't Daddy go with us to Aunt Vicky's or the mall?" the kids used to ask. Now they don't ask anymore. They just accept Jim the way he is. I'd like to tell them that because of the war their

father just can't take crowds and loud, noisy places and parties, but I just don't know how.

I came to therapy complaining about Jim's numbing, not realizing that, over the years, I had become numb myself. Just like Jim, I am afraid of the feelings inside me—the years of pent-up anger and hurt and my sense of loss about what I thought my marriage would be and what my marriage really is.

Sometimes I cancel my therapy sessions because I don't want to face my feelings. When I face the truth about my life, it hurts so bad I pray for the numbing to come back.

—WIFE OF A COMBAT VET

Numbing

Have you ever cut yourself and not felt the pain immediately? Have you ever suffered whiplash in a car accident but not felt the soreness or fatigue until several days later? The body often emits a natural anesthetic that permits us some time to take care of our wounds and to do whatever is necessary to protect ourselves from further injury. When the pain is overwhelming, we may even go into shock and lose consciousness entirely. Our bodies simply cannot tolerate the pain, and nature, mercifully, spares us.

Just as the body may temporarily anesthetize itself against physical pain for self-protection, the psyche can numb itself against onslaughts of unbearable emotional pain. As described in chapter 1, soldiers need to put aside their emotions during combat. Acknowledging feelings would be both personally confusing and life-threatening. Connecting with grief or other powerful emotions would lessen the ability of most soldiers to give and take directions or otherwise figure out what to do next in order to save themselves and others.

This deadening, or shutting off, of emotions is called *emotional* or *psychic numbing*. As described in chapter 3, numbing is a central feature of PTSD and can be present in other forms of combat trauma as well. Numbing or dissociation also has been found among survivors of the Nazi holocaust and the bombing of Hiroshima; victims of earthquakes, floods, and fires; and victims of sexual and physical assault.[1]

In the face of a life-threatening event, numbing is not a matter of personal choice but the result of biochemical reactions to danger which are hardwired into the human brain. Yet even after having been presented with scientific evidence showing the biochemical basis and survival value of numbing, many veterans continue to feel ashamed of becoming numb during combat and to view it as a sign of cowardice or mental or physical weakness. Our culture tends to value action over inaction. Hence not only combat veterans but many others as well erroneously equate numbing or "freezing" with passivity, surrender, or even stupidity.

Numbing is not "stupid," it is life-preserving. Like human beings, many species of animals go into a fight-flight-freeze mode when they encounter danger. Animal studies have shown that some species, from fish to lions, go into an inactive or "freeze" role rather than an action or "fight-flight" role if they see little chance of escape. However, even if a good escape route is available some animals freeze for a number of reasons: predators tend to detect moving prey more than static ones; if one stands still, a predator's attention may be diverted to noisy or moving objects; and moving prey tends to entice predators into attack mode.[2]

In addition, part of going numb involves a release of biochemicals that reduce the sensation of pain, both physical and mental. This physical and emotional analgesia, it is argued, permits the animal or the human being to focus on self-defense or on finding a viable means of escape by reducing the distractions caused by high levels of fear or by intense physical or emotional pain. Furthermore, should an animal or person be killed as the result of being attacked, this analgesia helps minimize the physical and emotional pain of dying.[3]

Nevertheless, numbing can create serious problems when the individual remains in that state long after the original traumatic event, or when he or she responds to current non-life-threatening situations by going numb. Some veterans find it difficult to discuss relationships, financial situations, and other problems without going numb. This can be exasperating for partners who are trying hard to resolve certain issues and who may view the veteran's numbing as "not caring" or "not taking responsibility." However, the veteran's numbing may be a carryover from combat days, when there was no such thing as a minor problem and every interpersonal or other problem was life threatening, or potentially so.

Numbing can also interfere with parenting. A recent study of the effects of PTSD on parenting found that of all the symptoms of PTSD, it was the veterans' numbing (as opposed to their startle response or other hyperalert symptoms, or to their nightmares or other re-experiencing symptoms) that seemed to cause the most relationship problems. Furthermore, two aspects of numbing—emotional detachment and disinterest in others—caused more relationship disturbances than a third aspect of numbing, purposeful avoidance, or the veteran's conscious decision to avoid reminders of combat.[4] According to partners, of the many possible causes of relationship problems in the following list, emotional or psychic numbing is perhaps the chief source of their emotional pain.

How Combat Trauma Can Damage Relationships

1. Feelings of vulnerability; loss of sense of orderly or fair world

2. Loss of positive self-image: guilt, shame, feelings of helplessness
   a. Shame regarding loss of control during fight-flight-freeze and other involuntary biological reactions experienced during trauma or in response to reminders of trauma
   b. Shame regarding loss of control over one's thinking/feeling reactions during the trauma or in response to reminders of the trauma
   c. Loss of confidence about one's ability to protect oneself
   d. Loss of confidence about one's judgment and ability to handle stressful situations
   e. Shame at feeling "needy" (negative value in Western culture)

3. Betrayal by other people/agencies during or immediately after the war

4. Possible financial, economic, social, health losses; possible physical disfigurement

5. "Blame the victim" attitudes in the family, community, or professional world

6. Physiological and emotional reactivity to reminders of the trauma

7. Hyperarousal and persistent expectation of danger

8. Numbing: limited emotional, physical, sexual, and mental energy

9. Unexpressed anger and grief

10. Survivor guilt and other types of guilt

11. Loss of innocence: feeling "contaminated" or different from others as the result of witnessing or participating in any of the many horrors of war

The tendency for veterans to numb themselves emotionally with respect to their wartime experiences is reinforced by two outside factors: military experiences that tend to dehumanize the enemy and punish soldiers who experience or express fear, sadness, grief, or tenderness by giving them a derogatory label such as "sissy"; and a society that for the most part does not want to hear about the brutal realities of war. While there is usually interest in heroic war stories, often there is little interest in a veteran's emotional experiences and traumas. The vet's soul-searching questions, if he or she dares to ask them, may be even less welcome.

Often families and friends wish to be supportive, but don't know how. One wife explains how she and other wives wanted their husbands to

> simply get on with their lives . . . to bury whatever it was they had seen and felt, to become "normal" again. We refused to allow them to defuse. We didn't know how to hear men cry; we were unable to find out how they had changed.
>
> We weren't being cruel. We just wanted to love them as they had been and still were in our fantasies. We hoped that we could make them smile. But . . . we were the first to see that the problems would not disappear in some wash-day miracle, would not respond to our nurturing.[5]

Vets often complain that upon returning home they were expected to resume "life as usual" almost instantly. After combat duty, however, life can no longer be "as usual" for them or for their families. In addition, having to pretend to have been untouched by being in a war imposes yet another psychological strain on the already stressed veteran.

Psychic numbing exists in different degrees, in different ways, in different vets, at different times. There is no set pattern. However, to the extent that numbing creates emotional distance between a veteran and others, it poses a formidable obstacle to that veteran's efforts to form meaningful sustained emotional connections with others, especially with an intimate partner.

The Effect of Numbing on Relationships

The last time Lisa and Allen held hands was two years ago. Their last hug was five years ago. "And that's only because he forgot my birthday again and I reminded him," Lisa explains. "Allen was never that sentimental, but since he went overseas, he's done nothing about my birthdays or our anniversaries."

After several years of having their anniversary passed by unnoticed, Lisa finally insisted that Allen take her out to dinner. Allen was reluctant, but finally agreed. On the way to the restaurant he couldn't help reminding Lisa that birthdays, anniversaries, cards, and flowers no longer held much meaning for him. Allen's low tolerance for formal dinners and other social formalities was born overseas, where he had witnessed the suicide bombing of a restaurant, seen children starving to death, and at one point been near starvation himself.

Lisa was not heartless. However, she was tired of hearing about the war.

> While we were waiting for the waiter, all I heard about was how combat vets hardly ever ate in fancy restaurants, about how the restaurants were booby-trapped, about how lucky I was to be civilian and have escaped going to war—the whole bit. I wanted to leave right then and there, but then I figured it was probably better that he talk about the war than go into numbing.
>
> Besides, if I had suggested leaving, Allen would have either become furious with me or tuned out entirely. So I sat there pretending, wondering how I was going to get through three hours of this, when we had to leave early anyway because the restaurant's air conditioner blew a fuse. Allen had suffered immensely from the heat overseas and he can't stand being hot, not even for ten minutes.
>
> When I looked disappointed about having to go home, he got upset

with me for not being "understanding." This is the thanks I get for years of being a loyal wife.

Numerous research studies support the existence of feelings of detachment and numbing in interpersonal relationships among combat veterans with PTSD and other post-traumatic reactions.[6] It must be remembered, however, that many of these studies are based on male combat veterans and their family members who seek help at Department of Veterans Affairs medical centers or at Vet Centers, not on women veterans or combat veterans who seek help from private mental health professionals, lay counselors, or spiritual advisors rather than from the military. Therefore, the results of these studies cannot be generalized to all combat veterans and their families, especially to women veterans. It may be the case that veterans who suffer from severe numbing or other post-traumatic symptoms and their family members who seek help constitute most of the subjects of these studies.

Degrees and Types of Numbing

In the most extreme cases, the numbing is so pervasive that the veteran has great difficulty reintegrating into mainstream society. When combined with financial or personal difficulties, numbing can result in homelessness.[7] In other severe cases, vets work two jobs or ten- to fourteen-hour days, filling their lives with work, not people. Such a heavy work involvement may be an economic necessity. Some partners report that during nonwork hours, when the vet could be with the family, he or she may chose solitary pursuits or "blank out" in front of the television.

In my experience, the majority of partners do not describe their veterans as being chronically numb, but rather as fluctuating between being emotionally present and emotionally distant. "My husband has periods where he is an involved family man, followed by times where he walls us out with an invisible sheet of ice," says Lisa. Even when her husband is physically present, he may be emotionally unresponsive or suddenly freeze, stare into space, or leave abruptly, especially when politics or war is mentioned or if there is some trigger from the war, such as a passing airplane or a sudden noise.

Some veterans freeze during intercourse as well, perhaps because of an intrusive memory or because the emotional and physical closeness is intolerable. When veterans retreat into their shell, their partners may be left frantic, wondering what to do next and questioning their sexual desirability.

Numbing and Family Life

"I can tell the minute he walks through the door whether or not his 'wall' is going to be up for the night," says Lisa. "If it is, there's no chance of sex or any kind of communication." Typically, Allen wants two or three hours to himself after work before he can join the family. Sometimes his need for solitude conflicts with the children's schedules, so that he often misses spending time with them.

Lisa has read about combat trauma and understands Allen's need for this amount of peace and quiet. But on some level, she still wonders if there is something she does or says that causes Allen's emotional detachment. The children have little comprehension of their father's problem. Like their mother, they have come to accept their father's numbing as "normal." A depressive blanket seems to cover the family, and the major weight of the family's emotional life falls on Lisa.

> *If the kids and I plan a picnic or game and Allen, at the last minute, decides not to go, I've learned to go ahead without him. It's hard . . . but it's better than forcing him to go or staying home and depriving the kids and myself of some fun.*

When Lisa first sought help, almost all of her complaints about Allen's numbing had to do with the effects on their children, not herself. "I don't care about me, only the kids," she would repeat. Eventually, however, Lisa was able to experience her own deep sense of rejection and hurt at Allen's walling her out.

> *Allen would take the bullet for me. He says that all the time and I believe him. Yet it's painful to love a man, who although he might love you, has such trouble showing it. And it's not the big rejections—the major blowups—that do me under. It's the hundred little ways he ignores me every day. One hundred little rejections equal one big depression.*

While the veteran in numbing may not intend to shut out his wife, she often experiences his numbness as a personal rejection. Even when she learns in therapy that her husband's emotional distance from her has more to do with his war experiences or his family background than her own emotional or sexual desirability, she may still feel rejected. Partners of women veterans encounter the same dilemma. "Intellectually, I know it's the numbing, but emotionally, I need more from a marriage," states the husband of a naval officer.

Partners often complain about not knowing whether they are "on" or "off." The anxiety of not knowing whether one is going to be greeted with smiles, irritability, or a blank look is especially prevalent among partners who are adult children of alcoholics. For example, as a child, Lynn used to help calm her alcoholic father after his drinking binges and soothe her mother after her parents' frequent fights. Even before Lynn reached puberty, both parents were turning to her for "mothering" and comfort. As a little girl, Lynn needed to be taken care of by her parents rather than to be thrust in the role of their caretaker. However, Lynn repressed her natural child desires and received so much praise from her parents and other relatives for her abilities to make her parents and her siblings feel better that eventually she came to believe that the continuation of the family depended on her.

She also came to believe that if she wasn't perfect, the family might fall apart. Whenever one of her parents was upset, she interpreted it as the result of something she had failed to do or had done wrong. As a child she had a persistent nightmare in which her home was blown up because she failed to please one of her parents.

Today, as the wife of a vet who suffers from intermittent numbing, Lynn is experiencing the same emotional instability in her home as she did when she was a child. Once again, she feels responsible for the continuation and the well-being of the family. During her frequent anxiety attacks about whether or not she can take emotional care of her husband and children, she hyperventilates, perspires, and burns much of her emotional energy. Often she runs in two directions, trying to cheer up her husband and smooth things out for her children as well. When home life isn't happy she fails to see how her husband and children contribute to the situation and focuses on her own real or imagined inadequacies and minor imperfections instead.

Because her present home situation is similar to her childhood situation, Lynn's anxiety attacks tend to be intense and, at times, frighten her immensely. As a result of her exposure to pop-psychology talk shows and magazine articles, she has diagnosed herself as "compulsive," "co-dependent," "controlling," and "overly reactive." Such negative and erroneous self-evaluations create even more self-doubts and anxiety.

Partners can encounter additional problems with a veteran's numbing as their children grow older. Teenagers who have heard about combat stress or seen media presentations on the subject can use the veteran's symptoms or knowledge of the war as a club against the veteran in their attempts to assert their independence or in the usual clashes with parents over schoolwork, chores, and other teenage issues. A teenager might call her veteran parent or stepparent a "psycho" or a "nut job" in retort for being disciplined. Or she may say: "You can't even sleep through the night without having a nightmare. So don't tell me how to run my life." Or she may challenge her nonveteran parent's directives by calling that parent stupid, as proven by the fact that he or she married a "weirdo vet."

Such statements can easily trigger the veteran's anger toward, or withdrawal from, that child, and perhaps from others in the family, at least temporarily. From the veteran's point of view, he or she has been "zapped" by friendly fire. Rather than retaliate, the veteran may become numb and withdraw or retaliate verbally and then withdraw or become numb later.

Whereas younger children might feel rejected by a veteran's numbing, older children may reject their veteran parent because of his or her numbing or unpredictable moods. They may arrange to see their friends outside the home or when their veteran parent is not around because they fear he or she may begin to stare into space, cry, sulk, yell, or otherwise embarrass them in front of their friends. In one instance, the daughter of a combat veteran did not want her father to attend her engagement party. She knew her father hated crowds and formal affairs, such as she had planned. She had seen him go numb at previous formal family functions. While she loved her father very much and was understanding of his combat trauma, she just could not take a chance that he would ruin her special day. Even if he acted appropriately, she felt she would have to watch him constantly to be certain he was not becoming overly anxious or depressed.

Intellectually the father understood his daughter's position, but inside he seethed with anger, shame, and hurt. His wife tried to effect a compromise between her husband and her daughter, but both were rigidly entrenched in their positions. At one point, the veteran asked his wife to choose between him and their daughter. When she could not make this impossible choice, he threatened to commit suicide and left home. Outside intervention was necessary to help this troubled family.

Repressing Grief

Psychic numbing involves the repression of some powerful emotion, especially grief, perhaps the most painful of all human emotions. Grief repression has been cited many times as central to those times when a veteran is unable to or must struggle to connect with others emotionally.[8] The wall around some veterans that keeps others at a distance is essentially a reflection of a wall that exists around their own hearts to shield themselves from their own pain and grief. It bears repeating that combat veterans do not consciously decide to erect such walls. As with any trauma survivor, those walls are erected by an inner protective mechanism that seeks to shield an individual from being rendered dysfunctional by certain feelings should they be experienced in full.

Some vets are afraid to grieve. Having repressed their grief through numbing, they fear that once they begin to sorrow over one memory or incident, they will be flooded by other memories and drown in grief. So they fight their grief, trying to keep a tight lid on it, rather than experience the pain.

In some cases depression may involve repressed grief. It is often easier, or more comfortable, to be depressed than to hurt or suffer actively. Although depression is a way that grief can be expressed, it is not actually grieving. In order for healing to occur, the grief must be experienced in full, perhaps a little at a time and usually more than once, before the individual can become more fully involved in the present.

Vets with combat trauma often find themselves feeling emotionally numb inside or deeply depressed every year around the anniversary dates of the deaths of friends or certain other traumatic experiences. Although they may continue to go to work, their working capacities are often impaired. At home, their involvement with the family may come to a standstill. At such times, some partners curtail their outside activities and stay close to home in case their veteran needs them. This act of love can increase the tender feelings a veteran has for his or her partner. Even if a word is not spoken between them, the silent support offered by the partner's loving presence can be powerful and appreciated by the veteran. For many couples, the mutual acknowledgment of the sorrow involved in the anniversary event helps to forge a stronger bond between them.

On the other hand, being together at such times can lead to certain tensions. For example, Joanne didn't ask her boyfriend to give up his spinning class to stay home with her on the anniversary of the night that she was almost killed. He did so voluntarily. Yet she felt guilty because he gave up one of his favorite activities just for her. As with some veterans, the guilt made Joanne irritable, leaving her boyfriend to wonder why Joanne didn't seem to be comforted by his presence. He then mistakenly concluded that he had somehow failed her.

In similar situations, instead of feeling inadequate, the partner may become annoyed or angry at the veteran for not being more grateful that she broke a commitment to someone else or gave up an enjoyable activity in order to stay home and be there for him. Even if a veteran isn't irritable or doesn't act negatively toward his partner, the partner may come to feel inadequate if her presence doesn't seem to lift his spirit. This can lead to the partner becoming angry with herself for not having said or done the "right thing," or becoming angry at the veteran, whom she may now come to view as being "stubborn" and "unwilling to let go of the past."

Another possible source of tension arises because some veterans have more difficulty performing household duties or keeping their commitments to their partners when they are feeling numb or depressed. "That makes more work for me. But how can I remind her that she agreed to pick up the dry cleaning when she's doing all she can to keep herself together enough to get to work the next day?" asks the husband of a combat nurse.

While some partners are understanding, others wonder if their veteran's psychic numbing is an excuse to escape responsibilities. Even some counselors at veterans hospitals and Vet Centers, some of whom are combat veterans themselves, recognize that some vets use their post-traumatic symptoms as a way to get their partners to do more of the work, especially chores they dislike. In some cases, it is relatively easy to determine whether the veteran is using combat trauma as an excuse. But in others, the situation is complex. For example, Mike refuses to drive his fourteen-year-old daughter to cheerleader practice or to her basketball games. This angers his wife, who works full time and must add another trip onto the end of her already long workday. "Why can't he do it?" she shouts in a marriage counseling session. "After all, I do all the cooking and cleaning and work forty hours a week just like him. What is this? The dark ages when women did everything?"

But Mike insists that his sanity will snap if he sees one more basketball or pom-pom girl.

When Mike's daughter first became a cheerleader for her junior high school's basketball team, Mike begrudgingly did all the chauffeuring. Even though he had been a basketball champ in high school, he did not approve of his daughter's participation in basketball cheerleading. The sexually suggestive nature of the cheerleader uniforms and dance routines revolted him. Not only did he view them as sexist and inappropriate for such young girls, but they reminded him of the child prostitutes he had seen begging in the streets during his combat days. Nevertheless, he could not fight his daughter's desire to join the cheerleading squad or his family's reaction to his objections.

It was not until the third or fourth basketball game that Mike finally discovered yet a deeper source of his dislike of basketball. During this particular game, one of the players was knocked down. His kneecap was broken and his nose began to bleed profusely. As he was carried off the gym floor, he moaned loudly and left a trail of blood.

Mike's daughter began to weep. "Look at the blood! Look at the blood!"

As Mike looked, the heads of the basketball players seemed to pop off and, within seconds, their young bodies had become dismembered corpses strewn around the gym floor. Then, when his daughter leapt into the air yelling a cheer, Mike imagined her uniform full of bloodstains and her legs bleeding with knife wounds. Howling in pain, she died in midair.

The sight of the blood and the young boy falling had brought to the surface combat memories that Mike had almost totally repressed. It so happened that the number of combatants involved in a particular firefight, and their distribution and location on the battleground, was remarkably similar to the number of boys on the basketball team and their location on the gym floor. Furthermore, a member of Mike's basketball team, a friend whom Mike had encouraged to join the military, had died in that fight.

Mike had never dealt with his grief regarding that fight or his guilt regarding the death of his friend. Neither had he ever dealt with his horror at seeing the legs of a teenage prostitute being hacked with knives. Soon afterward, he sought help at a local Vet Center.

One year later, Mike was still in therapy working on his combat experiences. His overworked wife was still waiting for the day when Mike would be able to relieve her of some of the chauffeuring. Furthermore, her son was going to join a Little League the next year. Then, she asked, which "war problem" was going to prevent Mike from helping out with the driving? Would Mike at least allow his children to join a car pool? Up to this point, Mike did not trust his children with anyone but himself or his wife.

Mike's wife felt he was paranoid and impossible. Mike, on the other hand, felt he was only being cautious. "No one outside the family can be trusted," he insisted. Besides, if anything happened to one of the children, he would never forgive himself and probably end up in a mental ward. He'd go after the offender, too.

Mike's wife explained,

> *It's not the work I mind. It's Mike's attitude. Our daughter knows he doesn't like her being a cheerleader and feels guilty about going against her father. In fact, she was ready to quit the team after Mike broke down during that game. But I made her stick with it.*
>
> *She deserves to have a normal life; so does our son, even if our family isn't normal because Mike was in the Army. In fact, our kids need outside activities more than most kids because Mike's depressed and I'm depressed, too. We're struggling to keep our marriage together and make ends meet. I don't know how we're going to end up, but I do want our children to have as many good memories of their childhood as possible.*

As a compromise, Mike agreed to assume additional household chores and not make derogatory comments about sports. He also agreed to pick up his daughter, provided that he could wait for her in the parking lot and not have to observe any games. His daughter would also have to change from her cheerleader uniform into regular clothes before she got in the car. Mike never wanted to see that uniform again.

Repressed grief can also be triggered by expected life transitions, making these normal changes in a family's life exceptionally painful, if not retraumatizing, for the veteran. When the veteran reacts with increased numbing or other symptoms to normal life transitions, the stress the other family members are already experiencing as the result of these transitions is increased. For example, the time when a child leaves home for college, a military career, a job, or marriage can be difficult for many parents, even under the best of circumstances. Often there are mixed feelings. On the one hand, there is cause for rejoicing; parents can credit themselves for having succeeded in raising a child to the point of near maturity.

But on the other hand, the child's departure is an emotional loss for the parents. It is also a time of some fear. The child, now almost an adult, may fear facing the world without a protective parent nearby. The parents, on the other hand, may fear allowing their child to venture forth into a world of people, few of whom have the same attitude of parental love and protectiveness toward their child as they do.

As Doug Scaturo and Peter Hayman write, "For the combat veteran who has frequently observed the loss of significant friendships often instantaneously, randomly, and brutally on the battlefield, the normative transitional events of family life may take on exaggerated emotional proportions by the standards of those who have never been traumatized." Thus the event of children leaving home is experienced not only as a step toward the child's independence and maturation, but also as agony and betrayal. A child's leaving, however appropriate or innocent, brings to the surface the veteran's "feelings of total abandonment, isolation, and helplessness previously experienced during combat."[9]

The situation in Peter and Nora's home illustrates the difficulties combat veteran families encounter when a child leaves home for college. Peter's son had won a sports scholarship to a well-known but out-of-state college. Peter himself had loved sports as a youth, until a war injury prevented him from pursuing any sport whatsoever. He could barely walk, much less run. Unconsciously, perhaps, Peter's son excelled in sports not only for himself, but for his father.

Peter was always so enthralled when his son excelled in another game. At the same time, his son rejoiced that he could bring some joy to his semi-crippled, suffering father.

Peter had supported his son's applying for sports scholarships at various out-of-state colleges. Consequently his son could not understand the intensity of his father's grief and anger when he announced he was going to accept a scholarship from a college five hundred miles from home.

"How can you leave us?" Peter growled at his son.

"But Dad, you helped me apply for the scholarship yourself."

"Get lost! I never want to see you again. Maybe I'll kill myself."

Peter's son was angry, hurt, and confused. Peter's wife, Nora, was livid. She berated Peter for spoiling their son's victory in winning a major scholarship. Calling Peter selfish and inconsiderate, she insisted that he make amends to their son by helping him pack and move into his dorm.

Peter was in no mood for orders and called his wife selfish and inconsiderate for asking him to engage in physical activities, such as moving, which he could not perform well due to his war injuries. Peter stormed out of the home, furious, but also feeling guilty and ashamed. He knew he had mistreated his son, yet he felt so cheated and betrayed by life that he couldn't help but become enraged at the thought of having to separate from someone so precious to him.

Memories of dead war buddies flashed through Peter's mind and he began to tremble, thinking that his son might fall into harm without his protection. Within minutes, his rage had turned into tears. What if his son would die, away from home, like his buddies did?

"I'm overreacting. I'm overreacting," he told himself, but he still could not make himself feel differently. Inside he was shaking and bursting with emotions he could not name.

Nora requested an emergency meeting with Peter's counselor. Peter wept openly in front of his son about the pain of saying good-bye, not only to him, but to others who were now dead. For the first time, Peter's son understood that his father's reactions to him were not signs of disapproval or rejection of him as a son, but expressions of his father's profound love for him, his father's deep fears for his safety, and his father's war grief.

For Peter, the son's leaving home for college was a reliving of his war experience where he lost many friends. Although Peter had several good friends, his family was the center of his emotional life. Now one of the major purposes of his life, his son, was walking out the door. No wonder he was shattered.

Nora was hurting, too. Like her husband, or any parent saying good-bye to a child leaving home, she was wracked with feelings of pain and loss. Yet Nora had never gone through months of deep depression with the only joy in her life being her usefulness to her son. But Peter had clung to life many times only because he knew that his suicide would devastate his son.

Once I had a flashback of an enemy attack where twelve guys died. I was driving at the time and losing control of the car. So I tried to stop the flashback, but I couldn't. My car almost went off a cliff and I nearly hit some people.

Driving home, I decided I was a danger to society and should kill myself. But when I got home, my son, who was six at the time, was waiting outside for me. "Daddy, Daddy, where have you been?" he asked. "I've been waiting for you a long time. Hurry up, Daddy. I want to show you the 'A' I got on my homework." After that, I realized I couldn't kill myself. My son needed me.

Now that his son was leaving home, Peter would have to find new people to love and additional purposes for living. So would Nora. It would be hard for both of them, but harder for Peter because of his combat trauma.

In a later counseling session, Nora suggested that Peter join some veterans organizations or make some other attempts to find new friends. Or he could become involved in some educational or social projects in which he could have direct contact with other children who needed attention. He could even start paying attention to her. She needed attention, as did their marriage. Now that their son was gone, they would have more time for each other.

But Peter would not consider any of these ideas. This made Nora so livid she stood up in the middle of the counselor's office and shouted, "See! He won't do a thing to help himself. All he does is moan and groan about the pain and make us all suffer, but when I give him a positive suggestion to make things better, he refuses to even try. All he wants to do is hide from life, all alone in his little room."

Nora then began to sob. "Peter's not the only one who is heartbroken that our son is going away. I'm going to miss him, too, even if I was never suicidal in my life. Now with our son gone, I'll need my husband even more. But he won't be there for me. Why? Because I'm not important. Why? Because I didn't fight in a war?"

"Peter, just because I'm not a combat veteran doesn't mean I'm a nobody. My feelings matter too."

Peter remained unmoved.

"Your eyes are fixed on the floor and you have a sad look on your face. Are you feeling anything now?" the counselor asked Peter.

"I don't know. I just can't react. I want to respond to my wife, but I can't. I'm numb."

"What do you think of your wife's ideas?" asked the counselor.

"They're good logical ideas, but they are unacceptable to me."

"Why?"

"Because acting on them would insult my friends who died serving their country and my son, too. No other boy can replace him."

"Explain to me how making new friends is a betrayal of your dead war buddies. I really want to understand," said the counselor.

Peter could not explain, but deep in his heart he was certain that there was a strong connection. For many war survivors, including soldiers, refugees, and concentration camp inmates, fully grieving and saying good-bye to the dead "perpetuates the hell" they experienced when they saw that the dead among them were not recognized or appreciated. Therefore, on an emotional level, embracing the new can be experienced as abandoning the dead, which is tantamount to discounting and forgetting one's own memories of what was a permanently life-changing experience.[10]

While society might want combat veterans to forget the past, they cannot do so without annihilating a part of themselves. Peter's reluctance to make new friends after the departure of his son is not only a way of honoring the dead but also, on some level, an act of self-preservation. Yet, to his wife this seems like a needless sacrifice that leaves both of them relatively isolated.

At a transition time, when couples need each other's comfort and support, Nora was left standing alone. The devastating impact of the son's departure left Peter with little to give his wife as she faced a now empty nest. Peter's reasons for not being able to be there for her were legitimate and, to a large degree, out of his or her control. Yet that does not mitigate the fact that Nora was not receiving the tenderness and affection she needed and expected from her husband at this time. In such situations, there are no "good guys" or "bad guys." Instead there are two hurting people who could provide each other with considerable support if only the legacy of war wasn't standing in their way.

Fear of Loss

Veterans in a state of psychic numbing often can function quite well at work or in other situations where emotional awareness and responsiveness are not required. However, at home, where emotional exchange is essential, they often struggle to communicate. Their "wall" might not always be up, but some partners are convinced that on some level it is always there.

For some veterans it is easier to be among relative strangers than among those they love, in whose presence they might forsake their wartime vow to never become attached. "I swore I would never again let anyone matter to me, so I couldn't ever hurt that much again," states a veteran, remembering the combat death of his best friend.[11]

In times of family trouble and loss, some veterans become increasingly numb, while others become the rock on which the entire family leans. However, even the most helpful veteran may have difficulty being emotionally present during a crisis unless he or she has learned to deal with loss, frustration, and other difficult emotions (in therapy or by other means). It is not clear why some vets respond to family crises by helping and why others distance themselves. A veteran's response may depend not only on his or her upbringing but also on the sheer amount of death and destruction encountered in combat. The ways a veteran reacted to loss on the battlefield can sometimes provide clues to his or her response to current family or other crises.

Veterans who had responded to the death of a comrade or a malfunctioning weapon by becoming more aggressive may have angry outbursts when there is a loss or crisis in the family. If they had responded by overindulging in alcohol, food, or drugs, they might respond in the same way in the present. If they simply shut down emotionally on the battlefield, they may react similarly in the present.

There are also veterans who are helpful during family crises, except for those crises which they feel are their fault, in whole or in part. The added burden of guilt, in addition to the other stresses involved in a crisis, can be so overwhelming that emotional distance is needed to preserve one's sanity and to control one's rage, not only toward the situation but inward as well. This holds true even if the guilt is irrational, that is, if the veteran had little to do with the negative event or if the veteran is exaggerating his or her role in it. If a vet's father dies of cancer, for example, and the veteran assumes no responsibility for the father's illness, the vet is likely to be emotionally present. If the veteran's child dies of the same cancer, but the veteran believes the cancer was caused by a toxic substance or illness to which he or she was exposed (or suspects that he or she was exposed) in the military, the veteran's guilt, although irrational, may cause him or her to become emotionally distant from the child. Similarly, if a teenaged child runs away from home, becomes involved in criminal activities, or develops an alcohol or drug problem, the veteran may blame his or her real or perceived deficiencies as a parent for these events. Partners and other family members may also blame the veteran, which only increases the veteran's burden of self-hate, shame, and guilt.

On the other hand, a veteran's sense of responsibility for a negative event can propel him or her to make every effort to help. Lorraine accumulated a huge debt to pay for her son's health care and gave up lucrative job offers to care for him. Before Lorraine gave birth to her son, she had ten miscarriages. She blames the miscarriages and her son's leukemia on her exposure to malaria, parasites, and certain dangerous chemicals while on active duty. Some physicians agree with her analysis; others do not.

Lorraine is full of sadness and anger. Yet after years of therapy, she has yet to show any real emotion. Her therapist explains:

> Lorraine is highly functional in so many ways, but her feelings are strangers to her. She talks about her feelings, but she's never really felt them. For example, she talks about how sad she is about being in so much debt and about her son's being so ill. Yet she's never shed a tear or even looked sad. She doesn't even sound sad, and when she talks about her anger with certain doctors, her voice is so calm you'd never know she feels like dashing their brains out.
>
> Lorraine will do anything for her husband and family, but because she's so numb, they call her the "ice woman" and shun her. To top it off, Lorraine thinks she deserves this rejection. According to her logic, all those miscarriages prove that she's a failure as a woman, and her son's illness that she's a bad mother, too.

Sometimes veterans distance themselves from others in order to protect them from harm. Consciously or subconsciously, they may fear that the "bad karma" or "death taint" they acquired during battle may have followed them home, and therefore everything they touch may wither and die. So, they conclude, it's best to "stay away." When a family member is injured or ill or meets with some misfortune, a veteran may assume the blame, even if he or she had little or nothing to do with the negative event. A veteran might view the death of a family member or friend as a punishment or "payback" for something he or she did, thought, or felt while on combat duty.

Mike, for instance, was certain that God was going to punish him for accidentally killing an innocent child overseas by taking away one of his own children. Shortly after Mike married Barbara, Barbara's daughter by a former marriage developed a tumor. From the time the girl was first diagnosed until her death, Mike refused to drive Barbara to the hospital, talk to the doctors, or help in making any of the necessary decisions about the child's treatment.

At night, when Barbara reached out to him for comfort, he would either get angry with her or lie next to her like a mummy, looking at her as if she were crazy. "You're overreacting" would be his only comment.

As the little girl deteriorated, Mike became colder and colder, absenting himself from the home even more. A few times he promised to visit his stepdaughter in the hospital or come to a doctor's conference, but he never appeared. "I just can't stand hospitals," he would say.

Since Mike had been close to his stepdaughter, Barbara knew that his seeming indifference was not due to his insensitivity, but due to his inability to feel his grief. One night, after the child had taken a turn for the worse, Mike began cutting himself with a razor blade, angrily shouting that he would make the doctors "pay—big time" if the child died. Then his voice began to tremble as he repeatedly begged his wife to forgive him for, in his view, he had contaminated the child and therefore caused her death.

After that evening, however, Mike showed no further emotion, not even at the funeral. Despite her understanding of combat trauma, Barbara was enraged. "He didn't help with any of the arrangements, hold my hand—nothing. I can forgive him for lots of things, but not this. At that moment, when I was burying my child and needing him the most, he wasn't there for me. I know he has PTSD, but this is carrying it too far!"

Mike had an almost identical reaction when Barbara's grandmother died. Immediately after the phone call announcing the grandmother's death, he left the room. He ignored Barbara all day, even though she was weeping. When dinner wasn't ready on time, he said, "Okay, I'll forgive you for crying this time, but you should be over this thing by now."

In abusive homes where veterans engage in physical battering, they may also engage in economic battering. For example, they may deny their partner or other family members the money necessary for medical care, punish that family member for seeking medical attention without their expressed permission, or deny a family member the funds to visit a sick relative or to attend a family funeral. In cases of such extreme abusiveness, the vet's behavior cannot be explained by his or her fear of loss stemming from combat trauma. His or her mistreatment of others more closely fits the personality profile of someone who has a character disorder or another disturbance than someone who has PTSD, depression, or other forms of combat trauma.*

See chapter 8 for more information on battering.

A combat vet guilty of child molestation tried to convince the court that his combat-related PTSD caused him to sexually assault children. Anger and irritability are official symptoms of PTSD and depression as listed in the DSM-IV, but child abuse, wife abuse, animal cruelty, and other forms of violence are not. Combat may have traumatized this veteran and taught him how to use weapons and force. However, his unacceptable behavior cannot be explained, much less justified, by having fought in a war.

Preliminary research has found that at least in some homes PTSD-afflicted veterans experience fewer or less intense startle responses and other PTSD symptoms when their partners are around.[12] This suggests that for some PTSD-afflicted veterans, their partners serve as "safety valves." Therefore, when a partner is not available, especially if the veteran is in a physically or emotionally weakened condition due to illness, injury, or another type of crisis, life can feel more dangerous for some veterans. As a defense against this increased sense of vulnerability, they may shut down emotionally.

As a result, the partner must deal not only with his or her own medical or other problems, but with a vet who is becoming increasingly emotionally distant and, depending on the extent of the numbing, increasingly dysfunctional. If the veteran is highly dependent on the partner, emotionally or financially, the veteran may become more helpless and dependent and, in some cases, more antagonistic to others in the home. This is also a time when veterans with substance-abuse problems may increase their use of alcohol or drugs. In a few extreme cases, veterans can begin competing with other family members for their partner's now-limited attention or begin acting in an extremely childlike manner. While some emotional upset is to be expected during a family crisis, such childlike behaviors are usually not the result of combat trauma, but of other psychological problems.

For some veterans, the pattern of withdrawal from the family during injury, death, or another crisis is cyclical. "There are months, or years, where he's right there for me during times of trouble. But there are other months, or years, where I can't rely on him at all for help," explains one wife. Other veterans are described as being helpful initially, but ultimately abandoning the scene of the crisis—the hospital, the funeral parlor, or wherever—because they could not tolerate the pain. However, some of the very individuals described above have demonstrated loving, caretaking behavior toward sick children and their partner, after their partner or a friend or counselor pointed out to them what behavior was needed.

Social Isolation

"It doesn't take much to remind me of that war," says Arnold, who has been in counseling for depression and PTSD for over two years. "And when I remember, I don't feel like going out and pretending to be happy either. I used to pretend—to please my wife—but now I'm sick and tired of it."

His wife, Dakota, however, is sick and tired of staying home. "We can't go to parties because Arnold can't stand small talk. We can't go to movies either, because sad ones make Arnold depressed. Comedies depress him, too, because they remind him of his depression. Basically, Arnold isn't interested in people or fun anymore."

"I feel different from everyone else," Arnold explains. He's also afraid of how he might react if someone mentions the war in which he fought, particularly if they make a derogatory comment about veterans or a statement betraying gross ignorance about the events and circumstances of that war. In addition, Arnold feels it is inconsiderate of him to impose his depression and cynicism on others. "Why should I ruin the party with my depression?" he asks. Like many depressed persons, he feels socially undesirable when he is "down" and only wants to be with others when he is "up," which, due to his mood swings, is often unpredictable.

Since being discharged from the military, Arnold has visited his father only twice. Arnold went to war very much a "hawk," preparing to make the military his life. He also wanted to make his father, a career officer, proud of him. Yet some of his military experiences made him question procedures and personnel. Although Arnold still feels that the war was justified, he did not reenlist and abandoned his plans for a career in the military. Despite his exceptionally high I.Q., Arnold has chosen to stack cans at a local grocery store rather than go on to college. He has also chosen to stack the cans at midnight so as to keep his interactions with others to a minimum.

Arnold's father does not understand his son's survivor guilt and nightmares, nor his alienation from society. To him, Arnold is a disgrace to the family, not only because Arnold isn't a better provider for his wife and son but because Arnold was not "tough enough" to endure the stresses of war. Arnold's father helped liberate the Nazi death camps. He also lost a leg in World War II. "If I can get over that, why can't Arnold get over what he saw?" he asks. "Besides, what's a mental problem compared to a wooden leg?"

As Arnold's case illustrates, social isolation and alienation are frequent characteristics of veterans afflicted with depression or PTSD or both. Researchers found that as compared with veterans who did not have PTSD, veterans with PTSD had higher rates of social phobia, the fear and avoidance of social situations.[13] The researchers offer several possible reasons for this social alienation: fear of bodily harm, fear of being negatively evaluated by others, fear of being triggered and subsequently behaving inappropriately, and a lack of interest in other people caused by negative homecoming experiences, by numbing, or by the fatigue, hypersensitivity, and negative outlook on life that are part of depression.[14] In Arnold's case, his social isolation not only reflects his depression, it perpetuates it. Deprived of human companionship, Arnold sinks deeper and deeper into himself and into negative thinking. His reduced interest and ability to relate to others, however, is not only detrimental to him, but to his wife and children.

In light of Arnold's war zone experiences, social gatherings and other occasions often appear meaningless or superficial to him. Sometimes he belittles Dakota's desire to see her friends and asks her to stay with him instead. Other times, he urges her to accept invitations. Yet often she stays home anyway, feeling morally obligated to be with her husband. Although partners may not like their veteran's social isolation, some may also come to accept it and give up trying to pressure their veteran into attending social or family functions. Dakota says:

It's too much pressure, not only on Arnold, but on me. If I insist that we go out, then I have to worry about whether or not Arnold's going to make a scene or feel so uncomfortable away from home that he'll get even more depressed and then blame it on me. Now I automatically say "no" to every invitation. It got too embarrassing to be always canceling out at the last minute and coming up with new excuses all the time.

Therapy and medication have helped Arnold, but his emotions still aren't stable. I never know what kind of mood he's going to be in before we go out. Neither does he. If something about some war comes on the news or if one of his war buddies calls, I can usually just forget our plans. Besides, we usually fight before we go out anyway. So now we don't make any plans. Nobody calls us anymore and we're stuck with each other.

Arnold has dropped most of his old friends from before the war. While Dakota has kept some of her friends, Arnold doesn't feel he has much in common with them. Dakota usually gets together with them on her own. Most of their mutual friends are other combat veterans.

"But they're mainly his friends, not mine," Dakota explains.

And when they start talking about their combat days, they expect me to leave the room. I guess they don't think a woman can take it. I used to leave meekly. But now I protest. After all, it's my living room they're sitting in—my food they're eating. After a while they forget I'm there and I fit right in. It's okay, I guess, but it would be nice to have conversations with people about something else besides war and the negative part of life.

Despite Dakota's wish for a broader scope of friends, she is grateful that Arnold at least socializes with other vets. Some vets do not even have this outlet. Some are virtual loners with few contacts except for their partners and perhaps a few select friends.

Arnold socializes primarily with other veterans because he feels safe with them. They understand him and won't attack him psychologically. Communicating with similarly emotionally scarred vets is meaningful to Arnold, whereas light social banter and most forms of "chit-chat" are not.

After Arnold received his 100 percent service-connected disability for combat trauma, he spent more time with his veteran friends and became heavily involved in efforts to help homeless veterans. These involvements gave meaning to his pain and enhanced his self-esteem. At the same time, Dakota felt Arnold should be spending some of that time with their children or helping her around the home. After years of being a "superwoman," she was tired, and due to the demands on her—both at work and at home—she had no time for social or recreational clubs or outings.* The only group she was able to attend was her Vet Center women's group, and even that required a major effort on her part.

*See chapter 7 for more on multiple roles.

When wives and girlfriends first come to group, they often feel relieved. At last, they don't have to explain their situation in great defensive detail and can communicate almost instantly with the other women. They can also share their conflicting feelings about their veteran's social isolation and the social isolation which their veteran's problems impose upon them. On the one hand, they may feel that their first obligation is to their husbands and boyfriends. The more they learn about combat trauma, they more they want to be supportive. On the other hand, they may feel lonely or cut off from certain friends and relatives.

Even if they have friends outside of group, partners often do not feel free to share the emotional and other realities of their lives with these friends. Like their veteran husbands or boyfriends, they do not want to impose their hardships on others. Nor do they wish to be told by others that they are "co-dependent" or "masochistic," or that they should be ashamed of themselves for giving their veteran "too much" or "too little."

Summary

Psychic or emotional numbing is a natural and normal human response to being relatively helpless in a situation of great danger. In order to cope with the crisis, individuals tend to shut down emotionally and focus all their attention on surviving. Problems arise when the emotional numbing lasts beyond that needed for survival or is extended to situations that are not life threatening.

Numbing almost always causes havoc and misunderstandings in intimate and other relationships requiring the expression of deep feelings. The difficulties veterans have in acknowledging their feelings and their fear of loss often hinders their ability to establish emotionally close relationships with their partners and other family members. Even partners who know that emotional distancing is a normal part of combat trauma can feel shut out, alone, and unwanted when they encounter the veteran's protective "wall." As a result, over time, some partners are dismayed to find that they have built up their own wall of emotional defenses and become numb to their own emotions, just like their veteran.

I'm fifty-five now—finished, drained, and dry. Finished doing my duty—finished with Zak and his combat stress.

The kids are gone. Now it's my turn to live. Right? But now my face is falling. Right?

Sometimes I think I should have left Zak twenty years ago, when I was still pretty. On my thirtieth birthday I remember looking at myself in the mirror and wondering if I could put up with one more mood swing or one more ruined night out.

But Zak was just starting therapy and I didn't want to set him back by leaving. The kids were young then, too, and I knew he loved them dearly.

"He can't help it. It's all that war stuff. I'll give him two more years, until he finishes group therapy," I thought. But then I sobbed for two hours.

The two years became three years, then four and five. Counseling helped Zak a great deal, but now he had depressive episodes instead of drinking binges. Instead of yelling at me, he started crying in front of me. Instead of me worrying about him getting cirrhosis of the liver from all the alcohol, I started worrying about him shooting a hole in his head.

Therapy had taught him how to stop being so cynical and sarcastic, but it still didn't feel like a marriage. Yet I didn't have the heart to leave him, not when he was trying so hard to treat me better and conquer his symptoms. "You want too much. No marriage is perfect. You've been a good military wife for so long and you're as tough as he is. Why abandon ship now?" I told myself. Yet in my gut, I knew these were excuses.

Slowly I became immobilized and stayed with Zak yet another ten years. With each year, my feelings for him shrunk, the romantic feelings that is. Although Zak and I were more like friends than husband and wife, we became exceptionally close friends after my mother died and my father took sick.

Zak was like an angel to me. For three years, he drove me to the hospital, argued with the doctors, and held me in his arms as my father shriveled

away before my eyes. Today I feel loyal and grateful to Zak for all his sup-
port. but I still don't love him the way a woman should love a man. At fifty-
five, I should be all grown up by now, but when some of the younger military
wives ask me if I think I made the right choice in staying with my marriage,
I still don't know what to say.

5

"Sex now? Sex never?"

Combat Trauma and Sex

Note: All couples struggle with a variety of sexual issues, but this chapter focuses on concerns specifically related to combat trauma, such as sexual disinterest and sexual urgency. You, or your veteran, or both of you may be troubled by one or more of the concerns described here and perhaps additional concerns as well. The purpose of this chapter is to describe some of the sexual struggles common among couples where one partner suffers from combat trauma, not to promote or critique any particular religious or philosophical views of human sexuality. Skip over any parts that you find uncomfortable. You can skip the entire chapter and still benefit from this book.

In addition, the case examples in this chapter are not meant to be representative of all help-seeking combat veterans, but rather to illustrate some of the possible ways that combat trauma can intrude upon a couple's love life. However, combat trauma is not an excuse or explanation for sexual or physical abuse. To the extent that sexual deprivation and sexual withdrawal are means of controlling or punishing one's partner, they can be considered forms of sexual battering. Sexually humiliating or emotionally degrading a woman during sexual activity or requiring her to "prove" her love by engaging in longer or more frequent sexual activity than she desires or by trying certain sexual positions or practices she does not desire are all forms of sexual abuse. As described in chapter 8, these behaviors are not symptoms of combat trauma and are best understood as stemming from psychological problems and experiences other than military duty.

> Come here, lie with me
> And take away the pain
> Then go away
> I never want to see you again.
> —ANONYMOUS COMBAT VETERAN

Bruce's body is covered with scars, but he is still a very sexy man. Even if he wasn't a vet and endowed with all the aura (and the muscles) of a warrior, he would still be sexy to me. Bruce is a terrific lover, but when I get into bed with him, I get into bed with his war memories, too. Sometimes I wonder if Bruce is using sex to forget. Other times, he gets so down, he's not interested in sex.

When Bruce doesn't want sex either he acts like I don't exist, or he starts a fight just to keep me away. I used to think there was something wrong with me because he didn't want me, until in a therapy session, he explained that sometimes he just can't handle his combat trauma and his job, much less the emotional and sexual demands of a relationship. At such times he wants—and needs—to be alone, free from other people, to "get himself together."

But on any given day, he can't predict how long a period of "cooling out" he may need. Sometimes all he needs is an hour or two. Sometimes the whole evening. Meanwhile I'm supposed to take care of the kids and everything else and then be ready for that magic moment when he decides he wants me. And when he wants me, he wants me right then. No matter how tired I am from a rough day at work or from being home with sick kids, when he's ready, I'm supposed to turn into a heated sex kitten.

Sometimes I give in to Bruce. Sometimes I don't. But if I give up other plans or push myself to have sex with him and then he all of a sudden stops right in the middle due to some war thing, I get mad. Maybe it's selfish of me, but I'm tired of having to be understanding all the time.

I like sex, but for me it's hard to keep up the passion unless I feel cherished and loved and emotionally close to Bruce. But Bruce has periods where he can't communicate and if I insist on talking, he'll just withdraw even more. At such times, when he wants sex, I hate to turn him down, even if I'm angry with him, because his wanting sex is a sign that he's trying to get out of his depression and isolation. At least he's reaching for pleasure instead of pain. So I go to bed with him even when I don't feel like it, even when we haven't talked for days, or there's all this silent fighting going on. Sometimes I fake orgasm, too, just to make him happy.

In this day of women's liberation, it's not easy to admit such things. It's even harder to admit that many times I go along with Bruce sexually because it's easier that way. Sex reduces his anger level and stops him from picking on me and the kids. Over the years, I've learned that if Bruce has his sex, for the next few days there's more peace at home for me and the kids.

—LAURA, WIFE OF A COMBAT VET

Sex is important both as a physical means of releasing tension and as a means of communicating affection and love. Sex is also a means of reducing individual loneliness. Through physical merger with another person, human beings seek not only physical thrills and the pleasure of sensual excitement, but also validation and appreciation of themselves as unique individuals.[1]

According to Masters and Johnson: "The way we express ourselves sexually—our most intimate way of relating to another person—reflects how we value ourselves, how we value the other person, how that person values us. It reflects all the things that mean warmth, love, affection and security to us—and which we therefore seek and cherish."[2] Before the "sexual revolution" of the 1960s, many women were taught to equate sex with love and with emotional, if not financial, security.[3]

Undoubtedly today's women, especially younger women, are not shackled by the sexual taboos of the past. Yet there is ample evidence that the double standard of sexual behavior still is operative, although perhaps in more subtle form. Although today's women are permitted, if not encouraged, to make themselves as sexually appealing as possible, there is still more condemnation of women who engage in premarital sex or who commit adultery than of men who engage in the exact same sexual behavior.[4]

Regardless of their age, most veterans' partners seen thus far hold relatively conservative sexual values. Even if they were not virgins when they met their veteran, they tend to feel that their sexual expression should be reserved only for men with whom they have a strong emotional commitment. While some soldiers come home to find their partners sleeping with other men, the women I've counseled are almost always those who remained sexually and emotionally faithful while their man was away and who continue to remain true no matter how many relationship problems they are experiencing. Even if their vet has or has had prolonged periods of sexual apathy, sexual flings, or some type of sexual obsession, few of the women seen thus far have ever seriously considered having an affair with another man. In fact, when approached by other men, most of the women I have worked with felt guilty as well as exhilarated at being seen as sexually desirable.

Dora, for example, jokes about sleeping with the handsome young teller at her bank who propositions her almost every time she makes a deposit. "If my husband stays out all night again, I'm going to meet that teller for drinks," she often says. Once she even made a date with the teller, but, as expected, quickly broke it. Not only did guilt overpower her, but she did not want to complicate her life or invest her emotional energy in a relationship—even a primarily sexual relationship—with another man. Besides, her major desire was for love, not sex.

Sexuality is a vital source of human physical and emotional gratification. To date, however, there are fewer than a dozen studies on the ways in which combat trauma might affect the veteran's sexuality and that of his partner. In all but one of these studies,[5] researchers found that veterans diagnosed with PTSD reported reduced sexual capacity and interest and problems such as erectile dysfunction and premature ejaculation, which were not related to medical problems.[6]

However, since most of these studies were completed on male Vietnam veterans, the results cannot be generalized to women veterans or to veterans from other eras. Furthermore, in some of these studies, questions about sexual intimacy were mixed with questions about other forms of intimacy, making it difficult to draw any conclusions specifically about the relationship of combat trauma to male sexuality. In addition, some of the studies were based on surveys with return rates of less than 50 percent, leaving us with little information about those veterans who did not respond.[7]

In general, it is difficult to draw firm conclusions from formal research. Studies of prisoners of war from previous wars have found that the prison-camp experience often results in long-term sexual disinterest, impotency, and other sexual dysfunctions, especially if severe malnutrition and physical abuse were involved.[8] However, some of the partners of POWs who have sought counseling report that not only are their veterans sexually interested and almost always sexually potent, they insist on sex on a daily basis.

Once again, I want to stress that there is no "typical" veteran or "typical" partner of a veteran. In sexual matters especially, there is wide variability. Some combat veterans have no problems with their sexual functioning. However, in my limited sample, several areas of sexual concern related to the veteran's combat trauma emerged, including sexual disinterest, problems in sexual performance, insistence on sex on demand, the separation of affection and romance from sexual activity, the need to stay in control, and various forms of sexual obsession. While these patterns can be found in persons who aren't combat veterans and in women as well as men, combat appears to have played a significant role in their development and have given these patterns unique characteristics that reflect the combat experience.

These patterns are not necessarily constant over time for any given veteran. For example, some vets experience periods of sexual apathy or impotence when suffering from clinical depression or PTSD. When they find some relief from these conditions, their sexual functioning returns to normal. Similarly, some vets desire great control over their intimate moments. Partners who view their veterans as being "controlling," however, also describe their veterans as having periods where they can let go of directing every sexual move and be "normal." According to the women, the veteran's need to be watchful during sex or to reenact his role in combat in the bedroom seems to be related to increases in symptoms of combat trauma caused by an anniversary or another trigger. Given such fluctuations in her veteran's sexual behavior, a woman may not know whether to put on her flannel nightgown or her sheer negligee.

Remember, the first step in coping with any sexual concern is a thorough medical exam. Because most sexual problems are rooted in personal or in relationship problems, a close look at your satisfaction with yourself and with your relationships (not only with your partner, but with others) is also in order. The second step is to learn more about human sexuality in general and your sexual concerns in particular or consult with a qualified sex therapist.

Sexual Impotence and Apathy

"Sex, what's that?" more than one woman has said, describing her veteran's longstanding sexual apathy or sexual impotency.

Some of the possible major causes of lack of sexual interest or abilities in traumatized veterans include symptoms of combat trauma (especially depression, emotional numbing, the startle response, and irritability), addiction, combat-related medical problems, and the impact of the losses that usually accompany midlife and aging. Depression and emotional numbing, especially when they involve anger turned inward or repressed grief, can lead to sexual disinterest, anorgasmia (lack of orgasm), or other sexual problems, not only in the veteran, but in his partner as well.[9]

Some women find it hard to feel erotic if they feel burdened by the many demands made upon them at home and at work or if they are in a state of mourning about their own lives—about the years spent loving and caring for a man who does not, or cannot, return their love in kind or about the years spent taking care of others while neglecting themselves. In a parallel manner, some veterans find it hard to feel sexual because of all the psychic energy they must expend to manage their PTSD symptoms, their depressions, and other combat trauma reactions. Like their women, for all the reasons described and to be described in this book, they may also be in a state of mourning about their lives. Under such emotional conditions, it is very hard for veterans or their partners, as for most people, to achieve high levels of sexual arousal on a consistent basis.

In the early years of her marriage Dora used to masturbate when her husband withdrew from her. Today she hardly ever does so.

I used to think I stopped because I was approaching forty, but that's supposed to be a woman's sexual peak. I guess it's my husband, not my age. Since I've numbed my anger at him, it's no wonder my sexual feelings have also gone dead. Funny, now that I think about it, the last time we had good sex was after a fight when we both told each other how much we hated each other. Maybe the sex was good because we finally let out our feelings.

As described in the previous chapter, psychic numbing occurs on three levels: the emotional, the mental, and the physical. Physically, the muscles constrict. According to Wilhelm Reich, author of *The Function of the Orgasm,* this muscular constriction can result in genital disturbances. Furthermore, "sexual energy can be bound by chronic muscle tensions."[10] When medical causes are ruled out, this muting of sexual feeling and pleasure can perhaps be related to the overall numbing of emotions in the veteran, his partner, or both.

Some female partners of veterans experience little feeling, either on an emotional or sexual level, during sexual intercourse. Others have pleasurable sensations, even orgasm, but are distressed to find that they experience their sexuality in a detached and distant manner. "It's like my body doesn't belong to me," explains one wife, whose statement reflects a severe degree of psychic numbing. Similarly, her husband describes his penis as "numb" and his orgasm as "dead." Furthermore, sexual pleasure and potency can be inhibited, if not totally obliterated, in almost anyone—man or woman, veteran or nonveteran—by anxious or painful thoughts or memories.

Have you ever begun to worry about your bills or the health of a family member in the middle of making love? What was the effect on your sexual interest? If you were the victim of rape or some other form of sexual abuse, how easily could you blot out the memory of being violated? Wouldn't it take time to be able to respond sexually again, even with someone you loved and trusted?

If a woman has had painful sexual experiences, memories of her past may intrude on her present sexual experiences. Similarly, vets who were sexually assaulted at some point in their lives or who witnessed or participated in sexual acts associated with pain or violence may recall these events when they begin to become sexually excited. On the simplest and most innocent level, perhaps gunfire went off while the veteran was making love. Or perhaps he witnessed or participated in rape, or he or a comrade was attacked or "set up" by a prostitute or girlfriend.

Such memories, even if they are not in the veteran's conscious awareness at the time he is initiating sexual contact, may decrease his level of sexual involvement and ability to achieve and maintain an erection. Survivor guilt can also play a role in the veteran's sexual relations. "Here I am, making love, when my buddy will never make love again. Just the thought of it kills my desire," explains one vet. Unless his partner is aware of the many possible causes of erectile failure in men, especially in men with combat trauma, she may interpret the vet's sexual problems as a sign of her lack of sexual attractiveness. This is especially the case if a few sexual failures precipitate a vicious cycle of sexual withdrawal. After the veteran experiences two or three sexual failures, he may erroneously conclude that he is a sexual failure. In the future, rather than risk another sexual failure and experience all the subsequent shame, he may be reluctant to initiate sex or to respond to his partner's sexual overtures in the future. After repeated sexual "failures," he may withdraw from sexual activity altogether. This can create tension between the couple, making it difficult for them to connect emotionally or sexually. Once this vicious cycle has begun, some women resign themselves to sexless relationships or, just like their veterans, come to see themselves as sexual failures also, which only perpetuates the negative cycle.

When Dora and her husband first began experiencing sexual problems, they went to a sex therapist who advised them that it wasn't necessary for a man to have an erection in order to pleasure his wife. He could simply use manual or oral means of stimulation or even sex toys to help her achieve orgasm. This advice sounded logical, but when Dora's husband didn't seem interested in sex, she found it difficult to ask him to follow the therapist's suggestions. Not only was Dora somewhat shy about making such requests, but in her years with her husband she had learned the following:

> When my husband can't make it [have sex], that means his war stuff is bothering him and I know better than to press him for anything, much less sex. He pretends he's sleeping, but I know he's awake, thinking. The depression, or anger, just oozes out of him.
>
> If I ask him to touch me, I'm afraid he'll call me "selfish." Here he is suffering, and what am I thinking about? Myself. A few times I did ask him and he did what I wanted. But he did it mechanically, without any emotion whatsoever. It was no fun and made me feel like a whore.
>
> So I don't ask anymore. If our sex gets interrupted because he gets into a mood, I just roll over and pretend that I'm asleep. He's left me hanging sexually so many times, I've learned not to get too turned on

when we start. Slowly but surely, my interest and enthusiasm for sex has diminished.

Sexual problems can result when a veteran's war memories are evoked by the mere sight of a naked body or any scars resulting from the war. Hence women, especially those who have invested considerable time and energy in maintaining trim figures or other forms of attractiveness, are often disappointed and in some cases devastated, to find their men almost immune to their loveliness. They often fail to understand that every time the veteran takes his clothes off, or sees a woman disrobe, he may begin to—automatically and unwillingly— think of dead, wounded, or mutilated naked bodies.

Before his tour of duty overseas, Dora's husband had associated nudity primarily with pleasure. But now it is paired in his mind with pain and violence. He came home without a scratch, but for those vets who were injured, especially if they were physically scarred, disrobing and exposing the parts of their bodies that were wounded or disfigured may serve as yet another reminder of the war. If, in addition, a vet was wounded in or near his genitals, nipples, or other sexually sensitive areas, the mere sight of his scars may contribute to his sexual difficulties.

A vet may value his injuries as signs of masculinity, or perhaps his scars engender only pain and anger. Many of the vets I have counseled dismiss their injuries as "nothing," ever mindful of the fact that they managed to survive while others died, or that they could have been injured more severely, as were others. "Sure there's a hole in my leg, but at least I have one," says Sam. "Some guys lost both or everything."

Psychic numbing can contribute to a denial about the losses inherent to injury and disfigurement, and, in some cases, an intolerance and condemnation of veterans who do acknowledge their losses. For example, Ron, who would always adamantly insist that the loss of his arm "didn't bother him at all," had only contempt for "crybabies." Quite possibly his sense of superiority over vets who were angry or sad about their injuries may stem in part from the fact that he had never acknowledged or grieved the loss of his arm.

While some women say that their veteran complains about his injuries almost constantly, other women report that the "no talk" rule applies to war injuries as well. Ron's girlfriend explains:

Ron's not only missing an arm, but his body is covered with scars and punctured with gunshot wounds. Looking at his body objectively, it is ugly, horrible really. But I love him and don't mind caressing his ugly spots. I just close my eyes and kiss parts of him that would make most people shudder.

I only wish he had told me about his body before we had sex the first time. I was shocked. But since he didn't say anything, I didn't either. Besides, I knew he was testing me. He kept staring at me to see how I would react.

We've been together five years. Our sex life was great in the beginning, but now it's almost dead. We never talk about his scars, or his combat experiences. After the first couple of months together, he couldn't get an erection. I told him I didn't mind, that I just wanted to hold and love him anyway. But he'd push me away and sometimes wouldn't come to bed at all.

I've caught him masturbating a few times, so I know he's not impotent. But he's definitely disinterested in me. I thought—hoped—his disinterest would be temporary, but now we're just like two friends living in the same house.

In therapy, Ron slowly began to confront his long-suppressed feelings about his war injuries and their negative effects on his sex life. Even vets who were not injured can be in so much emotional pain or are so cynical about other people, governments, or the military, and, by extension, life itself, that sex seems unimportant, if not meaningless.

Harvey went to Vietnam an idealistic nineteen-year-old. Combat had made him and his unit so numb they were able to fry steaks and make jokes while watching entire villages being blown to bits. At one point, Harvey was attacked by a group of Vietnamese women carrying razor blades. They were aiming for a particular artery in the leg, which, if slashed, could make a person bleed to death. Rather than shoot the women, he kicked them in the face, which made him wonder if he was a "good guy" or a "bad guy."

At the same time Harvey marveled at the women's motivation. Didn't these women in ragged pajamas know he could have blown them away in a minute? Why were they willing to risk their lives just to kill a handful of American servicemen?

Harvey's questions about the U.S. involvement in Vietnam severely conflicted with the patriotic fervor that had sent him to Vietnam in the first place. Since he could find no way to resolve this conflict, Harvey entered a state of mental numbing that only compounded his emotional numbing, rendering him sexually disinterested.

After returning to the United States, Harvey discovered that his wife had taken a lover. He forgave her but she continued to betray him. After he divorced her, he had a short period of promiscuity followed by a long period of celibacy. In his present wife, Sue, Harvey feels he has finally found a loyal and loving partner. But Sue is allowed into Harvey's world and into his bed only a little at a time. Harvey wants Sue to actively pursue him. Yet sometimes he feels threatened by the very sexual assertiveness that he asks of her.

"Does he want me or not?" Sue wonders. She also wonders why she must pay the price for Harvey's past experiences with women. When she's physically ill or emotionally troubled, Harvey becomes highly anxious and then withdraws. At such times Sue wants moral support and physical affection, not a cold or empty bed.

There are many valid reasons for Harvey's behavior toward Sue, but Sue's emotional and sexual frustrations are equally real and painful. Already she is experiencing a lessening of sexual desire and other signs of depression. Before she met Harvey, she liked to have sex almost every night. Now if they only make love once or twice a month, she says she "doesn't miss it." But when she's honest with herself, she admits how much she longs for the soothing effects of the sexual embrace.

After many months of no physical contact, not even a hug, Sue woke Harvey at 4 AM in hopes that he would make love to her. Here is his response:

Damn her! That bitch! I told her not to wake me up in the middle of the night. She knows I have trouble sleeping. But a few weeks ago, it was I who woke her up at 4 AM and told her that was my best time for lovemaking. Maybe she thought she was doing what I wanted.

I don't know and I don't care. I never thought I'd get so calloused that I wouldn't care how my wife felt. But right now her desire for me is an outright nuisance! I wish she'd just go away.

I've been thinking about the war lately. The thoughts just interfere with everything. My depression takes over and I'm an utter flop in bed.

My wife never minds when I can't perform. She always says she loves me just the way I am.

Yet I can't stand to even talk to her and I despise her for loving me, maybe because I despise myself somehow. I turn my back on her, too, because I want to hide what's going on inside of me—the fear, the anger, the hate. I want her to go away, but without her I have nobody.

After she woke me up, I had nightmares. I tried to turn them off. I could actually feel myself trying to maneuver my eyelids so that the ugly drama would stop. But I couldn't stop the dreams, the horror. When I woke up, I wanted to kill somebody, something. The last thing on my mind was sex.

In one of my nightmares, I'm standing in the middle of a street, lost, confused, just like the first day I got back from overseas. I don't know where anything is, when suddenly my wife appears. She wants to help me, but I want her to go away because she can't possibly understand what I've been through.

In my mind, I begin reviewing all her faults. Yet I know it's not her little flaws that make me so mad. I'm angry at her because she didn't have to go, because her life has been so smooth in comparison. Sure, she's had her share of problems, but nothing like what I went through. I'm mad at her too because, despite all her love for me, she can't take away the fear and anger in me, can't stop the panic.

When I get like this, I feel crazy—here I am, pushing away one of the few people in the world who really cares about me.

Although Harvey and Sue do have many tender moments, Harvey resents the ways his combat experiences have interfered with his ability to feel romantic toward his wife. He explains:

Romantic love died in the battlefield, right next to my friends. After you've seen enough death, injustice, and horror, you can't believe in love anymore, at least not the mushy kind of love that's in the media and songs.

For me now, romantic love is a joke. How can I think now that getting lost in someone's embrace is going to take away my pain? When I hear love songs now, I get angry, then sad. I'm angry because I remember the times before the war when I was young and innocent and half-believed those songs. But the stress over there and the stress back here since has rotted me out so much I'm no longer capable of feeling like that any more.

Like her husband, Sue also has come to view romantic love as an adolescent fantasy. For her, as for other partners I've seen in counseling, the demands of having major responsibilities both inside and outside the home and of the intrusion of the war upon her life has nearly eradicated her romantic dreams. Sighing, she often says:

I wish I could feel romantic toward Harvey—he deserves it. But there's just too many holes in the wall, too many bills to pay, and too many hurt feelings on my part. I still love him, but it's sad, sad, sad, not to be able to love him like I used to.

Some vets are in touch with their sadness about their impaired capacity to experience loving tender feelings and express those feelings sexually; others are not. Either way, this can result in veterans wanting to avoid or leave media presentations that have a romantic theme or gatherings where romantic music is playing. Sometimes they tell their partners that they can't go to certain events or need to leave them early because they can't tolerate the superficiality or "phoniness" of the situation. On another level, however, they may also be distressed by their own anger and pain or the feeling of being different from everybody else.

Their partners can feel different, too. Sue explains:

At parties, I watch Harvey like a hawk. The minute I see him getting too hot—or too cold—I know it's time to make some excuse and get him home. My friends wonder why I can't relax and make small talk at parties. But how can I? I'm always afraid that someone will say the wrong thing about the military or the war and make Harvey go off or turn into a zombie.

Some veterans accept diminished sexual interest and activity as part of their combat trauma. Others use a variety of means to sexually stimulate themselves, including Viagra and other sexually enhancing medications, alcohol, marijuana, cocaine, or other illegal drugs, pornography or strip bars or other "men's clubs."

In my experience, men who cannot achieve erection and orgasm "naturally," as they put it, often feel ashamed of their sexual limitations. Those who seek to stimulate their sexuality by watching pornographic videos or going to topless bars sometimes feel conflicted about these activities. On the one hand, there is the relief in knowing they can do something to help restore their sex interest. On the other hand, there may be a sense that such means are "wrong" or "immoral" and they have some degree of shame at having to depend on external props to function sexually. Furthermore, should there come a day when these external props no longer work, some veterans may panic and seek professional help. Others may decide to be celibate or begin to withdraw from others, especially their partner.

After experiencing several sexual failures with his partner, Antonio began to frequent topless bars in hopes of being aroused. For a while, his efforts proved successful. After viewing women at the bars, he was able to go home and make love to his wife. Eventually, however, his go-go dancers failed him. No matter how voluptuous they were, he couldn't "get it up." His subsequent desperate search for younger and more attractive go-go girls also failed. It was at this point that he began to acknowledge his depression, not only about combat but also about certain life situations prior to his tour of duty.

When a veteran tries to achieve sexual arousal through pornography or other means, his partner can easily feel insulted and humiliated. Is she not enough? Why does he have to look elsewhere for sexual stimulation? She may also feel reduced to the status of a sexual plaything and wonder if he's having sex with her to express his affection toward her or to prove his masculinity instead. A partner who also contends with her vet's extramarital affairs can feel slapped in the face.

A woman whose veteran suffers from sexual problems may feel not only sexually disappointed but also emotionally abandoned. In her intimate relationship, she had hoped for a man's tenderness, adoration, and protection. But instead she found war: flashbacks and nightmares, emotional walls and emotional pain, power trips and insecurities, and, perhaps, the raw male sex drive, devoid of the usual preliminaries or of any romantic gestures. If she is unable to acknowledge and grieve her disappointments or take some positive action to improve her life, she may become depressed, develop other symptoms, or find ways to avoid her veteran sexually.

She may simply be cold toward him, always be tired or busy, humiliate him in front of others, or start arguments with him. Or she may gain significant amounts of weight. Some mental health professionals might view her weight gain as an attempt to "punish" the vet. In my view, however, if her veteran's lack of sexual responsiveness toward her makes her feel like a sexual failure, she may be overeating as a way to punish herself, not him. Her overeating could also be an indirect means of expressing her anger, disappointment, and other feelings about the current status of her love life.

Staying in Control

During the war, the veteran needed to be on constant alert. Combat readiness—if not overt paranoia—were qualities necessary for survival. Carol Vercozzi, in "The War That Refused to Die: Vietnam Again," explains:

> If the message of the military was black and white, the soldier's world was a hundred shades of green. Everything he had learned about order and logic and reason, even the things he had been taught about the war . . . fell apart . . . [during combat]. Nothing was real. . . . He stopped trying to apply reason, accepted that what you expected would not happen, that no one can be trusted, that everything outside yourself is subject to no rules you can ever uncover. . . . Death was the new "reality principle" and the paranoid combat-readiness state was the only hope of staying alive.[11]

In the bedroom, however, states of combat readiness are hardly conducive to satisfying sexual relations. Should the veteran's hypervigilance become so intense that it borders on paranoia, he may begin doubting his partner's love or faithfulness or become too frightened of her, or the sex act itself, to have sex. Not all veterans become hypervigilant in the bedroom; among those who do, the intensity and frequency of this pattern varies from one vet to the next. Some almost always are hypervigilant; others are on guard some days, but not others. Still others are described as undergoing monthly or cyclical changes, alternating between periods of emotional stability and "normal" sexual relations and periods of troubled sex.

The root of combat readiness (and the paranoia that can go along with it) is fear, fear of being attacked or losing control. Certain aspects of the sexual relationship may serve to trigger such fears in the vet. Simply taking off his clothes or lying down may make a vet feel vulnerable and defenseless. He may also be threatened by shutting the bedroom door or by having the lights off. If his partner wants to close the door for privacy reasons or turn the lights off or down for romantic or other reasons, conflicts can ensue.

More fundamentally, however, sex can be threatening to a vet, as it can be to any man or woman, because it involves giving in to sexual desire. Many people hold back during sexual relations for fear of being overpowered by this strong biological need, especially since it requires some degree of "giving in" to another human being. While a man might very much desire sexual pleasure, he may fear the loss of control that such surrender implies. Or perhaps he views surrender as "feminine."[12] Similarly, women who have difficulty achieving orgasm have often been described as unable to "surrender" to their partner or to their own sexual impulses. Just as women sometimes have trouble "letting go" sexually for fear that their partners will hurt them, men can have the same fears.

"What if she bites me?" asks one vet, explaining his fears about oral sex, fears he never had prior to combat. For him, as for many other people (including civilians), letting go sexually is difficult because it increases both physical and emotional vulnerability. As the result of his combat experiences, however, for him this vulnerability often feels not only emotionally problematic (as it is for many people), but life-threatening as well. In addition, for him, as for others (including civilians), sex is the only time he feels emotionally close to his wife. Only during sex are his defenses down. While he describes the intimacy he experiences as sweet, he is also frightened by it. "I'm afraid to let her under my skin," he says, "so I limit the sex. I don't want to get hooked on anybody anymore. What if I lose her, like I lost others?"

For some vets, giving in to a woman's sexual requests, or even to their own desires for the woman, feels like "giving in to the enemy." Yet the "ability to surrender" is a "prerequisite . . . for orgasm."[13] In some bedrooms, the woman actually can become the enemy. Perhaps she disappointed or "disobeyed" the vet in some way, thereby crossing the line from friend to foe. Her vet may view her as someone to be conquered. Yet the very process of sexual conquest requires that the vet let down his defenses and surrender to her.

For a few of my patients, such surrender has been impossible. As a result, they experience various degrees of impotence. Or they arrange their sex lives so that they maintain almost total control over the sexual situation. For example, he may try to protect himself by making it clear that only he, not his wife or girlfriend, is allowed to initiate sex; by never looking at her face and only having intercourse facing her back; or by not permitting her to stimulate him, orally or manually, and using her only for penetration. By stimulating himself, he not only protects himself from the possibility that the woman might hurt him, deliberately or by accident, but he can also monitor his own level of excitement and exert greater control over the timing and intensity of his orgasm.

If he does allow the woman to stimulate him, he may be very specific about how she is to do so. She may be allowed only to touch certain areas of his body or to exert only certain amounts of pressure at various places. In one instance, a woman was instructed to caress only one particular segment of the rim of her husband's penis and no other part of his body, with only one of her fingers, not her entire hand. When she failed to follow these directions, she was accused of trying to hurt him and sex was discontinued.

In some instances, the veteran specifically requests that sex be separated from affection. Perhaps this is a way to control the degree of closeness between himself and his partner. "If we have sex, we can't cuddle and talk. It's just sex, nothing else. But when he wants to be close and have us just hold each other, then the rule is that we can't have intercourse," explains one partner. "I guess my vet can handle only one form of contact at a time."

When the veteran rushes sex, when he wants to strictly control every sexual move, or in other ways enters into combat mode, his partner is likely to experience little emotional satisfaction or sexual arousal. Like a soldier on the battlefield, she's wondering what will happen next and is focused on how to help the situation, not on how to enhance their sexual experience. Should she be passionate, or become quiet? Should she stay in the bedroom, or excuse herself? Under such conditions, sex becomes sexless, at least for the woman. Her sexual needs may not be considered. Insufficiently aroused and substantially diverted, both mentally and emotionally, from experiencing the sensuality of the moment, she may have difficulty enjoying sex as a sensual experience or achieving orgasm.

Sex Now

In some homes, sex is a rarity; in others, it can feel like an imperative. Some women describe their mates as almost always insisting on sex; others say their partners alternate between their "regular selves" and their "warrior selves" who demand gratification as their due. The urgent quality to their desire cannot be attributed solely to their need for sexual gratification. In the sex act, their men seem to be seeking not only sexual release but security, self-esteem, and, in some instances, perhaps a sense of superiority, or "victory," as well. When refused by their partners, they feel desperately unloved.

Among veterans who are socially isolated, the intense need for sex may reflect loneliness. Like any other socially isolated individuals, even veterans who choose to be socially isolated can become "stroke-deprived." They do not receive the smiles, the hugs, the compliments, or any of the visual, verbal, or physical "strokes," large or small, that can come about during interactions with supportive others. In this state of deprivation, the vet may turn to sex to meet not only his sexual needs but also his friendship and other social needs.

Peter calls sex the "total stroke." For a long time, he believed that sex would satisfy all his hungers: his hunger for sex as well as his hunger for companionship and a greater sense of purpose in life. Like many persons, he confused sex with love and with emotional closeness. When sexual activity without tenderness or communication left him unsatisfied, he increased his sexual activity. Yet he continued to feel restless and empty inside. Eventually he found that in order to help fill his inner void, he needed to spend time talking with his partner, socializing with other people, and thinking more deeply about his life.

On another level, an intense need for sex may reflect the fact that, biologically, sexual release is the "antithesis of anxiety." As has been repeatedly proven in studies of both men and women, anxiety interferes with sexual performance, especially with orgasm.[14] Conversely, it is difficult, if not impossible, to be anxious while highly sexually aroused.

Hence, for some vets, sex is more than sex. It is a tranquilizer or sedative for their anxieties and other tensions, providing not only a physical peace, but an emotional peace as well. "Sex takes away my anger," explains Peter. "After satisfying sex, for a few moments at least, all seems well, both within and without."

In this sense, sex can be used like a mood-altering drug. When the vet begins to feel pain, fear, or confusion, he may fear becoming overwhelmed, not only by the specific emotion itself but also by the strength and power of that emotion. If he hasn't been taught how to manage strong emotions, simply experiencing their power can make him feel out of control. That his emotions are throwing him off base and won't go away on command also may threaten his sense of masculinity. "Real men" are supposed to be in control of their emotions, not the other way around. While it may be acceptable for women to be dominated by their feelings, former warriors are not supposed to let emotion get the upper hand. This fear of strong feelings is especially prevalent among veterans who lost control over their emotions during combat, especially if their loss of emotional control resulted in certain behaviors that are now causing them guilt or shame.

At this point, the vet needs a means of cooling his emotional waters, feeling in control, or asserting his masculinity. Sex can help discharge the excess physical energy created by fear of losing control. It can also temporarily mitigate, if not obliterate, emotional upset and personal insecurities, as well as affirm the vet's sense of manhood. Regardless of how emasculated a man feels in other areas of his life, when he is with a woman, he can at last "feel like a man." At least one person, his wife or girlfriend, is (literally) "under him."

Like alcohol and drugs, sex and sexual obsessions can be used as an escape from emotional realities as well as other realities, such as children, bills, and other responsibilities. In addition, for some vets, orgasm functions as a form of shock treatment for their depression. "Without three orgasms a day, I get so blue I can't stand it. The minute I start feeling down, I reach for my wife. If she won't cooperate, I do something else," explains Peter. When his wife refuses him sexually, he suffers from more than sexual frustration, he suffers the full weight of his depression.

Peter's wife protests:

I'm tired of being his pill! Peter and I don't have a relationship, we have a "sex-ship." I'm supposed to be ready to jump in bed whenever he needs me, no matter what else is going on. I could be upset, the kids could be crying, my mother could be on the way over—it doesn't matter. He wants it when he wants it. Sometimes once a day isn't enough. He wants sex two or three times a day. I just can't do it!

Sex, Midlife, and Aging

As veterans and their partners enter and pass through midlife into their senior years, inevitably their sex life, like every other aspect of their life, will be affected by the many changes associated with aging. As with any other couple, the state of their emotional and physical health and their financial stability will play key roles in their interest in and ability to respond sexually to each other.

Veterans with progressive illnesses, whether war related or not, or whose war injuries become aggravated by the aging process or by subsequent injuries or medical problems, may be so preoccupied with their health or in so much physical distress that their sexuality is negatively affected. Or they may be taking a medication for diabetes, hypertension, anger, anxiety, depression, insomnia, or some other condition that suppresses sexual responsiveness. For this reason, some veterans refuse to take these medications or stop taking them around the time they want to have sex. "I would rather be a raving maniac or go into the black hole [of depression] than lose my sex drive," states one veteran.

Rage, anxiety, depression, and insomnia can also diminish the sex drive. The less fatigued, depressed, or anxious a veteran becomes as the result of properly administered medications, the more interested he may become in the sensual aspects of life. With increased control over his moods and his traumatic reactions, he may feel more confident about his social abilities and hence may interact more frequently and more meaningfully with his partner. As their communication improves, so will their sex life. On the other hand, sometimes even such improved personal functioning cannot overcome the negative sexual side effects of certain medications. This creates a double bind for the veteran who values his sexuality as well as his emotional and physical health.

Sexual interest and abilities have also been found to wane at midlife among vets with long histories of alcohol or drug addiction. While their bodies may have been able to sustain the negative physical effects of substance abuse when they were young, as they age the toll addiction has taken on their health usually becomes increasingly evident. Not only do alcohol or drugs have direct detrimental effects on physical health, but the lifestyle associated with substance abuse is often fraught with poor nutrition, inadequate sleep, and other forms of poor physical self-care. Along with any number of health problems due to substance abuse may come diminished sexual interest and ability.

Simply stopping the drinking or the drugging does not repair the physical damage wrought by years of self-neglect. In order to regain physical health and sexual stamina, proper nutrition, rest, and attention to medical problems need to follow. Yet for a veteran to restore himself to physical health, he needs to feel he deserves to be well. Only then will he spend the time, money, and energy to take care of himself. If he is suffering from intense survivor guilt, self-hate, or low self-esteem, or if on some level he is punishing himself for something he did or did not do during or after the war, he may deprive himself of good self-care. Hence he may not take advantage of available services and opportunities for medical or psychological help. In some cases, however, the services he needs do not exist, are not readily available, are of poor quality, or are beyond his financial range. Even if he seeks medical care, he may not follow the food, exercise, or other recommendations of his physicians.

Money worries can also diminish the sexual interest of both the veteran and his partner. If the aging process worsens a veteran's traumatic reactions or physical problems, resulting in employment problems, the veteran may find himself increasingly financially dependent on his partner. The psychological impact of this on men who were trained to see themselves as family breadwinners and as protectors of women and children can be devastating, creating guilt and worsening any existing depression or PTSD. Vets whose partners are or have been the major or stable source of income may find themselves increasingly uncomfortable with this arrangement as their partners age and tire more easily from the strain of dual roles—one at home and one on the job.

The women may also be resentful of the economic and emotional burdens they have had to shoulder over the years. Women over forty also are at greater risk for developing depression and various medical problems. A partner's cancer, heart condition, or increased fatigue due to aging and stress can bring a couple closer together or drive them further apart. When a partner's impaired health increases a veteran's sense of guilt over his unwanted but nevertheless real limitations, this can lead to increased loving attention toward the partner; or it can lead to conflicts, such as those which beset Sarah and Will.

Upon his return from combat duty, Will worked as a mechanic. During his soldiering days, dishonest leaders and poor mechanics had endangered his life and the lives of others. As a result, Will made every effort to pro-

duce quality work. It was almost a matter of life and death for him, as it was during combat. Will was such a skilled mechanic he could command high wages, but he would eventually quit a job if one of his superiors or coworkers proved incompetent or corrupt. Will changed jobs so frequently, he was not able to maintain any company-based life or health insurance for very long. Therefore his wife, Sarah, felt compelled to keep her job for insurance purposes, even though, after their children were in high school, she wanted to go back to school and move ahead vocationally.

Although Sarah felt frustrated with her career and struggled to establish emotional intimacy with Will, she described their sex life as "fantastic." Even when Will would isolate himself for days, Sarah wouldn't even think of divorcing him. "He's the best lover I ever had," Sarah explains.

When Sarah was forty-five, her mother became seriously ill. Sarah wanted to leave her now much-loathed job to help take care of her mother, but she could not because her family needed her health care coverage. After work, Sarah would spend many hours helping her mother, but she made a point of being in bed with Will as much as possible. Since they usually made love around 11 PM, by 11 PM Sarah was usually showered, perfumed, and ready.

But Will wasn't ready at all. Guilt had overpowered his sex drive. Will believed that his work patterns had prevented Sarah from leaving a job she disliked; he believed that Sarah looked older than her years as the result of decades of strain caused by his inconsistent earnings and his PTSD; and he could not assist Sarah in taking care of her mother. After all the death he had seen during his combat days, Will could not tolerate being around sick or dying people.

To make matters worse, he adored his mother-in-law. She had always been kind and nurturing to him, a far cry from his own mother who had neglected him and his siblings. Will had spent most of his childhood "mothering" his alcoholic mother and parenting his siblings. He had received little emotional support and loving care until he met Sarah and her family. Sarah was caring and nurturing toward him, but her mother was even more loving. Now Will's mother-in-law was thin, bald, and coughing up blood, and Will couldn't stand it. Between his guilt and his grief, Will shut down, emotionally and sexually.

Sarah thought Will no longer desired her physically because her face was aging and she no longer had the figure of her youth. When Will refused her sexual overtures, Sarah wept uncontrollably. She wept not only because she felt sexually rejected but also because she was grieving the loss of her youthful energy and appearance and the loss of the illusion that she would live forever.

Will had confronted the reality of human mortality many times on the battlefield. But Sarah's first meaningful encounter with death was her mother's illness. In sex, Sarah, like many other people, including veterans, wanted not only sex and love but also comfort and affirmation of her existence. In her time of grief, she needed Will's arms around her more than ever. The only way she knew to be held was in sex.

Sarah's tears were a plea for Will to hold and caress her. But the more she cried, the guiltier Will felt. He knew Sarah needed him and now he felt inadequate as both a provider and a lover. Will did not know how to put his feelings into words and experienced his guilt and sense of inadequacy internally. As the pressure mounted, Will exploded—unfortunately, at Sarah.

"What's wrong with you? Your mom is about to die and you want sex? What kind of woman are you anyway? And how come you are crying? Your mother's the one who is dying—not you," he said.

Sarah was now humiliated to the core and furious. Who was the one who spent hours caring for her mother while he, King Will, sat home and watched TV? And who worked at a job she hated for the sake of the family while he, King Will, switched jobs whenever he wasn't happy? Why, if she left a job every time she was discontent, their family would be in the poorhouse.

As Sarah continued to lash out, Will lashed back. Sarah would retaliate, followed by another insult from Will. And so the evening went until one of them left the bedroom and slept on the couch.

There is such needless pain and suffering in this story. The tragedy here is that Sarah and Will could have given each other so much love and comfort, if only they knew how to put their feelings into words and how to ask each other for what they needed. As veterans and their partners go through the various crises of midlife and aging, their sexual drive and abilities may be diverted and perhaps diminished by the physical and other life changes inherent to growing older. Yet a couple does not need to be deprived of the much-needed pleasures of touching and caressing simply because one partner is (at least temporarily) experiencing difficulties in their sexual responsiveness and abilities.

A veteran who is over forty may not have the "instant" erections of his youth and may need additional sexual stimulation from his partner in order to achieve and sustain an erection. However, he may be reluctant to accept that he needs this help and (in some instances) she, in turn, may be reluctant to provide it. Some women feel that certain kinds of sexual activities, such as oral sex, are immoral or unfeminine. Or they harbor resentments against their veteran which they express by refusing to be active during sex.

Sex education of a new sort is needed for the couple in midlife, including an expanded definition of sexuality. Sexuality needs to be seen in its fullest form, including a larger range of sensual activity than genital contact, for example, massage and various forms of sensual touching.

As a veteran and his partner say good-bye to their youth, they may need each other and their intimate moments even more than when they were younger. Fortunately there are many excellent books on the subject of sexuality for middle-aged and older persons. Even more fortunately, wrinkles and gray hairs do not kill the sex drive. It is my wish that couples reading this book not be deprived of what can be a source of tremendous satisfaction in their middle and later years—a mutually gratifying sexual and emotional intimacy with one another. (See appendixes A and B for resources and suggested readings.)

Women's Responses

In general, women have trouble being intimate with a man who is unhappy, angry, emotionally distant, or verbally or physically abusive. Other women, however, especially physically abused women, cling to sex as a major means of keeping their relationship alive. While it is impossible to make global generalities about the sexual response of partners of veterans with combat-related sexual problems, several patterns do emerge.

Sexual Avoidance

Some women respond to their veteran's sexual dysfunctions, to his insistence on sex on demand, to his obsession with sex, or to his sexual flings by turning off their sexuality. They may go to bed with him, but over the years they may lose touch with their own sexual rhythms and desires. They may even deny that they have any sexual drive or desires at all. When they do engage in sex, it is usually in response to their veteran's need, not their own. In this, they are similar to many other women, who learn to adapt their sexuality to their man's timing and tastes.

The partner of a combat vet, however, is under special pressures. She knows her vet is troubled, and if sex is paramount to him, she may go along with his sexual desires to help promote his mental health and keep the peace at home. When she is assertive or aggressive in bed, her behavior may not be a reflection of her own sexual desires, but a response to her veteran's request that she be more active sexually. Hence sex becomes more like work than play.

In recent years, with the onset of the sexual revolution, sex has become an achievement situation for women as well as for men. It is no longer enough for a woman to lie in bed passively. Now she may feel pressured to "perform" by having an orgasm or at least displaying heated passion. In addition, a relatively new phenomenon has emerged— women insisting on their "right" to sexual fulfillment and demanding that men bring them to orgasm.[15]

However, women who make such demands on their veterans are, in my experience, relatively few in number. In most cases, the woman allows her sexuality to be monitored by her veteran's desires. As a result of all the concerns described in this chapter, a woman's sexual desires and most certainly her sexual spontaneity might become inhibited, leading eventually to her avoidance of, if not outright hostility toward, sexual activity.

Decreased Self-Esteem

When a woman experiences love during sex only on occasion, she may begin to feel like a whore even though she is with her own husband or boyfriend. Yet even when she feels she's being used as a sex machine, she may have sex with her veteran because she feels it is her duty, because of her veteran's insistence, or because he is, or seems, desperate. "Sex is the only time he feels alive. How can I deny him?" is a statement I have heard over and over. Some women fear that their veteran will regress further and further into his PTSD or depression or "go crazy" if they do not comply.

After years of counseling, Jean can clearly see the ways in which her veteran's combat trauma contributes to their intimacy problems. Despite this intellectual understanding, Jean, like many newcomers to counseling, often attributes the sexual problems in her relationship to her real or perceived inadequacies. "If only I was 'better,' then he would love me more" is her underlying thought. More specifically, "If only I knew how to relate to him better," "If only I was prettier," or "If only my breasts were fuller, or my thighs slimmer [or whatever], then he would respond to me." Jean's self-esteem continues to suffer because, as a woman, she has been socialized to look to male approval and male responses as a measure of her self-worth.

Even women with significant career achievements can find it difficult to love themselves or to validate themselves as women when the man they love avoids them sexually, treats them like a sex object, or fails to give them the love and affection they desire. A woman's confidence can also be eroded by the confusion of having strong but conflicting thoughts and feelings about the causes of the sexual difficulties in her relationship. She doesn't know whether to blame herself (for not being "adequate enough"), the war, or him. Anger at the self, anger at the veteran, and feelings of betrayal can exist right alongside a deep compassion for the veteran's suffering, leading to a dilution, if not total obliteration, of sexual interest and response.

The situation becomes even more complex in relationships where the woman experiences her veteran as being loving and attentive at certain times, but not others. "Sex is great when Tyrone is his regular self. But when he's under pressure or something snaps him back into the war zone, the regular Tyrone disappears and a warrior takes his place. He begins to heave and the blood in his veins visibly pulsates. Then I never know what to expect, in bed or anywhere else," says Beau. Like other partners, Beau experiences many pleasurable times with her husband, who can be extremely tender and loving as well as self-centered and cold. His "PTSD moods," as she calls them, are unpredictable. Sometimes they last for days, at times for months. When she wonders whether or not to stay married to Tyrone, she does not know on which Tyrone to base her decision: the regular Tyrone or the warrior one.

Some women are so devastated by their mate's sexual apathy, they desperately pursue him sexually. If they can but engage him in sex, even purely carnal sex, then they feel loved and assured of their worth. So far, this pattern has evidenced itself only among a few of the battered women seen in therapy. As Lenore Walker, the author of *Battered Woman* states, battered women typically use sex to create an illusion of love and as a means of establishing harmony in the home. Yet the price they pay is loss of self-respect.[16]

Sexual Deprivation and Depression: A Vicious Cycle

Women who blame themselves for the sexual problems in their relationship tend to forget that when they want sex, their mates may be sexually disinterested or impotent as the result of combat trauma, certain medications, the effects of poor self-care or prolonged substance abuse, or other medical or emotional problems. They also tend to forget that if there were more communication and emotional intimacy in their relationship, their sexual interest might soar. Unfortunately, both veterans and their partners can find themselves in the midst of a vicious cycle: the diminished frequency and quality of their sexual relationship can serve to increase and complicate the emotional distance, communication problems, and conflicts between them, making it that much more difficult for them to be together sexually.

The lack of sexual contact or meaningful sexual activity can also perpetuate, or even increase, any existing depression or other emotional problems or any stress-related medical problems, in either the vet or his partner. While they may be depressed for different reasons, both suffer when their sexual relationship is suffering.

Since sexual activity and orgasm require energy, they are often seen as draining. However, suppressing sexuality and fighting the need for sexual release also require energy. While a person may feel depleted immediately after intercourse, ultimately the sexual release functions to create more energy and an elevation in mood. When a woman states that she is too tired for sex, part of her fatigue may stem from the very lack of sexual touch and fulfillment itself.

Summary

Sexuality is an issue in many homes, but especially in the homes of veterans who suffer from combat trauma. Veterans' sexual responses may be diminished or altered by the intrusion of wartime memories or survivor guilt into their intimate moments. Some veterans may fear the physical and emotional vulnerability inherent in disrobing and in the sexual act itself. When these (or any other factors) diminish the ability to enjoy their sexuality, eventually some vets may come to avoid sex altogether. As the result of these and other effects of combat trauma, partners can also experience diminished interest in sexual relations with their veteran.

While some vets have periods of sexual disinterest, others are interested in sex almost all the time. An intense need for (or preoccupation with) sex may reflect a need to combat depression or anxiety or to forget not only war experiences but also current problems. Sex may make them feel good, if only briefly. However, their partners may feel like sex machines or human tranquilizers. When veterans alternate between being sexually disinterested and sexually demanding, their partners may feel like sexual rejects as well. Whether veterans avoid sex or are obsessed with it, their partners' self-esteem may suffer, especially when they don't feel cherished by their mate.

In homes where the woman does the majority of the housework and child care, sheer fatigue may deplete her sexual energies, especially if she also has an outside job. And underneath the fatigue and role conflicts, which are real, may lie resentment. Even if she can't admit it, her difficulties responding to her veteran sexually may stem from her anger at him for any inequalities in their workload or for disappointing her sexually. The anger stemming from her sexual disappointment is further increased when she feels her vet has not met her need for intimacy and emotional bonding.

Women in sexually unfulfilling relationships sometimes turn to their children, to their work, or to church, community, or other activities to find comfort and fulfillment. Some women can openly acknowledge their disappointment and anger; others deny these and other negative feelings, bury them with excess food, or express them through a physical or emotional symptom or an addiction. The possible negative impact of combat trauma on a veteran's sexual happiness and that of his partner can be viewed as yet another casualty of the war.

6

"I didn't feel entitled to be angry"

Anger, Grief, and Guilt

Before Joel started therapy, whenever he was reminded of the war or we had financial pressures, the littlest thing could set him off. If he blew up at me, afterwards he'd always apologize and say he didn't know what came over him. But by and large, his anger at the time was not really focused on me, but on what he thought was wrong with the world and with people who slighted him. Sometimes he really was slighted, but other times he was overreacting.

For the most part, I passed off Joel's anger as his way of grieving for some buddies who were blown up by a land mine and his guilt about that and about other things that happened in the war. Joel didn't talk much about the war, but the few incidents he did share with me were enough to help me disregard his anger—whether at me, the computer, or the traffic—as unimportant. That's not a healthy way to deal with things, but most likely he and I would not be together if I hadn't.

I thought therapy and medication would help, and they have. But lately it seems that all that talking about the war in therapy has made him more on edge than ever. There are times when it's the eggshells under the feet, constant tension, a constant testing of the atmosphere to decipher Joel's mood, whether it be angry or depressed, that keeps the whole family wound up. I'm confused about how at the same time that therapy is helping Joel acknowledge his emotions and take responsibility for them, he's also starting to blame me for more and more of his dissatisfactions. If a line is too long or one of the kids cries too loud, that's my fault. If his mother forgets to call or calls too much, that's my fault, too. Maybe now that Joel is aware of his combat trauma, he wants to run away even more. But he has no place to go, and that's my fault, too.

At my very first counseling session, the therapist suggested that I was a very angry woman. The idea was totally unacceptable to me. To me, anger was ugly and to be an angry woman, well, that was almost the same as being a "bad" one. "Good" women, I had been taught, forgave quickly and did not harbor resentments. They were also experts at turning lemons into lemonade and at keeping their mouths shut when their husbands were upset.

Because my husband had seen so much death in the military, and I was still pulling shrapnel out of his skin, I didn't feel entitled to be angry. My problems seemed petty compared to his. I was also afraid that if I aired my grievances with him, his entire storehouse of anger from the war might land on me or the children. Many times it has been in my best interest and in the best interests of my children to follow my grandmother's advice and keep my mouth shut.

—ANDREA

Anger

Most of the women I've worked with in individual or group therapy have usually found it easier to admit to feeling anxious or depressed than to being angry. Anger is a major problem for them, as it is for their veterans.[1] Despite popular psychology books that often suggest "let your anger out," old religious and societal sanctions against expressing anger still exist for women, especially those who were raised to believe that anger wasn't "feminine."

Andrea, for example, was taught that anger was a sin and that God would strike her dead if she ever talked back to her parents or any other authority figure. While Andrea now laughs at this old-fashioned thinking, emotionally she is still bound by it, as are many other women. They fear that if they express their anger, especially toward their partners, they will be struck dead by a thunderbolt. In most cases, the thunderbolt the women fear the most is not a physical attack, but an emotional one. For many women, especially those born prior to the women's rights movement of the 1970s, self-esteem is closely intertwined with their partner's view of them.

Perhaps today's young women are being taught differently, but many seem to be affected by the same message that governed so many of their mothers and grandmothers: anger is not desirable in women, and expressing anger can result in alienating or even losing the man they love. In addition, many women, regardless of their age, were raised to assume the traditional female role of family peacemaker. They fear that expressing anger will cost them what they have been taught to value most—family peace and harmony. Some report that when they shared their frustrations, they were called "selfish" or "uncaring" by their veteran or reminded that they, like other civilians, could not possibly comprehend the horrors and deprivations of fighting in a war. More than one woman has received the same guilt-evoking message from her veteran's family and friends: she should put her own feelings and needs aside until the veteran "gets himself together." She should especially keep her anger to herself, since the veteran is already upset enough.

Some women are in touch with their anger, others are not. Often they are ambivalent. When they feel overburdened or rejected, they feel entitled to their anger. However, they also feel that they should be more understanding and patient toward their veteran because of all the hardships he endured in the military. If their veteran is in therapy, they may not want to interfere with his recovery efforts. Some partners keep quiet because their veteran has talked about suicide, a real possibility in some cases.*

*See chapter 12, "Suicide and the Veteran Family."

However, this pattern may change when a woman reaches midlife and begins to re-evaluate her life. Upon such reflection, she may begin to both appreciate—and resent—what she has sacrificed for the sake of others or for the sake of her value system. She may feel cheated and betrayed, yet proud of her determination to keep her family together. Just as her veteran may feel he gave his all in the name of patriotism, only to be troubled by inner turmoil and not receive the recognition and benefits he was told he would receive or he thought were his due, she may feel she gave her all for the sake of family values, only to be unappreciated by her family. She may also encounter people who devalue her for having been "old-fashioned" and invested so much of herself in her relationship with her veteran instead of in material or career success. In addition, as she ages, she, like most mature women in this society, is likely to be deemed increasingly physically undesirable and expendable, as if she was a wounded soldier unfit for battle.

Combat Veterans and Anger

Many women readily describe their partners as angry. Some even call their men "human volcanoes," ready to erupt at any moment. Perhaps it is primarily those women whose veterans have a problem with anger who seek help. Therefore, it cannot be assumed that anger is a problem for all combat veterans. Yet anger and rage reactions are characteristic of inadequately treated mental health problems, such as depression, PTSD, and substance abuse, and medical problems, such as chronic pain, physical disability, closed head injury, or chronic illnesses, which afflict many combat veterans.

Furthermore, research completed on help-seeking Vietnam combat veterans diagnosed with PTSD reveals that anger was and continues to be a major problem for them. Studies conducted on veterans shortly upon their return from Vietnam, as well as studies conducted decades later, have consistently found a close relationship not only between anger and combat-related PTSD, but between anger, social isolation, and impaired relationships with partners and children.[2] However, the high index of anger found in these studies may apply primarily to help-seeking Vietnam veterans with PTSD, not to all Vietnam veterans or to all combat veterans. The high levels of anger found among the Vietnam veterans who participated in these studies may reflect not only their combat experiences but also their unwelcome homecoming and their difficulties finding appropriate mental health care upon their return.

To date, little research has been completed on anger in veterans since Vietnam. Given that most of the more recent troops were not subjected to the societal rejection encountered by many Vietnam veterans, it can be argued that their degree of anger may not be as great. On the other hand, it could also be argued that their level of anger may be just as high, but for a host of different reasons. For example, perhaps among the men and women in the Reserves or the National Guard are those who, despite their patriotism, did not expect to be called to war and resent the disruption this caused in their lives. If, in addition, they were deployed not once, but several times, or if they came home to find themselves without a job or family support, they may be just as furious as those Vietnam veterans whose "welcome home parades" consisted of antiwar protestors calling them "baby killers." However, given the lack of research in this area neither of these possibilities can be verified.

A "Catch-All" Emotion

Although the degree of anger experienced by a veteran may be affected by personal, political, and social factors, the combat experience itself is a breeding ground for many types of anger. On the battlefield, soldiers needed to suppress their grief, fears, homesickness, self-doubts, and many other emotions. Anger, however, was one of the few emotions they may have felt free to express, and it was often the expression for a wide range of feelings, especially grief and guilt. For many soldiers anger became a "catch-all" emotion.

On the psychological level, combat trauma is basically a problem of unresolved anger, unresolved grief, and unresolved guilt. Some experts feel that the main issue is the grief. Others argue that it is the anger or the guilt. Still others insist that the root of the problem is the sense of powerlessness that lies beneath the veteran's anger, grief, and guilt. These experts point out that while many people find it difficult to confront feelings of powerlessness, for most combat veterans such feelings are totally unacceptable in that they undermine the image of soldiers as brave, tough people who can successfully handle almost any situation. The debate has yet to be settled.

In my view, the relative importance of grief versus anger versus guilt varies from one veteran to the next. One veteran may be volcanic in his rage but has yet to shed a single tear over his losses. Another veteran may have grieved profoundly but has yet to confront his anger. Yet another may allow himself to be mistreated or overgive to others as a form of self-punishment, or he may develop certain medical or psychological symptoms, yet never recognize how guilt may be playing a role in such problems. Some veterans try to stifle their feelings of anger, guilt, grief, or powerlessness with alcohol, drugs, or some other substance. Others try to distract themselves from these emotions with overwork or some other compulsion.

Grief

Anger and Grief—The Intimate Connection

For combat veterans, like other trauma survivors, anger and grief are intimately related. The losses endured as a result of the war inevitably generate a lot of anger, especially if combat involved the loss of numerous comrades; friendly fire or other human errors; permanent injuries or torture; the shattering of cherished beliefs about one's self, human nature, or the nature of the universe; or, in the soldier's view, some form of social injustice. Hence, on one level, the anger is pure rage at whatever force caused damage or death. On another level, however, the anger reflects grief for personal losses, as well as any sorrows and disappointments that may exist over the failure of certain government, religious, or other institutions to live up to their stated purposes and standards.

For example, a decade ago drunk drivers who were responsible for the deaths of pedestrians or other motorists frequently received ridiculously light sentences by today's standards. Relatives of the victims were consequently enraged not only at the drunk driver but also at the court system. Even more infuriating was that sometimes drunk drivers would leave the court free to drink and drive again, perhaps to kill more innocents and themselves. As with relatives of victims of drunk drivers in the past, some of a vet's anger may be a legitimate response to experiences with injustice, and some of it a defense against their grief.

Isn't it easier to be angry than to be sad, especially if one is a combat veteran? Anger makes one feel powerful and full of energy. In contrast, when one is grieving, one feels weak and helpless. Grieving involves mourning specific losses as well as one's helplessness. In grieving, one is acknowledging the reality that nothing he or she can do can resurrect the dead or restore what was lost.

This close connection between anger, grief, and helplessness can also hold true for combat veterans' family members. Often wives and girlfriends are shattered when they realize that, contrary to the popular myth, love does not conquer all. Perhaps they devoted themselves to their veteran, showered him with tenderness and affection, or gave up opportunities for personal fulfillment only to find that he still couldn't sleep through the night and that his capacities for intimacy and involvement in certain family and social functions remained painfully limited. Some women entered their relationship with their veteran believing that if only they were giving enough, then their veteran would be happy and all would be well. Many have tried to be the "perfect" wife or girlfriend and have expended a great deal of psychological energy trying to make their veterans feel better. Some have even become frantic in their attempts to "fix" their partner.

Yet, they learned that their love was not enough. While they were wanted, they were also not wanted; while they were needed, sometimes desperately so, they were also functionally useless in the face of symptoms of PTSD, clinical depression, and other forms of combat trauma. Yet if they expressed their frustrations and anger, only more anger or rejection may have been sent their way. Their veteran, struggling with combat trauma, simply could not tolerate the emotional overload.

Similarly, children who believe that by being perfect they can "cure" or "save" their veteran parent may be crushed when they realize that their model behavior doesn't have the power to heal the wounds of war. When the feelings of helplessness are too painful for family members to bear, they may emerge as anger or rage. The fury born from their sense of powerlessness may be directed inwardly toward themselves (in the form of low self-esteem, depression, or self-destructive behavior), outwardly toward others, or both.

Like their veterans, partners may suffer irrevocable losses. Women who put certain personal goals on the back burner in order to tend to their veteran sometimes find that when they are finally ready to resume pursuing some of these goals, the opportunities to do so no longer exist or are significantly diminished. For example, Andrea (whose story opened this chapter) had planned to continue participating in tennis competitions after she married Joel. However, the normal demands of marriage and children, combined with the emotional and other stresses of living with a troubled veteran, resulted in her not having the psychic energy, or the time, to stay in shape or maintain her tennis skills.

When, at age forty, she decided to take tennis lessons, Andrea realized that she would never be able to play as she had when she was younger. However, she did assume that after a few months of lessons and regular exercise, she'd be able to qualify to enter some local matches. To her dismay, Andrea found that she would have to work much harder and much longer than she had expected to regain even a small percentage of her former skills. She also recognized that the main barrier to reclaiming her skills was not her age, but the cumulative effects of years of emotional stress, inadequate sleep and nutrition, overdoing for others, and not taking time for herself.

Andrea's sense of loss was enormous, yet it did not express itself first as grief, but rather as fury—first and foremost toward Joel. The Andrea who was raised to believe that anger was a sin found herself chastising her husband at every turn. A few times she even threw things at him and refused to cook, do laundry, and perform other chores she had done routinely for years.

In couples' therapy, Andrea learned how to use words to express her anger. In one session, she read Joel a list of all she had given up to take care of him and their children. Andrea emphasized that while she had made certain sacrifices willingly, now she was livid. Not only had she shouldered more than her fair share of the work and received less than her fair share of appreciation, many times Joel had been unfair by making her the target for resentments he had about the war and other issues unrelated to her.

Andrea had another list—that of all the dreams she had for her life. But instead of reading it, she crushed it into a paper ball and said: "Why bother? It's too late for some of these dreams to come true." She was about to throw the paper ball at her husband when she began sobbing, "Good-bye, sweet dreams." As Joel rose to embrace her, Andrea glared at him and told him to get lost. She continued to sob uncontrollably for almost a half an hour, at which time she reached out for Joel's hand. When he gently kissed it, Andrea began crying even harder.

"Maybe you have to say good-bye to some of your dreams," he said to her, "but don't say good-bye to me. I'll watch your back, Andrea, like you've been watching mine. You kept me alive more times than you'll ever know. You're not only my wife, but you're my best buddy."

Ironically, Andrea's expressions of anger resulted in greater understanding between her and her husband. Joel explains:

Lately Andrea's been acting like I did during my worst explosions. She's yelling and screaming at me like never before. But I guess I deserve it. Before these couples' sessions, I never really listened to her when she tried to tell me what was going on with her. Maybe if I hadn't shut her out back then, she wouldn't have to rant and rave to make me realize how selfish I've been and how much she gave up for me.

It's strange, but even though Andrea is mad at me almost all the time these days, she finally understands how cheated and frustrated I've been feeling all these years and, of course, I know all about lost years and hopes that can never be. So, guess what? We're closer than ever.

Anger as Part of the Five Stages of Grief

In her landmark book, *On Death and Dying,* Elizabeth Kübler-Ross explains that the grieving process consists of five stages: denial, anger, bargaining, depression, and acceptance.[3] Not only people who are dying but anyone who suffers major losses in life can expect to experience these five stages of grief. These "stages" do not always occur in precise order. A person can be in more than one stage at a time, and the length of time spent in each stage varies from person to person, as does the depth of feeling. Throughout the five stages, feelings of fear, despair, disorganization, guilt, and anxiety, and even adrenaline surges may be experienced.

Denial

In the first stage—denial or shock—the loss is not acknowledged. For example, the first time Joel saw death, he felt he was dreaming instead of living real life. For a brief while he even denied the reality of the death that surrounded him by unconsciously hoping for miraculous resurrections.

Anger

Once a person's denial is cracked, he (or she) can expect to be flooded with anger. He may be angry at any person, place, or thing he feels contributed to his loss; angry at life in general for giving him such hardships; or even angry at himself for not having been able to foresee or prevent the loss. In some cases, people of faith may find themselves angry at the deity of their understanding.

Bargaining

The bargaining stage of grief is characterized by fantasies of "what if" and "if only." It is also characterized by excessive and irrational self-blame.

Depression

Periods of depression are a normal part of the grieving process. Even though the depression is temporary, it can still be intense and painful and may include symptoms such as difficulty concentrating, low self-esteem, changes in eating and sleeping habits, feelings of futility and hopelessness, or various physical problems such as backaches, headaches, vomiting, or constipation.

Acceptance

Acceptance does not mean that a person no longer thinks about or no longer feels sad about the loss. It simply means that a person has stopped fighting the reality of the loss and the emotional toll it has taken on him or her and any others involved.

It bears repeating that conceptualizing the grieving process as consisting of five stages does not mean that a person will progress neatly from stage to stage. Human emotions never come in neat packages. There are transitional states, where one moves from one stage to the next. Also, a person can be in more than one stage at a time. For example, the acceptance stage is often colored by anger, depression, and bargaining. Or a person may have reached the acceptance stage, only to have the anniversary date of the loss, another major life loss or trauma, or some other trigger act as a setback to an earlier stage. In the words of a career officer:

> No matter what the shrinks say, there's no such thing as "coping with grief," at least not for me, who's been through three wars. Oh yes, there's plenty of times I'm ever so confident that finally I can pay full attention to the living rather than grieve the dead. But then, out of the blue, grief floods me as if I just realized how much those men mattered to me. Then comes the numbing, the anger, and all the rest. Will I be going around these emotional circles forever? I hope not, but maybe that's how it is.

Because grieving is a process, it takes time. Neither the veteran nor his partner can simply decide to set aside a few hours that week to grieve and be done with it. There is no timetable or schedule for grieving. There are no published statistics about how long it takes to finish grieving a loss. Much depends on the nature of the loss. The depth and length of a person's grieving process will depend on the extent and meaning of those losses to that person. It will also depend on cultural background, personality, and the number of other demands that are placed on his or her time and energies.

Combat veterans, like other trauma survivors, typically have longer and more intense periods of mourning than nontraumatized people. Similarly, partners with histories of child abuse, suicide, homicide in the family, or other trauma can also expect that people and situations that remind them of their trauma can trigger a renewal of both grief and anger. Also, like their veteran, partners can expect that they may react more intensely to new losses and other stresses than they feel is warranted. They may be correct in their assessments.

However, there is no need for combat veterans or any other trauma survivors to beat themselves over the head for "overreacting." Neither do they deserve to be shamed or humiliated by comments such as "get a life" or "get over it." There are numerous reasons, both biological and psychological, some of which involve forces beyond human control, which explain why trauma survivors can be more reactive to subsequent grief and loss than persons who have not been traumatized. Here are two such reasons:

For people who have been traumatized, losses involve images of horrific events as well as perhaps memories of their own near-death encounters. These images can easily trigger involuntary biochemical reactions that bring to the fore memories of past traumas and losses. Hence for a combat vet, as for any member of the veteran's family who has also been traumatized, mourning one loss involves mourning previous losses as well, thus intensifying and prolonging the grief. A second reason is that being traumatized can expand a person's ability to experience intense emotions. Consequently, should that person become involved in a minor car accident, he or she might react with more depression and sorrow than others who were present.

Many of the grieving veterans I've counseled have shared with me that they keep their grief to themselves lest they be accused of "wallowing in self-pity." However, there are differences between true grief and chronic self-pity. Self-pity, anger, guilt, and depression are all parts of the normal grieving process. But if self-pity, anger, or guilt comes to dominate one's personality or determine most of a person's behavior over a prolonged period of time, then that person may be suffering from more than grief.

Guilt

VA psychologist Edward Kubany defines guilt as a negative feeling state triggered by the idea that one should have acted, felt, or thought differently.[4] The death, injury, or insult of another, as is common in war or any type of traumatic experience, is a breeding ground for guilt.

Just as anger can be a defense against grief, it can also be a defense against guilt (and the losses and feelings of powerlessness that are often associated with guilt). In some instances, however, the reverse is true: guilt can be a defense against anger, grief, or feelings of powerlessness. To feel guilty about a certain situation implies that one had some control over the outcome of that situation. Many times during war or other traumas a person may have few, if any, choices, and the outcome of the situation is shaped largely by forces beyond that person's control. However, by feeling guilty, a person can maintain the illusion of having had more power and control than were actually available to him or her.

Should that person ever come to realize how little power he actually had, the feelings of guilt may shrink considerably. However, he may then find himself consumed with anger, or grief, or both. Perhaps his strong feelings of guilt had distracted him from acknowledging his powerlessness and fully grieving his losses. Guilt might have also helped him put a lid on the storehouse of rage he may have been suppressing regarding a particular event. When the guilt lifts, he then must face the challenge of mourning his losses and finding constructive outlets for his anger and pain.

Types of Guilt

There are many types of guilt, some of which are listed below. Not only combat veterans but also their family members may struggle with one or more of these types of guilt.[5]

Survivor Guilt

Survivor guilt is perhaps one of the most common forms of guilt experienced by combat veterans. Survivor guilt refers to feelings of guilt about staying alive in situations where others died or about being less injured or harmed than others. It often involves the wish to suffer for the person who has been injured or killed, as well as guilt for being grateful that one was spared the suffering. Survivor guilt also refers to feelings of guilt about something one did, thought, or felt in an effort to stay alive or to protect him- or herself from psychological or physical harm.

Combat veterans often wonder why they suffered less than someone else with whom they served in the military or why they lived while fellow soldiers died. Vets with survivor guilt often wish to join or to change places with the dead or injured and mistakenly believe that if they had suffered more, others would have suffered less.[6] In most life situations, even traumatic situations, it is difficult if not impossible for someone to change places with another person in order to spare that person death or injury. In certain extreme situations, such as war, there may be some opportunities to take the place of another who is condemned to death or torture or abuse. In some prisoner-of-war cases, for example, soldiers could offer themselves to be abused or killed so that another soldier, innocent civilian, or other person might be spared. This may work, but there is no guarantee that the power holder will hold to the agreement and not harm both the soldier and the person the soldier is trying to protect.

In situations such as normal bereavement, illness, and serious accidents, it is virtually impossible for anyone to serve as a substitute. Even if someone made him- or herself ill or committed suicide, that would not necessarily restore another person to health or spare that person from death.

Nevertheless, soldiers, or anyone who is sincerely confused about why they fared better than someone else, may begin to reevaluate their spiritual, existential, or religious beliefs. However, questioning and perhaps coming to doubt, alter, or reject previously held beliefs or the beliefs of their family or community can create yet another set of guilt feelings.

Failure to Meet Parental Expectations

Guilt begins in our childhood when as infants and young children we are completely dependent on our parents and other adults for our well-being. Since our survival depends on pleasing our caretakers, when they scold or become angry with us, we fear that we will be abandoned or neglected. Along with that fundamental fear comes guilt at not having pleased the parent or caretaker.[7]

The guilt you felt as a child when you were reprimanded or rejected by your parents or other caretakers for not pleasing them motivated you to change your behavior in order to avoid parental scolding or neglect. Through direct teaching as well as parental admonitions, you probably learned the morals and rules of your household and society. Over time, you may have come to automatically feel guilty when you violated parental or societal norms. Even when your parents or caretakers weren't around to scold you, you probably scolded yourself for disobeying their rules.[8]

As people grow older, they can also transfer the childhood guilt regarding not pleasing their parents or caretakers to other authority figures, such as teachers, clergypersons, work supervisors, military superiors, political figures, or others with religious, political, economical, or vocational status or power.[9] Hence even a forty-year-old reservist could feel guilty about not meeting the expectations of his commanding officer, to such a degree that he feels his commanding officer has the power not only to harm his military standing but also to obliterate him. This fear can exist even if the possibility that the commanding officer could give him a particularly dangerous assignment or duty is remote. Hence this fear not only of being scolded or shamed in front of his unit by the officer for not meeting a certain standard but also of being annihilated by the officer stems back to infancy and childhood. At that time being judged as deficient in some way could have led to being rejected and neglected, which could have led to death itself.

Guilt at not meeting parental expectations can compound survivor guilt in instances where an individual's failure to obey or please an authority figure resulted in the death or injury of another. For example, Tyrone was raised to believe that children were supposed to obey their parents. In the military, he learned to obey commanding officers. In one instance, however, Tyrone balked when his commanding officer ordered him to fire at a group of supposed enemy soldiers in the distance. Based on reliable sources, including information from other soldiers, Tyrone thought the soldiers were Americans, not the enemy.

Tyrone refused to fire, only to discover the commanding officer had been right: the soldiers in the distance were indeed armed enemy troops. During the resulting firefight, some of Tyrone's comrades were killed. Tyrone's guilt for having stayed alive was compounded by his infantile guilt at disobeying an authority figure, his commanding officer.

Like Tyrone, Camry, a military nurse, suffers from double guilt. She was on the front lines nursing a wounded soldier when the enemy attacked again. A speeding bullet grazed her face and killed a soldier next to her. She then used the soldier's corpse as a shield against the continued fire. To this day, decades later, she feels she should have died with the soldier (a form of survivor guilt).

But Camry also suffers from guilt for violating her father's repeated admonitions about respecting the dead. Her father had been a soldier during World War II. He had served under a general who insisted that his troops respect not only their own dead but also enemy dead. Soldiers under this general were harshly punished if they mutilated the bodies of the dead. Camry's father had instilled in all his children the value of consecrating the remains of the dead. As a result, Camry feels as if she betrayed her father and all that he stood for when she used the corpse for protection.

Failure to Meet Societal Expectations

Parents and caretakers aren't the only origin for demands to meet certain standards. Society also places pressures on people. Regardless of how independent anyone thinks he or she might be, almost anyone can be made to feel guilty for not living up to the cultural expectations their culture places upon them.[10]

For example, many women in Western culture feel guilty about not being slender enough, even if they grew up in homes that paid no particular attention to female body size. Our culture tends to measure the worth of a man by the size of his bank account. Hence men who are unemployed, such as disabled veterans, or who are burdened with financial hardships, such as some soldiers, may experience guilt for not being financially successful. Even men who grew up in homes where military service was valued over the acquisition of material goods may experience some level of guilt for not living up to the cultural expectation that, as men, they should have plenty of money in the bank.

Childhood Omnipotent Guilt

Another form of guilt is childhood omnipotent guilt—a well-documented tendency of young children to think that the world revolves around them and that they control everything that happens. Young children think that if they wish something, it might come true. For example, when children become frustrated with a parent or sibling, they often think or say, "I hate you—I wish you were dead!" which is a perfectly normal expression of aggression. But, if for some reason that parent or sibling subsequently becomes ill, dies, or leaves the family, the child thinks that he or she caused this person to become ill, die, or leave. This is called *magical thinking,* because hating one's parent, sibling, spouse, or friend, or even wishing another person dead does not cause these people harm unless the aggressive wish is acted upon.

No matter how old or how mature we may be, a part of us—consciously or unconsciously—may still be engaging in magical thinking or seeing ourselves as omnipotent. When someone we know is harmed or killed, the child in us may feel we harmed or killed that person because we sometimes harbored hostile feelings toward him or her.

But hating people doesn't kill them or make them sick. In themselves, angry, hateful thoughts, feelings, or wishes cannot cause the physical death, illness, or injury of another, with one important exception: if you severely or continually maltreated someone, and then that person acquired an illness or injury directly related to your behavior, some of your guilt may be appropriate. If not, some of the guilt you are experiencing may fall into the category of childhood omnipotent guilt.

Superman/Superwoman Guilt

In adolescence and adulthood, childhood omnipotent guilt can be transformed into a type of guilt called "superman or superwoman" guilt. In order to cope with a traumatic or extremely stressful situation, people can come to believe that they have superhuman qualities.[11] The more helpless and powerless people feel in a life-or-death situation, the greater the need for superhuman powers. One theory is that during traumatic conditions, people tend to revert to childlike thinking, including the tendency toward childhood omnipotent guilt.[12]

It is not unusual for survivors of traumatic circumstances to experience guilt and feelings of failure for not knowing what no human being could have known and for not having abilities that are beyond human capability.[13] Examples are medical staff who feel guilty for not being able to save everyone, soldiers who feel guilty for not having foreseen all enemy assaults, and relatives of seriously wounded soldiers who feel guilty for not knowing the outcome of certain medical procedures.

Contributing to superwoman/superman guilt is a tendency for people with survivor or other types of guilt to exaggerate the importance of their role during a traumatic or stressful event or series of events.[14] However, in most cases, no one person is usually the sole cause of a negative or devastating situation. For example, a military nurse who feels such intense survivor guilt about soldiers who died while under her care that she frequently dreams of dying in her patients' place needs to realize that a host of factors determine the quality of patient care.

Certainly her competence on the job was a factor, but other factors were involved as well, including the competence of other staff members; the organization of the hospital as determined by the administrators, state and federal laws, and the military and medical boards; the potency of the medications; and the reliability and quality of support services, such as electricity and gas. Just as she would not take sole credit for helping to save a soldier's life, she could not realistically take sole blame for causing the death of a soldier unless, of course, she purposely murdered the soldier.

In addition, it is very easy to think that because you could have or might have done something to save a person from harm, you caused the harm.[15] In the example of the military nurse, it was important for her to realize that even though she might have done something to save a particular soldier's life—for example, she could have been more careful in administering oxygen—this doesn't mean she intended or caused the death.

Existential/Religious Guilt

Religious guilt is frequently present with survivor guilt. For example, it is not uncommon for soldiers to experience guilt about violating the religious code of "thou shalt not kill" by being warriors. Like some abused women and children, sometimes soldiers can be coerced into lying, stealing, or committing cruel or sadistic acts toward others. Anyone who is coerced in these ways can suffer from severe religious guilt.

In some cases, persons who have lost a loved one or a friend to a violent death attribute the death of this person to their having violated a tenant of their faith. For example, Randy still suffers from survivor guilt over the suicide of his war buddy some fifteen years ago. However, his survivor guilt is compounded by his religious guilt for having an adulterous affair during his tour of duty. On some level, he feels that the death of buddy is divine "payback" for violation of his marriage vows.

Another type of religious guilt is almost the exact opposite of the religious guilt described above. This guilt involves rejecting previous religious and spiritual beliefs and traditions. Hence veterans whose family members or war buddies died particularly horrible deaths may have stopped believing in the God or Higher Power of their understanding because their prayers for the well-being of their loved ones were not answered or because the God or Higher Power of their understanding did not provide them the help and rescue that they needed during their trauma.

However, there can be guilt in abandoning or rejecting one's former religious or spiritual beliefs, especially if family members or significant others are critical of this change. Hence, persons who come to reject the tenants of their faith as the result of a severe trauma or stress may feel guilty about not being able to truly believe what they used to believe or not being able or willing to attend services as they used to.

Guilt of Being

Guilt can arise from violating a religious taboo or not living up to a moral code espoused by one's religion of choice, regardless of the particular religion. This type of guilt is called the "guilt of doing." However some religions—for example, those in the Judeo-Christian tradition—also foster another kind of guilt: "the guilt of being."[16]

The guilt of doing involves the sense that you cannot live up to a certain religious or spiritual ideal because of something you did wrong or something you failed to do right. In contrast, the guilt of being refers to the sense that you cannot live up to your religious and spiritual beliefs because of what you are—a vulnerable, frail, and, according to some faiths, by nature a sinful human being.

In the Judeo-Christian tradition, the guilt of being derives from the notion of original sin. In other religions, such as Islam, there is no parallel to the idea of original sin. While guilt of being can originate from religious ideas about the inherent sinfulness of being human, it can also arise from being the emotional scapegoat in a family or group. White supremacists make African Americans, Asians, and other non-white people the scapegoats for their internal ills and problems in the world which they feel powerless to remake according to their own desires. Most hate groups, regardless of who they hate, think that if they only eliminate a certain kind of person, then they will feel happy and peaceful inside and the world will be put in good order.

Hate groups blame their problems on the sheer existence of people of a different color, national origin, religion, or sexual orientation. The guilt of the people who are different from one's self is the guilt of being alive. This is the guilt of being.

For example, it doesn't matter to a white supremacist what an African American does or feels. He or she could be a brilliant doctor or a street thug. It's all the same to the white supremacists because, in the extremist mind, the African American is a criminal who needs to be punished if not obliterated simply because he or she exists. Of course, if the African American commits a crime or makes a mistake or somehow fails in being a modern-day saint, that adds fuel to the fire. But it isn't the cause of the fire.

In certain families, social organizations, work groups, or military units, the same process of scapegoating can occur. Often one person is selected. However, in some families or groups more than one person can be placed in the role of scapegoat. There can be so much emotional and verbal abuse of the scapegoats that they can easily begin to feel they should have never been born. This sense of guilt at being is even greater if those who are being emotionally scapegoated are also being physically or sexually mistreated.

Scapegoated persons who become the objects of frequent or ongoing verbal or other forms of abuse need to develop coping strategies to survive, some of which may be dysfunctional. For example, a scapegoat with little support and no way out may start to drink, use drugs, overeat, lie, or steal, or they may have memory problems and make frequent mistakes. These behaviors then become the object of criticism by the others in the family or group, and the scapegoated person may criticize him- or herself as well. The self-criticisms and the criticisms of others lead to guilt of doing, which only reinforces the scapegoat's fundamental feeling of guilt of being.

Another important factor in such situations is the humiliation involved in being the recipient of verbal, physical, or sexual abuse. The awareness that one is being used and that others have power over one's body, emotions, or thoughts erodes the integrity, which can make one feel like a thing, not a person. This vulnerability to the verbal and other forms of attack from others can create a sense of powerlessness and worthlessness that can lead to a sense that one does not deserve to live and a feeling of guilt at simply being alive. One soldier explains:

I've been criticized from the day I was born. My mother told me she was ashamed to have such an ugly child. My dad wasn't happy with me

either. I felt I shouldn't have been born and should never have existed.
I felt guilty for being alive—for breathing, eating, sleeping, having fun,
working, anything. Even today I can feel guilty about anything I do, even
being a good soldier, because I feel like I shouldn't have been born.

Shadow Guilt

Related to religious guilt, but somewhat different, is shadow guilt. According to psychologist Carl Jung, the human personality has many parts. One part of our personality—the person we present to the world—is called "the persona." The person has learned socially acceptable traits and knows how to modify certain instincts and desires in order to fit into society and not be punished for breaking societal rules.[17]

Another part of the personality is called the shadow. The shadow is the reservoir of many of our desires and feelings that we, or society, feel are unacceptable. Hence the shadow contains our lust, greed, vanity, aggressiveness, pettiness, selfishness, capacity for violence and evil, and all those parts that are "bad" and should definitely not be acted upon.[18] Also contained in the shadow are qualities that are not considered "evil" but are socially undesirable, for example, vulnerability and emotionality in men and aggressiveness in women.

Some people are relatively unaware of their shadow. They don't even know it exists. If you ask the average person if he or she has ever lied, cheated, wanted to kill someone, or lusted for someone who was not his or her mate, most likely that person would say "no." That might not be the actual truth, but to that person, most of the time it is the truth because he or she is not aware of his or her shadow. It is too horrible to contemplate. The idea of being murderous or lustful is so unacceptable that the shadow is suppressed out of awareness.

However, even though our shadow is usually repressed and even if we do not act on the impulses and desires in the shadow, we are aware that we have secret desires and temptations which we, or others, judge to be immoral. Our awareness of our shadow, however vague, unclear, or confused, breeds a sense of guilt. "In an existential sense . . . man feels guilt with regard to himself . . . because there are within him obscure forces, impulses, and inhibitions which neither his will nor his intelligence or his knowledge can master."[19] In addition, no matter how much we suppress our shadows, the primitive urges and feelings contained in it continue to emerge. They are very powerful.

One way to handle the shadow is to deny it exists but to satisfy it by watching other people act as if motivated by their shadow. That's one reason why movies with lots of sex, killing, and other socially unacceptable behavior are so popular—people release their shadow urges by watching others act out those urges.

The average person wouldn't dream of robbing a bank, plotting a financial swindle, killing, raping, or wishing a family member or coworker dead. But people spend time and money to watch television programs and movies where such things are commonplace. In other words, one way to handle the shadow is to allow it to live vicariously through reading books or watching dramas where people act in ways we wouldn't dare for fear of being condemned by society. Another way is to admire people who act out or who are thought to act out their shadow. For example, a recent study concluded that voters "secretly" want presidents and elected officials to be adulterous and have sexual escapes.[20]

However, people who have been in stressful life circumstances involving the harm of others have often encountered the shadow not in movies or in distant political figures, but in real life. They may have seen people act out their shadows and may have been in situations where they were forced to act out their shadow or where their shadow urges were activated.

Anyone who has been witness to war or other forms of violence has seen people who are acting out shadow urges. Anyone who has been exposed to injustices based on prejudice due to race, gender, sexual orientation, religion, or disability, and anyone who has grown up in a home with emotional or other types of abuse, or where one or more family members suffer from an alcohol, drug, or food addiction has seen people whose shadow selves are damaging not only their own lives, but the lives of others. Those who have been forced to go against their own moral standards in order to save their own lives or the lives of others were forced to act out parts of their shadow.

Even if you were not forced to betray your values during your stressful experiences, if you have ever felt vengeful or murderous toward those who hurt you or someone you loved, you have met your shadow. Having self-destructive thoughts is also a part of the shadow personality.

To go through a stressful life event and not encounter the shadow in oneself or another person is impossible. In fact, it is encountering the shadow in others and oneself that makes these life situations so stressful, if not traumatizing. Your experience has taught you the capac-

ity of others for evil, deceit, or negligence. You have seen these qualities in others and, in one way or another, whether you have had to act
on them or not, you may have seen them in yourself. Veterans and other survivors of man-made traumas are acutely aware of the possibility
of human evil. However, even people who have suffered as the result
of the expected loss or illness of a loved one, an unjust personal or job-
related situation, or an act of nature may have been exposed to human
error and malice.

Even if you have never acted on a shadow impulse, you may experience shadow guilt because when you are honest with yourself,
you realize that no matter how hard you try you cannot eliminate the
shadow part from your being and because you sense that the shadow,
although repressed, has the potential to erupt and cause havoc in our
lives. The fantasies and desires of our shadow, whether they be sloth,
murder, greed, lust, or self-aggrandizement, "defy the censorship of our
will. It is another self which is in us, which we cannot stifle, and which
we fear will be discovered."[21]

Moral or Atrocity Guilt

Moral or atrocity guilt refers to guilt feelings resulting from participating in or even merely observing abusive violence or atrocities. In
combat zones, soldiers and civilians sometimes participate in or witness morally questionable activities. In war, soldiers are exposed to or
engage in atrocities or in cruel and sadistic forms of torture of people
or animals. As a result of being exposed to the "monster" or "beast" in
oneself or in others, they can come to feel they are tainted and to view
all other aspects of their personality as being evil or despicable. There
is also a feeling of being cut off forever from society because of what
one did or saw. The kind of guilt involved in having witnessed or participated in atrocities has been called moral pain, moral guilt, or atrocity guilt.

The agony of this guilt is much worse if one actually committed
a morally questionable act than if one merely witnessed it. However,
even soldiers who simply observed an atrocity or immoral act can feel
contaminated by what they saw or heard. It's as if they absorbed the
evil they witnessed into themselves, even though they did not conceive of or participate in the atrocity. On some level, they feel responsible for the event simply because they were physically present.

Another aspect of this type of guilt stems from being unable to protest the atrocity or stop it. Yet there are circumstances where stopping an atrocity may be virtually impossible without endangering one's own life or the lives of others. In some circumstances, even sacrificing one's life to try to avert the atrocity would be ineffective or might even spur the abusive individual to become even more abusive of others. Under these circumstances, the choice with the least negative consequences is compliance, as morally unacceptable as that might be. It bears repeating that being held captive by hostile forces that present the captives with a set of morally questionable or personally dangerous options is the essence of trauma.

This section on moral or atrocity guilt is not intended to indict or chastise or to excuse or make rationalizations for individuals who participated in morally questionable behavior during wartime. The purpose of this section is to present yet another consequence of war that leaves a long-lasting imprint on soldiers and other combat military personnel.

Competency Guilt

Competency guilt refers to feelings of guilt for not having acted as efficiently or wisely as one thinks one should have. An individual with competency guilt often tends to suffer from hindsight bias. Hindsight bias means believing you could have known what was going to happen before it was possible to know or believing that you dismissed or overlooked clues or signs that "signaled" what was going to occur.[22] Because you believed you *should* have known certain things or *should* have acted on clues or signs that a jury of reasonable people would probably not view as definitive information but rather a vague hint, intuition, or superstition, you decided that to some extent you caused the tragedy.

For example, Raphael, a soldier, asked his commanding officer (CO) to be relieved of guard duty one night. He wasn't feeling well and had a "bad feeling" about being on duty that evening. Raphael had never asked for any favors before and was an especially skilled and dedicated soldier. But the commanding officer refused his request. His men were always having "bad feelings." After all, they were in a war zone. It would be abnormal for them not to have bad feelings. For a brief moment the CO considered taking Raphael's place that evening, but he decided against the idea. If he gave in to one soldier's request, then in fairness he'd have to give in to the requests of others, and he could not do that without seriously compromising his ability to perform his duties and creating chaos. The CO refused Raphael's request, only to find out the next day that Raphael had been killed five minutes after assuming guard duty. To this day, the CO feels that he killed Raphael and should have died in Raphael's place.

The CO is committing the error of hindsight bias thinking. First, he had no knowledge of what was going to happen on guard duty that evening. Second, he was feeling guilty for not following an intuitive feeling (or, in other instances, a hunch or premonition), yet the norm is for people to base their actions on high-probability outcomes, not low-probability outcomes, which is the standard for hunches, intuitive feelings, or premonitions.

In the CO's experience, hundreds of men had "bad feelings" on certain days and there was little relationship between a man's bad feeling and his fate in battle. Some men with premonitions that they were going to die that day actually did die, but others did not. Conversely, some who were confident of returning alive were killed whereas others with confidence returned alive and unscathed.

It has been suggested that people tend to view thoughts or intuitions they had during a stressful event (but disregarded) as omens, premonitions, or warning signs because this gives them a sense of control or mastery in situations where they did not have enough control to prevent the death or injury of another. It has even been suggested that in some cases people change their memory of the event to include omens and premonitions in order to avoid feeling helpless or powerless.[23]

Negligence Guilt

Negligence guilt refers to feeling guilty due to some form of negligence in performing assigned duties or in executing a designated role.[24] Under conditions of war or other traumas, making mistakes is to be expected. During traumas, especially war, time is limited and confusion reigns. Seldom is there the luxury for extended gathering of evidence, consultation with experts, and careful weighing of options. Also, as described in chapter 3, under conditions of trauma, people are subject to fight-flight-freeze reactions and other biochemical changes that can negatively affect their mental and physical capacities. These reactions are not voluntary.

"Catch-22" Guilt

"Catch-22" guilt refers to lose-lose situations where all the choices available are unacceptable or involve a violation of personal ethics. No matter what choice one makes, one is betraying oneself or an important value, and the outcome is undesirable.

It isn't fair for you to judge yourself for what you did or didn't do against "non-existent fantasy choices that would . . . [have] kept everyone safe and alive."[25] While we all wish for miracles, or at least for a superman or superwoman, to provide a magic rescue out of a horrible situation, the hard truth is that there are situations where it is impossible to preserve the life, health, or integrity of all involved. Judging your actions against what a superman or superwoman could have done is a form of "superman guilt."

Trauma has been defined as a situation where all of the alternative courses of action are unacceptable or painful. If you are in a traumatic situation, the choice of safety and happiness for all is not available. The best choice is the choice with the least negative consequences. Persons who suffer from "Catch-22" guilt feel guilty because they violated a personal standard of right or wrong. Yet they needed to violate that personal standard of right and wrong in order to uphold another standard of right and wrong.

Responsibility Guilt

Responsibility guilt stems from confusing having a responsible role toward others with the ability to protect them from harm.[26] Military officers, parents, and medical workers, for example, can easily confuse their sense of responsibility due to their role with the idea that they had the power to cause and control the outcome of negative events.

It is easy to confuse your role or job with "an ability to determine outcomes."[27] There is a difference between feeling responsible about your role as an officer, physician, teacher, or some other role involving the care and protection of others and having the ability to prevent terrible events from occurring. Just because you are in a responsible role for another person doesn't mean you have the power to protect that person from all harm. If you had the power to protect that person from negative events, such as sniper fire or a car accident, then you should also have the power to create positive occurrences, such as arranging for that person to meet the love of his or her life. Although highly desirable, that kind of power simply does not exist among mortals. While your reasoning may quickly tell you that you cannot orchestrate a series of blissful events for the people in your charge, if you suffer from survivor guilt, you need to use that same reasoning to remind yourself that you cannot always shield your charges from life's harms.

True Guilt

Many of the types of guilt described above result from not measuring up to societal expectations or the expectations of others. However, guilt can also arise from not meeting one's own standards. The term *true guilt* has been used to describe the guilt that stems from letting yourself down, whether in the form of not taking care of yourself, allowing yourself to be mistreated, not pursuing your personal dreams, or in some other way not being faithful to yourself. False guilt derives from "fear of social judgment and the disapproval" of others, but true guilt derives from not being faithful to ourselves.[28]

Men as well as women can be pressured by a significant other into actions they do not want to take. Bill, for example, had a vasectomy at his wife's insistence.

> *Since I was exposed to toxic fumes and substances overseas, my wife and I decided not to have children. We were too afraid of birth defects. We planned to use several means of birth control, but my wife insisted I have a vasectomy, too. I didn't want that vasectomy, but I thought I'd feel too guilty if I didn't do what she wanted. What's worse, I gave in to her on other important issues too. Maybe they weren't important to her, but they were to me. I believe compromise is necessary for a good marriage, but I was doing all the compromising. Sure I'm still married, but I lost my self-respect.*

Bill feared the guilt involved in disappointing someone he loved and, quite possibly, in incurring his wife's anger and rejection. In this respect, he was guided by false guilt when he acquiesced to his wife's demands. However, today he feels the pangs of true guilt, a guilt based on not acting on his true convictions and not standing up for himself.

True guilt is widespread, for few people are always faithful to themselves. In fact, true guilt can be as repressed as our shadow or other antisocial impulses, because to acknowledge the ways in which we have let ourselves down can be excruciatingly painful. When we are true to our inner callings and personal convictions, we run the risk of being criticized or even ostracized by others. In some cases, being true to ourselves can cost us our lives or the lives of those whom we love. On the other hand, to not be ourselves and to not actualize our dreams has another penalty: the horror of letting oneself be "paralyzed by fear, fashioned by environment, petrified by routine . . . [or] sterilized by conformity" and permitting oneself to simply copy others instead of being and developing oneself.[29]

True guilt has sometimes been called authentic guilt or guilt that arises from your own standards rather than guilt that arises from someone else's standards. Yet some people find themselves in situations where there is massive pressure to abandon their own beliefs and conform to others. The resulting spiritual or moral guilt is a major cause of survivor guilt, depression, and a host of other trauma-related disorders.

Guilt and Relationships

Like excessive anger, strong feelings of guilt can present a major obstacle to developing satisfying relationships. Relationships, especially intimate and family relationships, can be negatively affected when intense or long-term guilt feelings result in any of the following:

1. A deep feeling that one does not deserve positive supportive relationships.

2. A fear of intimacy based on (a) fear that one's guilty secrets will be revealed, or (b) fear that once another person discovers the truth about oneself, one will be rejected.

3. Guilt-related addictions and compulsions, which take away time and energy that could be invested in relationships and which also directly interfere with the stability and emotional depth of a relationship.

4. Permitting oneself to be exploited (financially, sexually, emotionally, vocationally) as an expression of unworthiness or a form of penance/atonement.

5. Over-giving or over-protectiveness in relationships.

6. Lack of assertiveness, where one feels that others are more important than oneself or that one doesn't deserve to have one's needs met.

7. Alienating/distancing from others by not returning calls, frequent canceling or not keeping dates/promises, fighting over trivia, irritability, or some form of abuse.

8. Difficulties with separation.

9. Associating with dangerous people.

10. Ending relationships because they are becoming too intimate or loving.

Aggression and Anger, Grief, and Guilt

Anger and aggression are not the same. Anger is a feeling; aggression is an action involving some type of verbal or physical attack on property, a person, or another living being. It is possible to be angry without becoming verbally or physically violent. Indeed, civilization as we know it depends on the ability of human beings to control not only their sexual impulses but also their aggressive ones.

As is obvious by the high rates of family violence and crime and by the numerous wars that have besieged humankind throughout the centuries, it is often difficult for human beings, both as individuals and as groups, to control their aggression. Even well-rested affluent civilians who are not stressed by the horrors of war sometimes find it difficult to stop themselves from lashing out at another person. For combat veterans, controlling aggression is vastly more difficult than for most people for reasons such as military training and experience, the alarm state, combat addiction, berserking, and impacted anger.

Military Training and Experience

Both in their basic training and on the battlefield, soldiers learn how to react quickly, and violently, to any danger, real or perceived. As a result, for some soldiers responding with violence becomes almost automatic. While this quick-action response is useful for surviving combat situations, it is no longer useful (or condoned) upon return to the United States. Hence veterans must quickly unlearn the violent tendencies that had been expected of them and served them so well during the war.

The Alarm State

A major barrier to unlearning the quick-action response is that combat veterans, especially those who suffer from PTSD or depression, tend to react more strongly to stresses in their current lives than persons who have never been traumatized. Because of their prolonged exposure to life-threatening situations, combat veterans can enter a state of alarm and terror more quickly than civilians, especially those who have never been traumatized. For example, sometimes even a well-meaning question or comment can feel threatening and set off a stream of physiological changes in vets that make them less able to control their behavior.

Once in the alarm state, the part of the brain responsible for abstract thinking and reasoning begins to shut down, which can create more alarm.[30] The increased alarm can lead to more terror and panic, which can elicit the aggressive response to fear learned in combat. A further complication is that the alarm state can be triggered not only by stresses or real or perceived threats but also by emotions such as grief, guilt, or feelings of powerlessness. For the combat soldier, such emotions may be perceived as being life threatening because they can distract one from doing what is necessary to stay alive, help protect one's unit, or fulfill one's mission. Hence, when a veteran experiences the first glimmer of sadness or guilt internally, he or she may panic, thus setting the stage for an aggressive act. Alternatively, since anger is a "catch-all" emotion for many soldiers, guilt, grief, and other feelings may be experienced as anger, which is also conducive to aggressive behavior.

Combat Addiction

Another barrier to controlling the quick-action response is *combat addiction,* which recently has been used to describe the excitement, "rush," or "high" that some veterans experience in combat and which some may continue to experience when they recall their combat days or when they engage in dangerous activities.[31] According to some researchers, the biological changes that occur in soldiers when their lives are on the line can minimize their awareness of danger and of physical and psychological pain and discomfort and help them to move rapidly and powerfully. The resulting state of excitement can be overpowering and extremely pleasant.[32]

Berserking

"Berserking" is an extreme form of the loss of restraint of aggression. Just as not all combat veterans experience combat addiction, not all combat veterans experience the berserk state. Dr. Jonathan Shay describes the berserk state as "flaming ice."[33]

> No one has ever drawn a syringe of blood or cerebrospinal fluid from a berserk warrior nor mapped the electrical activities of his nervous system. No one knows how much of the large literature on the physiology of extreme stress can be applied to berserking, on which there is no established physiological literature. It is plain that the berserker's brain and body function are as distant from everyday function as his mental state is from everyday thought and feeling. . . .
>
> Veterans are well aware of the sensations that accompany the berserk state. . . . The heart pounds, the muscles tense, the senses are on extreme alert. This is widely known as the "fight or flight" reaction. . . . There may be a "burning in the gut" or a feeling "like electricity coming out of me." . . . Bodily strength at such times seems superhuman. . . .
>
> Prolonged combat also brings bodily changes that deaden pain, hunger, and desire, resulting in an emotional coldness and indifference. The neurochemical basis of this change may be the release of opiate-like substances by the brain itself in response to terror and pain. . . .
>
> The true physiological relationship between the burning rage of the berserker and his icy deadness remains uncharted territory. We see the paradox that the same human being may burn with fury while cold as ice, incapable of hunger, pleasure, or even pain from his wounds.[34]

Impacted Anger

While it may be difficult for some veterans to unlearn their well-learned quick-action response, the major problem presented by help-seeking vets is their fear of *becoming* violent, rather than actually *being* violent. Having learned what they could do in terms of killing and maiming others during war, veterans may strive to suppress their anger, even over legitimate grievances in their current lives, for fear of hurting family members or others.

This "impacted anger," however, is a powder keg, which on occasion is ignited and can explode. Sometimes the anger emerges dramatically. Vases are smashed, employers are cursed, or family members are denigrated. But in my experience, more often the anger emerges less violently, in the form of small cutting remarks or verbal outbursts over relatively trivial matters. These minor outbursts, however, can do as much to erode a relationship as a major physical assault.

Partners can also suffer from impacted anger. If a woman has repressed her anger over time regarding a series of incidents, then each new conflict with her veteran brings to the surface not only the anger belonging to that particular incident but also all the built-up angers from the past. Like her veteran, the woman becomes afraid of erupting and tries to keep her anger to herself. She may hesitate to speak up even about minor incidents for fear of "thunderbolting" her veteran with all her past angers or with threats of leaving. At some point, however, like her veteran, she may no longer be able to restrain herself from unleashing all the anger she has been carrying inside for so long.

Stalemates often occur in homes where one person (whether the veteran, his partner, or his child) criticizes, yells, or screams at another family member on a regular basis. Over time, the recipient of the anger learns to "tune out" the hostility being directed toward them. Just as a woman may become relatively immune to her veteran's angry comments toward her, he may become immune to her volcanic eruptions toward him. Children, too, may come to ignore a parent's anger toward them. Such stalemates also tend to occur in homes where the critical remarks or other forms of anger are too painful or overpowering to be absorbed.

However, disregarding an angry person's anger may only result in increasing that person's anger. At this point, the angry person may withdraw or, alternatively, may escalate the verbal criticisms in order to obtain the partner's or child's attention and regain a sense of power and control. In some cases, a family member may feel the need to resort to violence in order to be heard or command respect. In my clinical experience, the usual pattern after an ugly outburst of rage is for the angry member to redouble his or her efforts to suppress the anger, which in turn leads to a further buildup of impacted anger. Unless the real causes of the anger are dealt with directly, the possibility of another wounding outburst of pent-up anger in the future is imminent. (See appendix B for helpful books on anger management and on processing trauma-related anger, guilt, and grief.)

Summary

Anger, grief, and guilt are issues not only for combat veterans but for their partners as well. Anger is a natural response to situations involving social or personal injustice. It is also a natural response to feeling unappreciated, overworked, misunderstood, cheated, or mistreated. However, part of a person's anger may be an indirect expression of grief, guilt, or feelings of powerlessness.

Anger and rage reactions have been found to be problems for many returning vets who suffer from PTSD, depression, or another traumatic reaction. To some extent, this may reflect the fact that, in a war zone, anger may be one of the few emotions that is permitted expression. Generally, in the military, as in other dangerous occupations, grieving or having any emotion that makes one vulnerable may not only be unacceptable but also highly impractical, if not life threatening, to oneself and others. However, the quick-action response of anger and aggression, so useful on the battlefield, creates havoc in civilian life, especially in intimate relationships. For veterans with serious cases of combat trauma, anger management is seldom enough to reduce anger. Identifying and grieving one's losses and identifying and dealing with one's guilt feelings are usually required as well.

Some female partners of veterans are in touch with their anger, others are not. Often they are ambivalent about their anger, especially if they were raised to believe that anger was not feminine. Just as for combat veterans, anger for their partners can be a defense against grieving and guilt. Anger can also be a defense against mourning their losses and disappointments in life and in their relationship and a defense against feelings of guilt for not having done more for their veteran or family. Like their veterans, partners can suffer from impacted anger, which can lead to problems such as depression, stress-related physical problems, or addiction.

My name is Guadalupe and I'm an "old-fashioned," yet "liberated" woman. I love my job as a loan officer and I love cooking for my husband, too. My coworkers rave about the El Salvadoran specialties I sometimes bring to staff meetings. But I've also been asked if I iron my husband's underwear, if he beats me, and how many dozens of children I plan to have. When I look offended, they assure me that they are only joking.

When my husband volunteered for combat duty in Iraq, my supervisor said, "Oh really? I thought only 'real' Americans could join the Army." I suppose that was a "joke," too. I wanted to blurt out that both my parents and Miguel's were naturalized citizens and that none of them had ever taken a dime in government handouts. They never cheated on their income tax either. But it probably would have been a waste of time. In his small mind, anyone with brown skin who speaks Spanish is probably an illegal freeloader or is too dumb or lazy to be in the military.

Miguel's parents lost many relatives during the cruel civil war that devastated their homeland. Yet when Miguel decided to join the Army, they were glad that someone in their family would be serving the country that had saved their lives. Miguel became a captain in record time. His military record, like his English, was flawless. Yet he still felt he had to prove he was a "real American." Maybe that's why he volunteered for the most dangerous missions.

When Miguel was gone, my period stopped and I went to Mass every day. Once he was missing in action for three days. All I could do was pray and sit by the phone and wait for news of Miguel. Crazy as it sounds, I hoped that being by the phone would make it ring sooner or that if I sat close enough to it, Miguel could hear me saying, "I love you."

Miguel came home without a scratch on his body, but his heart and soul were shattered, or so it seemed to me. Like many vets, my Miguel didn't talk much about what happened over there. I can only imagine the horrible things he saw. Having grown up on stories about how some of his relatives in El

Salvador had been killed because they were mistaken for disguised militants, it was probably torture for Miguel to have to decide if people dressed like civilians were really civilians or were secretly armed or on a suicide mission.

Some of the men under Miguel's command were Hispanic, some were not. Under enemy fire, most of them didn't think about class or race. But there were a few who held on to their prejudices and it was these few that drove Miguel crazy. He was "too" Hispanic for some of the non-Hispanics but not Hispanic "enough" for some of the Hispanics. Yet he needed the respect of all the soldiers under his command, not just because of his pride but because any lack of cooperation, however small, could compromise the mission or result in deaths.

When Miguel tried to hide his Hispanic side for the benefit of certain non-Hispanics, he felt like he was betraying his origins. On the other hand, when he showed his Hispanic side, he feared certain non-Hispanics would view him as less competent. The only one who understood his dilemma was Tyrone, a light-skinned African American man who was "too black" for some of the whites and "not black enough" for some of the African Americans. Tyrone was killed in a suicide car bombing on April 13.

Today is April 13, the anniversary of Tyrone's death. Tonight my family is gathering at the church to prepare for my niece's baptism. Baptisms are big deals in our culture, and I'm the aunt. I have to be there, but I know Miguel needs me. He'd never admit that he wants me around, but I know that he does. If I make up some excuse to tell my family about why I can't come, they'll know I'm lying. Then I'll get the lecture about how Miguel's unhappiness would go away if I quit my job, paid more attention to him, and started having babies.

But it's Miguel who doesn't want children. Yet, to take the heat off him, I let the family blame me and my career for all our problems. Also, I don't tell Miguel about some of my raises and bonuses—it would hurt his ego. He doesn't ask where the extra money comes from, but he knows. Yet we can't talk about it or any other issue that is even remotely related to Iraq.

I have these kinds of dilemmas all the time, and until I joined a woman's group at a local Vet Center, I had no one I could really talk to openly about *my life. All my relatives ever told me was that I was failing Miguel as a wife, and all my non-Hispanic friends and my Anglicized Hispanic friends ever told me was that Miguel was "crazy" and that I was even "crazier" for loving him. When I first joined the group, I felt guilty revealing "family secrets" to "strangers"—that is, nonfamily members. But the women in group don't feel like "strangers" to me anymore. To me, they're my "emotional sisters."*

With their help, I'm learning that I'm not the cause, or the cure, for my husband's unhappiness and that I don't have to allow his situation to totally dominate my life. I'm also learning that I have issues of my own to work on, issues remarkably similar to Miguel's: for example, repressed grief and anger, and identity confusion stemming from living in two worlds—the Hispanic and the non-Hispanic.

Most important, I'm learning to listen to my own heart, not the opinions of others. For me, this listening to myself and respecting myself is the true meaning of women's liberation—not whether or not I work outside the home or whether or not I do my husband's laundry.

7

"There's no time for me"

Multiple Roles

*As the wife of a combat vet with a flaming case of untreated combat
trauma, I have several full-time jobs. My full-time office job is just one
of them. In fact, it is the easiest one of all.*

*First, and most important, I am a mother, and being the wife of a
vet whose emotions are still raw from the wounds of war, this means
that usually I function like a single parent. I don't know whether it's
his combat trauma or male chauvinism or a combination of both, but
the bottom line is that I am responsible for almost every detail of my
children's lives. I pack their lunches, go on their field trips, and iron
their clothes. When it's time for them to go to college, I'll probably do
all the applications work, all the packing, and all the crying.*

*I am also responsible for most of the details of my husband's life—
arranging his medical appointments, explaining and protecting him
from his parents, my parents, the social workers, and the neighbors. I
take care of all the family finances as well.*

*When my husband is in a good mood, he vacuums, does the dishes,
and irons my blouses. But I never know how long his good moods are
going to last, and I can't count on anything getting done unless I do
it myself. I hate to start a fight over something as trivial as an undone
chore.*

But all those undone chores pile up, and before I know it, I'm work-
ing all the time. Sometimes I get so tired I can't even fall asleep. But oth-
er times I purposely stay up until three in the morning just to have a lit-
tle time to myself, and a little peace.

I wish I could do more for myself, but I don't have time. Seems like
everybody is used to me being around most of the time to take care of ev-
erything.

I do everything for everybody else. I don't do anything for myself be-
cause that would be selfish. Yet when I do what everybody else expects me
to do, no one ever says "thanks." Sometimes I feel so unappreciated that
I want to run away from home.
   —DESTINI, MOTHER OF THREE AND WIFE OF A COMBAT VET

Most of the women I've seen in counseling are employed outside
the home, some for personal fulfillment, but most out of economic necessity. Some women enjoy their jobs; some don't. Yet even those who
look forward to going to work every day sometimes feel so burdened
by their domestic responsibilities and the challenges of living with a
traumatized veteran that they speak of quitting their jobs or working
fewer hours. Still others feel they've outgrown their present positions
and wish they had the resources to pursue a vocation or avocation that
better suits their current interests. However, if their vet is medically,
emotionally, or financially unstable, they may be reluctant to give up
the economic security provided by their current job.

Even women whose salaries are not essential to keep the family
afloat often hesitate to cut back on their hours, lest at some point in
the future their veteran's emotional or medical war injuries worsen
and decrease his earning power. For example, a veteran with a relatively minor combat-related back or leg injury or with a few moderate symptoms of depression can still be a model employee. However, if
over time his symptoms seem to be increasing in frequency and severity, his partner may not be certain how long he will be able to maintain
his solid work status.

Even veterans who are in fairly good physical health and are dedicated to their field may be subject to anniversary or other trigger reactions that can negatively affect their work performance. In more severe
cases, a veteran's work record may be marred by frequent or unplanned
absences (due to bouts of depression or to sleepless nights plagued by

nightmares or flashbacks) or by one or more outbursts of temper on the job.

In such instances, it is not only the woman who fears that her veteran's job may be in jeopardy but the veteran himself. Often a vicious cycle is created whereby a veteran's shame about not living up to his own expectations as a worker and his fears about losing his job increase his stress levels, which can lead to more numbing, anxiety, insomnia, or other symptoms. The increase in symptoms, in turn, can lead to more problems both at work and at home, resulting in even higher levels of stress, leading to more symptoms, and so forth.

Ironically, a veteran's earning power can be disrupted not only by a work-performance problem arising from his combat stress but also by a financial or vocational success. It is not unusual for a veteran with combat trauma to apply himself at work as if he's on a military mission where the safety of all depends on his doing his job in the most competent and responsible manner possible. Yet when his hard work and dedication earn him an offer for promotion, he may decline the opportunity. Or he may suddenly quit his job or abandon his business at the height of his financial or vocational success or after receiving an award.

This seemingly irrational behavior may be the result of a veteran's survivor guilt, which tells him that he does not deserve to enjoy the fruits of his labors. It can also stem from an association of responsibility and authority with death. Promotions, awards, and other forms of financial or vocational success usually bring with them not only more income or status but also additional responsibilities and the need to master new skills. This can cause panic in those veterans who are convinced that a mistake they made while they were in the military contributed to the injury or death of a comrade or of an innocent civilian. Or perhaps they observed the ghastly consequences of an error made by a military or other superior. As a result, these veterans may fear that the inevitable errors they will make while they learn new skills or adjust to a new work role might have calamitous results.

To the outside observer, a veteran's refusal to accept an advanced position or his decision to abandon a successful business or profession makes little sense. Yet in the light of his combat experiences, his actions make perfect "trauma sense." Tina, whose husband, a Reservist, has been called to active duty several times, says:

Most of our arguments are about money. We're always short, but I can't get a higher paying job unless I take time off work to get some training. Gene says we can't afford that right now. But we could afford it if only he'd take the training that's being offered to him for free at his work. Then he'd automatically receive a pay raise. But he won't do it.

The training isn't even that hard. I keep telling Gene that he already knows so much about the subject that he could probably teach the training himself. He agrees, but he won't budge. Only in couples' therapy did I find out why: It's not just that Gene's afraid of change, which he is, but he feels guilty about having good things in his life because his cousin died in combat and never had a chance to enjoy life.

When I tell Gene that he couldn't have saved his cousin and that his cousin would want him to be better off, Gene just clams up and won't talk to me. Then I do the absolute wrong thing and start yelling at him for not letting go of the past and moving on. I hate screaming at him, but how can he be so worried about money all the time, then not take advantage of the chance to make more?

I have to apologize for yelling at him about ten times before he'll come out of his shell. Then he'll start crying about how guilty he feels about his cousin and how scared he is that if he does anything different on the job from what he does now—tasks which he knows so well he can do them in his sleep—that he might make a mistake. In the military, you just don't make mistakes or someone gets hurt. That's how his cousin died—because someone made some tiny mistake.

I'm beginning to understand Gene. But I'm still angry—and scared. Will we always be strapped for money? Will we ever be able to afford another child or a better home? Will I be working full time until I'm an old lady?

For some veterans, job dissatisfaction stems from a heightened sense of justice. The minute they see a coworker being mistreated, a customer being deceived, a safety precaution being ignored, or the slightest hint of corruption, they want to walk off the job. Other veterans have employment difficulties because their current jobs lack the adventure, power, or sense of purpose that was part of their military experience. A former officer explains:

Overseas I had the power of life and death over dozens of troops. Now I push paper in an office where I have to take orders from a man who can't even spell. Overseas I commanded millions of dollars' worth of equipment and I made my own decisions. Now I have to write memos before I can do practically anything.

As horrible as it was to see so much destruction, I loved the people I fought for and I admired and was humbled by how they kept up their spirits in the midst of such poverty and adversity. I miss them and I miss all the action. I never want to kill again, but it depresses me that nothing I do as a civilian can replicate the challenge and the adrenaline high of combat.

This officer's wife did not have to work for economic reasons. Yet she dared not give up her full-time job as a computer programmer to pursue her dream of becoming an artist. What if one day her husband got so frustrated on the job he just quit? Then she, like the partners of veterans who are unemployed, underemployed, or trapped in low-paying jobs, would be the family's primary or sole source of reliable funds.

The strains of having primary responsibilities both inside and outside the home are obvious. Yet they are often overlooked, in part because of media images of the working woman as one who glides from one role to the next without anxiety, conflict, or effort, with her makeup intact and her figure perpetually slim. In addition, there is the cultural expectation that a woman should be able to do it all, or at least most of it, without complaining. "I don't know why we think that we have to do it all, but we do," the women often say.

Handling a full- or part-time job in addition to home means increased demands on time and energy, which often result in overload and fatigue. With additional roles come additional commitments: more people to respond to, more appointments to keep, more deadlines to meet. In addition, a woman must come to understand and grapple with any office politics as well as her interpersonal dynamics at home.[1]

The woman who works outside the home faces the exhaustion of having at least two full-time jobs: one at home and one at work. She may also have a third job: that of making the arrangements necessary to execute all her various roles; for example, the phone calls regarding child care and the transportation of children to and from school and other events. Try as she may to avoid conflicts between her domestic and her wage-earning roles, the logistical difficulties involved, especially when children are young, can be enormous.

If her sleep is interrupted by her veteran's nightmares or by his medical problems, she may come to work already tired. If she fears his anger, she may need to spend the night at a friend's or in the car. If his emotional capacities are impaired due to his combat trauma, she may be the emotional center of the home. Both her veteran and her children may look to her for nurturing, guidance, and strength.

She may also have a fourth job: taking care of her veteran. Recent research has shown that partners who function as caregivers of veterans with chronic PTSD show poorer levels of psychological adjustment than partners of veterans without PTSD. If, in addition, there is violence in the home, the caregiver's mental health suffers even more. These findings held true regardless of the amount of social support the woman was receiving.[2]

Even if a veteran does not have long-term PTSD, his partner may have added to her many responsibilities the role of actively encouraging him to seek help, arranging his therapy appointments, or helping him obtain his benefits. If her veteran cannot tolerate bureaucratic procedures or waiting, it may be she, not he, who contacts medical or veterans benefits offices or who waits in line at the pharmacy. If he is hospitalized, there are frequent visits and, in some cases, participation in family therapy or conferences with doctors, all of which require time, energy, and effort.

Her children might also have special needs. They may need to attend therapy or Alateen meetings. Children from violent homes may have learning problems that require tutoring or extra parental assistance. She also may be making special efforts to involve her children in recreational or social activities in order to offset the depressive mood in the home or to compensate for their father's emotional numbing. In any of the above cases, the working woman's scheduling problems are even more complex.

At the same time, she may not be able to afford services that would make her life easier, such as maid service or professional nursing help for an elderly or infirm relative. If money is tight, she must also consider economic factors in executing her multiple roles. For example, she may need to shop at discount stores, even though the stores are out of her way and the lines are long. If she cannot afford convenience foods, her time in the kitchen is increased.

Consequently, the veteran's wife feels pressured for time. Yet she often feels she cannot complain about her time pressures to her partner
because they seem trivial compared to his trials overseas. This is especially true of women whose cultural background limits women to traditional roles. Isabella, whose grandparents immigrated to the United
States from Bolivia, explains:

> *If I mention to Edwino that I feel pressured, he just laughs at me and*
> *says: "You should have been in my unit. Then you would have seen real*
> *pressure. Why, when I was overseas . . ." and on and on. Or he'll start*
> *in on how grateful I should be that, unlike my aunts in Bolivia, at least*
> *I have stores to go to and a car to get there with . . . and on and on.*
>
> *All I know is that my life is not my own. During the weekdays, my*
> *job consumes me. Then at night, I do everything and spend all my time*
> *getting me, and everybody else, ready for the next day. My weekends and*
> *holidays are not my own either. I clean, cook, take the kids shopping.*
>
> *Sure, I'm not surrounded by enemy fire, but my daily list of "things*
> *to do" would blow away the minds of most men. All they have is one*
> *job — I have at least six: cook, laundress, chauffeur, cleaner, shopper, bank-*
> *er, not to mention my full-time job, being a mother, and being a "good"*
> *daughter-in-law. My in-laws are from the old country where women wait*
> *on men hand and foot. If they see Edwino doing the dishes or changing*
> *a diaper, they scold me for not doing my job. I can't serve microwave din-*
> *ners or carry-out food either. Unless I cook dinner myself and have sever-*
> *al courses, my in-laws go into an uproar about how I'm starving my fam-*
> *ily, how they came to the United States to get away from hunger, and on*
> *and on. . . .*
>
> *Edwino laughs at my lists, but I couldn't survive without them. He*
> *doesn't understand that I'm working practically all the time. Neither do*
> *my kids.*
>
> *I don't know if they learned it from TV, their grandparents, or what,*
> *but they complain when I'm a few minutes late to take them where they*
> *need to go, as if I'm late because I was taking a bubble bath or doing my*
> *nails.*
>
> *No. I'm usually late because I'm finishing up chores they said they*

would do, but didn't do. Yet I hate to nag the kids because they've got
enough on them with their dad so unhappy and troubled. But I do blow
up at them sometimes. Then I feel guilty because I really do want to be
a patient mother and give them quality time. But how can I be patient
when I have so much to do?

Sex-Role Stereotyping

Sex-role stereotypes die hard. Often the woman faces the dual problems of a partner who is unwilling or unprepared to share domestic tasks and her own difficulty in giving up the traditional homemaking tasks that once defined her value to her family. As the previous example illustrates, women whose cultural or religious background includes the belief that a woman's career and other outside roles are peripheral to her central role as wife, mother, or homemaker may find it exceptionally difficult to break free of sex-role stereotypes.[3]

For example, when Isabella's in-laws grew too old to take care of themselves, there was no question that they would come live with her. That meant that now she was responsible for their daily care and their medical needs. It was also expected that she would serve them traditional breads and other specialty dishes from their homeland.

Quite predictably, soon after her in-laws came to live with her, Isabella began showing signs of clinical depression. Yet even when she felt half-dead inside, she'd rise every morning at 4:30 AM to prepare the special foods for her in-laws, as well as breakfast, lunch, and dinner for her own family. It would have never occurred to her, her husband, or anyone in her family to say "no" to the grandparents' requests or to offer Isabella some help.

In today's world, with the exception of certain strongholds of traditional sex roles, men do help with domestic chores. Yet, according to most of the women, veterans who share domestic responsibilities often view themselves as merely "helping" or doing the woman a favor rather than sharing responsibilities. Women also complain that after having promised to do something for the home, their vet may "forget" to keep his promise or decide to do it later. The woman then has the dilemma of choosing to press him to keep his commitment and risk being called a nag or a bitch, or to suppress her resentment and do the work herself.

Even the partners of nonveterans experience this type of dilemma. However, the partner of a combat vet may have special difficulties in getting her veteran to complete his responsibilities at home or to assume more of them. She may know that after having followed so many orders in the military, he may react negatively if he feels he's being "ordered around" at home. "He'll say he has too much pressure at work or from his PTSD to do anything more around the house," one wife reports. "He'll just get mad and walk out," says another. "If I push him too far, he might get into a funk and make me feel guilty," says yet another.

A mother may find herself needing to choose between overextending herself or seeing a child's needs go unmet. Suppose her husband promised to drive one of their children to a birthday party, but at the last minute he says he cannot take the traffic. He's had an exceptionally hard day. By accident, he saw some war footage on television and it set him back emotionally. It was enough for him to manage his emotions so he could stay at work all day without him now having to go out again. He needs to be alone, to collect himself. What his partner is asking him to do seems minor compared to the pain, anger, or frustration he feels inside. Perhaps he also believes that taking kids places is "women's work."

His wife might have had a hard day, too. But she cannot disappoint her child and she may have empathy for her veteran's pain and not want to add to his burden. Also, she may realize that if he is in such a negative mood, even if she insists that he keep his commitment, she will most likely not get what she wants. Furthermore, there will also probably be a scene between them, which will only upset her child and other family members.

In order to spare everyone (herself included) the stress of yet another marital conflict, the woman usually ends up doing the driving. Furthermore, the child may expect the mother to do the driving. After all, isn't this what mothers do, take care of children? Never mind that the mother has worked all day. She is expected to be a source of boundless energy at night and compensate for the fact that she works all day by doing whatever she can for her children at night.

In addition, in some homes, children are acutely aware that their father has endured many sufferings because of his military service. Hence they may perceive their mother's demands on their father as "pushing" or "stressing" him, even if her demands are legitimate. Children may particularly resent their mother asking their father for more help if he has war injuries. Janet says:

> *If our son is supposed to go to a game and Keith and I argue over who is going to take him, our fight ruins his fun. By the time we decide who's going to take him, he's decided not to go. He knows that his father has back problems from the war and doesn't like to drive. On the other hand, I work longer hours than my husband, so I feel he should help about more at home.*
>
> *But it doesn't matter who's right or wrong. When Keith and I fight, our son gets hurt and doesn't want to go anywhere. Bad enough my husband is almost a recluse and is trying to turn me into one. But I don't want our son to be a hermit. So I do all the driving.*

In other homes, however, there is a complete or almost complete role reversal. If the vet is unemployed, partially employed, or on permanent disability due to war injuries, he may become a house husband while the woman works full-time. In some instances, the role reversal works smoothly. Says one wife:

> *It took a lot of training, but I finally got my husband to have dinner ready on time and to do the dishes afterward without me having to tell him ten times. At first he used to call me at work to ask me about every little thing. But after I told him that if he could figure out how to survive in a war, he could certainly figure out the vacuum cleaner and the mop, his phone calls stopped.*

But some women find that their vet does not become a househusband automatically; the men need to be reminded to complete certain chores. Sometimes the woman tires of doing all this reminding and begins completing some of the chores herself. Eventually, one chore at a time, she may reassume most of her previous domestic responsibilities.

Furthermore, if the veteran suffers from PTSD or depression, despite his good intentions, he cannot always be relied upon to keep his commitments. If there are no children in the home, the woman can let go of certain nonessential household chores until her veteran regains his strength. But if she has children, much of the work cannot be left undone. The woman has no choice but to do it herself.

For example, Yin-Ying, who worked full time, and her husband, Lee, who worked ten hours a week, established an elaborate division-of-labor chart. Lee's heart wasn't in it, yet he realized that the old days when men could read the paper while their wives cooked dinner were over. Yin-Ying wanted to rest after work—"not too much, just a little bit."

The first week Lee attempted to do his chores. But he wasn't used to doing three things at once like Yin-Ying. Furthermore, when he got tired or bored, he wanted to quit, even if he hadn't completed everything on his list. After all, he reasoned, he had stressed himself enough in combat. He was home now, not in the military. Breaks and slight infractions of the rules were permitted here. Besides, folding the laundry was really not a life-and-death issue compared to loading machine guns with ammunition.

The first day Yin-Ying came home from work, she found Lee taking a nap. She was angry that he had only completed half of his chores but also glad to see that Lee was able to get some rest. He suffered from insomnia and nightmares, and Yin-Ying worried about him. The next day, however, the chores weren't done and Lee wasn't sleeping. He was out with his friends. Once again, Yin-Ying was resentful over the chores but a part of her was glad. In fact, she was delighted that her husband was socializing, rather than isolating himself, which had been his pattern. On the other hand, she was determined not to do his work for him.

The next day she picked the children's clothes for school out of the laundry but left her clothes and the filled dishwasher untouched. That night she quietly confronted Lee and he promised to do better next time.

Two days later the laundry was still unfolded and the dishwasher was still full. At this point Yin-Ying wondered if it wouldn't be easier for her to do Lee's tasks rather than to keep prodding him only to hear him say she was making "a big deal about nothing." In fact, just in terms of time, it would probably take her longer to nag Lee into doing the work than to simply do it herself. But she left the chores undone, set the table with paper plates, and wore a dirty blouse to work.

She planned to confront Lee once more, but he looked so dejected that particular evening that she felt it best to drop the subject until a better time. A few days later she considered approaching him again, but he seemed so emotionally shut down that she once again decided to wait. In the meantime she quietly unloaded the dishwasher and did Lee's laundry chores.

For the next few days, she waited for Lee to be in a good mood and for the right time to talk to him about the chores. The right time never came. Meanwhile, the household's needs continued. Despite her anger and resentment about the situation, within weeks Yin-Ying had reassumed responsibility for almost all the chores that had been Lee's tasks.

In some instances it is not only the veteran's resistance to helping with the domestic work which burdens the multiple-role woman but also her own difficulties in giving up traditional homemaking activities. In assuming responsibilities outside the home, a woman might experience the loss of a clearly defined, socially approved feminine identity provided by the traditional female role.[4] When she finds that she no longer has time to volunteer for charity fundraisers, she may be criticized by others. If she tells her veteran she cannot attend yet another veterans' reunion, he may criticize her, too. But, more important, she may berate herself for not being able to be the type of partner, mother, or family member she could have been were she not employed outside the home.

The social system may not support the woman either. Despite some improvements in recent years, she may still have difficulty finding adequate child care, part-time work, or a flexible work schedule. At the same time, her colleagues and superiors may question her investment in her work, given that she is simultaneously committed to a family. If they are aware that her vet is on disability for depression, PTSD, or another combat-related psychological problem and they are not informed about combat trauma, they may falsely assume that at any moment her veteran will "go off" or "lose his mind." Therefore, they may conclude, she is not suitable for a promotion or for special training that would lead to a promotion.

Like her veteran, the multiple-role woman may suffer from loneliness. Typically, she has little time for recreational, social, religious, or community activities. At work she may not fit in with younger, single workers. In her neighborhood or in certain social groups, she may not fit in with full-time homemakers whose interests, responsibilities, and schedules are different from hers.

For many of the women who have attended counseling, it has been a monumental achievement to recognize that they have needs and ambitions outside of the family and to begin taking steps toward meeting those needs or goals. Setting aside all the tasks they had yet to do at home or at work in order to attend individual or group therapy was often the first big step. Afterwards, some women began scheduling time to meet with friends or to participate in social or community activities that nourished them. Others decided to take courses that would promote their careers or other interests even if this meant being out of the home an extra evening or morning a week. Often they had been putting off taking such courses until their veterans recovered from combat trauma or until such time as their personal goals would not inconvenience their families. However, after years of waiting, they decided to take action. One wife explains:

> My "real job," for which I'm not paid, is at home. But I am paid and receive more recognition and respect for my other "real job" at the office. When I wanted to take a cooking course, nobody in the family objected. But when I wanted to learn computer programming to advance my career, you should have seen the fireworks.
>
> My mother-in-law refused to babysit for the kids, saying: "Isn't it enough you work all day? Now you have to go out at night, too? Who's going to mother those kids and take care of that husband of yours? Put your career off for later." But when I took the cooking course, she thought it was great.
>
> I'm surprised that her guilt trip sunk in, that it's still hard for me to do things for me, just for me. I was brought up to think I belonged to the family, but I thought I had outgrown that. I guess I haven't. But I'm not going to beat myself up for not being "liberated enough." I'll just go ahead and take the course anyway, guilt and all. If I have to go to school guilty, well, I'll just go there guilty, because if I put it off any longer, I might never get to it.

When the Veteran Is Physically Disabled or Becomes Medically Ill

When a veteran is physically disabled or becomes ill, in addition to her other roles, his partner may find herself in the role of nurse or medical case manager. Albert had five physicians, each for a different medical problem. He never went anywhere without a small bag full of medications. The list inside this bag, specifying which medications had to be taken when and under what conditions (for example, with or without food or water), was written and continually revised by his faithful wife, Penelope.

The frustrations involved in calling five doctors every time there was a medical change or problem was too much for Albert. If he was put on hold for more than a few minutes by the doctor's office, he would either hang up or curse the receptionist. Penelope decided it was easier to make all the calls herself than to deal with an angry husband or an equally angry doctor's staff. Yet calling all these doctors and trying to coordinate their efforts often added several hours of work to her week.

Even more taxing for Penelope were the times when Albert need-ed hospitalization. His PTSD symptoms always increased at these times because Albert associated hospitals with war. Hospitalization also forced Albert to confront the issue of trusting authority figures. In the mili-tary, Albert had trusted certain authorities with his life, only to witness them making foolish mistakes that nearly killed him. Now Albert was trusting his life to medical authorities. What if they made mistakes or let him down as had other authority figures in the past?

To the extent that an operation or a major medical procedure rep-licates the veteran's combat experiences, the normal stresses of inten-sive medical care or hospitalization are heightened. At such times, the veteran may make even more demands on his partner for loving atten-tion and selfless care. However, at the same time that she's being asked to give more to her veteran, she may not be receiving whatever emo-tional and other support he had been giving to her and the family.

A partner may also find herself in the role of "psychological nurse" (and the term is not used in a derogatory manner) to her veteran. Af-ter many years of counseling, Albert achieved a workable peace with his past. In fact, he was so grateful for his newfound life that he want-ed to share it with other veterans by giving them hospitality and emo-tional support. Penelope, however, was not quite prepared for her role as hostess and informal counselor to Albert's friends, and a part of her resented having to share him with other veterans. Yet she knew that her husband's mental peace depended on his reaching out to other veterans who hurt, and she did not object when Albert allowed fellow veterans to stay with them if they were suicidal or having severe anniversary reactions. Penelope not only cooked for these men but also listened to them and helped her husband bear his grief as he began to lose his friends to premature heart attacks, suicide, addiction, PTSD, depression, or other combat-related medical or mental illnesses.

Albert and Hassan met in alcohol rehab and became good friends. They identified with each other as combat veterans and supported each other in the struggle to stay sober. After they had both succeeded at several years of sobriety, however, Hassan's father was murdered by a street thug. This loss sent Hassan into a drinking relapse, which result-ed in his wife seeking a divorce. After his wife left, Hassan sunk into a catatonic depression.

With medical help, Hassan eventually emerged from his nearly veg-etative state, but he was not the same Hassan who had joked and gone fishing with Albert in the past. The loss of his father and wife had bro-ken Hassan's spirit. He was staying alive only for the sake of his moth-er and his children. His speech was slurred and he was afraid to leave home lest he have a panic attack. There were no more fishing trips with Hassan and no more long phone conversations in the middle of the night. Both had meant so much to Albert.

To help ease Albert's loneliness, Penelope went on fishing trips with him even though she didn't like fishing. As hard as she tried to hide her dislike, it showed. When Albert pointed that out to her during one trip, she felt so unappreciated she lost her temper. They spent the rest of the trip arguing, during which Penelope made it clear to Albert that she did not have the time to be his fishing buddy as well as his wife and medical case manager.

The next "casualty" was Albert's best buddy, Floyd. Floyd and Al-bert had met in a PTSD inpatient unit and had stayed in close touch for many years. At one point, Floyd was facing severe financial troubles, but the economic stress did not result in increased symptoms of PTSD or depression. It resulted in schizophrenia, an illness with which Albert was totally unfamiliar.

As Albert watched Floyd increasingly withdraw from the real world into an imaginary world of his own, Albert was horrified. "I've lost him. I've lost him," Albert moaned inside. Albert also felt angry, abandoned, and helpless. Not only was he losing one of his few good friends, but he was also unable to help him.

While Albert grieved, Penelope kept the home running and pro-vided her husband with extra emotional support. Yet there was no one to give her additional doses of love or attention when she needed a boost. She was emotionally depleted and resentful that, once again, she was giving more emotionally than she was receiving. Yet she loved Albert and she felt she did not have the right to complain because he was disabled and so distraught. Also, she feared that if she spoke up, Albert might become depressed, and possibly suicidal, and she did not want to burden him with her difficulties. In her view, he had enough of his own.

Penelope found solace in her music and her faith. She was encouraged to stay in touch with her own family of origin, which luckily was very supportive of her, and to try to make as much time as possible for those activities that strengthened her emotionally or spiritually.

Responses to the Multiple-Role Dilemma

One common response to the problem of competing demands is the attempt to be "superwoman." Because in many instances the new values for women have not eliminated the old values, but have been merely superimposed upon them, many women expect to work outside the home while fulfilling a traditional family role to the same extent as if they did not have job responsibilities.

Another not-uncommon response to the multiple-role dilemma is overeating. Even if a woman's extra pounds have not created health problems for her, psychologically the excess pounds usually decrease her self-esteem and her sense of control over her life. A woman may turn to food for comfort or as a way to alleviate stress. If she has little time or energy for pleasurable activities or if her sex life is sporadic or unfulfilling, she can easily be tempted to turn to food for gratification. This does not mean, however, that the veteran's combat trauma is responsible for his partner's eating problems.

Just as the alcoholic or drug-addicted veteran is responsible for what he does to his body, his partner is responsible for what she puts in her mouth. Food is a fast fix; it is also an easy fix. Since women tend to do the shopping, cooking, and feeding of the family, food is readily available. Furthermore, unlike drugs or alcohol, food is legal but it can serve the same purpose. Food can sedate the emotions and anesthetize the woman to pain, anger, and hurt. Food can also be used to quell inner turmoil or as a way of dealing with—or not dealing with—relationship difficulties and external stress. The physical act of eating is not only pleasurable but also tension reducing.

Dora is overwhelmed with demands, both inside and outside her home. Her sex life with her husband is troubled, as is her entire marriage. In the midst of feeling overwhelmed by responsibilities and wondering what the outcome of her marriage will be, she turns to food to lift her mood and to give her the energy she needs to do all she has to do. But she doesn't really need the calories to complete her work. Furthermore, any good sensations she gets from eating something delicious usually vanish when she looks in the mirror and decides that she is fat.

Yet Dora can't stop eating. For her food is a way out. Like many partners, Dora feels that her whole life is being "gobbled up" by the needs of her husband, her children, and her full-time job. In response, she gobbles up whatever she can find.

When Dora gets home from work, she simultaneously juggles making dinner, helping her son with his homework, and worrying about her husband. What psychological state will he be in when he gets home? Will he get home at all tonight? She has situations at work that she needs to figure out. She is also exhausted. But she can't just finish the dinner dishes and go to bed. She has to pay the bills her husband "forgot" about and do the laundry he promised to do.

Dora is tired of worrying about her husband, of constantly placating him, of doing his work for him, and tired of all the fighting. When her son asks her to take him to the crafts store to buy clay for a school project, she wants to scream. Instead she gulps down the leftovers from his lunch box and finishes off the ice cream. Then she has to go to the grocery store to buy more ice cream so her husband doesn't find out that she binged and yell at her again.

Under the intense pressure of so many obligations and feeling unsupported by her husband, Dora often gives up. "I might as well eat, what else is there for me?" she sometimes asks, not realizing that what she really needs is more rest, more love, and more time for herself. Like many partners, Dora wants desperately to exert more control over her life but doesn't know how to do so. Feeling powerless, she turns to binging, but that only makes her feel less in control and gives her less, not more, physical and emotional energy with which to cope with her multiple roles.

Helping the Multiple-Role Woman

The purpose of therapy for a multiple-role woman is not to teach her how to be more efficient so she can do it all faster, but to help her learn to appreciate herself more for what she does. She is also encouraged to examine how she might structure her life so that all her various roles are expressions of her individuality rather than her conformity to a stereotype about the ideal woman. Specifically, women who work outside the home usually need help in:

1. Understanding that family problems are due not to personal inadequacy but to characteristics inherent in her multiple-role situation.

2. Accepting conflict as inevitable.

3. Making choices and reconsidering assumptions about the female sex role.

4. Acknowledging personal strengths and assets.

5. Acknowledging legitimate dependency needs and feelings of helplessness.

6. Learning to ask for help.

7. Learning self-nurturing.

8. Exploring alternative ways of fulfilling roles.

9. Expanding career horizons.

10. Expanding social and other personal growth horizons.

Most of the women I have counseled have high expectations of themselves. They want to be thorough and excellent workers, as well as loyal, sensitive, giving partners and mothers. When problems arise, the woman mistakenly tends to define the problem as her inability to manage or cope. Given a lifestyle that includes the schedules and tasks involved with work, school, child rearing, marriage, and homemaking, as well as the intense emotional needs and unpredictable behavior of a veteran who is suffering from a stress disorder, occasional interruptions in the routine and unfulfilled expectations are inevitable. The woman needs to be reminded that these occurrences are natural, not signs of her personal failure.

She also usually needs help to appreciate the complexity of her life-style and the weight of the many responsibilities she is carrying. Part of her burden stems from the traditional assumption that it is the woman's responsibility to take care of everyone's needs. Not only does she tend to believe this, but her veteran, children, parents, and other relatives do also. Therefore, it is often difficult for her to ask her veteran or others for help.

At the same time, the woman may fear success in her career. Often she anticipates that her achievement will threaten her veteran, who is perhaps struggling emotionally and financially. If she or her veteran come from a culture with traditional views about the female role, she may also fear being ostracized as a "women's libber."[5]

Summary

All working women who are also partners or mothers struggle with the burden and the conflicts inherent in having two major commitments—one to their families and another to their jobs. In our society, women of all ages, especially middle-aged women, may also find themselves caring for older relatives or for grandchildren. In addition, women are usually assigned the job of arranging all their roles so that they do not conflict with one another so that the needs of the entire family can be met.

Unfortunately, in many families when the woman assumed a working role outside the home, there were few subtractions made from her home roles. This is especially the case in homes where there are traditional values about the woman's role and the veteran is reluctant to or has a limited ability to participate in child care and housework due to psychological, medical, or physical problems. Consequently, even the most hardworking and efficient woman will inevitably have times when she is overwhelmed by the demands on her time and energy. Beneath the surface, she may also be angry and resentful of all that is expected of her in her multiple roles.

Her multiple-role dilemmas are similar to those experienced by other working women. However, her burden is increased by her veteran's combat trauma, medical problems, and any resulting employment or emotional dysfunctions. Often the partner of a combat vet carries with her to work the mental agony of worrying about her veteran's medical status or his psychological condition and possible self-destructive behavior. At the same time she must be careful to be productive at work and in no way endanger her job since her income may be essential for the family's survival.

Also, depending on the severity of her veteran's medical or psychological symptoms, she may assume major multiple caretaking functions with respect to her vet. She may arrange his appointments and serve as a buffer between him and the world. To the extent that he is unable to shoulder the responsibilities of parenthood, she must assume the massive responsibilities of being both mother and father to their children. She also has the responsibility of explaining her veteran's actions to the children, as well as coping with the children's reactions to their father and her veteran's reactions to both their children and their reactions to him.

Self-care, fun, and pleasurable activities fall by the wayside as the woman goes endlessly from one chore to the next, from one crisis to the next. When she becomes tired and depressed, she may wonder what's wrong with her. When she encounters conflicts and stresses in her life, she tends to interpret them as reflecting some personal deficiency on her part. Yet many of her problems are inherent to the multiple-role lifestyle and the challenges of loving a troubled combat veteran, not the result of some inadequacy or personality problem on her part.

LORRAINE'S STORY

My husband slit his wrists in the shower with one of the knives from Iraq he had sometimes used on me. I almost left him after he used me for target practice one night. But I blame Iraq for this, not him.

Len had been a medic in Iraq, where he had seen so many soldiers— women, too—become amputees. He talked about Iraq night and day, but not to me. He read every book on the subject, but I was not allowed to do the same. Not until the day of his funeral did I find out any details about what he had experienced or why he finally decided to end his life.

At the funeral, his war buddies told me that the week before, Len had made some mistakes on the job. They weren't life-and-death mistakes, but his errors in reading certain lab results had messed up some patient's treatment plan. Len was a dedicated lab technician. He simply could not handle the guilt, not on top of all the survivor guilt he felt about the people he couldn't save or who had lost an arm or leg in Iraq. Len used to hear their voices in the night.

I also found out that Len had gone to great lengths to save a certain Iraqi family. The family was massacred anyway. Len blamed himself.

Is that why he made my life miserable? When Len was angry, nothing was safe. Furniture flew, curtains were ripped, toys were smashed. The name-calling was vicious, and PTA meetings, visits to the grandparents, and all shopping trips for the children were canceled. I could hardly ever take the kids to the movies, and we never invited anyone over for dinner.

If I felt a beating coming on, I'd lock the children in their bedrooms or, if there was time, drive them to my mother's. Eventually, however, Len would wear out and everything would be peaceful. Sincerely repentant, he would shower us with love and many gifts.

I'm sorry Len is dead, but a part of me feels released. I was tired of walking on eggshells and having one anxiety attack after another. My think-ing had become distorted, too, as I was always trying to find answers to prob-lems over which I had no control. I was always irritable and depressed, and when he'd be gone for hours, wandering aimlessly in the streets, I didn't know who was closer to suicide, him or me.

Not knowing how I could change my life, I started taking valium and then alcohol. When I realized that my drinking was making me neglect my children, however, I went to AA, and I have been a sober and good mother ever since. But Len remembered my drinking days and my mothering mistakes and sometimes used them as excuses to physically abuse me.

Over time, I became increasingly passive and numb to my own emotions, as well as psychologically depleted from dealing with my husband's Dr. Jekyll/Mr. Hyde personality. He would be the brute one day and Mr. Wonderful the next, leaving me in a constant state of confusion about whether to stay with him or leave him.

Now that Len is gone, I miss him. I think he was basically a good man, but a misguided one. There were times he was so loving, so giving, so charming that he melted my heart. I still have trouble reconciling my affection for him with his abuse of me. I can't blame Iraq for all his problems, but I am certain that if he hadn't seen war, he would have been a different man.

I have never set foot in Iraq. Yet I consider myself a veteran also. I lived, breathed, slept, and fought with that war for years, and it will probably stay with me until the day I die.

8

"Why do I stay?"

Battered Women

I met Bill right after he was discharged from the Army. He seemed kind and was extremely charming. My parents, however, protested my seeing him. They felt he had a "dark side." But I thought they were just prejudiced against military men. In their view, men who joined the military were "losers" who couldn't find a job anywhere else.

Six months after the wedding I found out that Bill really did have a dark side. The abuse began slowly and insidiously. I didn't count his slapping me and sitting on top of me as abuse. Even when he threw things at me or locked me up in rooms, I didn't consider myself battered.

Me, an educated woman with a master's degree, battered? My shrink had to be out of her mind. When she first used the word battered, I was not even fully aware of what she was talking about. Sure, Bill and I had our difficulties. But didn't every married couple? He wasn't that bad, was he? If Bill was angry, it was my fault, or that war's fault, I supposed. All I had to do to make things better was to keep improving myself and help Bill readjust to civilian life.

Last Memorial Day, Bill pushed me out of the car into the rain. It was midnight and he had taken my house keys, my credit cards, and my paycheck. At that moment, I realized that maybe my shrink was right: maybe I was an abused woman. After all, my life seemed to revolve around avoiding Bill's anger and doing whatever I could so as not to "set him off." I couldn't even make a doctor's appointment for the children without obtaining his "permission" first, even though I earned most of the money in the family.

Up until this point, I had lived in denial, just like he did. Together we minimized my physical injuries and my mental sufferings and blamed everything on the war. I firmly believe that Bill's war experiences did play a role. Bill was a trained killer who had somehow not gotten the fight out of him. Being in the Special Forces, he had been asked to kill certain people. That wasn't always possible without innocent people being harmed as well. Having learned violence as a problem-solving technique in the military, he felt free to use it in our marriage. The war had also taught him that it was okay to push around women.

I left Bill several times, but he would always hunt me down. Once he kidnapped me and the kids from a friend's home. Breaking into my friend's house was peanuts to him. He was skilled at scaling walls and other such tactics. After each episode of violence, however, he was the most loving and wonderful husband and father imaginable. The children would scold me for having wanted to leave him. Since Daddy was being so "nice" now, they felt I should forgive him as I did them whenever they misbehaved.

When I try telling people about my marriage, they usually turn around and tell me that I am as "sick" as Bill is. Even my therapist thinks I'm crazy. Very few people, it seems, understand the powerful forces that keep a woman trapped in an abusive situation. They also fail to understand how war can change a man. Sure, Bill had problems before the war, but I am certain that my life with Bill would be altogether different if he had never gone to war. There is a lot of good in Bill, despite his abusiveness.

—TESSA, WIFE OF A SPECIAL SERVICES OFFICER

Not all combat veterans batter their partners. Yet domestic violence is a problem in some military and veteran homes, as it is in society at large. Because women are the primary victims of battering, this chapter is addressed to women. This is not intended to minimize the harsh reality that men are also battered by their partners and that battering can be found among gay and lesbian couples as well as heterosexual ones. Furthermore, male, gay, and lesbian victims usually find it even more difficult than heterosexual women to ask for help and find support.

What Is Battering?

While definitions vary, most researchers agree that a battered woman (or man) is one who has received at least two or three deliberate and severe physical assaults within an intimate or bonded relationship. The physical abuse can include a wide variety of bodily assaults: slapping, hitting, punching with fists, attacks with broken glass or weapons, burning, biting, pushing, slamming against walls, and shoving down steps. In many states, not only the violent act but also the threat of violence is considered a crime. Psychological humiliation and degradation almost always accompany the physical abuse. However, the threat of violence must exist in a relationship if it is to be considered a battering one. The woman must know that her partner is capable of directing blows at her and perhaps, ultimately, of killing her or someone else—for example, one of her children, family members, or friends.

Yet it is not necessary for a woman to be continually beaten in order to feel terrorized or humiliated into a submissive posture. One or two beatings or threats of violence, accompanied by infrequent inflicting of physical pain or actual torture, are sufficient to establish a pattern of male domination by force. One wife was beaten twice soon after her husband's return from combat. For years since, she has kept quiet, hiding her innermost needs and feelings from her husband for fear of being hit. A few months ago, she summoned the courage to assert herself and ask some questions about a touchy issue. As expected, she was assaulted and now lives in fear. These infrequent assaults are enough to "keep her in her place."

For a pattern of battering to be shown, there must be at least two deliberate, severe physical attacks. Almost any aspect of abuse can occur once or twice. But if it occurs three times and the woman is still in the relationship, the relationship is considered a battering one. Abuse occurring once or twice could reflect an isolated instance of lack of control or extreme circumstances. However, three instances indicate that the woman has become emotionally, socially, economically, spiritually, or otherwise entrapped by her mate.

The Multidimensional Aspects of Battering

Although physical cruelty must exist in order for the relationship to be considered a battering one, battering is multidimensional. It includes not only physical and emotional abuse, but economic, social, sexual, and, for some, spiritual abuse as well. Economic battering refers to the use of money as a coercive tool by the abuser. Social battering refers to the abuser's attempts to isolate the woman and severely limit or control her interactions with others, including neighbors, friends, coworkers, relatives, or even her own children. Sexual abuse refers to any form of coerced sexual activity or to any use of sexuality as a means of manipulation or humiliation. Spiritual abuse refers to using religious or spiritual beliefs as a way of punishing or degrading a woman. It also refers to using physical force or psychological manipulations to control a woman's spiritual or religious beliefs and practices.

Here are some specific examples of these types of abuse:

Physical abuse: Pushing, shoving; being held down or locked in the house to be prevented from leaving; slapping, biting, kicking, choking, hitting, punching; having things thrown at you; being abandoned in dangerous places; rape, threats of harm; being subjected to reckless driving or being prevented from driving; being refused help when sick, injured, or pregnant.

Social abuse: Lack of freedom to chose friends; attempts to isolate you from others, including family members; verbal humiliation before, during, or after social events; refusal to attend social functions you want or need to attend; social events used as weapon—delay in making commitment to attend; attendance as a reward for compliance to demands; unpredictable behavior with reference to social events; control over health care.

Economic abuse: Control over family finances, including victim's earnings; control over whether or not victim works and choice of job; on-the-job harassment; calling victim's employers and coworkers to make threats or demean the victim; control over monies for health care, children's needs, and family obligations/events such as calls, gifts, visits, attendance at birthday parties, funerals, weddings, and other family social events or events of religious significance.

Emotional abuse: Ignoring your feelings, ridiculing or insulting women as a group; insulting your cherished beliefs, religion, occupation, race, heritage, or class; withholding approval or affection as a means of punishing you; criticizing/calling you names; shouting at you; insulting your family or friends; refusing to socialize with you; humiliating you; refusing to work or share money; punishing the children or other loved ones when he is mad at you; threatening to kidnap the children if you leave; abusing pets to hurt you; manipulating you with lies and contradictions; making all the decisions.

Sexual abuse: Making demeaning remarks about women or your sexual desirability; insisting that you dress in a more sexual way than you want; minimizing the importance of your feelings about sex; criticizing any aspect of your sexuality; forcing sex (in general, after a beating); forcing sadistic or other unwanted sex acts; withholding sex and affection; insisting on unwanted touching; publicly showing interest in other potential sex partners; having affairs with others after promising monogamy.

Spiritual abuse: Mocking your religious or spiritual beliefs; deliberately distorting such beliefs so as to undercut your self-confidence; using your beliefs to coerce you into an unwanted activity; obstructing your attendance at or participation in religious observances and services; forcing you to commit acts that contradict your religious or spiritual standards; repeatedly reminding you of ways you have failed to live up to these standards; insisting that his abuse of you serves a religious or spiritual purpose.

The Battering Cycle

The battering cycle characterizes many battering relationships. In her work with thousands of battered women, researcher Lenore Walker found that battering is neither random nor constant, especially when the abuse occurs in the context of a marriage or sexual relationship. Instead, in many but not all cases, battering occurs in a repeated pattern with three distinct stages: the tension-building stage, the acute battering incident, and the phase of kindness and contrite, loving behavior—the "honeymoon" stage.[1]

In stage 1, the tension-building stage, tensions arise between the partners that ultimately lead to stage 2, the acute battering incident. Then follows stage 3, the honeymoon stage. Typically in this stage, the man is loving and kind and promises never again to hurt the woman or in some other way implies that the violence may be over. The abuser's repentance is totally believable and the woman has faith that there will be no more violence. The abuser may also believe that he will never again be violent. (In contrast, veterans whose abusiveness is linked only to combat trauma, not other factors, live in dread of their next outburst of violence. They have little confidence in their ability to control themselves, which is the source of much shame.)

Stage 3 is powerful. In the case of the battered woman, it is in this stage that her drama of love and romance is renewed. In hopes that her marriage or relationship is not really dead, she forgives her partner and stays. This stage accounts for the enigmatic ability of abuse victims to quickly forget painful episodes, sometimes almost as soon as they occur, or to minimize them.

The battering cycle disproves the theory that battered women are masochists who stay in abusive relationships because they like violence. Most battered women stay for the kiss, not the fist: that is, for the love and attention of stage 3, not the anxiety and physical and emotional pain of stages 1 and 2. Hence battered women who have difficulty breaking away from their abuser or who have mixed feelings toward him should not be considered "sick." They may have protective, loving feelings toward him because of the stage 3 affection he has showered upon them.

How Prevalent Is Battering?

Current estimates are that anywhere from one-tenth to one-third of all married couples engage in spousal assault.[2] More than one million abused women seek medical attention for injuries caused by battering each year.[3] Some studies show that at least 20 percent of the visits to emergency rooms by women are the result of battering. Since battering by intimate partners causes more injury to women than auto accidents, rapes, or muggings, it may come as no surprise that four women a day in this country die as the result of domestic violence.[4] However, many researchers, as well as official military and other government documents, note that wife abuse, like child abuse, tends to be underreported.[5] There are also couples where the woman perpetrates the violence or where both partners are abusive. However, male-to-female violence generally results in more serious injuries and death than female-to-male violence.

Men from all social groups batter—rich men, poor men, white men, men of color, professors, and even clergymen. There is some evidence, however, that there is a greater prevalence of woman battering among low-income people.[6] This difference may reflect the negative effects of poverty. It may also reflect the fact that statistics about battering are gathered not only from police reports but also from publicly funded facilities and clinics that tend to be frequented more by poor and low-income women than those women who can afford help from private doctors or facilities. Some studies have also found more family violence among African American and Hispanic families than among European American families.[7] However, these ethnic differences are related to differences in income level. When rates of partner abuse are compared for families with similar income levels, ethnic differences all but disappear.[8]

To date, we do not know whether veterans batter their partners more or less than any other group of men. Several studies have found battering to be more frequent among male Vietnam veterans with PTSD than those without PTSD.[9] However, these studies involved relatively small samples of combat vets and veterans from the Vietnam era only. Hence the finding that combat veterans had higher rates of partner abuse than nonveterans cannot be generalized to all Vietnam combat veterans nor to veterans of other wars, for whom there are few statistics on domestic violence.

In the general population, rates of wife abuse tend to be highest among couples in their twenties and thirties and to decline as the couples enter their forties and fifties.[10] However, studies completed in the late 1990s found that some 3 to 6 percent of Americans over fifty are being physically abused by a family member.[11] How many of these older persons are partners of combat veterans or combat veterans themselves is unknown.

Why Women Stay

It is easy to understand women who leave violent homes and much harder to understand those who remain with their batterers. Women stay for numerous reasons, chief among them being the battering cycle (described above) and finances. Many battered women are economically dependent on their husbands. Even if they are employed, they might not be able to support themselves and their children on their salary alone. This is especially the case if the abuser has control over the family finances and she cannot expect her fair share of the marital assets should she leave. Military wives may fear that if they report the

228 "why do i stay?"

abuse, their husband will not be promoted or may be expelled from the service, resulting in the loss of his income and military benefits for the family.

Another compelling reason women stay is because they've been warned that if they leave, they will be injured or killed, or that one of their children or relatives will be harmed. Indeed, statistics indicate that women are more likely to be attacked, or killed, by their batterer after they leave him than when they are at home with him. Some women stay because the batterer has threatened suicide. In my experience, the departure of the battered spouse often precipitated severe depressions, suicidal thoughts, panic attacks, alcohol binges, or other significant psychiatric problems in wife-abusing veterans.

Some women are more vulnerable to entrapment in long-term abuse than others. The more vulnerable women include those who:

- believe that love, that is, their love or the strength of their will to make a marriage work, "conquers all";

- believe in traditional roles for women: not that being a wife and mother is important, but that being a wife and mother is *all important* and that it would be a *terrible crime or sin or a sign of deep personal failure* not to be a "good" wife and mother (*"good" wife and mother* being defined as willing to try hard enough and willing to sacrifice enough so that a marriage or relationship lasts, no matter what the costs);

- have strong religious or spiritual beliefs against separation and divorce;

- have few skills, little education, or for other reasons have few economic alternatives to marriage;

- are physically or mentally disabled: women in wheelchairs, deaf and blind women, women with MS, mentally retarded women, and so forth;

- have few legal rights due to being illegal immigrants or involved in lives of crime;

- live in communities where wife beating is accepted and/or communities with few resources for abused women, such as in many rural communities;

- become progressively isolated from family members and friends

(Note: Once the pattern of increased isolation begins, the woman has fewer and fewer connections with outside sources of validation of her worth and competence and the abuser's negative view of her becomes more dominant.);

• grew up in a violent home or were in prior violent love relationships that were somehow more violent or abusive than their current (abusive) relationship;

• believe on some level that they are unlovable, worthless, not "good enough," flawed, scarred, or inadequate due to prior emotionally (and or physically) abusive relationships, especially if the negative messages about the self were instilled during childhood;

• have learned to dissociate or "go numb" or into denial when abused because this was a coping mechanism from prior abusive relationships;

• feel shame about some trait they feel is negative or have a history of eating disorders or other addiction (which may have been the result of some kind of abuse situation);

• feel indebted to their husband/lover because he helped rescue them from a negative situation;

• are emotionally vulnerable because they have prior feelings of guilt or inferiority on which the abuser plays; because they are young in age or young emotionally and don't have a strong sense of self due to their limited experiences, protected upbringing, or other factors;

• have a poor support system: lack supportive friends, family members, ministers, or communities; lack civic, legal, and police support;

• have venereal diseases or feel they are unattractive;

• are actively alcoholic, have an eating disorder or drug addiction, are clinically depressed, or suffer from a severe anxiety or dissociative disorder or psychosis;

• become physically or mentally impaired due to the abuse (once they have been negatively affected, it is harder for them to mobilize the resources, energy, and will to leave);

- are in a relationship where the abuser threatens not only them but also their relatives, children, coworkers, pets;

- are in a relationship where the abuser is a pillar of the community or well thought of;

- came from families where there was marital conflict and are trying to undo memories of childhood by having a "perfect" marriage —no matter what the cost; and

- are in a relationship where the abuser provides something she desperately needs: affection, financial support for herself (or her family), help in her career, and help with child care.

Why Men Batter

Perhaps the most common question asked about the battered woman is "Why does she stay?" This question seems to put the responsibility for the violence on the victim rather than on the power holder. As described above, there are many reasons why women stay. However, the more important issue is not why women stay, but *why do men batter?*

There is no single cause. Woman battering usually stems from many factors, some of which are described below. If you are being battered by the man you love, some of these reasons may apply to your situation; some may not. In general, abuse is especially prevalent in homes where the veteran is addicted to alcohol or drugs, where he suffers from a neurological disorder or untreated medical problem, or where he has a character disorder or is overtly paranoid. It also tends to be more prevalent in homes where the veteran suffers from an untreated combat-related condition.

Combat-Related versus Noncombat-Related Battering

Unfortunately the media has helped to perpetrate the false notion that having been in combat turns a man into a woman or child beater. However, battering is not inherent to nor is it a symptom of PTSD, depression, dissociation, or any other form of combat trauma. Yet some vets do batter, and for some the battering is combat related.

In some cases, woman battering is the direct result of the vet's confusing his partner with enemy soldiers in the midst of a flashback or a paranoid state resulting from an extreme state of hyperarousal due to being severely triggered. In other cases, a wife or girlfriend may be assaulted because—without prior warning—she approached her veteran from behind, thus stimulating his startle response, which put him into "combat mode."[12]

As described in chapter 3, irritability, hyperalertness, hypervigilance, and proneness to angry outbursts are common signs of hyperarousal. When a PTSD-afflicted veteran feels threatened—for example, if he experiences someone as being hostile toward him—his body automatically goes into "survival mode." In this state, his abilities to accurately assess the situation, as well as his abilities to control his verbal and physical aggressiveness, are severely compromised.[13] Hyperarousal with its resulting readiness to attack may have served life-preserving functions in combat. However, it can wreak havoc in interpersonal, especially intimate, relationships. When hyperarousal is combined with alcohol, which for some men loosens inhibitions against aggression, emotional and physical abuse are even more likely.[14]

Veterans who batter can be divided into two groups: veterans whose battering is a direct result of combat trauma, and veterans whose battering cannot be attributed primarily to combat trauma and who would have probably become violent toward their wife or girlfriend even if they had never seen war. Combat may have intensified their need to batter, and some of their battering may be related to PTSD or to some other form of traumatic stress. However, the root of their aggression stems more from a history of family violence, a personality disorder, or any number of other sources. For the purposes of this chapter, this second group of veterans will be referred to as "typical" batterers in that they more closely resemble civilian batterers than men who would probably never have battered if they hadn't fought in a war.

There are many similarities between these two groups. There are also many important differences. Battering that stems from combat trauma is usually sporadic and is associated with situations that trigger a veteran's combat memories or that are related to a distinct symptom of PTSD, depression, or dissociation. Unlike the typical batterer, the vet doesn't feel entitled to hurt the woman he loves. Neither does he blame her for his behavior. Instead, he takes responsibility for the assault and suffers from intense feelings of shame and guilt afterwards.

In contrast, the typical batterer blames his aggression on the woman. Afterwards, he may minimize the impact of his behavior or deny it altogether. Statements such as these are common: "You're imagining things again. I didn't hit you. You probably bruised yourself on purpose just to make me look bad in front of the kids." Or: "Okay, so I pushed you around a little. I was only joking. I didn't mean to hurt you. Besides, you aren't hurt that bad." In contrast, the veterans I've worked with whose violence is primarily combat related not only recognize but also sometimes exaggerate the extent of the injuries they've inflicted. Because they are trained killers, they're often terrified by how much more harm they could have caused. Veterans who battered in the midst of a state of dissociation or emotional numbing or in the midst of a flashback or nightmare are especially frightened of themselves.

The typical batterer may experience and express remorse. Even when the remorse is genuine rather than manipulative, it is usually short-lived. He also tends to forget his past acts of violence. In contrast, the veteran with combat-related battering tends not to forget his actions. Quite to the contrary, he tends to dwell on it for quite some time, usually with much guilt. Often he lives in dire fear his PTSD or other form of combat trauma may result in his lashing out at the woman he loves once again. In some cases, he may decide to leave his wife or partner rather than risk losing control in the future. In contrast, the typical batterer does everything in his power to hold on to the woman, even to the point of mutilating himself or threatening suicide.

Other differences between the two groups are that unlike veterans whose battering stems primarily from combat trauma, veterans who more closely resemble typical civilian batterers may force their partners to do illegal things; display extreme jealousy; use jealousy as an excuse to batter; threaten to spread rumors; have a past history of violence (including cruelty to animals); and blame all their problems on others. They also tend to employ all the various forms of abuse described above (that is, physical, emotional, sexual, spiritual, economic, and social abuse) to entrap the woman. In contrast, battering that is primarily combat related involves physical abuse and emotional abuse, but not all the other forms of abuse.

When battering is severe and persistent and when it involves the full spectrum of abuse that constitutes a true battering relationship, combat trauma is not the culprit. In such situations, a veteran's need to batter his wife or girlfriend may have been intensified by his war experiences, but it stems primarily from other sources.

In cases where an untreated combat-related condition (such as PTSD or depression) interacts with another disorder (such as alcohol or drug addiction, neurological damage due to war injuries, or untreated diabetes or another medical condition), it is difficult to determine which is primary: the traumatic reaction or the other disorder. However, the result is the same—a physically abused and emotionally scarred wife or girlfriend.

The Role of Alcohol

Many studies of battering in the general population have found a clear relationship between alcohol consumption and marital psychological and physical violence.[15] In addition, there is some evidence that the quantity of alcohol consumed, especially if it is beer or hard liquor as opposed to wine, is more predictive of abusiveness than the frequency of drinking: that is, men who batter don't necessarily drink more often than men who don't, but batterers tend to drink larger quantities of alcohol.[16] A study of Vietnam veterans also found that the drinking quantity, rather than drinking frequency, was related to some limited extent to physical and emotional abuse.[17] However, this study was conducted on fewer than four hundred Vietnam veterans who admitted their violence toward their partners. Hence its results cannot be generalized to all Vietnam veterans or to veterans of other wars, for whom there is little or no information on the relationship between substance abuse and battering.

Traditional Views about Men's and Women's Roles

Batterers frequently adhere to the traditional male sex-role stereotype, which dictates that "real men" should appear unemotional, always strong, and never confused.[18] A veteran who holds this stereotype might panic when his feelings about the war rise to the surface. Feeling out of control and emasculated (by his own emotions, which, except for anger, he may view as "feminine"), he may attempt to regain a sense of control and affirm his manhood by battering. Battering also helps release the mounting adrenaline caused by his pent-up emotions and inner turmoil.

He may also try to feel "manly" by attempting to control his wife or girlfriend by other means, such as by making excessive demands on her, by restricting her financially, or by isolating her from others. However, if she resists his attempts to control her, or otherwise frustrates him, he may resort to violence in order to assume a position of dominance.

In my experience, violence in the home seems to erupt when the woman does not meet the veteran's expectation that she can make life smooth for him, when he feels threatened by her need for intimacy, or when he somehow feels emasculated by her strengths. While these dynamics also exist in nonveteran homes, they are especially prevalent in homes where the vet is still struggling with an untreated traumatic reaction or with untreated substance abuse. They are also especially prevalent in homes where the veteran holds to what are now severely challenged, if not totally outmoded, notions of the woman's role. Due to his particular upbringing or mode of thinking he may still believe that women should be submissive partners, or wives and mothers and little else. When his partner's behavior or attitude contradicts his beliefs about how a woman should be or act, he may batter in an attempt to reinstate the traditional sex roles with which he is more comfortable and which assign him a position of dominance.

Economic and Emotional Dependence

While battering is not limited to any particular population of men, it has been found to be more prevalent among families experiencing financial pressures, frequent moves, and isolation from peer groups and family support systems—characteristics of some veteran families. A related problem is that in some homes, the vet is economically or emotionally dependent on his wife. He may sense his dependency and resent it. It insults his masculinity and sense of control. As a result, he may batter to maintain superiority.

Childhood History of Family Violence

In my experience, some of the most severe and long-term cases of woman battering exist in homes where the vet came from a violent family where he saw his mother being beaten and, perhaps, was beaten also. Because he was socialized to see violence as normal, it may be harder for him to unlearn violence as a coping mechanism, especially if he still harbors unresolved feelings regarding the abuse he saw or endured as a child. In addition, if his mother spent most of her time avoiding beatings, or recovering from them, the vet may have suffered from inadequate physical and emotional nurturing as a child. In his partner, he may hope to find the mother he never had. When she fails to meet his needs, he may become quickly furious.

The fact that boys who grow up in violent homes are more likely to have problems with aggression as children and more likely to batter their wives and children has been supported consistently by research studies conducted on both civilian and military samples.[19] Although most abused boys do not become abusive adults, they are up to a thousand times more likely to abuse their wives than boys from nonviolent homes.[20]

On the other hand, many boys who grow up seeing their fathers beat their mothers develop such a repugnance for violence they have trouble disciplining their own children in even the mildest ways. As small boys, they may have tried to stop the violence or, at the very least, wished to do so. Because they were physically incapable of controlling their father's aggression, they may have felt like failures. However, as adolescents they may have been physically able to protect their mother by standing up to their father or even assaulting him. I have worked with many veterans who grew up with abuse who have made every effort to avoid repeating the cycle of violence with their own families, to treat their wives as they wished their father had treated their mother, and to give their children the warm loving home they never had.

Military Training and Combat Experience

Combat veterans who batter are similar to other abusers in that they may batter out of a need to control and feel masculine and because they have few other means of expressing their needs and frustrations. However, physically abusive veterans differ from other batterers in that their military training and experience not only gave them permission but, in some cases, encouraged them to give in to, rather than to restrain, their violent impulses. In addition, most vets received intensive training in a variety of fighting techniques.

Untreated PTSD, Depression, or Other Traumatic Reactions

One psychological factor leading to woman battering among combat veterans can be the unresolved grief and rage that underlie the symptoms of PTSD, depression, or other reactions to combat trauma.[21] For some men, it is easier to lash out at a wife or girlfriend than to deal with the seemingly insurmountable amounts of pain and anger within. Some of their pain and anger may be left over from combat, but some of it stems from their frustration and disappointment with the present, as in the case of David.

"Why do I hit her when she's all I got?" asked David.

"Why do you think you do?" I asked.

"Because she's there, the safest available target."

"Who do you really want to hit?"

"Some of the jerks I served with, my CO, my boss, myself."

David entered therapy in an extreme state of psychic numbing. As his emotions began to surface, he began to panic. The feelings seemed to overwhelm him at times. He felt out of control, almost powerless, over his inner life.

Most people do not like to feel powerless—over anything. For combat veterans (both male and female) being overwhelmed by emotion may be experienced as shameful evidence of cowardice, incompetence, lack of loyalty, and other forms of personal failure. Some may batter their partners as a defense against such feelings. (These dynamics may be similar for those female veterans who feel they must prove to their comrades that they aren't "emotional" or "hysterical" women unfit for military duty but that they are just as emotionally controlled as male soldiers allegedly are.) For example, David frequently felt powerless in Afghanistan. Once he was ordered to shoot into a deserted hut. David objected, but his CO insisted. As it turned out, inside the hut were two abandoned toddlers.

"I swear, I didn't know there were two kids in there, I swear," David bawled in one session. "And I could have killed my CO." But David didn't kill his CO. He never even spoke to his CO (or anyone else) about the incident. Soon afterward, however, as a means of atonement, David began befriending children in a nearby orphanage. Five weeks later, guerrillas blew up the orphanage. All the children were killed. "After that, I gave up," says David. "I didn't care about nothin' except getting home alive."

Upon David's return to the United States, his wife did not want to hear about Afghanistan. He could not find a job he liked and hadn't anticipated that filing for his government benefits would require so much paperwork. Once again, he decided "not to care."

He claimed to have put Afghanistan out of his mind until his wife unexpectedly became pregnant. He was also in the midst of a career crisis. With a baby on the way, David desperately needed a raise. In his line of work, however, only those who were willing to socialize with potential clients during the evening and travel to conferences could hope for a pay raise. David didn't like to be away from home for extended periods of time. His home was his sanctuary, his refuge from the stresses of the day, one of the few places he felt safe.

He also detested business lunches and gatherings because they involved protracted interactions with business associates and others who weren't combat veterans, people whom he felt had taken the easy way out by choosing not to serve their country. The few times David did try socializing as the job required, he was so exhausted by the massive effort it took for him to control his anger and contempt for some of the people he was with, he broke out into hives.

After the hives subsided, he was so distraught by his inability to handle the situation and his realization that his combat trauma was impeding his career that he was unable to concentrate on his work for weeks. He then became afraid that his slide in work performance, if noticed, would endanger his job, thus exacerbating his feelings of inadequacy as a breadwinner. Under these stressful conditions, he began hitting his wife and threatening to throw her down the stairs or puncture her ovaries if she ever became pregnant again. Or, fearing his anger, he'd withdraw from her altogether and spend his nights in a park or go to the mountains for days.

If she would not consent to an abortion, he planned to leave her. On the other hand, he felt that abortion was a form of murder. Seeing no solution to the problem, he became angrier and angrier at his wife, who he felt had tricked him into impregnating her. His wife, however, claims that the pregnancy was a total surprise.

As David's case illustrates, unresolved PTSD can play a key role in abuse, with a greater frequency and severity of battering occurring among couples where the veteran has yet to deal with his grief, guilt, and rage. For example, incidents can be precipitated by the death or serious injury of a family member. The veteran, in a state of psychic numbing, may show no apparent emotion. However, when his partner begins to grieve or openly react, the veteran may batter her as an attempt to cope with the pain which her emotional response brings to his awareness.

In one instance, a vet's sister-in-law died in childbirth. He showed no emotion until his wife picked up the phone to make arrangements to attend the funeral. Screaming that there was no need to make any reservations because the sister-in-law wasn't really dead, he pulled the phone out of the wall and punched his wife in the stomach and face. In another instance, a child received second-degree oil burns in a kitchen accident. The vet refused to accompany his wife to the hospital. In his view, the child was not injured. Even when the child returned home in bandages, the vet was emotionless and said nothing. The next day the wife began to cry as she changed the dressings on the child's wounds. The vet accused her of overreacting and choked the cat. When the wife intervened, the vet choked her.

Beatings also may occur on patriotic holidays or when a veteran encounters frustrations with bureaucracies—like waiting in long lines and other delays—even though the wife may be the veteran's righthand partner in the process of obtaining his rights. Mary Elizabeth, for example, was constantly contacting veterans benefits offices for her husband, Walter, who became irrational or depressed when he had to deal with government officials. Since being discharged, Walter had been unable to work and she also was the sole support of the family. Yet Walter abused her, especially on patriotic holidays.

One Fourth of July Walter tied her to the bedpost for two days. Using one of his combat knifes, he scraped the names of dead buddies on her stomach. He later left to buy some beer, and he came back with a dozen live crabs also. He put Mary Elizabeth in the bathtub with the crabs and tried to re-create water tortures he had seen overseas. When a neighbor unexpectedly came to the door, Mary Elizabeth somehow managed to slip away and lock herself in her bedroom. Now she wanted to kill herself.

My suggestion that her desire to commit suicide might reflect her suppressed anger toward Walter was not well received. Mary Elizabeth insisted that she understood why Walter was violent and listed all the traumas he had experienced during combat which, in her mind, excused his behavior. Similarly, Amy, who arrived at her first counseling session with a black eye and two missing teeth, felt that the military was responsible for her boyfriend's outbursts. He had been wounded overseas, and when he was in pain from his injuries, he would prevent her from leaving the home and, sometimes, batter her.

While not all women are so "understanding," many blame anything but their partners for the violence. Such thinking, however, is a form of denial that only serves to help the woman "forgive" and resigns her to a life of violence.

Other women report that their husbands or boyfriends hit them and then ask for forgiveness because, after all, it was just their combat trauma acting up. There is, however, no excuse—not even PTSD—for a beating or any other form of abuse.

Combat-related battering is sporadic and lessens when the vet learns to identify and constructively express his leftover anger, grief, and guilt from his war experiences and when he learns to root his sense of mastery, competency, and achievement in developing his skills and talents rather than in dominating a woman. He also must learn to accept his own emotions and see them as part of the human condition rather than as signs of "feminine weakness." Renewed pride in himself, as a combat vet and as a competent person, usually reduces his need to batter in order to feel powerful, important, or masculine.

Summary

After their firsthand experiences with blood and death, some vets recoil from all forms of violence. Others, however, find themselves "on guard" and "ready to attack" even at home. Yet there are important differences between a veteran who batters his partner or child primarily as the result of his combat experiences and the one whose tendencies toward violence may have been exacerbated by conflict, but originate in noncombat-related emotional problems. In the former, violence is infrequent; is usually followed by prolonged periods of guilt, self-blame, and withdrawal from the partner; is usually restricted to physical and emotional abuse and rarely involves economic, social, or other forms of abuse; and typically occurs during certain flashbacks to combat-related experiences, in times of family loss or injury, or when the vet is feeling powerless over his emotions, his finances, his personal relationships, or some other aspect of his life. Sometimes physically attacking a family member is an attempt to recapture a sense of control and to affirm one's strength and masculinity.

In contrast, battering that stems primarily from noncombat-related issues tends to be frequent or long-term; occurs in the absence of current stresses or of reminders of war (as well as in response to such triggers); and involves social, economic, spiritual, and sexual abuse as well as emotional and physical abuse. Here batterers take little or no responsibility for their violence and blame the woman for "provoking" them. Although they may express some remorse, it is short-lived. If they do withdraw from their partner following a beating, their withdrawal is usually short-lived as well. Soon they resume their effort to monitor and control her. If they became anesthetized to violence in combat, they may trivialize her injuries and thereby support her denial that she isn't hurt "that bad."

Like women being abused by nonveterans, the battered partners of combat veterans often fail to realize the extent to which they are being abused until they are severely injured, or until one of their children develops a problem. Even if children do not become directly involved in the violence, they will suffer psychological damage from living in a home where they see their mother being abused. Since domestic violence tends to escalate over time, eventually the children will witness or discover the parental "secret" and imitate the parental patterns of victim, aggressor, or both. Like children from alcoholic homes, children from violent homes tend to feel responsible for the family turbulence and, in some cases, suffer from long-term guilt over what they did or didn't do to cause or to prevent the assaults.

When they become adolescents, children from violent homes may act out the violence they have seen at home by being violent either toward themselves, others, or both. Some may run away from home or stay absent from the home for long periods of time. Just as their mothers can develop a severe depression, PTSD, or another traumatic reaction (and perhaps a substance problem as well) from living in a state of constant danger, children from violent homes can also develop traumatic reactions or addictions of varying degrees of severity.

RAY'S STORY

Two weeks after Samantha came home from the Persian Gulf, her boy-friend called her a "baby killer" and moved in with another woman. Funny, I was glued to the TV during that entire war but I never heard anyone, even war protestors, call the Gulf troops "baby killers," especially female troops.

In fact, my Sam never fired a shot. "I'm no hero," she says. "All I did was pick up dead bodies and dig graves for dead animals." Sam was stunned to see that some of the enemy dead were small boys or old men. Sam grew up on a farm, so she felt sorry for the animals, too. The first time she collected pieces of American dead, she wet herself and vomited. Then and there Sam decided she was a coward.

Sam doesn't drink much, but one night she had a few too many. It was then she told me about how after a while sometimes she'd look at her buddies and imagine them being blown to bits. Their body parts would scatter every-where, including all over her hair and face. One afternoon she had this vision about a soldier sitting next to her. An hour later, the soldier was blown to bits. Sam feels responsible for this death and I can't convince her otherwise.

Sam doesn't feel she deserves the medals she got. She doesn't even feel she deserves to have nightmares because, in her view, she never saw combat. She thinks she encountered less racism in the military than her father and great-uncle did and she feels guilty about that, too. Yet her dad thinks that the reason Sam never got to use some of her advanced skills was because of racist notions about African Americans making inferior soldiers.

It's because of all these crazy guilts that Sam keeps putting off our wed-ding. She's afraid that her punishment for being such a coward and for that soldier's death will be that something bad will happen to me. She's also scared that she might have been exposed to some of kind of slow-acting poison gas and that any day now she might suddenly die or become a cripple. Given that, it wouldn't be fair to me for her to marry me.

Every time I get the sniffles, she thinks that maybe she's infected me and calls me five times a day to make sure I'm okay. That drives me nuts. My boss doesn't appreciate it either. Once I got so annoyed with all the calls I told her to "get over that stupid war" and start acting like a "normal person." Later I apologized, but the damage was done. I had really hurt her.

But her unrealistic fears hurt me, too. Almost every time I want to do or go some place new, she comes up with a list of fifteen things that could go wrong. Her "danger list" plays on all my self-doubts and I can't make progress in my life. I think she's cynical, she thinks I'm naïve, and we fight all the time about this. I love her dearly, but her concerns about my well-being are suffocating me. She doesn't know how to have fun either, and that drags me down, too.

When Sam doesn't show up for a date, I never know if she was up half the night pacing the floor or off somewhere helping some veteran. But if I'm in a jam, she's there for me, every time. Sometimes her family calls her "Whack Job" or "our crazy lazy vet." Yet when there's a crisis, who do they call? Sam.

Last Christmas Sam's sister gave her a box of sand containing broken pieces of a doll. When Sam opened the box, her whole body started shaking, and then her sister laughed at Sam for a good ten minutes. But guess who this sister made executor of her will? Sam. When Sam's sister's ex-husband was dying, she turned to Sam, not to her brother or to her new husband, for strength. Sam was so busy on the phone with her sister and driving her back and forth to the hospital, she forgot my birthday. She even paid for the funeral with money she had been setting aside for our dream vacation.

With Sam, everything is a matter of life and death. We could be making love and if the phone rings, she has to pick it up. After all, it could be an emergency. If it turns out that someone needs something, she throws on her clothes, thanks me for being so understanding, then dashes out the door. At first I was understanding. But now I want to shove her cell phone down the garbage disposal and grind it to bits. Some of the people she helps are just using her. She says that she knows that but she can't refuse anyone in need, especially a veteran. It's her way of saying "thanks" for coming home alive and paying for her failures during the war.

I couldn't ask for a kinder, more considerate girlfriend. She adores me, yet there's distance between us because she's not telling me certain things. But that could be my fault, too. She can probably sense that I don't really want to hear about some of the awful things she saw overseas. I wonder, too, if some day her feelings of guilt and failure about the war will make her feel so unworthy of my love that I'll lose her altogether.

9

"I have to be twice as good"

Women Veterans: Achievements and Injustice

I was proud to have been one of the over 229,000 women on active duty in 1990 and even prouder to have been sent to the Persian Gulf. During Operation Desert Storm, some 40,000 of us military women flew airplanes, walked through minefields, stood guard over strategic areas, handled body parts and Iraqi prisoners, and lived in constant danger just like the men. These were crucial combat-support duties. Yet, like the women who put their lives on the line in Korea, Vietnam, Grenada, and Panama, because we did not engage in hand-to-hand warfare, many people (and even certain parts of the Pentagon) did not consider us as having been in combat. People back home in Kentucky still don't think I was a "real" soldier.[1]

 Growing up in my hometown, girls who got married right after high school were considered the lucky ones. We unlucky ones were expected to help relatives or work at some dead-end job until we finally caught a man. But with so many eligible men leaving because of the economy, our prospects for marriage grew slimmer every day. Unlike many of my friends, I realized that if I stayed put, I might die unmarried, unloved, and unfulfilled in many other ways. I didn't want to end up like my mom, who dropped out of high school, had five children, and never set foot outside of Kentucky, or like my baby sister who was emotionally and financially trapped in an abusive marriage to a raving alcoholic. I wanted to be someone. I wanted to see other parts of the world and meet new and different people. If I joined the military, I could get training, travel, and go to college, too.

But I was the one who helped my parents at home and at their store. And I was the one who took care of my nephews and nieces when my sister got beat up. "Isn't it better to be poor and be together, than to have money and not have a family?" my mom kept asking. My boyfriend begged me to stay, too. He promised marriage and swore he'd never hit me. But didn't his father start beating his mother when he lost his job? And hadn't his grandfather beat his grandmother? With only a high school diploma, eventually my boyfriend would be on unemployment, we'd be fighting over every dollar, and I'd end up hit with no way out.

So I packed my bags and joined the Army. I loved every bit of it—the training, the discipline, and the group spirit. Sure there were rules—lots of them. But there were lots of rules back home, too, and at least in the military I was learning things and advancing myself.

Having grown up teased by three brothers, it didn't bother me when some of the guys asked me if I ever got hysterical and threw things like the head nurse in M*A*S*H or if I joined the Army because I hoped that throwing grenades would make my boobs as large as those of Sarah MacKenzie in JAG. I didn't even get upset when civilians automatically assumed that being in the Army meant I was a nurse, a clerk, or some kind of hostess. "You're too short and too cute to be a soldier," they'd say.

Yes I was short—and thin, too—but I worked hard and could hold my own. Soon most of the men in my unit trusted me just like I trusted them. Yet I still felt I had to be twice as good as and work twice as hard as the men to feel competent and like I belonged.

Real war wasn't like the movies. I was totally unprepared for the heat, the filth, and, of course, the death. The low status of women over there grieved me more than any of my male comrades could ever understand. I was constantly dodging bullets, too. One afternoon another woman and I were jumped by a group of thugs. For what seemed like an eternity, they pounded us with bricks.

The attack left me with a closed head injury, three broken ribs, and a broken arm, and my friend was now blind in one eye. Next to us in the hospital was a soldier who had lost part of her face and half of her shoulder in an explosion. "I'll never be pretty again," she sobbed.

After the attack, I began having headaches that lasted anywhere from two hours to two weeks and unpredictable bouts of blurred vision and dizziness that sometimes caused me to collapse on the floor. My arm never healed properly either, so I was relegated to desk duty. I had good days and bad days. On good days, except for a mild headache or two, I was almost like a normal person. But on bad days I couldn't remember some of the simplest things, like how to get to the grocery store or what to put on first, my shoes or my socks. I prepared myself for my bad days by writing notes to myself and pasting them all over my house. Sometimes it took me two hours to get dressed and out the door, but at least I got out the door!

My therapist told me that my depression might lift if I allowed myself to grieve my losses. But every time I started getting upset about what happened to me, I thought of my friend who lost her eye and the soldier who lost part of her face and decided I had no right to complain.

"You got off easy. Because of your injuries, you'll no longer be risking your life on dangerous missions," I was told. But I had lost my pride and my purpose. I felt like an unheroic casualty with inconsequential injuries that I didn't have the right to mourn. Gone was my sense of power. Now remarks about my being a woman, something that had never bothered me that much before, seemed to sear my soul and gave rise not only to fury, but to despair. Although mostly it was men outside my unit who made these comments, I felt betrayed anyway.

"I don't care how many push-ups they can do, women should never be sent overseas. They're sitting ducks and can get the rest of us killed"; "Why didn't she shoot those guys? Goes to show you, women aren't any good at killing, even if they're dykes, and even dykes don't really know how to shoot"; "She better not get a Purple Heart for that little mugging of hers" certain male soldiers whispered loud enough for me to hear. Then they'd watch for my reaction. If I showed any emotion whatsoever—or said something about reporting them—they'd smirk and call me "touchy" *or "overly sensitive." They'd also be quick to remind me about soldiers who had suffered worse, as if I weren't already aware of that.*

Since my medical discharge from the military, whenever I visit my parents, they just shake their heads and said, "Now who's going to marry you?" After years of counseling for PTSD and depression, I'm asking myself a similar question: Will I ever be able to have a relationship with a man?

I never had a romance in the Army and I've outgrown most of the men back home. I make it a policy not to talk much about the military with my dates, but I probably intimidate them anyway, especially the civilians. Some military men also think I'm too "tough" or "masculine" to be a "real woman" (whatever that is). Then there's guys who see me as a "cripple" and want to take care of me.

Ha! I'm emotionally stronger than most men, even some Marines. I've bagged and tagged body parts and handled dead babies filled with illegal drugs. It's memories like these, more than my disabilities, that make me feel painfully different from others. If it weren't for other women vets, the guys from my unit, and one or two others, I'd probably be the loneliest woman in the world.

—TIFFANY, MAJOR, U.S. ARMY, RET.

Tiffany's experiences are not unique. Many women joined the service in order to expand their world, encountered both support and sexism in their military careers, and now bear physical or emotional scars from the hazards of serving in life-threatening situations. However, there are many women veterans whose personalities and stories are different from Tiffany's.[2]

This chapter describes some of the issues with which Tiffany and other women veterans commonly struggle—for example, sex-role stereotyping and sexual harassment. Yet for some women veterans, these and other issues described here may not be issues at all. Just as gross generalities cannot be made about male combat veterans, neither can they be made about female veterans. Since relatively little research exists on women veterans, the extent to which the stresses and joys of being a woman veteran described here are prevalent among women veterans as a whole remains unknown.

The Rise of Military Women

Women were serving their country even before they could vote! During the American Revolution, the War of 1812, the Civil War, and every war since, women have sacrificed, bled, and died for their country. Yet it was only with the establishment of the Army Nurse Corps in 1901, followed by the Navy Nurse Corps in 1908, that military women began to receive any formal recognition.[3]

The necessities of World War II resulted in the Army's WACs (Women's Army Corps), the Navy's WAVES (Women Accepted for Volunteer Emergency Services), the first women Marines, the Coast Guard Women's Reserves, and the WAFS (Women's Auxiliary Ferrying Squadron). The 1948 Women's Armed Services Integration Act opened the doors to women in the Navy, Navy Reserve, and Marine Corps. Now women had options other than joining a separate women's corps or organization—at least on paper. Although the 1948 legislation officially integrated women into the armed forces, it had many loopholes and heavily restricted women's roles in the military.[4]

The number of women in the National Guard took more time to grow. After World War II, there were no women in the Guard. In the 1950s women from the Air Force Reserve were permitted in stateside medical training centers in the Air Guard and the Army Guard. However, these women had to be officers, and they worked largely in medical capacities. In 1960 only fifty-eight of the over four hundred thousand personnel in the Army Guard Force were women. It was only after the 1967 legislation that opened the doors to women who weren't officers that the numbers of women in the National Guard began to swell. As of the writing of this book, women embody 10 percent of the National Guard.[5]

By 1975 the military academies at West Point and Annapolis and the Air Force Academy were opened to women. In 1992 women pilots were no longer excluded from combat zones; in 1993 women were permitted on combatant ships, and in 1994 Army women were permitted to serve in certain capacities in ground combat units.[6]

Overall, the number of military women has increased rapidly since the end of the all-male draft in 1973. At that time 1.6 percent of U.S. military personnel were female. By 1980 the figure had increased to 8.5 percent and nine years later was 10.8 percent. In 2004, 1.76 million veterans were female, with the total number of veterans in the United

States at 24.5 million. Sixteen percent of Persian Gulf veterans in 2004 were women. As of 2005 more than 17 percent of U.S. military personnel were female.[7]

Along with the increase in the percentage of women in the military came an increase in the number and types of roles available to them. During World War I women were either nurses or operators. Today about 80 percent of jobs and more than 90 percent of career fields are open to women. Whereas the first women admitted to the Guard were restricted to stateside medical work, the women in today's Guard can be deployed to combat areas and perform many nonmedical forms of combat support, such as maintaining aircraft, trucks, and other vehicles.[8]

Like Tiffany, women who have served in combat zones or in other dangerous areas can encounter the attitude that unless they've slit someone's throat, they don't qualify as "real" combat soldiers. Yet over time, the nature of combat has changed. Now it includes a multiplicity of ways of waging war other than ground troops involved in hand-to-hand combat, firefights, and other close-range struggles. With the advent of modern technology, war is increasingly being waged by highly sophisticated weapons and equipment rather than by bayonets and grenades. The operation of these various types of sensors, weapons, vehicles, and other machines and other new equipment does not depend on a person's genitals, but intelligence, training, and other skills. Some of these new inventions can even be operated autonomously. As Capt. Barbara Wilson, U.S. Air Force, writes, "Technology—not the Charge of the Light Brigade—is the answer."[9]

Almost Invisible

Despite their proficiency in new military technology and proven ability to play key combat support roles, today's women veterans and soldiers, like those who came before them, remain largely invisible. During the Revolutionary War, the War of 1812, and the Civil War, women donned men's uniforms and pretended to be men until their injury or death revealed their gender. When these fighting women were discovered, some of them, along with certain women doctors, nurses, and other medical workers, were awarded medals and pensions by grateful presidents and military commanders. Yet the contributions of these early military women are rarely mentioned in our history books.[10]

Even today, Web sites about the Korean War rarely mention the women who served there. We also know little about the women who served in Vietnam and Southeast Asia. There are no official records on how many women served, the honors they received, or the nature and extent of their emotional or physical injuries. Save for personal letters and books written by the women who were there and the efforts of a few dedicated researchers, we would know practically nothing about them.[11]

Even more invisible than military women and veterans are the many women who served (and still serve) in ways that were not (still aren't) seen as being officially "military," yet without which the official military would not have operated as rigorously and as efficiently. Just as many religious, social service, and political organizations would collapse without the support of dedicated volunteers or underpaid dedicated workers, the military would have suffered without the moral, physical, financial, educational, and other supports offered by innumerable women who were (and are) part of the Red Cross, the Women's Auxiliaries of the American Legion, and other veterans' service organizations and similar groups.[12]

The creation of the Vietnam Women's Memorial in Washington, D.C., helped to increase the visibility of women veterans, and certainly Tiffany and the women who served since the Vietnam era have received more recognition than those who came before them. Yet their contributions and the prices they pay for their efforts continue to be insufficiently documented or acknowledged. Studies on women's traumatic reactions and subsequent physical health problems, for example, are scarce.[13]

Good Girls versus Bad Girls:
The Madonna/Whore-Witch Dichotomy

In addition to being overlooked, military women and women veterans can, to one extent or another, find themselves saddled with military versions of some of the same myths about women that have plagued and continue to plague civilian women. One of these is the centuries-old "Madonna/whore-witch" dichotomy.[14] Here women are divided into two categories: good and bad. Women are either self-sacrificial saints with hearts of gold or unchaste "witches" whose selfishness, greed, and lust for power motivate them to control, corrupt, and even destroy others (especially men). The "Madonnas" are humble, honest, nurturing, and relatively passive and asexual. In contrast, "witches" are arrogant, hostile, and capable of using any manner of trickery and deceit to satisfy their ambitions. Some of these "witches" do not hesitate to use their sexuality to lure men into their traps.

Rose Sandecki, a Vietnam army nurse and the first woman to direct a Department of Veterans Affairs Vet Center, describes how women in Vietnam were often subjected to the "most extreme forms of sex-role stereotyping" in that they were "alternately treated as princess or prostitute." Even as late as the early 1960s, she writes, the military woman "was commonly thought of as a lesbian or prostitute."[15] In my counseling experience with women veterans, especially those who served prior to the Gulf War, there were frequent complaints of being stereotyped as a "dyke," as a "whore," or as someone who should not be taken seriously because the main reason she joined the military was to find a man or because she was a "loser"—that is, so physically unattractive or so mentally or emotionally deficient that joining the service was her only option.

Lurking in the background of history, ready to attack military women, lies the image of another kind of "witch"—the Amazon woman warrior of the past whom writer Phyllis Chesler calls the "universal male nightmare." Some of the most common ancient meanings of the term *Amazon* are "man-hating," "mannish," or "opposed to men." Hence military women, especially those who are not in caretaking roles, sometimes encounter the fears aroused by the legacy of these fierce fighting women who viewed all men as their enemies and had only one use for men—the fathering of their children. According to some accounts, the Amazons left their male offspring to die, gave them back to their fathers, or turned them into servile eunuchs.[16] Tiffany did not fit into any of these categories, yet she did not fully escape these negative stereotypes.

It's not just people back home in Kentucky who ask me how come I'm 35 years old and not married yet. It's people around here too—in Washington, D.C., the home of the military, where people should know better. More than one person has come right out and asked me if I'm a lesbian or a bisexual or if I had so many men while I was in the Army that I'm incapable of settling down. Other people put me on a pedestal. The ones I can't stand the most are those who pity me because they think that I sacrificed not only my health, but my ability to be a "normal woman" for the sake of my country.

Then there are those who tiptoe around me because they think that underneath it all I'm a homicidal maniac. Why do some people think that just because the military taught me how to fight that I'm ready to kill someone at the drop of a hat—and not feel guilty about either?

Sometimes Tiffany wonders if she's "paranoid" and misinterpreting how others respond to her. But—just in case—to avoid being negatively stereotyped, she doesn't tell people she's a combat vet unless she has to.

Because there is so little research on women veterans, the extent to which Tiffany's experiences are common among military women is unknown. Some women, such as military doctors, nurses, and other women who have traditionally feminine roles as caretakers, may have escaped being viewed as trigger-happy "witches" or man-hating "battle-axes." However, they haven't escaped entirely from being portrayed as readily available sex objects. In certain media productions— for example, *M*A*S*H*—almost all of the nurses are portrayed as competent dedicated workers able to withstand the emotional and physical strains of caring for the wounded. In some episodes, nurses refuse to be defined or limited by their gender. In others, however, nurses are depicted as being ready and willing to have sexual relationships with soldiers or doctors.

Tiffany was shocked to realize that the ancient "Madonna/whore-witch" dichotomy was still alive and well in the U.S.A., the country that had led the struggle for women's rights. Like many young women, she had assumed that because of the existence of laws protecting women's rights and the prevalence of women in politics, medicine, and other traditionally male-dominated professions and occupations, that sexism was a thing of the past.[17] Yet she encountered the sexist good girl/bad girl dichotomy and other sex-role stereotypes not only in certain parts of the military and in her current world, but within herself.

Double Whammy #1: Sex Roles and Sex-Role Stereotyping

Note: Not all women veterans struggle with the sex-role dilemmas described in this section. Perhaps it is primarily women veterans who are troubled by these dilemmas, rather than those who have resolved them or for whom they never were dilemmas in the first place, who seek help.

Acknowledging that she had moments of self-doubt about whether or not she was a "normal" woman was difficult for Tiffany. The very fact that she had self-doubts created even more self-doubts. In her view, soldiers were not supposed to have insecurities about their identity, but be self-assured and clear about who they were. What Tiffany had yet to understand was that in large part her self-doubts were socially caused; they stemmed from certain mistaken cultural beliefs about how men and women differ in traits, interests, and abilities. These beliefs, or sex-role stereotypes, affected how people responded to her and influenced how she viewed herself. Like many women, Tiffany had been taught to judge herself by how well she lived up to the stereotype for her gender.[18] Yet in the military, Tiffany was required to exhibit many abilities traditionally considered to be "masculine." Hence she faced the double whammy of being expected (and expecting herself) to meet the often opposite requirements of "the ideal man" and "the ideal woman." Tiffany also expected to complete this impossible feat without any anxiety or struggle. "I'm a soldier and soldiers can handle anything," she had always told herself. "If I can handle combat, I can handle this." Yet the emotional truth was that such conflicts caused her considerable distress, as they have other military women.[19]

According to the traditional male stereotype, the ideal man is physically strong, decisive, adventurous, self-confident, self-reliant, brave, stoic, rational, assertive, emotionally controlled, and not easily influenced by others. In contrast, the traditional stereotype for women depicts them as being gullible, childlike, timid, illogical, emotional, unstable, passive, submissive, and obedient. It also depicts women as being biologically inferior to men in strength and endurance, so jealous and immature that they are always squabbling among themselves, and so emotionally reactive they can't make sound decisions under stress. Therefore, they can't be trusted as leaders or relied upon as comrades-in-arms.[20]

Within the general stereotype for women, there are also subtypes based on social class, race or ethnic background, and weight and other aspects of a woman's appearance. For example, Hispanic women have been stereotyped as being "hot-tempered," Asian women as prostitutes or sexually exotic and subservient, and African American women as "controlling matriarchs," both oversexed and morally and intellectually inferior to Caucasian women. These derogatory images of minority women do not ease the readjustment of minority women veterans and can present further obstacles to the numerous minority women in today's military. (In 1990 38 percent of the total number of military women were from minority groups.[21])

Regardless of their social, economic, or ethnic differences, women traditionally have been expected to place a high value on their family and other relationships and, in general, to try to put their families first, before their careers or outside involvements. Except for situations where the family is dependent on the woman's income, traditional standards mandate that women do not allow their careers or other involvement outside the home to interfere with their roles as caring and responsible partners, mothers, or daughters, or with the physical needs of their households.

Military women can experience a clash between this traditional standard and the expectation that being in the military means making their military duties a priority. When women join the Reserves, they are aware that, if necessary, they may be deployed away from their families. Yet for some (not all) women, being thrust into a combat zone or other arena far from their families may have come as a shock because they thought being deployed was only a remote possibility. If so, the clash between a woman's commitment to the military and that to her family may be heightened. According to some researchers, the presence of women in the National Guard and Reserves who may experience such a clash may help to explain statistics that show that women deployed to serve in the Gulf and subsequent overseas combat zones have higher rates of depression, PTSD, and other traumatic reactions than men.[22]

Military men can also experience conflicts between their commitment to their families and to the military. However, their conflicts may be less severe in that the traditional measure of a man's worth lies more in his achievements and professional and financial successes than in his relationships.

Sex roles are changing, however, and our society has made many gains in expanding the definition of what it means to be a woman. In some instances, it is just as acceptable for a woman to be deployed as a man. Nevertheless, dozens of recent studies indicate that traditional sex-role stereotypes aren't dead yet. In fact, sex-role stereotyping has been found to be more extreme and more prevalent in the United States than in thirty other countries, including countries where women have far less economic, legal, and social power than in the United States.[23]

Another issue is that of valuation. In general, and especially in the military and other dangerous occupations, stereotypic male traits are valued over stereotypic female traits: that is, it is considered more valuable to be powerful than to be kind; to be able to think logically than to feel deeply; and to be stoic rather than emotionally expressive. In the military, stereotypic male qualities are not only more highly valued than stereotypic female qualities, they are also measures of a soldier's honor, courage, patriotism, and loyalty.[24]

As in many other careers, military women are required to exhibit certain "male" traits. Should they display what are considered feminine traits, they risk being seen as inferior, incompetent beings unsuited for military duty. However, if they don't display some stereotypical female behavior, they risk being viewed as "masculine" or "abnormal"—for a woman. Even when they display traditionally male traits, some may view their behavior in a negative manner.[25] For example, generally it is deemed "better" to stand up for one's self than to accept insults and indignities. When a woman does so, however, she runs the risk of being seen as whiny, aggressive, or controlling; when she doesn't, she's a wimp, a sissy, a pushover, a doormat, or even a coward. A good soldier is also expected to be logical rather than emotional. A female commander can be applauded for being rational and methodical in performing her duties, yet in the next breath be accused of being "cold," "antisocial," or "hard" because she isn't showing more emotion. Should she show some emotion, however, she may then be seen as "hysterical."

Hence the military woman can find herself in any number of unresolvable double binds. No matter what she does, the old stereotypes may come out and undercut her power and self-confidence. Whether she "acts like a man" or "acts like a woman," she may be disparaged and shamed, not only by male troops and superiors but by female troops and superiors as well. The double binds and the tensions caused by sex-role stereotyping are often greater for women who are expected by their partners, families, or others to "act like a man" when on duty but "like a woman" at home. Sandecki writes of the role confusion that can result from being expected to "'switch hats'" from "hard nosed professional to softly feminine."[26] Such confusion can be especially problematic for women whose religious or ethnic backgrounds emphasize traditional roles for women and for officers and other women who hold positions of authority in the military.

Sex-role stereotyping can create yet another problem. In an effort to do their duty and avoid censure, some women are careful to hide personality traits or habits considered to be "feminine." In some cases the pressure on military women to prove that they are equal to men can result in a woman rejecting her "feminine" side altogether. Yet there is value and usefulness in both traditionally male and traditionally female qualities. Studies indicate that the people who report the highest degrees of self-actualization and the most satisfaction out of life generally are not those who adhere rigidly to the sex-role stereotype for their gender. Rather they are able to use both traditionally masculine and traditionally feminine qualities to solve problems and manage their lives.[27]

If a woman internalizes the stereotypes of the ideal woman, ideal man, and ideal soldier, should she leave the military, she may carry these conflicting and demanding standards with her.[28] Hence she may struggle with these double binds as a civilian, especially if her partner, father, mother, or other important person in her life is in the military (or another career demanding stereotypical male qualities) or if she has a career or avocation that requires stereotypical male qualities.

When people are at war within themselves, even if they don't acknowledge it, they are at risk for developing or worsening any prior clinical depression, addiction, or stress-related emotional and physical problems. It is not psychologically healthy for any human being, male or female, to deny or suppress any part of him- or herself. Even if he or she wishes to change a certain part of him- or herself, that part must be acknowledged before it can be altered. Just as it is detrimental for male soldiers and veterans to deny and suppress any emotions, interests, or traits simply because they view them as "feminine," it is detrimental for women soldiers and veterans to attempt to try to obliterate any important part of themselves, whether that part be deemed "feminine" or "masculine."

Tiffany's reaction to learning about sex-role stereotyping and sex-role conflicts was mixed. Part of her felt immense relief to discover that some of her insecurities and emotional stress were caused by forces outside herself rather than personal deficiencies. Yet the realization that she was being affected by sexist social forces was painful. It was an admission of vulnerability, which violated the image of the ideal soldier. It also undercut her sense of control over her life and her belief that if she tried hard enough, she could overcome the barriers that stood in her way. While she could acknowledge the existence and effects of sexist sex-role stereotypes, she wanted to feel that only "other" women were affected by them.

"Learning all this stuff about sex roles makes me feel hopeless. I don't want to hear any more about it," she almost shouted at her therapist.

"That's fine. But it's hard to fight an enemy you don't understand. The only remedy for feeling so discouraged is action. But before you take action, you need to know what you are dealing with," the therapist replied.

With that, Tiffany's eyes lit up and she went on to read about sex roles, women veterans, and related issues. Over time, she grew to accept the reality of sex-role stereotyping and other forms of sexism as they applied to her personally. As a result, she was able to take the psychic energy she had been using to berate herself for some of her self-doubts and internal confusion and apply it to working toward her goals and enjoying her life. After she began working with other women veterans for positive change, she felt even more empowered.

Myths about Military Women

Military women and veterans are often saddled with myths about military women which impede their advancement in the military and devalue their contributions. Many of the myths listed below have their roots in the stereotypes for women described in the previous section. Some of the detrimental myths identified by Captain Wilson include the following:

- Women can't shoot and haven't had any weapons training.
- Women can't throw grenades because they're biologically different.
- Women can't endure the rough living conditions in a combat zone.
- Women have an adverse effect on unit cohesion and male bonding.
- Women are biologically weaker than men.
- Military operations and effectiveness are often compromised because so many women in the military become pregnant, which limits their usefulness and ability to serve in combat zones.[29]

All of these myths can be debunked by historical or scientific evidence. For example, while some women were undeployable during Desert Storm due to pregnancy, an even greater number of men were undeployable due to "substance abuse, alcoholism, court martials, sports-related injuries, off-duty fight-related injuries, and pending charges of domestic violence."[30]

Just as researchers tend to search for and emphasize differences between men and women rather than the far more numerous similarities between the sexes, the media and others have tended to focus on situations where mixing the sexes created tensions rather than on the many situations where mixed-gender units performed well. When under attack or united in purpose, soldiers tend to forget racial, class, and gender differences. During firefights and dangerous missions, soldiers (both male and female) usually care more about their comrades' dependability and capabilities, not their race, religion, or sex.[31]

For example, in the thick of action during Desert Storm and Operation Iraqi Freedom, sex differences often became irrelevant. Indeed, sometimes mixed-gender units were found to have operated more effectively than single-gender ones. Some American commanders, like those who served in Vietnam and El Salvador, found that in mixed-gender units "the women worked harder to gain approval and the men worked harder not to be outdone."[32]

Gender and PTSD

In terms of the general population, most studies report that women are more likely to develop PTSD and other traumatic reactions following a traumatic event than men. Studies have also found that these reactions tend to be longer lasting for women than for men. Most of the research conducted specifically on combat troops and veterans also has found higher rates for women. Similarly, studies of PTSD-afflicted Vietnam and Desert Storm veterans show higher rates of reported and officially diagnosed health problems for women than for men.[33]

It is noteworthy, however, that not all studies of combat troops and veterans have found higher rates of combat-related stress reactions among women. For example, two recent studies of Desert Storm veterans show no gender differences.[34] Keep in mind also that there are only a handful of studies on women's reactions to combat, many of which suffer from some of the same flaws as studies of male troops and veterans described in chapter 2, under "How many veterans really suffer from symptoms of combat trauma?" In some studies findings are based on one-time interviews by interviewers who are not trained mental health professionals. Furthermore, many questions remain about what these higher rates for women veterans truly mean. Are they really higher or do they reflect the fact that women are:

- more likely to admit to emotional distress than men?
- more likely to cope with their combat-related distresses by seeking help, whereas men are more likely to cope through substance abuse or violence (the rates of which are higher for men than for women)?[35]
- more likely to hold a lower rank and hence may be exposed to harsher living conditions?
- more likely to be younger and hence less experienced?

Among women veterans themselves, age and experience can play a role in the development of symptoms and in determining the severity of those symptoms. For instance, women who volunteered for Vietnam without having completed college or nursing school were more likely to develop PTSD and more severe symptoms of PTSD than women over twenty-one who came to Vietnam with a college or nursing degree or with several years of work experience under their belts.[36]

Double Whammy #2: Prior Traumas and Active-Duty Pressures

The higher rates of PTSD, depression, and other traumatic reactions among women who have served in combat zones also may reflect the impact of (a) prior traumas or (b) severe pressures and traumas experienced while on active duty, but which are not directly related to combat or to military operations. See appendix A for information on services for victims of military-related sexual or gender-based harassment or of physical or sexual assault.

Prior Traumas

Like some military men, some military women entered the military already suffering from the negative emotional and physical effects of prior traumas, especially child abuse or adult physical or sexual abuse. Given that the most common form of trauma in women is child abuse (with 17–33 percent reporting histories of physical or sexual assault) and that adult forcible rape is estimated to occur in approximately 10 percent of the general population, this should come as no surprise. There is also some evidence that military women are more likely to have been victimized before they entered the military than civilian women who are similar in age, social class, educational level, and other characteristics.[37]

Violence Against Active-Duty Women

During their military career, some women were exposed not only to the trauma of war but also to battering from their intimate partner, to gender-based job harassment, or to physical or sexual assault by military personnel.

Physical Assault

According to Department of Defense (DOD) data, between 1990 and 1995 over eight thousand active-duty women were victims of special abuse, and in half the cases, the abusive spouse was in the military as well.[38] For reasons outlined in chapter 8, there is cause to believe that sexual abuse, like rape, is a severely underreported crime. Hence, it is likely that there are more battered women within the military than the DOD data indicate. Also, the available statistics do not include physical abuse that occurs in cohabiting unmarried couples. According to a recent DOD study, 70 percent of active-duty women who are physically assaulted are not assaulted by their partner, a family member, or a friend, but by other persons.[39]

Sexual or Gender-based Harassment

In the early 1990s twenty-six women came forward regarding having been raped while on active duty in the Persian Gulf. Other widely publicized cases of sexual harassment and assault in the military followed. Since that time, the military has made attempts to curb these behaviors, and in 1992 the VA Public Law 102-585 came into existence. This law mandated the creation of mental health services for women victims and research on military-related sexual harassment and sexual assault.

In 1994 the Veterans Health Program Extension Act of 1994 repealed the 1992 provision that women veteran victims of sexual trauma needed to seek counseling within two years after discharge from military service and extended the availability of services through 1998.

This act also lifted the one-year restriction on counseling services for sexual trauma and provided for training counselors in sexual trauma and for the availability of a toll-free number for sexual trauma assistance. Then, in 2004, the U.S. Congress made permanent the Department of Veterans Affairs authority to provide counseling and treatment to women veterans who experienced sexual trauma during their tour of duty and expanded counseling services to include members of the Reserves who were sexually traumatized during training.[40]

VA Public Law 102-585 is a step forward for women victims; however, it defines sexual harassment as including only "repeated unsolicited verbal or physical contact of a sexual nature which is threatening in character."[41] This definition appears to imply that unwanted or uninvited sexual attention, pressure for sexual relations, or sexual assault (ranging from fondling to rape) constitutes harassment only when there are threats of punishment for noncompliance. Women's advocates and mental health professionals sensitive to the issues of gender and racial discrimination argue that these behaviors constitute sexual or gender harassment whether or not there were explicit threats of retaliation should a woman not cooperate.

For example, one published definition of gender harassment is "a broad range of verbal and nonverbal behaviors . . . that convey insulting, hostile and degrading attitudes about women." Hence, being shown pornographic or suggestive pictures or being exposed to objects or situations (or being told stories or jokes) that degrade women or that are sexually explicit or suggestive would all "qualify" as sexual harassment.[42]

Like active-duty women, active-duty men can be sexually harassed and can experience the same kinds of stress-related psychological, physical, and job-related difficulties as women. However, a 1995 DOD survey of military personnel found higher rates and higher frequencies of sexual harassment for women than for men. Also, numerous studies (completed on the general public, including an undetermined number of veterans) indicate that women are more likely to blame themselves and to be blamed by others for the harassment, thus increasing the negative effects of sexual harassment on women victims.[43]

Many of the women veterans I have worked with, especially those who served in Vietnam, did not realize that they had experienced sexual harassment until after they left the military. There are several reasons for this. Some women had an overly narrow view of what constitutes sexual harassment. Like many civilian women, they thought that only being repeatedly pressured for sex with threats to their job status or promises of rewards "counted" as sexual harassment.

In the context of war, surrounded by danger, death, and dying, some women considered being sexually harassed a relatively minor problem. Combat nurses and women in key combat-support roles were often so focused on their urgent and demanding duties, or on staying alive themselves, that they didn't have the time or energy to think about or react to being harassed. Some women saw the harassment as being caused by the combat-related stresses being experienced by whoever was harassing them, stresses these women well understood. Since, in their view, there was a valid excuse for the sexual harassment, some women decided the behavior should be overlooked or "forgiven."

Also, to have confronted or reported the harasser may have diverted his attention and the attention of the unit away from their crucial mission. If so, not only could military operations be compromised, but the lives of the woman and others in her unit could be even further endangered. Some women determined that it was in their personal best interest and in the best interest of all concerned to "not make a fuss" about any sexual harassment.

Military-related Sexual Assault

As you read the following findings, keep in mind that the existing studies on military-related sexual assault are few in number and none distinguishes between women who were assaulted in combat zones and those assaulted in more peaceful areas. Also, almost all of them are based on women veterans seeking medical or psychological treatment at Department of Veterans Affairs medical and mental health facilities. To date, it is not clear how representative women who seek help at VA facilities are of the total female veteran population. Assault victims may be more likely to seek help at VA or other facilities associated with the military than women who were not assaulted. If so, then statistics on the prevalence of military-related sexual assault may be inflated. On the other hand, it is possible that women victims of military-related sexual assault may avoid seeking care at the VA (or at the VA's smaller, more user-friendly Readjustment Counseling Centers) because these facilities remind them of their military experience. If so, then military-related sexual assault may be more widespread than the existing statistics indicate.[44]

Perhaps the largest study of military-related sexual assault was conducted between 1994 and 1995 on approximately sixty-three hundred
women VA outpatients from 158 different VA hospitals. Twenty-three
percent of these women reported military-related sexual assault. Several
other studies found similar rates. For example, in a 1996 study of approximately four hundred women veterans, some 31 percent reported experiencing some form of sexual assault while on active duty; 29 percent
reported unwanted sexual intercourse. A 1995 study of three hundred
veterans found that 25 percent of women under age fifty and 8 percent
of those age fifty or older stated they were victims of either completed
or attempted rape. A 1992 study of women who sought help at Readjustment Counseling Centers found that 40 percent of the women who
sought services reported being sexually assaulted while on active duty.[45]

The above findings indicate that women in the military are more
than twice as likely to be raped in the military than civilian women,
for whom the rate of forcible rape is estimated at one in every eight
to ten women. Furthermore, most authorities agree that the crime of
sexual assault is grossly underreported both in the military and in civilian life. The FBI, for example, estimates that only 25 percent of rapes
are ever reported.[46]

The Impact of Sexual Assault

Regardless of how many women experience sexual assault in the
military, the impact can be devastating and can involve not only many
forms of emotional pain, but any number of medical and physical
problems as well.

Reactions

After being sexually assaulted, many women find that their sense
of safety, their faith in their judgment, and their faith in their ability to protect themselves have been shattered. These can be disastrous
losses for any woman, but especially for one trained in fighting skills
and upon whose judgment hang the lives of many. Immediately or
soon afterwards some assault victims may be flooded with shame, guilt,
and other difficult emotions described below. Some may also develop
physical, sexual, and other problems. For others, these emotional, physical, and sexual problems may emerge months or even years later.[47]

There is no "right or wrong" time to experience the effects of the assault, just as there is no "right or wrong" way to react to it. After sexual assault, some women remain calm and controlled. Both reactions, the controlled and the emotional, are entirely normal.

Controlled Reactions

A woman may have a controlled reaction because her military training has taught her to be, her vocation expects her to be, and she expects herself to be like a sturdy oak that can weather any storm rather than a helpless victim. She may also have a controlled reaction because she is coping with combat duty or other life crises that feel more urgent. A military woman may also disown or repress any reactions to the assault that make her feel bad about herself, because at this crucial time, immediately after the assault, she desperately needs to affirm that even though the offender robbed her of her sense of safety, she still has her self-esteem and her emotional control.

A woman may also distance herself from any shame, guilt, or other feelings because she feels ashamed of being ashamed and guilty about being guilty. Generally in our culture and particularly in the military, self-confidence and emotional self-control are highly valued. Especially in combat zones, shame, guilt, and strong emotions are often viewed as psychological deficiencies that impede work performance and endanger the success of the mission and the lives of others. Therefore it makes perfect sense for an active-duty woman to hide or suppress her feelings for fear others might view her as "hysterical," "weak," "over-emotional," or "unfit for duty."[48]

Still other women disown feelings of powerlessness and humiliation because having such feelings doesn't fit in with their view of themselves as competent and assertive or with their history of advancement in the military or with other types of successes.

Emotional Reactions

Emotional reactions to sexual assault include fears of future sexual attacks on self or others, going out alone, sleeping alone, unfamiliar places, and others coming up behind the person who had been attacked; intrusive thoughts, mood swings, anger (at self, the assailant, and others) and grief; feeling dehumanized as if one is an object, not a person; loss of innocence and loss of faith in a just world; helplessness; hopelessness; and feeling overwhelmed and unable to cope due to changes in relationships or lifestyle resulting from the assault or from the symptoms created by the assault. Many assault victims suffer from feelings of guilt and self-condemnation as the result of one or more of the following beliefs:

- they should have thought, felt, or acted differently;
- as a result of the assault their entire self is now unacceptable or deficient and they are now "damaged goods," "a fallen woman," "a bad girl," "dirty," "defiled," "ruined," or otherwise contaminated; and/or
- they will forever remain "damaged goods."[49]

For all the reasons discussed above, the shame, guilt, and low self-esteem that can result from such beliefs can be especially intense.

Depression and PTSD

Clinical depression and PTSD are very common among survivors of sexual assault. Sleep becomes a nightmare of fear, restlessness, flashbacks, and terrifying dreams where one wakes up just at the point where one is going to die. A good night's sleep becomes an impossible dream. Depression, PTSD, and substance abuse are more prevalent among women who were violated as children or who, as adults, experienced multiple sexual assaults.

Studies of both civilian and military women who have been sexually assaulted reveal the following trends: About a third of survivors developed a major depression after being attacked, which is three times the rate of depression among women who have not been victimized. One in every four or five survivors will actively consider suicide at some point following the attack. Although many women experienced relief from severe depression after three months, eight to ten years post-rape, as a group, sexually assaulted women still evidenced higher rates of depression than women who had never been raped.[50]

Post-traumatic stress disorder rates for rape are higher than PTSD rates for any other crime. Some 90 percent of rape victims have been found to have PTSD symptoms the first month after the assault; about 50 percent for three months; and a substantial percentage for many months. Approximately 17 percent of survivors have been found to have PTSD symptoms for over seventeen years post-rape.[51]

Higher rates of PTSD have been found among survivors who blame themselves for the assault, who have sustained physical injuries, who have decided to testify in court, who were assaulted in a safe location, who were raped in a nontraditional or deviant manner, and who had access to fewer medical and psychological services.[52]

Somatic or Physical Aftereffects of Sexual Assault

As a society we tend to underestimate some of the physical effects of sexual assault. Yet assault can lead to a number of physical or somatic symptoms, create concerns about one's health, and aggravate any existing medical conditions. Recent data indicate that as a result of being raped, some 5 percent of victims become pregnant; 39 percent have acute nongenital injuries; over half sustain vaginal or perineal tearing; and 3 percent acquire an STD. In VA medical centers, some 20 percent of sexually assaulted veterans suffered from closed head injuries.[53]

Additional somatic aftereffects of sexual assault include pregnancy, fatigue, headaches, backaches, stomach pains, general body pain, nausea, rectal pain and bleeding, urinary tract infections, uterine pain, skin problems, severe PMS, irregular menstrual cycles, urinary burning, and vaginal infections, itching, discharge, and pain.

Alcohol and Drug Addictions, Eating Disorders

Sexually assaulted women, whether in the military or in the civilian community, have been found to have develop an addiction, such as an eating disorder, drug- or alcohol-abuse problem, or compulsive gambling, spending, or sexual activity. If they had one of these addictions before the assault, the assault may make it worse.

Assault survivors have been shown to be five times more likely to use prescription drugs, three times more likely to use marijuana, six times more likely to use cocaine, and ten times more likely to use other hard drugs than women who have never been assaulted. They have also been shown to be twenty-six times more likely to have serious problems with drug abuse and thirteen times more likely to have serious problems with alcohol. The more vicious the rape, the more severe the alcohol problem.[54]

Sexual Effects

The sexual side effects of sexual assault listed here include a wide range of reactions. A woman may experience some but probably not all of them. Sometimes a woman's reactions are inconsistent. For example, she may avoid sexual contact for a while, then become sexually active again, then return to celibacy. The most common sexual side effects of sexual assault include: feeling that one is no longer a woman or doesn't have the "right" to be a woman; fear of sexual contact, but not necessarily of hugging or holding hands; total or partial avoidance of sexual activity or the opposite, increased sexual activity; sexual indifference or the opposite, increased sexual appetite or increased preoccupation with sex; lack of pleasure during sexual activity; difficulties becoming aroused or achieving orgasm; avoidance of sexual positions and behavior associated with the assault; fears that becoming aroused proves that "I really wanted it" or "I secretly enjoyed it"; feeling confused, inhibited, dissociating ("tuning out" or "spacing out"); having flashbacks, fear, anxiety during sex; fear of penetration; vaginismus (involuntary vaginal muscle spasms) in anticipation of penetration (by a man, tampon, gynecological instrument, medication); pain (e.g., genital burning) during sexual intercourse; increased or decreased masturbation; sudden unexplained and unwanted surges of sexual arousal; fear of losing control or not being able to set limits on one's own sexual behavior or the sexual behavior of a partner; violent fantasies about sex during sexual activities and/or at other times; sexual arousal to violent images or images of sexual assault in the environment and/or masochistic and sadistic thoughts, images, or fantasies; indiscriminate sexual activity; if heterosexual, lesbian or bisexual desires and fantasies; if lesbian, heterosexual or bisexual desires and fantasies; fear of future evidence of sexually transmitted disease even if initial test results are negative; mixed or negative feelings about any resulting pregnancy; and mixed or negative feelings about having an abortion (or not having one).[55]

Cumulative Trauma: In Loving Memory of Dara, Military Nurse

Unfortunately, there are women who have experienced so much trauma as children only to be retraumatized by combat and then again by military sexual assault (and perhaps by other severe stresses or traumas as well) that the best efforts of dedicated therapists and doctors ultimately prove ineffective.[56]

Dara, for example, was physically and sexually abused by both parents. They forced her to torture and kill her pets and to molest her younger siblings and cousins. They passed her around to their friends. In order to keep her compliant and quiet, they poured alcohol down her throat and pumped her with drugs. At age five, she tried to run away. After being caught, she was locked in a closet for days without food and water.

Dara was constantly trying to find ways to escape. But as she got older she realized that if she did, her younger sisters and brothers would be abused in her stead. When she was seventeen, she couldn't take it anymore and fled. After working her way through college and nursing school, she joined the military and became a stellar military nurse. During combat, she did the work of three people. Others marveled at her emotional equilibrium.

Home from the front, however, Dara collapsed into alcoholism and deep despair. Now that she was no longer focused on saving the lives of others, her consciousness was flooded with images not only of wounded soldiers but also of the homeless, abused, wounded, and dead children she had seen in combat zones and in other areas to which she had been deployed. These images, in turn, brought to the surface repressed memories from her childhood. As she began recalling, and grieving, one incident after the next, she began to feel guilty. In her view, her sufferings as a child were inconsequential compared to the misery of the wounded soldiers and the children she had seen overseas.

"Doc, there were so many poor kids, not just one or two, but dozens. Kids with no eyes or no ears. Kids with no legs, no prostheses, using their arms to pull their bodies through piles of mud and body parts; four-year-olds taking care of two-year-olds because their parents were dead or missing; kids starving, dying everywhere," she sobbed. "That's why I didn't report the rape. What is a little rape compared to what those kids were going through?"

Dara had been raped by a military doctor outside the combat medical emergency station to which they had been assigned. In her view, the rape was her punishment for having run away from home when she was a teenager, thus leaving her younger siblings at the mercy of her parents. During the rape, Dara had automatically dissociated, just as she had as a child when she was being assaulted. Her state of dissociation was so severe, she couldn't think clearly, had trouble talking and moving, and was therefore unable to make any attempt to defend herself.

"I can forgive myself for being attacked when I was a kid, but not at my age. I have a black belt. I can shoot a gun. How come I just 'tuned out' and didn't fight back? Maybe what my parents said is true:

I wanted to be raped. I liked having sex with all those people and I deserved to be hit because I was a nasty girl who liked to do bad things," she said.

No matter how many times Dara was reminded of the involuntary nature and survival value of dissociation, she could not forgive herself. Also, many of the coping skills that help many veterans did nothing for Dara. For example, she could not visualize a safe place because she had never experienced one. She couldn't take up any sports involving balls because her father used her dead pets as "balls." Her childhood home was not safe, and even when she was stationed in noncombat areas, she was surrounded by wounded vets and suffering children. Counseling and AA helped her become sober. This enabled her to more clearly recall various events in her life and to begin experiencing her feelings about them. However, this increased awareness only made her feel more out of control, depressed, guilty, and angry.

Dara tried to learn healthy ways of expressing anger. But she had so much anger and so little experience in handling it that it spilled over into her relationships. She became increasingly critical and impatient with everyone—her friends, doctors, and other helpers included. Sometimes she'd explode at them. In an attempt to control her anger (and her sadness), she began drinking again. But alcohol provided only temporary relief. Over time, alcohol magnified her depression, rage reactions, and her thoughts of suicide.

There are numerous examples of individuals for whom the isolation of severe depression or PTSD is a stepping-stone to a clearer and deeper sense of purpose and an increased appreciation for life. Dara was not one of them. She had simply seen too much trauma for too long a time. The professionals who worked with Dara had hoped that because of her intelligence, her past record of having overcome seemingly insurmountable obstacles, her willingness to seek help, and her intense desire to contribute to the world, she would experience not only some healing but also post-traumatic or adversarial growth. Eventually, however, they reluctantly realized that the most they could do for Dara was to help keep her alive and sober.

Not all of the medical and other professionals who worked with Dara could deal with her outbursts of anger, with her horror stories, or with the sense of failure and helplessness that comes from trying to help such a severely traumatized individual. Some began referring her elsewhere or finding excuses not to see her. Some of Dara's friends could not deal with her anger either. Neither could they deal with her pain.

As some of her helping professionals and friends became increasingly distant, Dara became even more desolate. She said one day:

> It's my fault, Dr. M. I'm the one driving everyone away. But I can't help how angry I get. I try those things you try to teach me, deep breathing and all that, but none of them work. I'm sorry, Dr. M. You and the other docs must be so disappointed in me. Maybe in your next book you can have a chapter called "hopeless cases" and write about me. . . . And please, Dr. M., don't talk to me anymore about how smart I am and how strong I am to have gone through all that I've gone through and still be walking and talking instead of sucking my thumb in the lock-up ward of some mental hospital.
>
> Look at me, Dr. M.! I don't have a family and I've chased away half the people who cared about me.
>
> Look at me, Dr. M.! I can't work anymore. I can't even volunteer anywhere without getting triggered, then feeling like killing myself or blowing up at someone, and end up drinking again. What kind of life is that?

To some limited—but nevertheless noticeable—extent, medication provided Dara with some relief from her nightmares, anger, and other symptoms. But sometimes her periods of depression and dissociation were so severe that she forgot to eat, much less take her medications. She also felt she didn't deserve to feel better and within weeks stopped taking her meds. Soon afterwards, Dara wrote a thank-you note to those who had helped her. In it, she apologized for having wasted their time when they could have been helping others. Then she went into her bedroom and ended it all.

Nurses and PTSD

Approximately 27 percent of the 432 women veterans who participated in the National Vietnam Veterans Readjustment Study reported suffering from PTSD at some point since their return from Vietnam.[57] Since this study did not measure rates of depression, generalized anxiety disorder, and other symptoms of combat trauma, the 27 percent rate may have underestimated the extent of the distress experienced by women Vietnam veterans.

The majority of the women who served in Vietnam were nurses who had volunteered to go there. Many did not consider themselves to be veterans. Yet like the medical personnel who served in prior and subsequent armed conflicts, medical staff members in Vietnam were exposed to the same "psychological, emotional and moral pressures . . . as those who held guns." Neither were they safe from bodily harm. Medical units were often located near airfields or military bases and therefore subject to enemy fire and other attacks. Also, unlike in World Wars I and II, in Vietnam there were no "front lines" behind which people could hope to be safe. Similarly, in today's world of suicide bombers and the possibility of chemical or biological warfare, medical workers in allegedly "safe" areas are not safe.[58]

From the Revolutionary War on, nurses and women who served in medical capacities have been wounded, killed, and taken hostage. A few even became prisoners of war. Yet because they weren't sent to war to fire weapons, they have been (and in some cases still are) considered to be "noncombatants." During the Vietnam War, for example, none of the women who served there were considered "combatants" by the Department of Veterans Affairs. Yet male nurses who served there were often considered to have seen combat and their "classic symptoms of PTSD . . . [were] . . . usually taken seriously." Hence they were more likely to receive medical care, mental health treatment, and compensation than their equally deserving female counterparts.[59]

Today, the Department of Veterans Affairs, the Social Security Administration, and other agencies are increasingly accepting of the idea that "noncombatants" can develop symptoms of combat trauma. Yet the tendency to pass off the combat-stress reactions of women medical workers as some type of personality problem stemming from childhood (or from their failure to meet some stereotypic image of the ideal woman or nurse) has not been eradicated. Unfortunately, some women medical workers' war-related sufferings are still not viewed as "legitimate."

Attitudes toward Women Veterans' Traumatic Reactions

The myth that women are somehow biologically, emotionally, and physically inferior to men is centuries old. It persists, to one degree or another, not only within some parts of the military but throughout the world. Another myth, that women cannot be considered as combatants unless they engaged in ground fighting, is not totally dead yet either. Because these myths have such a long history and are so ingrained in our culture, even women veterans who find such myths infuriating may on some level have been infected by them.

To the extent that a woman believes these or any other negative myths about military women (even if she denies that she believes them or if she believes them only in part), they may affect her attitude toward her postwar problems. For example, she may feel her symptoms are not as "legitimate" or as important as those of ground troops. Or she may minimize the impact of her military service in producing her symptoms and attribute them instead (in whole or in part) to some form of "feminine weakness." Her mistaken attitudes will only be reinforced if she encounters medical or mental health professionals who, to one degree or another, do not regard her as a "real" combat veteran or who view her symptoms primarily as reflecting the stresses of marriage (or of being single), of motherhood (or of not having children), or of some type of menstrual irregularity or "hormonal" imbalance (such as menopause), rather than the trauma of war.

Teniqua had several therapists who held these and other misinformed attitudes about women and women veterans. Since she was married, they could not blame her PTSD symptoms on being single. However, since she didn't have children, they blamed her PTSD symptoms on that instead. Yet Teniqua feared that she had been exposed to toxic chemicals and substances while in the Persian Gulf and was terrified by the possibility that any child she bore would be deformed. "Every woman wants to be a mother, every normal woman that is," the therapist said. "If you're so afraid of birth defects, how about adopting a child?"

Teniqua considered the idea. But, like many combat veterans, she suffered from survivor guilt and felt that she didn't deserve the happiness of rearing a child. Because of her mood swings, anxiety attacks, and memory and concentration problem, she was convinced that she could not be a good mother. She also had nightmares about her child being sent to war where he or she surely would be wounded or die. Such thoughts triggered some of her worst war memories, which intensified her PTSD and depression to the point that she had little interest in sex, which made her feel like a failure as a wife. In one session she realized that she was consumed by guilt: she felt guilty for wanting children and for not wanting them; she even felt guilty about having survivor guilt.

Maxine, after twelve miscarriages, finally gave birth. Maxine wasn't sure if her miscarriages were caused by exposure to Agent Orange in Vietnam or by some medical problem which, in her view, made her a "defective" and "inadequate" woman. She already felt like a "defective" and "inadequate" nurse because, in her view, she hadn't done enough for the wounded and because, in her view, having PTSD meant losing her professional credibility. Like doctors, nurses weren't supposed to "break down." As a nurse who was responsible for the lives of others, she couldn't afford to pay attention to her own suffering either. The suffering of others came first. In her view, coming to therapy for herself was self-indulgent and selfish. She had no right to spend time on a "pity party" when she could be at home helping her family or looking for part-time or volunteer work as a nurse.

However, she had to come to therapy precisely because "whatever it was that happened over there" was preventing her from being the kind of loving and giving wife, mother, and person she wanted to be and had been prior to Vietnam. "I know I love my family, but I don't feel that love. I'd die for them, but when I say 'I love you' to my husband or child, I have no emotion. I feel like a hypocrite, a liar, and a cheat," she explained. Maxine, like many nurses and medical staff, had become emotionally numb while overseas. For most medical staff, such detachment was necessary in order to be able to function when overwhelmed with casualties or when confronted with horrendous wounds that their formal medical training had never mentioned.

"I'm always letting my family down. All it takes is seeing a Band-aid or someone getting shot on TV. Then all I can do is just sit there in a daze and do nothing but some mindless chore," Maxine continued. As is typical for someone with PTSD, Maxine had concentration and memory problems. It was not unusual for her to forget to pack a lunch for her child or to come for her therapy appointments on the wrong day. After months of counseling Maxine realized that she had yet to grieve the deaths of the young men and the civilians she had seen die in Vietnam and that some of her memory impairment and inability to focus stemmed from her repressed grief.

"How do I grieve?" she asked. "Nobody in my family ever cries."

"You don't have to cry," the therapist explained. "How about just telling me about some of the soldiers you tried to help but didn't make it?"

"But what if I tell you and I don't feel anything? If I don't feel sad or cry about those guys, what does that make me—some cold-hearted no-good nothing?"

"The feelings may or may not come. Maybe your inner wisdom intuitively senses that if you felt your feelings about the misery and death you saw over there, you'd be so overwhelmed that your memory and concentration problems would be even worse than they are now. You might not even be able to drive home. But if you want the feelings to come, it might help to talk about some of those young boys you cared about so much, but only if you choose to. If you want to try this, let's start with your telling me about one, just one, incident or soldier. And remember, you can stop talking anytime you feel like you're spacing out or it gets too painful—or any other time you wish. And you don't have to tell me why you want to stop. Just say, 'I need to stop,' or 'Let's change the subject.'"

As Maxine began to describe a soldier who had died in her arms, the feelings did come, as did the tears. As her emotional numbing began to thaw, Maxine began to feel more whole. Yet, like Teniqua, she continued to be almost paralyzed in making decisions or taking action on some of her ideas. "I'm afraid that no matter what I do, I'm doing the wrong thing and something terrible will happen, just like in Vietnam where if I made a mistake someone might die. So I do nothing, but then I feel like such a failure, I want to die. But I can't kill myself, because of my family," she wept in session.

Both Teniqua and Maxine dropped out of therapy at the very point where they had begun to recognize the irrationality of some of their guilt feelings and to feel the beginnings of some hope that they could regain enough self-confidence to go forward with their lives. Like any number of combat veterans (male and female), somewhere deep in their hearts Teniqua and Maxine believed that they didn't deserve to be the ones who made it out alive and that feeling better about themselves and wanting to have a good life was a dishonor to the dead and wounded.

Summary

From the Revolutionary War on, women have served their country in every war and armed conflict, not only in their traditional roles as nurses or caretakers but also as frontline soldiers. Today women have an increased presence in every branch of the military, on all levels, and many more positions are open to women as compared to the past. Since modern warfare is becoming increasingly dependent on technology and intelligence operations, the key roles women play in these areas are essential for the success of military operations. Yet if they do not engage in ground fighting, in some circles they are still not considered "combatants."

In general, women veterans evidence higher rates of combat-related post-traumatic stress, anxiety disorder, depression, and other forms of traumatic reactions. This may reflect not only research problems but also the fact that they are more likely than male recruits to encounter gender-based harassment and to have suffered from sexual or physical victimization both prior to or during their military career. The victimization rates for women in the military are appalling.

Women veterans, especially nurses, may suffer from the myths, attitudes, and stereotypes toward women in the military that devalue their contributions and that minimize their physical and/or emotional hardships. Today women veterans can find support, validation, and information about their rights and benefits from numerous women veterans organizations (see appendix A).

Tanya and I met in the Marine Corps. She's a nurse; I'm a computer specialist. When we got married, we were sure our love was strong enough to survive the separations and other hardships that are part of military life, and we were right about that. In fact, we probably got along better than most couples precisely because we couldn't be together all the time. We also knew that if one of us was sent to a combat zone, our days together might be precious few. So we made it a point not to argue about small things.

But everything changed after Tanya went to Somalia. She had always been a little high-strung, but I had never seen her so irritable and withdrawn. She hardly ever smiled. She'll snap out of it soon, I thought. Best not to talk about it.

But she didn't snap out of it and when I commented on her unhappiness, she told me I was imagining things. Sometimes I'd wake up at night and find her pacing the floor in the living room, her eyes red from tears. When I tried to comfort her, she'd push me away. "It's just allergies," she'd say. I knew better, but I also knew she would never admit to me, a fellow Marine, that she needed someone to lean on and love her.

I don't know what did her in over there—the wounded she couldn't save or the poverty, especially since the Somalian are black, like us. One night Tanya finally opened up to me and told me about her nightmare: "I'm sitting in a chair in a dark room when I notice that my uniform is full of blood. I'm about to get up to change when dozens of emaciated, wounded, dead or dying men, women, and children start coming into the room single file. As they go past me, they look at me. They don't say a word, but their eyes seem to be asking how come I failed them. Finally the procession stops. But no, there's one more dead person coming past me. That dead person is me, and then I wake up."

That night Tanya sobbed for hours and she let me hold her the whole time. She even let me rock her a few times. The next morning I was sure that Tanya would be back to normal. I guess I had seen too many television pro-

grams that showed a person getting over something terrible by simply spilling their guts to a therapist or to someone who cared about them. Not so. Healing is not a one-shot deal. In fact, telling me that nightmare only made Tanya worse. It affected me, too. Now I have the same nightmare as Tanya, only it's me sitting in the chair and the last person in line is me—dead!!

She refused to get help, even from our pastor, until she started having flashbacks in the operating room and realized that she was endangering her patients' lives. But she wouldn't go to any kind of counseling offered by the military. "That's for 'real' vets," she'd say. We didn't have the money for a private therapist. So I took out a loan and told her I had just gotten a bonus at work. She probably knew I was lying, but I'm not sure.

I've tried to be as supportive as possible, but it seems I'm always doing the wrong thing. If I make sexual advances, she feels guilty because she's usually too depressed or nervous to make love. But if I back off, she thinks that maybe I don't want her anymore. For a while I gave up some of my sports and other activities to be home with her. That made her mad because she thought I was treating her like a baby. Besides, she said, she needed to be alone a lot. Yet when I resumed some of my former activities, she felt abandoned.

I know I'm supposed to take care of myself, but I don't know what that means. Yes, I want to have a life, but a life with Tanya in it. Tanya, my precious Tanya.

10

"I long to lean on someone"

Military Couples

When my father was on combat duty, my mother received a tremendous amount of support from the other military wives and members of the military community. I didn't like the frequent moves, but the warm reception we received at each new base almost made up for the home and friends we had left behind.

I was proud to join the military and to marry a military man. We got along splendidly—until he came back from combat duty. When he started to overdo the gambling and began banging his head against the wall, I said nothing. Even when he seemed numb to my love, I said nothing. After all, as both a military wife and a military officer myself, I was supposed to be strong, keep a stiff upper lip, and stand by my man 100 percent, no matter how he might be destroying my peace of mind, as well as his own.

Given this atmosphere, I found dozens of clever ways of disguising the fact that my husband had symptoms of combat trauma and invented an ingenious list of excuses for not attending certain social functions. For my mother and other military wives of her generation, nonattendance at social and certain other military functions was a definite "no-no." Since I was active duty, there was less pressure on me to participate in wives' activities. But pressure or not, if my husband was severely depressed or being self-destructive, I had to be there to help keep him and our children together. Whenever my military duties took me away from home, I'd break out in hives from worry about what was going on at home without me there.

When I first came to the women's group, I tried to help everyone else. I had done a lot of reading on combat trauma and was quick to tell the other women to put themselves, not their husbands and children, first for a change. I was able to deeply feel the other women's anger and pain, but rarely acknowledged my own. As both a military wife and an officer, I was trained and expected to be independent and to hide my needs from others, especially my need to be taken care of, to be protected, and to feel loved. In my mind, as in the mind of my parents, my husband, my superiors, and others in the military community, such needs were signs of weakness and cause for shame.

Even though I considered myself quite liberated, in my heart of hearts I longed to lean on someone, "just a little bit." Quite frankly, I was jealous of the women in group who could cry, feel sorry for themselves, and express fears of "going crazy." I wanted to be a basket case, too, but I couldn't allow myself that. Instead I rigidly put my nose to the grindstone, day after day.

"If you can handle everything yourself, why do you come to group?" a group member once asked me. That question forced me to realize that having to be strong all the time had made me bitter and hard. There was no softness in me, no vulnerability. I didn't like what I had become, but it wasn't my fault. I saw no alternative to being an "iron woman" for the standards imposed upon me by the military were indelibly stamped into my psyche.

I know that if I act any differently, "femininely," I call it, others will see me as displaying "behavior unbecoming to an officer." Also it puts too much pressure on my husband if I show him I have needs. He can't take it when I have needs. He's the only one allowed to have needs. Yet I know that inside me there's a little girl aching to be held, aching to play. But I can't let her out. She has a lot of tears, too, but she's not allowed to cry.

—EVELYN, LIEUTENANT, U.S. MARINE CORPS

Military couples have always existed. The relatively few women who served prior to the recent rise of women in the military may not have joined to "catch a man," yet, as would be expected, their proximity to so many men often led to marriage. How many of these women continued to serve after marriage or motherhood is unknown. Yet even if they discontinued their military career, their familiarity with the structure of the military and with the demands of military service most likely benefited their marriages. Suzanne, a Korean War veteran, explains:

> *I had wanted to make the military my life career, but after I married, I didn't re-enlist. There were no role models for dual military couples back then. It was hard enough trying to combine family life with one military career, much less with two. But if I hadn't known the difference between a lieutenant colonel and a corporal, it would have been a disaster.*

Double Duty

As of 2004 there were more than twenty thousand military couples on active duty. (This figure refers to married couples only, not cohabiting couples.[1]) The number of women veterans who are married to or living with veterans or with men on active duty or in the Reserves or National Guard is unknown. Active-duty women married to active-duty men can find themselves carrying two sets of responsibilities: those belonging to their military role and those for military wives. Women veterans no longer involved with the military also can find themselves carrying the expectations of these two sets of duties into their civilian life, especially if their partner is on active duty or in the Reserves or the National Guard.

Like many military women and women veterans, Evelyn (whose story began this chapter) was brought up in a military home and indoctrinated into the "shoulds" of being a "good military wife" at a relatively young age. She was also brought up in a religious household, which emphasized the virtues of female submission, self-sacrifice, and the sanctity of the family. These "shoulds" were reinforced by her military neighbors and those in her (and her partner's) chain of command. Some of these "shoulds" include:[2]

- Always put her partner's career above her personal needs, her own career, and the needs of the family.

- Be willing to tolerate frequent moves and separations from her partner without undue complaint.

- Be prepared to bear and raise her children alone.

- Assume complete responsibility for the children, the home, the car, and finances during her partner's absences, but then allow him to feel he is the head of the household when he returns.

- Attend as many social events as her military duties permit and be careful to act in a way that promotes her partner's career.

- Conform to group expectations and especially any expectations or orders from the higher-ups.

- Always be compassionate, understanding, and obedient, and plan special homecomings for her partner.

- Keep her home spotless even though she is working full-time and doesn't have help.

- At all times, keep up the pretense of having a home life.

- Never, ever, under any circumstances, expose her partner's problems or defects of character.

- In general, be willing to accept a subordinate role at home (because not to do so would endanger her partner's status and potential for promotion) while at the same time fulfilling the often-contradictory expectations for the stereotypic man and the stereotypic female on the job.

The strains involved in walking the tightrope between these contradictory expectations are especially severe for women officers, who constitute about 15 percent of all active-duty women in all five branches of the military service.[3]*

*See "Double Whammy #1: Sex Roles and Sex-Role Stereotyping" on pages 252–59.

Military Couples and Trauma

The burdens of meeting the demands of being (or having been) both a military wife and a military woman are compounded when either the woman or her partner suffers as the result of having been exposed to combat or to other forms of trauma. With respect to combat trauma, there are several types of military couples:

1. Single-trauma couples, where one partner has been exposed to combat and the other partner has never been traumatized.

2. Dual-trauma couples, where both partners are combat veterans or where one partner is a combat veteran and the other veteran has experienced a noncombat-related trauma, such as a natural disaster, child abuse, adult sexual or physical assault, or a disabling accident.

3. Triple-trauma couples, where one partner has been traumatized twice (once by combat and once by a noncombat-related trauma) and the other partner has been traumatized either by combat or a noncombat-related trauma.

4. Quadruple-trauma couples, where each partner has been traumatized twice: once by combat and another time by a noncombat-related trauma. There are also multiple-trauma couples who struggle with the emotional and physical consequences of exposure to five, six, or even more traumas.

Political and Sex-Role Tensions

Military and veteran couples vary not only in the number and severity of traumas experienced by one or both partners but also in the degree to which one or both partners suffer from military- or nonmilitary-related medical or mental health problems as the result of these traumas or other situations. They also vary in the degree to which the partners have (or had) similar military duties and interests, similar ranks or rates of promotion; in the degree to which one or both partners seek (or sought) to make the military their career; and in the degree to which each partner is (or was) content with military life, military policies, or current political policies that influence military operations.

Political differences have the potential to create conflict in any couple. However, in a military couple, whose occupations are heavily influenced by governmental decisions, or in a veteran couple, whose lives may have been shaped by certain government policies, political differences have the potential to become explosive. Suppose the woman supports a particular government or military policy and her partner does not. Because her identity is bound up with the military, her partner's criticism of the policy may feel like a personal attack. In the extreme she may view her partner as being disloyal or hypocritical (for serving in the military even though he disagrees with some aspect of the military or the government).

The same could hold true when the woman is critical of a policy that her partner holds dear or for which he is willing to risk his life. Therefore, for some couples, political discussions and critiques of the military or the government are taboo. As one military wife explains, "It would be like being married to a doctor and being against medicine."[4] However, intimate partners are likely to have some sense of where one another might stand on certain key issues. Hence even unstated differences of opinion can become a source of underlying tension.

On the other hand, if a couple is united in both political views and attitudes toward the military, this can serve as a powerful bond. Their relationship may be even further strengthened if their military talents complement each other and if they are able to learn new military skills from one another. This assumes, however, that any tensions or competitiveness between them regarding differences in rank, military skill, or rate of advancement is minimal. In some cases, one partner may feel proud of the other partner's (current or past) higher rank or rapid rise within the military, yet harbor some degree of envy and resentment as well.

For example, sometimes the woman partner's achievements can threaten her man's sense of masculinity. Even if he does not feel particularly "emasculated" by her progress or superior rank, he may resent any teasing he may receive from others about this reversal of the usual situation (where the man commands more power and a larger salary than his female partner).

On the other hand, conflicts can also ensue from the opposite situation: where the woman is not being promoted to a desired rank as rapidly as she or her partner had hoped. As a result, she may see him as being a "better" soldier than herself, especially if he or others also believe this. If, in addition, either she or he fears that her falling short of expectations may impede the advancement of his military career, her inferiority feelings may be magnified. In her mind, not only has she failed to meet certain standards as a soldier, she has also failed in being a traditional "good military wife" whose role it is to enhance her husband's military status/career.

She may feel especially inadequate if she or others believe that there is no sexism in the military and that therefore her lack of anticipated progress is primarily a reflection of her inadequacies. Or perhaps she is aware of the subtle and not-so-subtle forms of gender discrimination and gender harassment and how they limit her professional growth. However, if her partner lacks this awareness and believes she is using sexism (or even military-related gender harassment or sexual assault) as an "excuse" to cover up her deficiencies, conflicts can easily ensue.

Common Challenges for Dual Military and Dual Veteran Couples

Regardless of their differences, all military couples face certain common challenges. As of 2004 approximately 79 percent of military couples were able to live together.[5] An unknown number of couples where one partner is a veteran and the other active duty (or a member of the Reserves or the National Guard) are also able to live together. However, at any moment, at least one partner can be sent elsewhere for a lengthy or indefinite period of time. Even separations that are not particularly dangerous (such as going to another location for specialized training) can be stressful. Such separations are especially problematic if they are indefinite in length; if they occur during the holidays or on special days, such as birthdays, anniversaries, or planned family reunions or vacations; or if they come at an inopportune time, such as while the couple is trying to conceive a child or is grieving the loss of a family member.

All these stresses are magnified when one partner is deployed to a combat zone or to another area fraught with danger, such as a rescue operation for a natural catastrophe. In such cases, the nondeployed partner (or the veteran partner who is no longer in the military) may agonize about his or her partner's safety. On the other hand, just as the nondeployed partner (or veteran partner) may have grown numb to fears about his or her own safety, he or she may grow or have grown numb to fears about the partner's welfare.

It is impossible, however, to block out the threat of harm entirely. "Always wondering, 'Is this the last time I'll see him?' drove me insane," said Rena, who served for four years in the Air Force. "If I don't squelch those kinds of thoughts the minute they pop into my head, then my fear takes over and cuts me off from all the good things I have in my life today." Rena feels she must be "strong" not only for her husband's sake, but because, as both a military wife and a member of the Reserves herself, she is expected not to admit or exhibit any fears or anxiety. Yet the possibility that both her husband's well-being and the course of her own life could be permanently altered by situations out of her control casts a dark cloud of emotional and financial instability over her life. Such an ominous cloud easily brings about anxiety, depression, and other forms of emotional distress for almost anyone, especially for the person who is economically dependent on his or her spouse or partner.

For couples where at least one partner is still active in the military (or the Reserves or the National Guard), threats to a partner's safety are not the only sources of stress. Military service often requires working extremely long hours, sometimes on an unpredictable basis. Military personnel of any rank may need to return to duty for an emergency at any time—even when off duty or on leave. If they are sent overseas or away from home, they may have only a moment's notice. Their return may be postponed, perhaps even more than once.

The partners who are relatively safe may be proud that their mates are risking their lives to serve their country or to help others. In fact, their prestige within the military and the community may rise because of their mate's mission and because they are proving their mettle as soldiers, former soldiers, or patriotic citizens by bearing up under such enormous emotional stress. Yet the unpredictable nature of military schedules makes planning—whether short- or long-term—difficult, if not impossible.

Even when a military couple is together, there are times when the emotionally or physically draining nature of their work and/or the aftereffects of any traumas they have experienced leave them utterly exhausted. The same holds true for veteran couples who may be psychologically and physically depleted as the result of combat or other traumatic experiences. At times, one or both may be too tired, restless, irritable, or preoccupied with their work or from their emotional and/or physical battle scars to be as close to one another as they might wish. If one or both of them has learned to cope with the combined effects of their current job stresses or past traumas by turning off their emotions, it may be hard to turn these emotions on when they are at home.

Since both partners may be experiencing (or have experienced) similar stresses, they may understand that their partner's lack of energy for their relationship has more to do with the pressures of one another's current or past military experiences than their feelings for one another. But emotionally, one or both partners can still feel rejected, disappointed, and lonely. Such obstacles to communication, intimacy, and the sharing of good times are especially prevalent among couples where one or both partners have been exposed to one or more traumas.

Dual-Trauma Couples

There are no statistics on the number of military couples where both partners have symptoms stemming from either military- or non-military-related trauma. Most of the information that exists on military or veteran multiple-trauma couples comes from clinical reports and the observations and impressions of therapists and others who work with help-seeking active-duty military and with help-seeking veterans. The extent to which these observations hold for non-help-seeking military or veteran couples remains unknown.

In my experience, one of the most common forms of dual trauma couples involves a male veteran suffering from combat trauma whose active-duty or veteran partner is experiencing traumatic reactions from childhood sexual or physical assault.* These and other dual-trauma military couples have many of the same relationship problems as couples in which only one partner suffers from combat trauma. Yet they have additional stresses.

*See pages 260–63 for statistics on the prevalence of combat-related and noncombat-related sexual and physical victimization among military women.

For example, the woman with a history of childhood sexual abuse typically was assaulted at night and while sleeping. As a result, she may suffer from nightmares and sleep disorders just like her man, and the couple may be kept awake quite often. In addition, the couple must cope not only with the combat veteran's flashbacks, emotional numbing, depression, and limited tolerance for emotional intimacy, but with the woman's similar symptoms. It is not only the combat veteran who may need to emotionally withdraw from the family, but his partner as well.

In dual-trauma couples, there is not just one set of anniversary times and other triggers, but two. While the combat vet may experience more PTSD, depression, or other symptoms on the anniversary of the date he entered the service, the date he was wounded, or the date of a particular battle, his partner may experience her symptoms on her abuser's birthday or the anniversary of the first assault. She may also experience symptoms during activities that remind her of the original trauma—for example, sex. This is especially the case if her partner is rough or assumes sexual positions or makes sexual demands similar to those of the woman's former abuser.

As outlined in the section "Sexual Effects" in chapter 9, women who were sexually assaulted (either as children or as adults) who have yet to receive help may develop a variety of sexual difficulties, ranging from an extreme aversion to sex to a tendency to sexualize relationships or to become promiscuous. In some cases, the woman flips back and forth between periods of puritanical avoidance or disdain of sex and periods of hypersexuality, neither of which are conductive to healthy sexual intimacy.

In one instance, a veteran who had been assaulted sexually for over eight years by her brother ran away from home as soon as she was sixteen. She worked as a waitress until she joined the Navy. Today she has an active sex life with her husband, also a former sailor. Despite his combat-related depression, he goes out of his way to please his wife sexually. Yet she has never experienced pleasure in connection with sex, much less an orgasm. For her sex, even marital sex, is dirty, horrible, and repulsive. Although she loves her husband, she wishes that sex was not part of marriage.

When this woman has flashbacks during intercourse or nightmares afterwards, sometimes she tells her husband and other times she does not. If he is in a bad mood or in "combat mode," she usually remains silent for fear of aggravating him further. However, even when her husband is feeling well, she hesitates to speak up for fear that he will become so enraged at her brother that he will seek vengeance against him.

She also remains silent because she wants to maintain her denial. "If I don't talk about it, maybe it will just go away," she says. "But if I talk about it, either to my husband or in therapy, that means I have to deal with it and I'm just not ready or willing to do that yet. Right now my priority is helping my husband cope with his combat trauma." Yet because she doesn't explain to her husband why she is sexually disinterested or unresponsive, he frequently interprets her coolness or indifference as rejection, which in turn aggravates his combat trauma.

During the years that she was my client, this young veteran was suicidal several times. So was her husband, who had yet to respond definitively to treatment for depression. When he became suicidal, his wife "pulled herself together" and became the family strong person. When she became suicidal, however, her husband quickly assumed the leadership role. Neither partner was willing to commit to an in-depth therapeutic process for him- or herself. Yet they both insisted that their partner not only needed but deserved help. "There's nothing more that I want in life than for my husband/wife (boyfriend/girlfriend) to get over this thing," they'd both say.

For some women, their partner's healing has become an imperative. "He's got to get better, he's just got to," they often implore. For both active-duty and veteran women, a partner may have the emotional status of a military buddy or comrade-in-arms as well as a mate. Just as these women might risk their lives to save a fellow soldier, they may be willing to go to any lengths to "save" their partner from psychological despair and suffering. On some level, the intensity of their desire for their partner to be healed also might reflect their own need for healing and their hope that if their partner can achieve some inner peace, so can they. It may also reflect the fact that combat trauma may be considered "more" traumatic and more "legitimate" than child abuse (or even than adult rape or battering), especially if the partner with combat trauma sustains a physical injury.

In general the losses and fears involved in combat are better understood and deemed more acceptable than those involved in child abuse or in adult sexual or physical assault. They are also more tangible. The distortion of one's sexuality and self-concept and the terror of being assaulted by an adult (especially by a family member) are real and have the power to change the course of one's life. Yet they may not seem as "real" or as "dangerous" as being attacked by enemy soldiers or as deserving of being mourned as losing comrades in battle. Hence the woman (or her partner or their family, friends, and colleagues) may consider the combat veteran's pain and suffering to be greater and more important than hers.

It bears repeating that the observations on dual-trauma (as well as triple-, quadruple-, and other multitrauma) military and veteran couples in this chapter are based on clinical experience with help-seeking couples where both partners are or were involved in the military. In my limited experience, these couples fell into two broad categories. The first group consisted of couples who broke up almost immediately after seeking help. Some only came for one session before filing for a divorce. The second group consisted of couples who stayed together through thick and thin—even when both partners failed to receive sufficient help with their trauma-related symptoms. There are many reasons for these two groups.

Combat veterans who find themselves socially isolated because of their PTSD, depression, their sense of alienation from others and society, or any other mental health or physical problems can become highly emotionally dependent on their partner. In some cases, their partner is not only their mate but also their best friend and one of the few friends they have in the world. In addition, men and women with histories of child abuse often cherish their marriages and intimate relationships because they were cut off, or have cut themselves off, from their families of origin. In addition, they are used to living in households where their needs are not always met. Even though life with a depressed, anxious, or PTSD-afflicted veteran may be trying at times, for some men and women with histories of child abuse, it may seem like heaven compared to life with an incestuous or physically abusive family member.

In dual-trauma couples that stay together, the partners tend to identify with each other. The fact that they have both been hurt by life and suffer deeply acts to bind them together. Typically the woman does not want to abandon her partner as she was once abandoned by her assailant and family. Since both partners may feel ashamed of their traumatic reactions and since they are both part of the military family, they may be more tolerant of one another. On the other hand, when they become angry with each other, they may experience a double anger, first at their partner and second toward the person (or institution) they feel let them down or used them in the past.

Triple- and Quadruple-Trauma Military Couples

Examples of military multitrauma couples include those in which one partner suffers from one set of unresolved issues regarding war experiences and yet another set of problems from childhood abuse or another trauma. At the same time, his partner has symptoms stemming from combat, from childhood or adult victimization, or from another type of trauma. Since traumatic reactions can also result from witnessing the murder, rape, or suicide of one's parent or sibling, if either partner was exposed to such events, that person may be suffering from traumatic reactions even if he or she was not injured.

For example, my caseload has often included women veterans with histories of child abuse or abusive relationships who were married or living with men who joined the military to escape a physically and/or sexually abusive family of origin. In one case, a male combat veteran had been sodomized by his father and two uncles. This veteran could not wait to become of age and enlist in the military where he hoped to find some peace and stability. In the military he found the order and discipline that was sorely lacking in his childhood. As he came to master various skills, he acquired an ever-growing sense of pride. However, after two tours of duty in a war zone, he also acquired another set of bad memories.

Other examples include marriages or relationships where the woman was abused as a child and then went on to marry or live with a physically abusive man (or was raped as an adult in either the military or the civilian community). For these women, traumatic reactions from childhood victimization can exist alongside symptoms derived from being victimized as an adult.

In my experience, active-duty and veteran women in triple- or quadruple-trauma relationships (like those in dual-trauma relationships) sought help primarily to salvage or improve their present marriage or love relationships and only secondarily to resolve their own past issues. Yet in order to work on their present intimate relationship, these women had to confront the psychological aftereffects of their past misery. For example, they had to work on their own emotional numbing, suppressed rage, tendency to isolate, passivity, sexual problems, and persistent low-self-esteem.

If it is difficult for civilian women to work on these issues, it is even more problematic for active-duty women or women veterans to do so. In the military, suppression of emotion is expected. It is not a "symptom"—it is normal. Also, the tendency to isolate may be difficult to distinguish from the usual obstacles military personnel may encounter in establishing and maintaining ties, such as frequent relocations, unpredictable duty schedules, and the demanding nature of military service. For women who serve (or served) in the military and who therefore are expected to be pillars of strength and self-confidence, admitting to low self-esteem, shame, or feelings of helplessness or powerlessness can be devastating.

In one case, Miriam, a combat veteran's wife, had a thirteen-year history of physical abuse by her mother. At age sixteen she ran away from home only to marry a man who beat her regularly. After she gained the courage to leave him, she contemplated a career in the military. Although she hesitated to make such a serious commitment, she longed to become "tough" and learn the fighting skills and assertiveness that would prevent her from being victimized again—by anyone, male or female. She also vowed never to marry. But a certain combat veteran won her heart and she remarried, then joined the Air Force.

She brought many interpersonal problems to her second marriage, as did her husband who had been sexually and physically abused by his parents in his formative years. After he completed several years of therapy for his war experiences, he found he was still not free of symptoms. His combat dreams now were replaced with dreams of his father beating him and calling him names. Eventually he came to see that even though he had made substantial progress in making peace with his combat experiences, he had yet another challenge before him in dealing with his childhood.

In my experience, like dual-trauma couples, triple-, quadruple-, and other multitrauma couples who participate in therapy for more than several weeks tended not to separate or divorce. While these marriage relationships were conflictual, with both partners complaining that their needs were not being met, each partner tended to identify with the other's pain and cling to the other as perhaps one of the few sources of affection in his or her life. Since they both had firsthand experience with the strains of military life, they also tended to attribute many of their partner's problems to the rigors and sacrifices often demanded by military duty. Hence—when they weren't furious with one another—they could be quite forgiving of one another's shortcomings.

The powerful bond that can be created between two people who have both experienced abandonment, betrayal, violence, and societal rejection can be illustrated by the myth of the multitrauma couple of Dionysus and Ariadne. The ancient mythological Greek god Dionysus, better known as Bacchus, god of wine, was the illegitimate son of Zeus, king of the gods. Zeus's wife, Hera, hated all her husband's illegitimate children, especially Dionysus because her husband had found Dionysus's mother particularly beautiful. Hera arranged for the death of Dionysus's mother and for Dionysus to be placed with foster parents, whom she caused to go "mad" and beat him.

As Dionysus fled from one abusive foster home to the next, he became addicted to alcohol and drugs and was plagued with dissociative episodes and both suicidal and homicidal feelings. But he also became a skilled musician and poet and, as god of ecstasy, he could have had almost any mortal woman (or immortal nymph) he wanted to be his partner.

But Dionysus chose only one woman to be his mate—a trauma survivor like himself—the princess Ariadne. This unlucky young girl had sacrificed her family and country to help a handsome young man who promised to marry her, then abandoned her on a deserted island to fend for herself. Like Dionysus, Ariadne suffered from depression and had no family and no home. Just as she was scorned by human society, Dionysus was shunned by that of the gods.

Dionysus roamed throughout the world seeking to find and rescue Ariadne. Once he found her, he never let her go and, despite his drinking, depressions, irrational rages, and bouts of manic madness, Ariadne stayed by his side until the day she died. In rescuing Ariadne, Dionysus was trying to save himself, and even though Dionysus was far from an ideal husband, Ariadne would be forever indebted to him as the one man who not only accepted, but on a gut level understood, her emotional pain and many fears.

"Come Close, Go Away"

I've seen modern-day versions of Dionysus and Ariadne—military or veteran couples where both partners had histories of child abuse—survive crises similar to those faced by this mythological couple—crises such as adultery, alcoholism, and drug addiction, financial problems due to gambling or overspending, violence, and suicidal depressions. Typically, as abused children, these partners were starved for nurturance and positive regard because physical or sexual abuse seldom occurs without concomitant emotional abuse and physical neglect.[6] Because their families of origin provided little nurturance, both partners may have an intense need for nurturance and love which they may hope will be fulfilled by their spouse or intimate partner. Yet they may also fear receiving nurturance and love since, in the past, loving care was associated with pain and they received both rewards and punishment from the same person.[7]

As a result, in the triple- or quadruple-trauma military couple where one or both adults were victimized as children, a pattern of approach/avoidance may develop toward intimacy and loving. Sometimes it is one partner who needs to withdraw or be angry. Other times, it may be the other partner who pouts and has the temper tantrums. Often the anger or withdrawal occurs after a particularly loving experience, as a defense against anticipated rejection or some other form of "punishment." This can be extremely confusing and painful to the other partner who, at that point, may threaten to leave or seek divorce.

Yet because this partner was also abused as a child, he or she may be accustomed to receiving double messages and therefore not act on his or her threat to leave. Undoubtedly his or her abusive caretakers said, "Get away from me," or "You're so bad you deserve the punishment I'm giving you," only to say eventually, "I love you" or "I need you."

Hence abuse survivors may be able and willing to stay in partially rewarding relationships because they are accustomed to living in households where they are scapegoated and where there is a cycle of being loved, then rejected or wounded in some other way. When both partners have military experience, they may also be bound by the military ethos of loyalty, enduring hardships without complaint, and commitment to duty. They may also feel it is their patriotic duty to take care of one another. Survivor guilt stemming from having friends or loved ones injured or killed in the service (or from not having been able to save another family member from abuse) can also play a role in maintaining their relationship.

If the couple also has children, they may want their children to have the loving, peaceful childhood they never had and hence refrain from divorce or separating. In giving their children the love, attention, and protection they craved but failed to receive as children, they somehow redeem their past pain. In addition, they can enjoy vicariously a normal childhood by providing their children with good care.

On the other hand, the tensions in triple- or quadruple-trauma couples can set the stage for child abuse. Under stress, one or both partners may find themselves acting like their abusive parent or caretaker and assaulting one of the children, even a highly cherished child. These outbursts of violence, however, are followed by periods of intense remorse and giving to the child who has been hurt.

Separation and Divorce

There have been divorces among dual-, triple-, and other multi-trauma couples where one or both partners have made significant progress in dealing with at least one of their traumas. At this point, either one or both partners may realize that they married or chose their partner for the wrong reason. For example, one or both of the partners may have had the unrealistic expectation that their partner would shower them with so much love and affection that they would forget the wounds of war or other traumas. Some may have married or become partners primarily as a means of escape from a violent or abusive home or as a means to avoid dealing with combat or another form of adult trauma. As one or both face the demons they have been running from, their self-esteem can grow. No longer "stuck" in their traumas, they are freer to develop as individuals. As their sense of self grows, they may find they have traits or new interests or attitudes that are incompatible with their present partner.

If their partner is not involved in a recovery process, is not progressing in that process, or is having ongoing problems with alcohol or another addiction, the partner with more recovery may feel he/she has "outgrown" his/her mate, or decide that the partner's traumas and traumatic reactions cannot be tolerated. The healthier partner may also resent the stress and limitations imposed by his/her partner's fears, negative thinking, or other trauma-related symptoms and may wish to find a partner without a trauma history. Or he/she may decide that he/she deserves someone "better" than his/her present mate.

Summary

Dual-military couples face all the challenges faced by couples where only one partner is or was in military service: the unpredictable separations, long work hours, and the many other demands of military service. However, the active-duty or veteran woman whose partner is or was in the military faces the additional stress of shouldering two sets of responsibilities: those attending her military career and those attending her role as military wife. Her difficulties are complicated if either she or her partner has been exposed to combat or another trauma and has developed traumatic reactions as a result, especially if both she and her partner suffer from the aftereffects of some form of military- or non-military-related post-traumatic stress reactions.

In dual-, triple-, quadruple-, and other multitrauma couples, the usual problems of emotional numbing, trigger reactions, depression, difficulties with intimacy, addiction, and anger are magnified due to the presence of more than one trauma in the home. Some active-duty women and women veterans consider their partner's combat trauma to be more severe and more worthy of attention than any child or adult victimization or other traumas that they have experienced. Because of the expectation that they will be silent heroines and unacknowledged pillars of strength, they may have difficulty asking for help and acknowledging any part of themselves that suggests vulnerability, helplessness, and need for attention and support.

To date there are few studies of military couples and their struggles and victories. Given the rise of women in the military and the increased number of military couples, such studies are clearly needed.

11

"Why can't you make Dad better?"

Children in Veteran Families

When Dad left for Vietnam I was not told too much why he had to leave and what he was going to be doing. . . . I cried terribly when he left, and emptiness and fear flooded my body and mind.

My father came home with a hearing impairment. . . . His resentment today toward his deafness is still eating him up inside, because it has gradually gotten worse over the years.

He had changed a great deal when he got home. His nightmares and diving in the bushes from his fear from the war were a few things I heard and saw. His drinking got a lot worse, and so did his anger. . . . Him being so unpredictable aroused a tremendous amount of paranoia in my daily living. . . . It seemed like he had his own war he was fighting inside himself, and with the effect of alcohol, he couldn't control his unbelievable rage that would explode in front of anybody.

My resentment toward my mother grew also. I felt she didn't care for us kids or else she would protect us from this insane man. . . .

A lot of bitterness, hatred, anger, resentment, and absolutely no pity for him was all I felt for quite a few years. I felt I was trapped in a vicious circle of fear with no way out and no one around to understand me and talk with. I became an extremist for destruction and hate and blame toward myself. I held myself responsible for my father's behavior because I felt I was unacceptable and hated in his eyes.

For over ten years it never dawned on me my father's behavior might be caused by what he went through in Vietnam. . . . I was ashamed of myself and felt extremely guilty for all the years of condemning my father to hell when he was already in a living hell of guilt, remorse, and hatred toward himself.

I can assure you I have been deeply affected directly from the war in Vietnam. I couldn't be excused from it because it came home with Dad and lived in our house for a good portion of my life.

Today, though, I am trying to learn and understand the destruction the war placed on our combat vets. . . . It tears me up inside to see their unmistakable misery within. I have seen it with my own eyes with my dad.

I will never forget the craziness and insane behavior from both myself and my father in the past. But my awareness and acceptance is the biggest asset I have today. I am working on all those feelings I have suppressed for several years and to me, this is the best thing I can do for myself. To keep trying and keep loving him for who he is and where he's been, and to understand it was not me who should be responsible any longer for his behavior.

—KID OF A VET[1]

Since research studies on children of combat veterans are few in number, this chapter is based primarily on clinical reports and clinical work with children of combat veterans. Hence the observations recorded in this chapter may apply primarily to children of help-seeking veterans and cannot be generalized to all children of combat vets.

Even among children of help-seeking vets, gross generalities must be avoided. The impact of a veteran's combat trauma on his children's development is complex. Combat veterans are not identical. Their parenting skills, their military experiences, their reactions to combat, their financial status, and numerous other factors that can influence the severity, nature, and course of any post-traumatic symptoms they suffer are not identical either.* Furthermore, a veteran's trauma is not the only factor

See "Why are some veterans more affected by combat than others?" on pages 48–53.

affecting a child's development. Other people (such as the child's non-veteran parent, other family members, teachers, and peers) also play key roles in a child's development, especially if they are struggling with unresolved traumas of their own.* Children can also be impacted by the media and social, political, or economic realities over which their family has little or no control.

See chapters 9 and 10.

Furthermore, children vary in their degree of emotional sensitivity, interests, and talents. Hence a child who is by nature emotionally reactive may be especially impacted by parental trauma. Furthermore, the effects of trauma do not just go from parent to child, but from child to parent and back and forth. For example, psychologist Kathi Nadir describes a World War II veteran who lost his hair after his son was sent to Vietnam. Upon the son's return, the father's hair grew back.[2] Similarly, I have counseled numerous World War II, Korean, Vietnam, and Persian Gulf veterans who sought help only after one of their children had been deployed to a war zone or was in danger of being so deployed. Most of these veterans had experienced some symptoms of combat trauma during or after their own tour of duty, but they had been able to manage them without outside help until one of their children's lives was at risk.

Nadir and other trauma experts also point out that a child's physical growth and emerging sexuality can activate a veteran's combat trauma, as can children's aggressive feelings, especially when directed toward the veteran or other family members.[3] Even when the vet tries to hide his reactions from his children, some children cannot help but observe their father's increased distress or symptoms. If they come to view their normal growth processes (or their aggressive feelings or their evolving sexuality) as wounding an already hurting parent, children can come to feel guilty about growing up or about having normal feelings, such as anger.

At the same time, they can be resentful because they feel they aren't being allowed to grow up and "be normal" like other children. Should the children's resentments result in their becoming defiant or withdrawn from the vet (or in problems with other family members or at school), the veteran's symptoms may be aggravated, which can increase the child's guilt and resentment, which can lead to more problem behavior on the part of the child and so forth, thus perpetuating a vicious cycle.

It must be emphasized that the descriptions of the various reactions children have to a parent's combat trauma presented in this chapter and throughout this book are not intended to portray a picture of all children of combat vets as suffering from severe or irrevocable psychological damage. Joseph Albeck, an expert on the intergenerational effects of trauma, stresses that children of traumatized parents should not automatically be seen as psychologically damaged because "not all effects of parental trauma are necessarily deleterious. The possibilities for growth as a result of trauma in both generations . . . must not be overlooked."[4] Just as veterans and their partners can develop certain admirable traits as the result of facing adversity, so can their children. For example, some children acquire an advanced degree of emotional maturity and other of the positive qualities as described in "What are some of the benefits of combat duty?" in chapter 2. While some children are negatively affected, with proper interventions they can heal.

Jesse and Linda's Story

Jesse, a combat surgeon, writes:

Birth reminds me of death. When I first saw the shriveled mass that was my newborn daughter, I felt pangs, thinking about how all the people who died overseas were once little babies like that. Some of them died like that—as shriveled masses. I hate to admit it, but right there, in the delivery room, I found myself pulling away from my daughter. Seeing her reminded me of all the surgeries I did on Afghan children who stepped on a land mine and lost a limb or two. If my daughter ever got killed or disfigured in an accident or by some attacker, I'd probably kill myself.

What's it all about? Why do we struggle so hard in this life, only to die in the end? Sometimes I wonder why I bother to live at all.

As Jesse's last statement reveals, he is severely depressed and, at times, suicidal. More than once his wife, Linda, has needed to lock up the firearms he brought home from Afghanistan and hide the key. Even though Jesse was never shot at or shot anyone, like many medical professionals who served in war zones he suffers from many of the classical symptoms of PTSD, especially survivor guilt.[5]

Yet Jesse finds it difficult to admit that he suffers any psychological effects from the war. During his medical training, he was taught to "develop a high degree of clinical detachment." Such emotional detachment, he learned, was absolutely necessary in order to make the "right medical decisions," but it also served to harden him to his own emotional reactions to the war. Jesse also is reluctant to admit to having emotional problems because he fears losing his colleagues' "respect, or worse [his] job or practice."[6]

If it weren't for Linda's insistence, Jesse would not have had the courage to seek help. Although therapy is helping Jesse with his depression, Linda still considers herself a "married single parent." Other mothers feel similarly. This does not mean that their vet doesn't love his children, but rather that his combat trauma interferes with his parenting. Often what appears to be disinterest or avoidance of children reflects an extreme concern for them.

For example, Jesse enjoyed taking his children on walks until one unhappy day when he found that instead of paying attention to them, he was searching for hidden land mines or booby traps. Shortly thereafter he began to dissociate or "tune out" at the sight of candy wrappers and other types of litter that resembled the tattered clothing and belongings of persons who had stepped on land mines. After that, Jesse feared, and legitimately so, that if his dissociation became severe, he might jeopardize the well-being of his children. One afternoon, for example, one of his children wandered away and he didn't even notice. Afterwards, Jesse refused to go on walks with his children, leaving them feeling disappointed and rejected and their father feeling like a total failure as a parent.

Many vets are extremely capable and involved fathers. However, help-seeking partners have voiced concerns such as the ones listed below. In many cases, the vet himself shares one or more of these concerns and seeks counseling specifically to improve his relationship with his children.

- The vet is emotionally withdrawn from the children; or the opposite, he is overly involved with them.
- The vet is excessively demanding, critical, or controlling of the children, treating the children "as if they were privates in barracks";[7] or the opposite, he overindulges the children and has difficulties disciplining them.

• The vet assumes little or no responsibility for child care; or the opposite, he feels so responsible toward his children he has trouble allowing them to take age-appropriate responsibility for themselves.

For Linda, as for other young mothers who have sought help, the image of the "liberated couple" where husband and wife happily and equally share the housework and the child care is an impossible dream. Linda would be grateful if Jesse would just show the children more fatherly love and be less critical of them acting like children—for example, for being noisy or contrary at meals. "Even when our daughter was two, she understood Jesse's blank stare. Jesse didn't think a two-year-old could understand when he wasn't responding to her, but she did. And he thought his children didn't miss him, but they did—and still do. He's their father and they love him."

When a child is hurting, that child's pain usually becomes the mother's major focus of attention, overriding her concern for herself or her vet. Even the incarcerated partners I have worked with, street-smart women who were heavily invested in presenting a tough image to the world, would almost always weep and ask for help when talking about their children.

Like many other mothers, Linda feels her children's pain. She even feels it when they aren't feeling it but denying it instead. Linda tries to compensate for her husband's parenting problems by giving her children extra attention and love. But she is tired of being her children's emotional Band-Aid and fears that all her love and extra efforts cannot undo the effects of Jesse's critical remarks. She says angrily:

How do you think I feel when I see Jesse Jr. giving up on a project because his father has called him "dumb" or "lazy"? No matter how hard I try to convince my son that he can succeed at a certain project, he has internalized his father's low image of him to such a degree that he gives up almost immediately. Here's me, doing everything, and here's my husband, the critic. Why am I to blame every time the children misbehave or have a problem at school?

Even though Linda knows her husband's view of her is inaccurate, she, like her son, has adopted Jesse's low image of herself. On some level, she sees herself as an inadequate mother, even though every piece of objective evidence points otherwise.

Jesse and Linda's story illustrates how the children, like their mothers, can suffer from self-blame, low self-esteem, difficulty expressing anger and aggression, and conflicts in establishing themselves as unique individuals apart from the family system. Like their mothers, some children assume responsibility for the vet's emotional well-being. If the veteran's combat trauma expresses itself in irritability, outbursts of temper, frequent flashbacks, or erratic behavior, the children are often frightened and anxious, not knowing what to expect next. "I've got to be home all the time to keep the children from falling apart in case he [the veteran] falls apart," explains Beth, mother of three. "Only when he goes on trips do the kids and I get a break."

While younger children may go to their rooms when Daddy goes "off," older children may leave for the evening. Or they may stay home and try to help their father. "Even if I leave home for the weekend, I take my father with me in my mind," explains Beth's oldest son, Tom, age fourteen, who is more troubled by his father's crying spells than by his anger. Tom has never been told why his father is so troubled or so distant. As a result, he often blames himself for his father's unhappiness and episodes of withdrawal from the family.

A Vet Center counselor explains:

> In the majority of these troubled families, the children have been given little explanation for their father's difficulties and the stresses of family life. Inevitably they attribute much of the blame and responsibility to themselves, just as do the children of divorcing, alcoholic, and otherwise troubled parents. The patterns of communication among family members are often very sparse so that there is little opportunity to acquire a more accurate or different explanation. Indeed, the child's sense of responsibility may be heightened by the frequent exhortations of "Be quiet. Be good. Don't upset your father." Thus, these children may grow up feeling alienated from their fathers, responsible for the difficulties in the family, and isolated from community supports.[8]

In Santonio's home, however, the father has recounted his traumatic war experiences so frequently that, by now, Santonio is bored with

them. "I can't stand hearing about war stuff anymore!" Santonio sometimes shouts. "Forget the past, Dad! Live in the present!"

But Santonio's father can't forget the past and his son's outbursts
engender father-son disputes, which leave the father feeling misunderstood and unloved by his own family and Santonio feeling guilty for
further upsetting his father and for not having suffered as much as his
father. Santonio willingly restricts his activities in order to be with his
father. At times, however, he resents the burden his father's emotional
pain has imposed on his life.

If the veteran is prone to rage reactions or flashbacks, the children
may fear inviting their friends home lest their friends witness the father's anger or disorientation. Their mother, who may greatly desire
that her children have a normal childhood, may discourage her children from having guests for the very same reason. She may also be
aware that the noise, play, and activities of children, especially if they
are young, may trigger her husband and increase his anxiety level.

The psychological problems experienced by children of veterans as
a direct result of the veteran's combat trauma can occur in one of six
types of family settings:

- Families such as Jesse and Linda's, in which the mother functions
  as a virtual single parent due to the veteran's emotional conflicts
  or withdrawal.

- Families in which the mother is so chronically stressed or
  depressed that she turns to one of the children for excessive
  emotional support.

- Families in which there is "secondary traumatization"—where
  one or more of the children overidentify with the veteran,
  exhibit some of the father's symptoms (or other symptoms), or
  attempt to "rescue" the veteran.[9]

- Families in which the vet overprotects or overvalues the
  children.

- Families in which there is physical, as well as emotional, abuse of
  the mother or the children.

- Families in which there is alcohol/drug abuse as well as
  untreated combat trauma.

These categories of families are not mutually exclusive, as will be shown by using some of the same families to illustrate different family problems. Families also vary in their degree of emotional closeness. Considerable emotional distance and anger exist in some homes. The children may respond to their parents' anger with anger of their own, or with various forms of emotional distancing. When Dad or Mom begins to yell, they may turn up the television or simply plug themselves into a DVD player using headphones. Vet Center counselor Ellen Salom found that when children drew pictures of their homes, sometimes they depicted each family member as being in separate rooms.[10] Such pictures suggest a high degree of emotional alienation and lack of communication in the family.

In other families, there are close attachments. Sometimes the bond includes all the family members; other times, tight subunits are formed between one or more family members, which to one degree or another seem to or actually exclude other family members. For example, the mother and a child may be so closely bonded the vet feels left out. Or perhaps the vet and one or more children form such a close subunit that the mother feels rejected.

The Effects of Distancing on Children

Being emotionally distant from another family member may be fleeting, may persist for several weeks, or may become a life-long pattern. Even when emotional distancing lasts only a few minutes, it is painful not only for the veteran's partner and children but for the veteran as well. In response to a veteran's emotional detachment, partners and children may find themselves emotionally distancing themselves from the veteran, too. Since feeling alienated usually coexists with a strong need to feel close, not only are these feelings painful, they may also give rise to guilt, self-doubt, and confusion in all family members.

Yet the veteran's distancing from his children may have little to do with his true feelings. Some of the emotional distance, for example, may be a carryover from his combat days.* It can also develop in situations of ongoing stress, even when there is no immediate threat to life. Thus, some of a veteran's emotional numbing may be due to the stress of his combat reactions, financial problems in the family, and other issues. Upon his return, to one degree or another, the numbing may persist because emo-

*Emotional numbing often develops during life-and-death situations (see pages 92–96).

tions cannot be turned on and off like water faucets. As time passes, the numbing may be compounded by the stresses of the readjustment process as well as the inevitable stresses of daily living and any subsequent major misfortunes or traumas.*

See "Why are some veterans more affected by combat than others?" on pages 48–53.

If a veteran's emotional distancing extends to the children, they will probably feel rejected. He may not be rejecting them at all, yet they may believe they are unwanted because they aren't good enough for their father. If they then begin to withdraw or create disturbances, they may become less approachable or less responsive to their father when he does show them love. Their negative attitude may wound him, especially if he dreamed about coming home to or having an idyllic father-child relationship.

In response, he may pay less attention to them or he may begin to scold them over minor matters or be irritable and impatient with them in other ways. In turn, the children may become even more withdrawn or unruly. Everyone may be feeling hurt but no one knows how to talk about it. Any negative behaviors that arise can be indirect ways of expressing the hurt, yet they can also be ways of connecting. Bickering and arguing, although unpleasant, are ways of getting a response from the other person and may be preferable to indifference or feeling unimportant.

A veteran may be an extremely capable and involved father. But if he hasn't had the chance to recuperate from his combat experiences or any other ordeals life has presented him, his ability to deal with the stresses of parenting may be limited until he is able to make some sort of peace with the past. In addition, just looking at his children may spark unwanted memories of dead or suffering children he encountered during the war or grief for the children of comrades who were left fatherless. Regardless of the reason, a vicious cycle can begin when emotional distancing on the part of one family member can perpetuate emotional distancing and irritability in another.

The child's reactions to the father's emotional distancing appear to be age related. Among preschoolers, there may be increased separation anxiety, evidenced by increased clinging to the mother, increased fearfulness, and even increased aggressive behavior. Mothers of slightly older preschool children have reported an increase in temper tantrums and a decrease in playing with other children following any periods of time where the father's emotional withdrawal or absence from the home is especially prolonged.

Between the ages of four and seven, children's understanding of the world is egocentric. In their view, the world revolves about their needs and they believe that their thoughts and wishes actually can cause external events. Hence they easily blame themselves for their father's alienation, anger, or depression. Even if they were given information about combat trauma, they would have difficulty digesting and comprehending such information. At this age, children still tend to believe that they are the major cause of all the activity around them. Furthermore, as author Melanie Suhr notes, "In times of stress, even adolescent or older children can revert to (such) egocentric modes of thinking."[11]

By the time children reach seven or eight, their capacity for concrete reasoning has increased.[12] Now they are able to see cause and effect more clearly. Yet unless they are told about the psychological and other effects of war upon the warrior and repeatedly reminded that their father's symptoms are not their fault, they may still personalize the father's alienation.

At this stage, children may also become involved in loyalty conflicts between the parents. A child may side with the mother or with the veteran, or have split loyalties. It is not uncommon for children who side with the veteran to join with him in any denial of his PTSD, alcoholism, or other problems. Since some children tend to idealize their parents, they may find it hard to admit that one of their parents has a serious problem. Just as some children scapegoat the veteran and blame almost all of the family's and their personal problems on him, children who ally with the veteran may blame their mother for each and every problem facing the family, especially for their father's symptoms and signs of unhappiness.

In several cases, a partner's attempts to encourage her veteran to seek professional help have met with resistance not only from the veteran but also from his "ally," one of the children. The resistance may be especially vehement if the mother is encouraging or insisting upon a treatment program that will take the father away from home, such as an inpatient war recovery program or an inpatient alcohol- or drug-rehabilitation program. "Why are you trying to send my daddy away to a hospital? He's not sick," children may protest. Some children erroneously think their mother is trying to punish them by taking their father away from them (sending him to an inpatient program), especially if the program is out of town. They may also fear that once their father leaves, he may never return. Or that some day their mother may send them away, as she did their father. These fears can usually be alleviated by careful explanations of what treatment involves and, if possible, visiting the treatment facility with the children.

At the age of seven or eight, children may not only begin to take sides but, if there is much quarreling in the home, as with children of divorcing parents, they may also come to distrust both parents. Without a parent to lean on, children can develop a host of insecurities, show signs of depression or an anxiety disorder, and begin rebelling against both parents.

Regardless of their age, some children learn to be quiet. The same inhibition of angry feelings has been found among children of Nazi Holocaust survivors.[13] These children have often kept their angry feelings to themselves because they did not want to cause additional suffering to their obviously already suffering parents. In a parallel manner, some combat veterans' children may not want to upset their already obviously upset father or their overburdened mother. In addition, a child may have been severely punished by the veteran for aggressive or defiant behavior. Given their military training and background, some vets equate anger with disrespect and tolerate little disobedience from their children, and the children's anger becomes repressed.

When Children Repress Anger

Children, including adolescents, may stifle their anger because of their natural dependency on their parents. Generally it is difficult for anyone, even adults, to express anger toward those upon whom they are emotionally or financially dependent, for if the anger is expressed, there is a high risk of alienating the person whose love and attention or support is so desperately needed.

Children's repressed anger can eventually emerge in the form of self-mutilation, depression, suicidal thoughts, sudden outbursts of aggression, or compulsions and obsessions—for example, with food or cleanliness. In my experience, temper tantrums, hostility, and aggression are far more common than self-mutilation. Nevertheless, in one case, a ten-year-old son habitually scraped his legs with razor blades, not enough to injure himself, but enough to leave noticeable marks. In another instance, a child scratched his head to such an extent that he became partially bald. Other examples of self-mutilation include head banging, self-burning, skin pinching, hair pulling, and extreme fingernail biting.

Self-mutilation can be a way of releasing repressed anger, as well as other forms of emotional pain. Suicidal depressions can also stem from repressed anger, with several children contemplating suicide as a means of making their dads "sorry" for not paying more attention to them or as a means of escaping the arguing and other forms of unhappiness at home.

In contrast to children who internalize their anger (in the form of self-mutilation, under- or overeating, compulsive hand washing or other activity, depression, or suicidal thoughts) are those who external-ize their anger by frequently destroying property, harming animals, or fighting with their siblings or classmates. Some children blame their mother for their aggressive acts. "You made my dad sick!" or "Why can't you make Dad better?" tormented children have cried out as they smashed tables, toys, or radios. In other instances, otherwise "perfect" daughters have been found tearing drapes off windows, shouting: "I hate you! I hate you, Mom," blaming the mother for all of the family's problems.

When children use emotional withdrawal as a means of punishing or manipulating their mothers, the mothers may wonder if their chil-dren learned this behavior from their veteran father. The mother of a teenager explains:

> My son was not a problem when he was young, but now whenever things don't go his way or he doesn't like the family rules, he threatens to aban-don me or totally tunes me out. I couldn't understand where this behavior came from, since it wasn't evident in his younger years, until it suddenly dawned on me that he's treating me exactly the way his father treats me.

In other instances, anger stemming from the family situation is displaced onto refugees or others who originated from countries in which the veteran fought. Such groups are relatively safe targets for the hostility which a child may feel toward a parent or the family situation but does not feel safe to express. For example, the son or grandson of a Vietnam vet may express anger and disdain toward Vietnamese neigh-bors or vendors, the child of a vet who served in the Middle East to-ward anyone with brown skin who looks like a "towel-head."

For example, Brian, age eleven, was referred for psychological test-ing when his grades began to decline after the fifth grade, the same time he began refusing to sit near children who were Muslim (or who he thought were Muslim) and starting fights with any children whom he felt were wrong about some matter. Right and wrong were big issues in his family since his father had become very sensitive to issues of justice and fairness as the result of combat.

When Brian's father returned from war, he was easily startled by sudden noises and often felt anxious around strangers. In a parallel manner, Brian became frightened by the ringing of the school bell and was highly suspicious of strangers, even the psychological examiner sent by the school. Nevertheless, Brian applied himself to the testing—until he was asked to put together puzzles of humans and animals. The cut-up pieces reminded him of the gore in his father's war stories and he was unable to concentrate on this part of the testing. He also showed signs of anxiety when asked to define words like *knife* or to deal with words and concepts having to do with aggression.

Whenever questions or pictures about vehicles came up, Brian became extremely afraid that the vehicles would be blown up or crash, like those in overseas war zones.

When Brian had trouble with these and other parts of the testing, he expressed fear that the examiner would yell at him, as apparently his parents did when he brought home poor marks. Even when he was assured he would have a second chance at certain items, he did not appear to believe the examiner and would give up.

As a result of the testing, Brian was placed in a special classroom environment where he received more individualized attention and less was expected of him than in a regular classroom. Consequently, he experienced many more academic successes than in his regular classroom. Over time he became more self-confident and was less aggressive toward other students.

In addition, seeing a therapist helped Brian separate his father's war realities from the reality of his own everyday life. Although Brian had trouble opening up to the therapist, eventually he disclosed that much of his mental life was spent fantasizing about his father's experiences in Iraq. Often his conceptions of what his father had experienced were severe distortions of what his father had shared with him. Some of Brian's ideas had become confused with news coverage and movies about war. In family therapy sessions with his father, Brian got a clearer picture of his father's war experiences, which enabled him to focus more on reality.

Brian also needed many assurances that his father was no longer in immediate (or imminent) danger, as he had been during combat and that the dangers his father had faced overseas were not prevalent in their particular neighborhood. Although Brian had been given these reassurances many times before, hearing them from his father was far more powerful than hearing them from his mother or his therapist.

The family therapy sessions also revealed that, in part, Brian was doing poorly in school in order to get his father's attention. Even being yelled at was better than being ignored. When it became clear to Brian that his father was willing to give him attention in other ways, Brian's school performance and emotional state improved.

However, one of the most significant breakthroughs for Brian was being able to articulate his anger at his father. Ever since he was a small child, Brian had been unable to show anger toward his father because he didn't want to aggravate him and because he feared his father's physical strength. Yet Brian's father had never hit either Brian or Brian's mother. On one occasion, however, he became so frustrated with his wife that he smashed the glass door at the entrance to their apartment building.

"Don't you know we might get evicted for that?" Brian's mother shouted.

"Don't you raise your voice at me, woman. I'm the man in the house," Brian's father shouted back.

"But the property manager is going to make trouble for us."

"I can handle that puny runt. Remember, I've stood up to armed men."

"But what if a child had been standing near you and had gotten hurt by the flying glass?"

"Then it would have been the kid's fault for being there, not mine."

Brian's father's last words were said in such a state of anger that he had forgotten he ever said them. But Brian did not forget—not the words and not the smashed door. He was afraid that if he made one wrong move at home, he would become the object of his father's powerful fist. Consequently, he acted out his aggressive feelings at school. Even the teachers and the principal seemed safer than his father. At home he was afraid to stand up for himself, even when he felt his father was drawing inaccurate and unfair conclusions about a particular situation. For example, Brian's father was so afraid for his family's safety that whenever family members went out, they were required to call home upon arrival at their destination. Sometimes after getting to a friend's house, Brian would quickly call home. "Hi, Dad. I'm okay, Dad. Bye, Dad."

His father, however, interpreted Brian's brevity on the phone as a sign of disrespect. Sometimes he accused Brian of hanging up on him, even though Brian had not done so. The root of the father's reactions to his son's phone calls was a wartime incident when a command control operator had muttered some information to him quickly, almost inaudibly, then hung up on him. This had left Brian's father with such incomplete information that he was not able to save some wounded Americans. As a result, he was intolerant of mistakes in his family as well as himself and became highly anxious whenever somebody spoke to him on the phone quickly or inaudibly.

In family therapy Brian learned how to talk to his father when he was in a hurry. "Don't get hyper, Dad, but I'm talking fast because I don't have much time to play with my friends unless I get started right now. If there's something really important you want to talk about, I'll stay on the line. But if you just want to talk about the usual stuff, I'd rather wait until later." In the presence of a third party—the therapist—Brian was able to speak directly to his father about things that were bothering him. The more he was able to do that, the less need he had to act out his anger in school.

Why the Veteran Distances from His Children

"In all honesty, I'd rather be alone," confesses Jeremiah, who harbors enormous guilt about his limited ability to tolerate his children. Similarly, a veteran treated by VA psychiatrist Sarah Haley suffers from chronic guilt for snapping at his wife and children "for every little thing." In fact, he considers himself "a poor excuse for a father" when his three-year-old asked why he looked so sad and yelled all the time.[14]

Parenting requires an enormous amount of energy, which some combat veterans lack due to a preoccupation with their war experiences or their combat-related symptoms. In this, they are like some of the survivors of the Nazi concentration camps, who, due to their focus on their traumatic experiences in the camps and their subsequent demoralization, have been found to lack the energy to parent.[15]

Vets with severe cases of combat trauma often feel they cannot handle the stresses of child rearing while simultaneously trying to recover from their combat trauma. As Haley writes, "Fatherhood may overtax the veteran's ability to resolve a trauma. Any point during the child's development can impinge upon the veteran's depression, withdrawal or conflicts."[16] As a result, the vet may allocate the job of parenting to his wife, not realizing that his very physical or emotional absence from the home is the source of many of his wife's difficulties with their children.

In some cases, the trauma of combat or specific injuries have caused physiological changes in the vet's central nervous system which make him more reactive, and hence less tolerant, of sudden noises and movements.[17]* Even without these biochemical changes, however, veterans often evidence the startle response to abrupt or unexpected noises or movements common for young children. Children may be strictly warned by their mothers not to surprise their father by jumping on him or in any manner approaching him from behind. The edginess some vets feel around others, especially children, can be seen as an exaggerated startle response.[18] Some veterans have come to fear children as the result of having fought in war zones where children were used to carry hand grenades or other explosives or were used as ploys to trap or kill American soldiers.

See "How can war affect veterans physically?" on pages 55–58.

Combat memories also play a role in a veteran's negative response to his children's aggressive play or to his or other children when they approach the ages of children they killed or saw killed while on active duty.[19] One vet's PTSD lay dormant until his son became nine, the exact age of a young boy he inadvertently killed during the war. This type of reaction is not atypical, even among noncombat veterans.[20] Jesse, like other combat medical personnel, often treated children. When his daughter turned two, he had to flee from her birthday party, remembering a two-year-old Afghan girl whose life he had failed to save. Some vets may not even want to have children as a result of such memories.

Sometimes the veteran's memories, not just of children but of anyone killed during the war, are activated by having children or simply watching children. Often it is the birth of a child that makes the vet realize that enemy soldiers and their supporters were human beings, too. Haley cites an example of a veteran who had "never thought of enemy soldiers as people, as parents with children or as people who would be parents someday" until he watched his own children at play.[21]

If, in addition, the veteran was attacked by or actually killed children during his combat career, he may "find it difficult to make the
transition to the roles of husband, protector, and nurturing parent."[22]
VA psychiatrist H. Glover, for example, has found that some vets who
killed women and children during wartime suffer from auditory hallucinations that "manifest themselves as the anguished cries of women
and children killed by the veteran. At times the vet may see the face
of a . . . woman or child while he is relating to a family member."[23]
In my experience, vets who witnessed or participated in the injury or
death of a child, even if the child was armed and dangerous, often relive such experiences in nightmares, intrusive thoughts, and in visual or
auditory hallucinations while they are awake, as well as while they are
asleep.

For some veterans, envy is yet another source of discomfort and irritability when they are around their children. "I'm jealous of my own
kids," Jesse admits reluctantly. Yet it has also come as a relief for Jesse to realize that the anxiety and impatience he feels toward his children do not stem from his lack of caring for them, but from a sense of
loss. When Jesse observes his children's innocence, he is reminded of
the innocence he lost overseas. Since this is painful for him, he sometimes wishes to avoid his children. He also wishes he had had someone to guide and protect him as he faced the challenges of war the way
he guides and protects his own children from life's challenges and obstacles. "Why didn't someone tell me what war was really like before I
went?" he often asks.

Jesse joined the military thinking he would help to save lives as
doctors did in World War II—in safely placed hospitals in demilitarized
zones. He was totally unprepared for rocket and other attacks on his
hospital, the volume of casualties, or the horrible types of disfiguring
injuries caused by guerrilla-warfare tactics. Furthermore, he had little
medical school training or other guidance in how to decide which of
the wounded would be helped to live versus who would have to be
allowed to die, decisions he was forced to make when there weren't
enough medical staff or supplies to take care of all the wounded immediately. To this day, taking his children to the pediatrician fills Jesse
with rage. He can't help but compare the excellent care his children
receive for relatively minor medical problems with what he saw in
Afghanistan: young Americans and Afghan children dying of various
forms of hideous, deforming injuries.

Military experience can also carry over into the veteran's attitude toward child discipline. Some vets underdiscipline their children; others overdiscipline them. In the extreme, some children are treated as if they were small soldiers. For example, in one family the children must be (or feel they must be) constantly "on guard" or "at attention" when their father is at home. But the minute he leaves, the children become extremely unruly, taking out all their rebellious feelings and repressed anger toward their father on one another and on their mother.

Their mother finds it difficult, if not impossible, to counteract her children's predictable reactions to being overcontrolled. Out of sheer exhaustion, she has given up trying to control her children when her husband is gone, fully aware that if her husband finds out about the children's unruly behavior, he might berate her for not being able to "control" the children. But her main concern is not being berated; it is that afterwards her husband might overpunish the children or try to control the children even more, which, she believes, will cause the children to behave in an even more negative manner in his absence.

She has tried to solve the problem by not telling her husband about the children's negative behavior. However, this has been a source of guilt for her. She feels it is wrong for her to keep this information from her husband and is afraid he'll find out some other way and then be even madder at her, and the children, than if he had been told directly. To this day, she hasn't figured out the best way to handle this situation.

Still other veterans are not disciplinarians at all; some may even overly indulge the children. However, they may have an exceptionally harsh response in one particular area: their children's aggressiveness. In some homes, when vets see their children destroying property or being cruel to a pet or another child, especially a new baby, it may "reawaken [for them] the painful effects of combat aggression and sadism."[24] If a vet committed atrocities overseas, he may react by being superstrict with his children, especially his sons, and may not allow even normal aggressiveness. Some vets even feel that their sadism and aggressiveness are being passed on to their children genetically.

Even veterans who were hardly ever emotionally distant from their children may begin distancing themselves from them as their children approach the age that the vets were when they went to war, and specifically from their daughters as they approach the ages of girls or women with whom the vets had traumatic encounters in the military. In some cases, veterans who witnessed or participated in the sexual assault, maiming, or killing of young girls or women overseas may experience a resurgence of their war memories when their daughters, nieces, or other females in their lives reach the ages of the girls or women whom they saw injured or killed during the war. Traumatic memories related to women may also be activated by media accounts of rapes and other forms of violence against women or by actual assaults on female relatives or friends.

When James was overseas, he witnessed the rape of a thirteen-year-old girl. James had considered trying to help the girl, but decided it was "none of his business." When the soldier subsequently shot the girl "for crying too loud," James looked the other way.

James forgot about the incident until his daughter turned thirteen. Suddenly, after several years of relative emotional stability, James became both suicidal and homicidal.

His daughter's thirteenth birthday triggered memories of the rape and intense feelings of guilt, shame, and horror. During the war, James had been so numb, he had not been affected by the rape. But now he felt like a moral coward for not having intervened on the young girl's behalf.

James's therapist explained that psychic numbing was almost automatic in combat. Furthermore, since the rapist was a soldier who frequently went "berserk," he might have attacked James if James had intervened.* Also, since the rapist was not the only soldier in James's unit who had ever gone "berserk," some of James's comrades might have considered him a "softie" or an oddball of sorts and ostracized him. In war, ostracism is lethal, given that one's life depends on the support of one's immediate comrades. Therefore, the therapist argued, James's not helping the girl was part of his survival instinct.

*See page 193 for a discussion of "berserking."

On an intellectual level, James agreed with the therapist's reasoning. But on an emotional and spiritual level, James damned himself and was certain God was going to damn him, too. Ironically, James no longer believed in God, yet he was certain that God was going to punish him for what happened to the girl and other civilians by arranging to have his daughter raped and killed.

James immediately purchased firearms and swore he would shoot the first male who looked at his precious daughter the wrong way. When alone, James contemplated suicide. Far better that he die to pay for the raped girl's death than for his daughter to be the sacrifice.

When James's thirteen-year-old daughter developed a crush on one of her classmates, James began having chest pains and forbade her from all contact with the young boy. She then began sneaking out of the house to call and to meet with her boyfriend. When James found out, he warned her that "all men were dogs" and that one day her boyfriend probably would rape and kill her. James made it clear that if she so much as spoke with any young man without his approval, he would throw her into the streets, where she would surely be raped and murdered.

As James's daughter began crying and begging her father to please be reasonable, James was reminded of the rape victim's moaning and her pleas for her life. This plummeted James into the world of his trauma even further, and he became even less able to think and to reason. When he began calling his daughter a "whore," his wife intervened. How dare James ruin their daughter's entry into womanhood by calling her a whore and tarnish her puppy love with talk of violent sex? Their daughter deserved a social life, and if James threw their daughter out because she was a normal teenage girl with normal teenage interests and hormones, then he would lose not only his daughter but also his wife.

James's response to the family turmoil was to dissociate and withdraw from the family. However, James's daughter did not view her father's withdrawal as his way of coping with stress but, rather, as a rejection—of her as a person as well as of her emerging womanhood. She began hating her budding sexuality. In her view, her sexuality had not only cost her her father's love and attention, it had also started a series of arguments between her parents where there was frequent talk of divorce. Her father's warnings about rape and murder reinforced her own fears about becoming a woman in a society full of violence against women.

As a result, part of her wanted to be a little girl again. She began sucking her thumb and wetting the bed, and she gained fifty pounds.

Mother's Helper

In homes where the mother is exceptionally stressed or lonely, she may in desperation turn to one of her children for emotional or other forms of support not appropriate for the child's age or degree of emotional maturity. Jesse and Linda's family provides one example of excessive reliance on a child for emotional support. When the birth of a fourth child triggered an increase in Jesse's PTSD, he began having intrusive thoughts and flashbacks in the midst of performing surgery. He promptly resigned from his position as chief surgeon and took a job writing medical reports. This new job carried less status, but Jesse didn't care. At least no one would be harmed by his difficulties concentrating because of wartime memories. However, the new job paid so much less that Linda needed to go back to work. While caring for an infant and three other children, she also found time to help her husband with his report writing. Says Joleen, Linda and Jesse's eldest daughter:

It started when I found Mom crying in the kitchen, saying: "God help me. I can't do it all. I just can't do it all."

"I'll help you, Mommy," I said, and from that day on I helped fix dinner and clean up. I felt proud to be able to help my mom, and when the new baby got old enough for me to hold, I took over being mom to him, too. I didn't mind not being able to watch TV after school, but I did mind having to quit Girl Scouts. But Mom needed me more and more, and I had to help her so she could help Daddy so our family wouldn't be poor and have to move.

However, it was not Linda's turning to Joleen for household help that was destructive, but rather Linda's sharing of her marital secrets and emotional pain with her daughter. As Joleen and Linda did chores together, Linda would often graphically describe to Joleen how disappointed she was with her marriage and warned Joleen never to marry a vet.

At the age of seven, Joleen was unprepared to hear her mother's secrets about her father. Yet Joleen also felt privileged that her mother would turn to her. Since her father was often emotionally detached from her, Joleen understood and quickly sided with her mother. Yet she still wanted and needed to believe that her father was a good man. Surely her daddy wasn't that bad. And if he was so horrible, didn't that make her, as his daughter, horrible, too? Joleen also felt she was betraying her father by listening to her mother's complaints and feared that if her father ever found out, he'd be so hurt he might punish her, or maybe even kill himself. But how, at age seven, could she tell her distressed, overworked mommy to stop?

As a child, Joleen had few defenses against her mother's feelings. She was easily overpowered by them, and they became a part of her personality. Instead of developing along her own lines and having her own feelings, Joleen took on her mother's personality and emotions. In psychological terms, Joleen became "enmeshed" with her mother. She would feel her mother's pain and sorrow as if they were her own and intuitively knew when her mother would be sad or unhappy. Often she would spend her allowance to buy her mother perfume or flowers, saying: "Someday Daddy will love you again and buy you presents. Meanwhile, you have me."

Starved for love and affection, Linda accepted the gifts. By the age of ten, Joleen was not only buying her mother gifts but also giving her pep talks and advice on how to handle her marriage, her in-laws, her job problems, and her friendships. Joleen could not imagine life without her mother and processed life through her mother's eyes. When she was twelve or thirteen, when children normally begin to separate from their parents, Joleen's natural separation process was stunted. She dared not be different from her mother, lest her mother crumble. Furthermore, because Joleen's relationship with her mother consumed so much of her time and psychic energy, she had few friends and participated in only one after-school activity.

When Joleen, at fourteen, developed an ulcer, Linda went for help. She told the group:

> *I know it wasn't fair of me to put Joleen between her father and myself. But before this group, I had no one to turn to. My parents were far away and the only women I knew were the wives of other doctors. I couldn't talk to them because it would have ruined Jesse's reputation. Besides, they would have never understood. All of their husbands were successful and none were having problems like Jesse. Of course, none of their husbands had ever been in a war zone either.*
>
> *I was so alone and afraid. Without Joleen I might have never been able to keep my sanity. And I needed her, I really needed her help. But I should have never had her take emotional care of me.*

In order to reverse the dangerous trend that had begun in Joleen, Linda ceased talking to her about her marital problems, insisted that Jesse and Jesse Jr. assume some of Joleen's chores, and put Joleen in therapy.

According to Joleen's therapist, Joleen suffered from depression and anxiety and nightmares due to repressed anger and fears surrounding her enmeshment with her mother. In one recurring nightmare, her mother's hairbrush and one of her father's guns fly together from one room of the house to another, sometimes clashing into one another, sometimes chasing Joleen, and sometimes destroying furniture along the way. The hairbrush was interpreted as symbolizing her mother's anger, the gun her father's. The dream shows that Joleen was afraid of her parents' arguing—as symbolized by the hairbrush and knife clashing into one another and destroying property—as well as her mother and father's individual anger toward her, as symbolized by both the hairbrush and the knife chasing Joleen.

Joleen believed that if she did not help and comfort her mother enough, her mother would be angry with her and even more angry with Jesse than she already was. This would lead to more marital arguments, which tore Joleen apart. By helping her mother, Joleen hoped to lessen the tensions between her parents and make life more peaceful for everyone in the family, including herself and her siblings.

In another dream, Joleen envisioned herself as a mummy glued to her mother's leg. She asked her mother to release her, but her mother said, "No." This dream depicts the symbiotic nature of the mother-daughter relationship and Joleen's desire to be her own person, not someone attached to her mother. It also represents Joleen's awareness that if she remained an obedient "mother's helper" and caretaker, she would never become an individual. Instead she would remain a reflection of her mother's emotions and problems.

Joleen's therapeutic progress was impeded by her brother's rebellion. Jesse Jr., now a teenager, was talking back to his parents and refusing to adhere to a curfew or to complete any of his chores or homework. Jesse Jr. even wanted to date an Afghan girl! There were numerous father-son disputes, with Linda threatening to commit suicide unless Jesse and Jesse Jr. came to terms.

In order to compensate for her brother's rebellion, Joleen tried to be even more obedient to her parents. She was tempted to enter the fights as family peacemaker and to give her mother emotional support, but she didn't know how to do that and support her father and brother, too. Joleen's therapist advised her to stay out of this family turmoil as much as possible. For example, she could go to her room while the others argued. She also encouraged Joleen to ask for time off from household duties in order to participate in more social and sports activities.

Depression and conflicts such as Joleen's are not unique to veteran families. In many families in which the mother (or father) is overwrought or dysfunctional, it is not uncommon for one or more of the daughters (or sons) to become a little adult or to take emotional care of the mother or father. The resulting depression has also been observed among daughters of refugee-camp survivors.[25]

There are many Joleens in the world. As they mature into young women, they may keep their "good girl" role of mother's helper and caring daughter, or they may become "bad girls" and abuse alcohol, drugs, and sex, or find other ways to show disregard for parental needs and rules. In some of the cases observed thus far, children who during their early years tried to "help" either their mother or their father sometimes began rebelling against their helping role as soon as their bodies began showing signs of adolescence. Others were physiologically mature for several years before they made the break from their old family role.

For example, girls as young as eleven have begun having sexual relations in their homes or in other locations where there was a high risk that they would be discovered by their parents. A few became pregnant at early ages, ran away from home, or developed severe addictions. In other instances, an adolescent boy or girl began dating or had a sexual relationship with a person from an ethnic or religious group that one or both of the parents disliked or with a person with attitudes or personality traits that one or both parents found unacceptable. In some, but not all, cases to one degree or another, these kinds of sexual and other behaviors can be viewed as ways of expressing anger at one or both parents as well as ways of rebelling against an overparentified role in the family. Reckless behavior also can be a means of expressing anger toward or rebelling against the parent or parents to whom the child or teen was formerly tightly bonded in a helper capacity.

When Adolescents Express Anger

Adolescence is a time in life when children try to establish an identity of their own apart from their parents' expectations of them. This process of separation and personal growth is called individuation. The tendency of adolescents to rebel against parental and other authority figures is, to some extent, a part of their effort to find out who they are.

In homes where the veteran father's life is dominated by combat trauma, normal adolescent tendencies toward separation and rebellion can combine with the children's need to distance themselves from the veteran's agony or anger. Problems arise when the children's need for distance or self-assertion takes the form of rejection or disregard for the veteran.

The adolescents' negative attitude toward their father might be their way of defending themselves against feeling overwhelmed by the father's emotions or against feeling helpless to help or "save" the father. Yet the veteran in the midst of a painful depression or trigger reaction may not interpret his son's or daughter's rejection or indifference to him in such an objective or insightful manner. Quite to the contrary, the hurting veteran is likely to perceive his child's negative attitude toward him as a form of "friendly fire."

Imagine how a combat vet feels when his fifteen-year-old son or eighteen-year-old daughter snickers at him or ignores him at the very moment he is feeling most vulnerable or out of control (such as when he is angry, numb, confused, or weeping due to a flashback, nightmare, depression, or anxiety attack)? Such behavior on the part of adolescents can deepen the veteran's depression and sense of isolation—as well as ignite his rage. The stage is then set for an ugly family fight where no one wins. The only casualties in this fight are the people who probably love and need each other the most—the family members themselves.

More than one mother's heart has been broken as she has seen her partner and teenage children snarl at each other and perhaps even come to blows. It is difficult for her to stand by and do nothing, no matter how adept she is at detachment. Yet when she attempts to intervene, she may be considered a "traitor" by all. Both her partner and her children expect her to be on their side and their side only.

During such awful moments when she sees the family life she has tried so hard to create being torn asunder, a woman may feel especially alone, helpless, and angry. All her sacrifices and efforts seem to be being blown to bits, not by enemy fire, but by some kind of emotional time bomb planted within the hearts of her family members by a war fought thousands of miles away from home.

"It's so sad," comments Margaret, who has seen her husband and teenage children "go at it" dozens of times.

*My husband would die for our children, but they have felt unloved by
him all their lives. When they were young, they accepted the way he
treated them. No questions asked. Now that they're older, they know
better. They know most dads don't spend a lot of time in the basement,
and they're angry that other kids have dads who go to school events and
take them places and their dad doesn't—or can't.*

*When they were little, they were too afraid to tell their dad how an-
gry they were. But no more. Last night my daughter said she'd get pregnant by a drug addict if my husband yelled at her one more time. Then
my eighteen-year-old son said he'd forget about college and join the Marines so he could go crazy . . . just like Dad.*

*I try and get my husband and kids to talk it out peacefully, but
they're all too raw to talk. One of them always says the wrong thing and
that starts the civil war all over again. All any of them wants is love. All
my husband wants is to think his kids care about him. All they want
from him is to hear him say: "I love you. I wish I didn't have these problems from the war, but I'm going to love you anyway—best I can."*

*And if my kids could just say, "Dad, we love you. We missed you
all those times you were in the basement. We thought you didn't like us,
and when we needed you we were scared to ask you for help. We might
be growing up, but we still need a dad. Please come be with us," my husband would probably start crying like a baby.*

*But my husband is too angry and too proud to talk like that and the
kids are just like him—angry and proud. And none of them realizes that
underneath all that anger is a lot of hurt. So all they do is fight and pop
one smart remark after the next.*

*When I try to intervene, they tell me it's none of my business. My
therapist tells me it's not my business either. But how can it not be my
business? They're my family.*

Secondary Traumatization

Joleen and her mother illustrate one type of mother-daughter enmeshment. Another type of child-parent enmeshment occurs when a
child becomes traumatized by the veteran's war experiences. This process, called "secondary traumatization," has been found not only among

children of Vietnam veterans but also among children of World War II veterans with symptoms of combat trauma and among children of the survivors of the Nazi Holocaust.[26] It has also been observed in clinical work with veterans from the Persian Gulf, Afghanistan, Lebanon, Bosnia, Somalia, and Iraq.

In secondary traumatization, the child, in some manner, relives the father's traumatic war experiences or becomes obsessed with the war-related issues that trouble the veteran. The child may even manifest symptoms similar to the veteran's. The child may have nightmares about war or worry a great deal about death and injury. Sometimes children as young as three or four years old have learned to imitate their father and hide under their beds when an airplane or helicopter flies overhead. In families of World War II veterans where there was secondary traumatization, "for some of the veteran's offspring, their father was, by far, the most important person in their lives. It is as if they were constantly together, constantly embroiled in a shared emotional cauldron. For these children, life seems to have been a series of anticipation of, and reactions to, their father's moods, impulses, and obsessions."[27]

Alan, the ten-year-old son of a Vietnam combat vet, did not have nightmares, but he had great difficulty sleeping because he "worried about being killed or kidnapped. His main fear was that he, his father, or both would be shot 'like in the war.' In many of his [Alan's] fantasies, it was as if he was living in one of his father's flashbacks rather than in his own reality."[28]

Like Alan, Ben was obsessed with power and violence. He was constantly playing war games, reading war comics, and attacking his siblings and neighbors with plastic swords or water bombs. It was impossible to have a conversation with Ben without his mentioning war and his father's various heroic feats. Despite his superior I.Q., he had trouble concentrating in school and was in frequent fights. His participation in sports was intense and, he admitted, a way to prove to his father, Dave, that he was as strong and brave as any veteran.

Children who suffer from secondary traumatization do not necessarily also assume a "rescuer" role in relation to their father. This role may be assumed by another child in the family who takes it upon himself to help make the father happy. Ben, however, did assume the rescuer role. When he wasn't playing sports or war games, he spent most of his time with Dave, who was not only his father, but his best, if not only, friend.

At the age of fourteen, however, due to the natural changes of adolescence, Ben began to want to separate from his father. Also, he became interested in girls, most of whom frowned on his interest in violence. Yet Ben felt guilty about experiencing the normal adolescent process of separating and becoming an individual, as if in growing up he was abandoning his father.

At the same time, Dave was experiencing his son's growing up—and away—as yet another loss, rekindling feelings of betrayal and abandonment associated with his war experience. In an effort to hold on to his son (who had been not only a son but also an admiring companion), Dave began to impose unnecessary restrictions on Ben's activities and to criticize Ben for minor imperfections, leading to further conflict between father and son, and more guilt on Ben's part.

Therapy helped Dave realize that punishments and critical remarks were not bringing his son closer to him, but driving him farther away and that losing children in their own lives is a normal part of parenthood, not a personal rejection. Yet Ben's becoming less interested in him and spending less time with him still felt like a rejection to Dave. At one point, his hurt was so great that he considered emotionally divorcing himself from his son and not interacting with him at all.

"You don't have to disappear from your son's life. You only have to recede gradually," his therapist advised him. "Your son still needs you and will continue to need you for the rest of your life. You are no longer in the forefront of his life as you were when he was younger, but this doesn't mean he doesn't love you. You need to learn to let go a little bit at a time."

The therapist's advice sounded easy, but Dave had difficulty tolerating the wrenching pain involved with allowing his son to develop his own interests and activities. Losing people is hard for anyone, but especially for combat vets because they have already experienced so many losses. It also threatens their sense of control and highlights their powerlessness over others, even their own children.

Yet this veteran was able to see that by not being so demanding of his son's attention, and by not creating friction over minor matters, Ben talked with him more and showed him more respect. The ultimate compliment came a week after being careful about how he interacted with his son. Ben said: "Gee, Dad, you haven't bugged me for a whole week. That makes me feel real good. Like I have a real dad."

On a day-to-day basis, however, it was hard for Dave not to be resentful and jealous when Ben rushed through dinner and then left to be with his friends. The pain of realizing that his son was growing up, and in small but real ways, progressively leaving him, filled him with anger and despair. "What my son is doing is all so normal," he told his therapist. "Why can't I adjust?"

"Turn the situation around and look at the positive. Isn't your son's growth beautiful? Didn't you play a part in producing such a mentally and physically healthy child? Would you really want your son to have no friends and be glued to you all the time? What if all your son did was hang around with you? Then you really would have a problem."

Jim presents another case of secondary traumatization. Like Ben, Jim listened to his father's war stories but, more important, was present while his father grieved and expressed great remorse for having been involved in the killing of women and children. Some of these women and children were warriors in disguise; some were innocents. Jim took on his father's guilt, as well as his sorrow, and at age fifteen began drinking heavily. While there were various reasons for his drinking problem, the internalization of his father's anguish and guilt was one of them.

Jim was hospitalized several times for alcoholism. After each hospitalization he attended AA meetings and other recovery groups. However, all his dedication to recovery did not seem to help him sustain sobriety.

Jim achieved sobriety only after the age of twenty-five, when he met and married an impoverished Vietnamese refugee woman who had been brutalized during the war. He adopted not only her children but also her three siblings, one of whom had lost both legs during the war.

"I've never been happier," says Jim. "And alcohol no longer calls my name. There are four people who need me now. I can't afford to drink."

Advanced training in psychology is not needed to see that in caring for these refugees, Jim found not only a purpose for staying sober but also a means of making restitution for the actions over which his father carried such tremendous guilt, grief, and shame.

Overprotectiveness and Overvaluation of Children

A vet may have difficulties being emotionally close to his children, yet still be extremely protective of them. He may even be overprotective in ways ranging from triple-checking their seatbelts to carefully screening their friends and activities to the point where hardly any person or activity seems safe.[29] He may also overvalue them. This doesn't mean he loves a child "too much," for there are no real bounds to parental love. Rather, overvaluation means that the child becomes the parent's major, if only, reason for living or that the child functions as a symbol or as a form of restitution for what the parent has lost.[30] Either way, the child may experience a tremendous pressure to fulfill the parent's need for a purpose in life or to achieve goals that the parent was unable to fulfill as the result of war experiences.

For example, when a vet whose life goal it was to become a musician lost his arm in battle, he did everything in his power to encourage his son's interest in music. He gave his son music lessons, took him to concerts, and in many other ways encouraged his son to develop his musical talents. When the son decided to become an engineer, the vet had to fully embrace his grief for the loss of his arm and his musical ambitions. For many years he had been able to keep these sorrows at bay by promoting his son's musical development.

Issues surrounding grief become more prominent as the veteran approaches midlife and wants to leave a legacy to the next generation. If his children, whom he values so much, turn out different from what he had hoped or, for some reason, fail to idealize him as a parent, the veteran's resulting despair may be great. For some veterans, a child's birth may symbolize the rebirth of a dead buddy or of a dead wartime girlfriend.[31] Even if the child does not have a symbolic identity for the veteran, the child may provide the veteran with his only real reason for living. Jesse, for example, frequently claims that if it weren't for his children, he would have killed himself long ago. With his professional skills and ambitions at a standstill due to his PTSD, and with his marriage now devoid of love and passion, without his children there would be no point in living.

When Jesse became suicidal, he pasted pictures of his children on his car dashboard so as to resist his temptation to drive his car off the road. His children were aware of the pictures and experienced their importance to their father as an awesome sense of responsibility for his well-being. If they happened to be delayed somewhere, for example, they would frantically call home to assure him they were safe lest he think the worse and then perhaps try to kill himself.

For many months after Jesse's suicidal crisis had subsided, his children continued to be mentally preoccupied with their father's well-being. After several years passed without any additional suicidal or other crises, the children slowly began freeing themselves of excessive concern about their father. The one exception was Joleen. Despite repeatedly being told by her therapist, her father's therapist, and both parents that her father was no longer suicidal and that she was not responsible for his well-being, she still felt that it was her role to watch over him.

Violence in the Family

Note: Child abuse is a widespread social problem affecting all social groups, not just combat vets. There are approximately three million reports of child abuse or neglect per year. Many researchers, however, suggest that the actual rates of child abuse are higher than official reports show.[32] Under no circumstances can child abuse or any other unacceptable behavior be denied or minimized. If there is violence in the home, it is important that it be stated that violence is wrong and dangerous and that help be sought immediately.* No form of abuse can be tolerated.

*See chapter 8 and appendix A for suggestions on getting help.

Mark was referred for psychological testing due to poor school performance. He was also in frequent fights with his schoolmates and enjoyed disrupting the classroom. Talking with Mark revealed that after his father, Nick, returned from combat duty, he began beating him and his mother. Despite his above-average I.Q., Mark had trouble concentrating on schoolwork because he never knew in what condition he would find his mother after school or whether he would be abused himself. His aggression toward his peers and teachers was, in part, a way to express his anger toward his father, whom he was too small and weak to oppose.

When Mark was told that punching his peers was wrong, he was puzzled. After all, his father had taught him, and showed him, that it was every man's "right" to beat his wife, girlfriend, or anyone who insulted him. The root of Nick's violence was low self-esteem. Although he was a decorated war hero and held a well-paying job, he didn't feel like a hero at all. In the Persian Gulf and later in Afghanistan he was shocked to find that some enemy soldiers were malnourished, ill-equipped teenagers. He saw nothing "heroic" about having captured or overcome these frightened ill-clad young boys. Nick had other self-doubts as well and expended much of his psychic energy trying to hide his insecurities not only from others but also from himself. Battering was his means of coping with his present life frustrations as well as with many of his unresolved feelings about his combat experiences.

Family violence is often multigenerational in that it tends to be passed down from one generation to the next.[33] Nick's father had been beaten by his father and then, upon becoming a father himself, continued the pattern. It followed that Mark would model himself after his father and use aggression as a means of feeling important, coping with daily living, and dealing with feelings. When Mark felt slighted by another child, he would instantly hit the child rather than feel the pain of being rejected; when a teacher gave Mark a low grade, she could expect to have her property vandalized.

While Mark admired his powerful father, Mark also hated him. When Mark was in kindergarten, he used to pray that his father would get drunk and pass out. That way he would not have to feel helpless and impotent as he heard his mother scream. Many times Mark tried to protect his mother only to be slammed against the wall and further emasculated by his father's taunts of "punk," "wimp," or "sissy."

In some abusive homes, one child is singled out to be abused; in other homes, some or all of the children are abused. In Mark's home, the boys were hit, but not the girls. Research shows that while girls are more often the recipients of sexual assault within the family, boys are more often the targets of severe physical battering.[34] "Boys are tough; they can take it. Girls can't," the thinking goes. Often the physical battering of boys is rationalized as a means of preparing them for the rigors of manhood. For example, ostensibly in order to "toughen up" his sons, Nick did not allow them to cry or show pain. If they did, they were beaten even harder.

Psychological testing revealed that Mark's chronic internal guilt and poor self-image began at the age of four, when his father cut his mother's arms three times as a punishment for Mark's poor table manners. Mark's table manners were but a pretext for the abuse, but Mark assumed the abuse was his fault. After this incident, Mark began feeling responsible for his parents' subsequent fights. On some level, he believed, he was also responsible for his own abuse. If only he was more lovable, smarter, or better, then his father would not beat him or his mother.

The three-stage battering cycle that helped to trap Mark's mother in her marriage also applied to Mark and his father.* During stage 1, the tension-rising stage, tensions rise between the couple, leading to stage 2, the acute battering incident. Afterward comes stage 3, the honeymoon stage, where the abuser repents and promises never again to hurt the woman he so loves. Usually this stage is accompanied by a profusion of gifts and ardent lovemaking, during which the woman's hopes for love and romance are renewed. Therefore, she forgives, and stays.

*Intimate violence tends to occur in a three-stage cycle (see pages 225–26).[35]

While this pattern of arguing and making up is common to many relationships, the distinctive feature of this cycle in battering relationships is what psychologist Lenore Walker calls a "sense of overkill."[36] The batterer is extreme, not only in his physical cruelty but also in his loving, repentant behavior. For example, during one honeymoon period, Nick presented his wife with a twelve-stone ruby ring that he had been waiting to give her at "just the right moment." He begged his wife's forgiveness. This time he was truly sorry. Surely it would never happen again. Just to prove it, he would go to church on Sunday.

This honeymoon period lasted three weeks. After the next incident, Nick came home with a gold-plated hairbrush and a bouquet of orchids.

The same battering cycle can be found in child abuse as well as partner abuse. For example, when Nick wasn't being cruel, he could be exceptionally charming, loving, and playful. After particularly severe beatings, he would come home with carloads of gifts for his sons. Sometimes he'd take them on camping trips or special vacations where he would lavish them with special attention. Other times he took them out to dinner or to a ball game, shared "top secret" war stories with them, or in other ways was the most wonderful father imaginable.

During these brief times, Mark's spirits soared. His dreams of having a "real father" were rekindled and he was determined to be the best boy imaginable so his father would continue to love him. But when his father would become abusive again, as he always would, Mark's self-confidence would crash. Starved for his father's affection and approval, Mark was determined to join the Marines when he came of age. Mark hoped that there would be another war by then so he could volunteer for the most difficult assignments and thereby prove his manhood both to his father and to himself.

Although Mark presented a tough-guy image, he never shared with anyone the fact that he had panic attacks and was frightened not only of the world but also of the monsters inside. The "monsters" he feared were his own feelings, specifically his murderous, vengeful impulses toward both his father and his mother.

Mark empathized with his mother's pain, but he also despised her for being too "weak" to protect him from his father. In addition, Nick had denigrated his wife so much that Mark lost much of his respect for her. It did not help that Nick blamed her for his abusive behavior toward his sons. "I'm only hitting you because your mother did _____," or "Your mother makes me hit you." Sometimes Nick would even claim that his wife had beaten herself up, even though Mark himself had witnessed the beating. Mark did not know what to believe, his eyes or his father's lies.

Mark also resented his mother because she never seemed to have enough time for him. So much of her time was consumed placating her husband, avoiding beatings, or recovering from them that she had less time for her children than they wanted and truly needed. In addition, although she was dedicated to her children, on some level she resented them, for it was her very dedication to them which prevented her from leaving her husband. On one occasion, unforgettable to Mark, she communicated the depth of her resentment.

When Mark was six, his father came home drunk and proceeded to beat his wife. Troubled by his mother's cries and by fantasies of hurting his father, Mark could not sleep. The next morning, Mark's father blamed his wife for making him drink and causing the beating. If she were not such an inept dumb-dumb, he would not have to discipline her to keep the family in order.

The moment he left for work, Mark felt sick to his stomach and ran to the bathroom. His mother ran after him, wincing with pain. Three of her ribs were broken. She cursed her husband for forbidding her to seek medical treatment, then took the twelve-stone ruby ring he had given her during a honeymoon period and threw it down the toilet.

Mark was horrified. "Dad will kill you for that."

She just glared at him, grabbed another honeymoon-period gift, the gold-plated hairbrush, and tried to flush it down the toilet, too.

"Stop, Mom!"

"You stop!" she growled back. "I wish I could flush you down the toilet. You, your brother, and that war, too. If it weren't for you kids and that . . . war, I'd have been out of here long ago. Now I'm trapped, a slave in my own home. Don't you ever cross me, Mark, or I'll whip you with this hairbrush."

Mark's mother never used the gold-plated hairbrush on her children. Other battered women, however, have used hairbrushes or other objects on their children, sometimes with deep, long-term effects. When abused women abuse their children, their behavior may stem from having been raised in violent homes themselves. Child abuse can also be an outlet for their anger toward their abuser, which they dare not direct at him.

Research consistently indicates that children who witness one parent batter the other frequently show signs of insecurity and emotionally immaturity, especially if they also are being intimidated or abused.[37] Some cling to stuffed animals, their blankets, or other security symbols long after their peers have abandoned such objects. Some become star students and try to be "perfect," fearing that if they don't behave in a model fashion, either they or another family member may be punished.

On the other hand, others do not achieve at their grade level. Mark's brother, for example, had so many academic problems that some school officials thought he was mentally retarded. Psychological testing, however, revealed that he had an average I.Q. Like his brother, Mark, his school performance was stymied by the violence at home and he frequently was involved in school fights. But unlike Mark, he did not attack other children. Rather, whenever he saw other children fighting, he would intervene to help protect the weaker one.

Existing studies show that a disproportionate number of runaway children come from violent homes. Perhaps life on the streets seems more benevolent than life at home, where the two people they love and need the most are tearing each other apart.[38] Some children side with the victimized parent; others identify with the aggressive one and eventually come to imitate that parent by abusing the victim parent and perhaps other family members as well; and still others feel loyal toward both parents and suffer internal conflict as a result. Many children also harbor ambivalent feelings toward both parents. "I don't know if I love my parents or if I hate them," explains Mark. "If they really loved me, they wouldn't fight."

Like combat vets, children from violent homes can learn to "tune out" and deny the violence. Some simply continue watching TV or studying even though a beating is going on in a nearby room. Should the victim emerge black and blue, they may act as if nothing happened. As they grow older, these children may turn to alcohol, food, or drugs as a way of furthering the pattern of denial and emotional numbing. Like combat vets, children from violent homes can develop post-traumatic reactions such as depression or PTSD.[39]

Combat vets who were also battered as children sometimes have two sets of traumatic reactions: one from their war experiences and another from their childhood. They have flashbacks not only about enemy soldiers, but about their angry fathers. After issues regarding combat are dealt with, vets who were battered as children often need to examine yet another level of trauma—that of being abused by a parent or caretaker.

Children and Parental Addiction

Large-scale studies conducted in the general population have found that among those diagnosed with PTSD, some 28 to 52 percent also suffer from alcohol abuse or dependence and an additional 21–35 percent from some other form of substance abuse.[40] Research conducted on Vietnam combat vets suggests that the rates of alcoholism and other forms of substance abuse may be somewhat higher.[41] There is little information, however, on rates of addiction among combat vets from subsequent armed conflicts.

Regardless of the rates of addiction among combat vets, or among partners who suffer from PTSD resulting from their own traumas, such as childhood abuse, when one or more parents or caretakers are burdened with an addiction, their children cannot help but be deeply affected as well. "I grew up in . . . [a war zone]," writes the child of an alcoholic vet. "I didn't know why I was there. I didn't really know who the enemy was."[42]

Like children from violent homes, children from homes where one or both parents or caretakers suffer from alcoholism, drug addiction, or another form of substance abuse frequently suffer from low self-esteem and guilt. Since many woman-battering cases involve alcohol or drugs, children are also at risk for being abused. Often they learn to suppress their feelings—especially their anger—and their emotional needs. Many erroneously feel that they are the cause of a parent's addiction. Girls especially may adopt a caretaker role toward the alcoholic parent, the nonalcoholic parent, siblings, or the entire family.

The above patterns are also common to nonveteran families where one or both parents suffer from some form of addiction. Yet when the addicted parent also has symptoms of combat or some other form of trauma, these patterns become intensified and more complex. In such situations, two powerful forces keep children emotionally stifled and feeling guilty about the troubled parent. For example, Lisa's father hardly drank at all while on active duty because he wanted to be as alert as possible. Afterwards, however, he used alcohol in order to deal with his combat trauma. Yet no one, not even he, suspected that his drinking might be related to his combat experiences.

Before her father joined AA, all Lisa had to worry about was whether or not her father would be too drunk to help her with her homework or drive her to her piano lessons. After her father became sober, however, his combat trauma emerged in full force and Lisa was confronted with her father's combat-related symptoms. When he had been drinking, he'd wake up in the middle of the night to have a drink. Now he was waking up to search for lost buddies. Now Lisa was more confused, and more embarrassed, than ever before. Somehow it was harder to have a father who sometimes acted like he was in a war zone than a father who drank too much. At least alcoholism was something with which her friends had some familiarity. Alcoholism was bad, but it wasn't "crazy," like PTSD. Who had ever heard of PTSD?

Helping Children Cope with Combat Trauma

The Pros and Cons of Disclosing the Trauma

Parents often wonder whether or not it is beneficial to children to learn about their father's war experiences and its aftereffects. There is no single answer to this question. Either way, there are advantages and disadvantages.

In his study of World War II veterans with PTSD, psychologist Robert Rosenheck found that many veterans were reluctant to discuss their war experiences with their children. "This reluctance derived from embarrassment and guilt about acts . . . they had committed as well as from the fear that they would become upset while discussing specific incidents. They were also afraid that unpleasant details would frighten and alienate their children." He also found that children of World War II veterans who were extensively and repeatedly exposed to detailed descriptions of their father's traumatic war experiences were more likely to develop secondary traumatization than children whose fathers deliberately kept their war experiences a secret so as not to negatively affect their children.[43]

This finding, however, should not imply that some of the veteran's military experiences and their effects on him and his loved ones cannot be openly discussed in the family. There is a profound difference between excessively exposing a child to descriptions of traumatic events and giving that child certain basic information on the nature of war and its impact on the human psyche. The potential negative effects of disclosing traumatic material can be significantly lessened if parents take the time to process this material with their children, help children cope with their emotional reactions to it, and identify some of the potential benefits of the combat experience, such as the kinds of skills and positive qualities their father (or other vets) developed in the military.

In homes where there is little or no talk about war or about why their father is so sad, angry, or confused, children then have to come up with their own explanations. Often they decide that their father's war-related problems are their fault. "If only I was a more lovable, more obedient, or more [something] child, my father would not be so unhappy," they may think. Or they may fantasize a reason. For example, if their father has scars from combat, children may surmise that he is very ill and perhaps dying. When their father is forgetful (due to his depression or intrusive thoughts about the war), they may conclude that he came into contact with toxic substances and may be going blind or deaf. Yet they don't know if their thoughts are true and hence may be confused.[44]

Sometimes children combine their fantasies about their father's war experiences with whatever partial knowledge they have about war in general and their father's war in particular. Their knowledge may come from history classes, the media, video or board games, or the Internet; from other children's accounts of or fantasies about their parent's or another relative's combat experiences; or from overhearing conversations about their father or about war.

For example, a child may have heard that some soldiers have shot children. The child's father may have never harmed a single civilian, yet the child may wonder if, in fact, her father did hurt children. If, at the same time, a child is struggling with jealous feelings toward a younger sibling, niece, nephew, or other child, then fantasies of the father's aggression can fuse with the child's own fantasies about hurting this other child. As a result, the guilt a child might feel about wishing to harm his or her rival may be intensified by any guilt the child might be carrying regarding the father's wartime actions.

The affected child may be young or an adolescent. For example, Susan, age eighteen, the only daughter of a combat Marine, was her parent's "little darling" until the arrival of her brother's baby girl. Then Susan's little niece became the center of the family's attention.

Susan felt she was too old to be jealous. Yet she was distressed to find herself fantasizing about killing her niece the way she imagined her father had killed children overseas. Imprinted in her mind were photographs of dead children from World War II, the Holocaust, the Rwanda genocide, and the Bosnian conflict which she had seen in magazines at her school library. She had also seen pictures of starving children in Africa on the evening news.

Susan knew her father had never been in World War II, Rwanda, or Bosnia. She also knew her father had nothing to do with children dying of starvation in Africa. However, these photographs had so horrified her that somehow she associated them with her father's war experiences. Susan knew practically nothing about her father's combat experiences. He never discussed them and, in order to protect her, he refused to answer any of her questions about what he did or did not do there. Susan interpreted his reluctance to talk about combat as possibly indicating that her father was trying to cover up some act of brutality, like having killed a child or not having helped save a wounded or malnourished child.

Susan wasn't sure whether her father actually had killed children, but she began to feel guilt over what her father might have done as a combat vet anyway. This guilt, combined with her own guilt over her own murderous wishes toward her baby niece, became an enormous burden, one she felt she had to carry alone. She was certain she would be seen as an evil person if she talked about her jealousy toward her niece and as a disloyal daughter if she expressed concerns about her father's combat role.

As this example illustrates, children, like adults, are not blank slates: they have their own issues and conflicts that interact with their knowledge of or fantasies about their father's war trauma.[45] Another area of concern for some children is their father's wartime sexual behavior. Exposure to news reports or media presentations about wartime rapes or the sexual mistreatment of prisoners has left some children wondering if their father witnessed or participated in any such events. They may also wonder if their father had a girlfriend, frequented prostitutes, or went to strip clubs while he was overseas.

These unanswered questions are problematic for all children, but especially for those in or approaching adolescence or for any children who are struggling with their own sexual issues. For girls, the pairing of sexuality with violence can become a source of anxiety and ambivalence about their sexuality.

Yet open communication between parent and child regarding such sexual matters is extremely difficult. Not only is sex a relatively taboo topic in many families, the subject may also trigger traumatic memories for the father. He may have trouble remembering or accepting certain sexual situations himself and therefore be unable to talk about them at all, even with his therapist, much less with his children. Also he may feel—justifiably so—that his children could not handle such harsh truths, and that if they knew about some of his sexual experiences overseas, they might lose their faith in him.

On the other hand, the children's fantasies about the father's behavior might be much worse than the father's actual actions. For example, they might wonder if he fathered children overseas. Such questions were sparked in children of some Vietnam veterans as the result of media coverage given to Amerasian children in the early 1990s and to the attempts of some vets to locate former girlfriends and children they had left in Vietnam. The 1990s also saw the emergence of films, books, and articles on these and other issues regarding sexual relations between Vietnamese women and American soldiers. Since Vietnam, such themes have continued in the media.

Children may feel disappointed in their father if they somehow suspect he had children overseas, then left them there. Children may then reason that if their father abandoned his overseas child, he might also abandon them. On the other hand, they might feel relieved that they do not have to contend with a stepsibling in the home.

Often, caring parents are caught in a double bind. Children from homes in which there are "no talk" rules often hunger to understand their father. If they know little about the father's war experiences, they are left to imagine what happened or didn't happen. Their fantasies, along with whatever information or misinformation about the war they derived from the media or other sources, can dominate their perceptions about the father's experiences. In some cases, children might be relieved to hear the truth because the truth is much more benign than their fantasies. In other cases, however, children may feel intruded upon and angry. Furthermore, their increased knowledge of the brutalities of war can cause some of them to feel the way some vets do: scarred, unlovable, tainted, or "abnormal."

On the positive side, however, after learning about combat trauma and its effects on the family, children are less likely to feel alienated from their father. They also are less likely to blame themselves for his problems.

Regardless of their ages, children repeatedly need to be told that they are not the cause of their father's or their mother's turmoil. In her work with adolescent children of Vietnam veterans, Ellen Salom found that they profited greatly from lectures and films about combat trauma and its potential effects on family life.[46] In her groups, children were helped and encouraged to identify the particular symptoms their father exhibited, the ways in which their father's specific symptoms affected them, constructive ways of coping with their father's combat-related problems, and their reactions to his problems.

Unlike adolescents, however, young children may not be able to grasp the nature of their father's war experiences, or to comprehend the meaning of these experiences to their father. While a young child will certainly not profit from gory descriptions of combat, even children as young as four or five can understand two of the basic feelings many vets have about their war experiences: sadness and anger. For example, a child can be told: "Daddy is sad (or mad) because somebody he loved died (or got lost, sick) in the war." Perhaps an analogy could be made between the father's feelings and the child's feelings upon having a bike stolen or losing a pet.

Mothers can also acknowledge to their children when their father is evidencing a traumatic reaction. If, in addition, she can make a clear connection between the veteran's war experiences and a potential or actual problem in the family, her children can be spared the self-defeating conclusion that the problem is a sign of their personal or moral failure, unlovability, or incompetence. These explanations must be stated without denigrating or ridiculing anyone, especially the veteran. For example, a mother can say, "In the war, Daddy learned that noises meant danger. That is why he jumps when you drop something. If afterwards he looks upset, it's not because you did something bad; it's because in war Daddy had to be ready to get up and fight when there was a loud noise in case the loud noise meant there was trouble." Or "Are you upset because you asked Daddy to sit next to you, but he sat by the door instead? Remember that in the war, Daddy learned to be afraid of strangers and new places. That is why he likes to sit near the door." Or "Daddy walks around the house at night not because he's upset with you or me, but because he can't stop thinking about sad and scary things that happened in the war." Similarly, if the veteran has an alcohol or drug problem, it is important that the problem be acknowledged in a matter-of-fact manner rather than denied.

Talking about Combat or Combat Trauma

If parents decide to have conversations with children about combat and its effects, they need to make certain preparations. For example, they need to think carefully about which topics would be helpful to discuss and which topics are best avoided, at least for the time being. Such decisions should take into account not only the child's age but also the child's personality and any stresses the child is currently experiencing. For example, if a child is ill or is suffering a recent loss, such as the death of a grandparent or a pet, it is probably best to wait until the child is physically and emotionally in better condition.

In making such decisions and in continuing to evaluate whether or not to continue sharing with children about combat and combat trauma, parents are encouraged to obtain feedback from at least two other people or sources. These individuals need to meet the following criteria: they must be knowledgeable about combat and combat trauma; they must be familiar with the unique circumstances of your family; and they must be trustworthy and sincerely care about everyone in your family. Trained mental health professionals who are knowledgeable about combat trauma can also be consulted, as can resources and books listed in appendixes A and B.

In addition, certain cautions must be observed.

1. *Be clear about your motivation.* The purpose of talking about combat and combat trauma is to help the child, not the parent. If a particular topic is being discussed because a parent is feeling so emotionally overwhelmed by it that he or she needs to release some emotional overload, that parent should be sharing those thoughts and feelings with another adult or with a trained mental health professional, not with a child.

2. *Keep in mind the child's age.* Any information about combat or combat trauma needs to be presented in an age-appropriate manner.

3. *Do not overwhelm the child.* Don't deluge your child with information. Give your child information or discuss issues surrounding combat trauma in small doses. Make a list of the information or topics you wish to share with your child, then rank order the items on the list according to how upsetting or threatening you think they may be to your child. Start with subject matter you judge to be the least upsetting to your child. If the child responds well, ask the child if he or she would like to talk about war-related issues again and if so, when. If the child agrees, you can proceed to the next least-threatening item at some appropriate time in the future.

4. *Correct inaccurate thinking or information.* Ask your children what they heard you say. Check to see if they heard and understood the information correctly. Be sure they know the meaning of the terms they are hearing or using. They may have a limited or inaccurate understanding of terms like *bombing, sniper attacks,* or *guerrilla warfare.* Or they may believe that Baghdad is two hours away by car. Their knowledge of other matters may be unclear, incomplete, or distorted.

5. *Observe your child's reactions.* A little upset is to be expected. However, if a child shows extreme signs of anxiety, like shortness of breath, sweating, dizziness, any of the symptoms listed in the "Cautions" section in the introduction, or any other problem that concerns you, stop all discussion about war or any other fearful topic. Try to calm the child, then follow the instructions provided in the "Cautions" section.

6. *Inquire about your children's emotional reactions.* In general, sharing traumatic stories or material or discussing sensitive matters with a child without also giving that child the opportunity to process this material and support in coping with it has the potential for creating as much emotional conflict and pain in the child as not knowing at all. Therefore, it is critical that after you verify that your children have an accurate understanding of the topic being discussed, you inquire about their emotional reactions to it. By doing so, you let your children know that they don't have to pretend that their father's problems or other family problems don't matter or should not be talked about. You can acknowledge the reality of their father's behavior (and of your behavior or the behavior of other family members) in a manner that is respectful of the veteran and of all concerned.

For example, you could ask, "How did you feel when I talked to you about _____ or when you see Daddy having a flashback (or anxiety attack, numbing episode, and so forth)?" If the discussion concerned family tensions, you can ask: "How do you feel when your brother slams the door because he and I had an argument?"; ". . . when Daddy and Mommy argue so much?"; " . . . when Daddy drinks so much?"; or " . . . when Mommy yells a lot?"

Prepare your children for the possibility that even if they aren't troubled or don't have any questions at the moment, it would be entirely normal for them to have questions or strong feelings later on that day or week. Then invite them to come to you with their questions or reactions. However, children, especially young children, often cannot identify their feelings, especially when they are coping with several emotions at the same time or when they are afraid they will be shamed or punished for their feelings. One way you can help children who have difficulty identifying or labeling their feelings is to tell a story that describes some of the emotions your children may be experiencing. The story could be about another person, about a hypothetical person, or about yourself, either in the past or the present.

"If I were a little girl or boy and my daddy got upset like that (or had trouble sleeping, etc.), I'd be worried about him. I'd wonder if he were sad or upset about something. But I'd also be mad at him for getting so unhappy (or angry, nervous, etc.) and not being able to pay attention to me or help me with my schoolwork (or, but I'd also be mad at him for leaving because I miss him). Sometimes I'd probably be so mad at him that I wish he would go away (or that he would never come back). But then I'd probably be sorry for thinking like that. It sounds funny, but I could be mad at him and love him at the same time. Do you ever feel like this?"

Or, if the subject is the impact of a parent's anger or of parental discord, a mother could say, "When Daddy gets mad at me, I feel scared and angry. I feel as if it was my fault that he is angry with me even though I know it wasn't."

She could also say, "When I was a little girl and my mommy and daddy looked like they were mad at each other, I was scared. I was afraid that maybe they would start arguing so much that they would forget about taking care of me. I was even afraid they might start hitting each other and one of them might get hurt. I was mad at them, too. But I was mixed up because I didn't know who was right and who was wrong. I wanted both of them to be right because they were my mom and dad. I wanted them to stop being so upset and be happy, too, but I was so sad because I didn't know how to make them stop arguing or feel better. Do you ever feel any of these ways?"

7. *Do not shame your children for their emotions; support them.* In our culture, people who aren't happy or who don't think positive most of the time are often seen as abnormal or inferior. As a result, children may already feel ashamed of being confused, afraid, anxious, or unhappy. Perhaps they have also been shamed by others. This makes it even more important that you assure them that having certain thoughts or feelings doesn't mean that something is wrong with them. Emphasize that they are responsible for their behavior, not their thoughts and feelings. Also emphasize that by talking about some of the thoughts and feelings they are ashamed of they might be able to change them or even eliminate them entirely.

Here are some examples of shaming messages:

"You are too old to feel that way." "Where's your head? It's ridiculous/silly to think (or feel) that _____." "If you want to grow up to be a man, you shouldn't be feeling _____." "Only babies _____." "Why are you talking to me about the same things you talked to me about yesterday?"

Don't compare your child to others or yourself: for example, "How come your sister/brother isn't as mixed up/angry/unhappy as you? How come you can't be tougher/braver/kinder/more forgiving like _____?" and "You say you want to be a _____ when you grow up. How can you expect to do that if you are so whiny, clingy, stupid as to feel _____ or believe _____?"

8. *Disentangle combat-related problems and issues from noncombat-related issues.* Combat-related discussions should not be combined with discussions about other issues unless there is a direct link between combat trauma and that other issue. When you are trying to help your children better understand and cope with the impact of combat trauma on their lives, don't stop to criticize a child, the veteran, or some other person. Also, don't bring up disciplinary and other parent-child conflicts unless they are related to combat trauma.

Summary

In homes where the veteran is unable to manage his combat-related symptoms, the children can develop low self-esteem and self-blame for their father's unhappiness. Some children assume a rescuer role toward their father; others may show symptoms similar to his.

Some veterans may withdraw from their children because they cannot handle the pressures of parenting or because they had painful combat experiences with children. When children interpret their father's withdrawal as rejection or as meaning that they aren't "good enough" for him, they may then feel unwanted, unloved, and inadequate. In some cases, children blame the mother for their father's suffering, and in other cases they cling excessively to her.

When veterans have major difficulties relating to their children, their partners may feel like single parents with the burden of their children's emotional and physical well-being on their shoulders alone. Some mothers try to compensate for their veteran's distancing or other behavior that separates him from his children by being supermothers.

In some homes, the financial and emotional pressures on the parents sometimes lead to child abuse, either by the veteran or his wife. More common than physical abuse is verbal criticism of the children. In many instances, the mother is a buffer between her children and her husband, finding herself unappreciated and misunderstood by both sides. On the other hand, some veterans with severe cases of combat trauma are deeply involved in protecting children from harm and fostering their development.

Children from homes where the veteran's symptoms dominate his life often suffer from mixed feelings about their parents and mixed loyalties. Their feelings of being different because of their father's PTSD are only compounded if he is also an alcoholic or violent. As a Vet Center counselor who works with these children suggests, "It is quite possible that the future will see self-help groups for Adult Children of [Combat Veterans] . . . similar to contemporary groups for Adult Children of Alcoholics."

12

"Is it my fault?"

Suicide and the Veteran Family

I was crazy about him. He was crazy about me. But why we were so attracted to each other, I'll probably never understand. I am beginning to understand, however, why Shawn killed himself.

I met Shawn seven years after he got out of the service. His face was all scarred, but it wasn't just from combat. It was from growing up in the slums of Atlanta, too. As tough as he looked, he was really very kind. He just didn't believe in himself, no matter what I said or did. He didn't believe in my love for him either.

For no particular reason, one day he woke up and said he was leaving me. He had to head up north where he could be free. I thought there was something wrong with me, but I never asked. Back then, I never asked men questions, I just accepted what they said.

For a year and a half I wrote him in Wisconsin. The first few months, he'd send me a postcard once a month. Then the postcards started getting shorter and shorter and fewer and fewer. When I called for his birthday, he refused the call. Then my letters started coming back to me unopened.

I gave up then and started dating other men. About a month after I married, Shawn's landlady wrote me that Shawn had committed himself to a psychiatric hospital, then escaped his ward, and thrown himself in front of a bus. The only reason she contacted me was because she had seen my letters, and no one else wrote to Shawn.

My first reaction was to blame myself. Was it something I had said or done? Could I have possibly prevented this? Was it my fault for marrying another man?

But Shawn hadn't even known I was engaged, much less married. And after all, he had rejected me, not the other way around. But I still felt guilty.

Bits and pieces of our conversations came back to me. Sometimes he'd make jokes about war . . . about how his first day there he saw some guy blow his brains out and what color the brains were . . . about some mother and child . . . about seeing heads mounted on sticks . . . about how even living in the slums of Atlanta hadn't prepared him for war. But he was always so funny about it that nobody realized he had a problem, even him.

After the news of his death, I went to a counselor. She told me to detach from the situation—not to blame myself and to try not to let Shawn's suicide upset me and my new marriage. But how can you detach from someone you loved? From someone you've slept with and given yourself to in so many ways?

I had nowhere to mourn him until I came to group. To many people, Shawn was just a "shiftless, crazy" vet. But I know there was more to him than that and that his death was something more than one guy's failure to cope.

—BRENDA, SHAWN'S EX-GIRLFRIEND AND NOW A
VOLUNTEER AT A VA MEDICAL CENTER

On June 1, when Jesse (the brain surgeon we met in chapter 11) mentioned suicide, his wife, Linda, went into denial. His statement of suicidal intent made her so anxious that she shoved it out of her mind. When Jesse made subsequent remarks about wishing to die, Linda trembled. She didn't know what to say except "Come off it," "Stop joking," "Let's talk about something pleasant," or in some other way dismiss Jesse's remarks.

Yet she was uneasy. She had read that all suicidal statements should be taken seriously and that in the United States, "a white Protestant man in his forties or fifties on a downwardly mobile social course, who has suffered a severe interpersonal loss in a relationship with wife or girlfriend, and who has used a gun" was at high risk for suicide. Physicians were also reported to have high suicide rates.[1] While Jesse did not have a gun and still had a marriage, he was a white Protestant physician approaching forty and definitely on a downwardly mobile social and occupational course. When Linda suggested having a small party for him, Jesse tore up his birth certificate. "Half my life is over and I've never truly lived. Don't talk to me about birthday parties. I need a death day party," he yelled as he stormed out of the house.

Despite Jesse's outburst, the possibility that her husband would actually kill himself was so threatening to Linda that she continued to believe that if she ignored Jesse's suicidal wishes, they would magically disappear. Also, although Linda would dare not admit it to herself, Jesse's suicidal statements made her furious. How dare he talk about suicide! Hadn't she been a good wife? Didn't he want to live—for her—and didn't she have enough to deal with—children, a job, a financial crisis, and his combat trauma—without him becoming suicidal, too? After all, Jesse was supposed to be the "man" in the family, and now he was falling apart on her.

"You'll feel better after you eat breakfast," Linda would tell Jesse when he'd wake up saying that he wished he had died in his sleep.

On October 1, Jesse announced to Linda that if things didn't get better, he would kill himself on New Year's Eve. There were other signs also: Jesse stopped attending group therapy, spent entire weekends in his bedroom, and lost almost all interest in sex. He also told Linda that since he was a physician, he could easily obtain any medications he wanted and knew exactly how many pills to take, and in what combinations, to die. Then she found out that Jesse had given his brother John a birthday present in advance, saying he would probably not be alive for John's birthday. Jesse had also asked John to help take care of Linda and the children after he was gone.

At this point Linda went into shock, but then she began facing the reality of Jesse's death wish. "No, no, it can't be true," she sobbed in group. "But it is true. What do I do now?"

Linda's first steps were to talk to Jesse openly about his suicidal plans and to contact his physician and therapist. In cases of possible suicide, mental health professionals are allowed to break the bonds of confidentiality and inform family members of their loved one's suicid-

al plans. Similarly, when a partner determines that her veteran is showing signs of suicidal intent, she should not hesitate to call one of his
physicians, his therapist, his spiritual adviser, or some other authority.
Depending on the circumstances, she may even decide to inform family, friends, or any other persons whom she feels could be helpful. Furthermore, she need not hide her actions from her vet. Linda told Jesse,
"I don't care whether you object or not, I'm letting your therapist and
your parents know. You can go kill yourself if you want to, but you're
going to have to fight us first."

Please note: In some cases, if the veteran is capable of violence or
extreme paranoia, the actions suggested above may not be advisable. It
is strongly suggested that a partner discuss the particulars of her situation with a qualified mental health professional.

In general, suicidal persons usually welcome such action—and the
subsequent attention. In many cases, they want someone else to take
over. If they were 100 percent intent on killing themselves, they would
have already done so. Instead, they chose to live and send out signals to
others, hoping that someone would take care of them, give them hope,
and affirm the worth of living.

The partner of a suicidal vet lives under immense pressure. Often
she tries to be especially careful about her speech and behavior toward
her veteran and tries to do whatever she can to minimize the stresses in
his life so as to avert a possible tragedy. Linda, for example, found herself
carefully monitoring not only her own actions, but those of her children. "Don't do that! Don't do this!" she'd say. "We can't let your father
feel bad." She also tried to make life easier for Jesse by not pressuring
him to attend certain social and family functions. At first she was willing
to go alone. Eventually, however, she stopped going out at all and became reclusive, like Jesse. It was only years later, after Jesse had made noticeable progress in his therapy and began to socialize again, that Linda
realized how detrimental the isolation had been to her mental health.

Even after an acute suicidal crisis has subsided and her vet appears
calmer and more elevated in mood, a partner needs to be aware that
suicide can occur at any time. Sometimes the veteran's seeming improvement is the result of his inner decision to commit suicide at some
future time and thereby terminate what he perceives as an unbearably
painful or hopeless existence.[2]

The veteran's suicidal state can also spill over to his children. It is
not unusual for children of suicidal veterans—even as young as thir-

teen—to threaten or attempt suicide themselves. This connection between parental and offspring suicidal behavior is not unique to veterans. As research has shown, one suicide in the family is a significant risk factor for suicide in the other family members.

At one time people believed that suicide was hereditary.[3] Although the genetic basis for suicide has yet to be scientifically substantiated, when a father commits suicide, or even talks about it, he conveys to his children the message that life is not worth living and that they aren't worth living for. Children can also acquire a sense of hopelessness and powerlessness. They may think, "If my father, who is bigger and stronger than me, a warrior even, cannot handle life, how can I, who am so much smaller and less experienced, ever hope to do so?" Should the father actually commit suicide, the children can develop symptoms of traumatic stress and a sense of guilt that can last a lifetime.

In some cases, suicide threats may seem manipulative in that they occur in some predictable fashion—on a monthly basis or when his partner disagrees with him, refuses him sex, or in some way doesn't meet his needs. For example, Julia's boyfriend threatened suicide at least a dozen times, yet never made a single attempt. After yet another "false alarm," Julia commented, "There he goes again—talking suicide—just to get me to do what he wants."

Although Julia has learned not to panic at every suicide note, she knows that just because her vet hasn't followed through on his threats thus far doesn't mean that he won't in the future. Even if most, if not all, of a veteran's suicide threats actually are manipulative, some day, somewhere, given the right amount of stress, he may, in fact, self-destruct. According to some researchers, approximately one-tenth of those who threaten suicide actually do follow through to completion. Furthermore, some 35 to 40 percent of those who commit suicide have made previous attempts. Some researchers have found that 80 percent of those who die had at least one prior suicide attempt.[4]

In several instances, vets threatened suicide upon learning of their wife's or girlfriend's decision to separate. Their partners are often confused, not knowing whether the threat is serious or merely a means of coercing them into staying. "Maybe he's just trying to scare me, but I also believe that if I leave, he might do it," says Susan, whose vet has suffered from depression ever since he left the military. They have no children due to his fear that he may have been exposed to toxic chemicals overseas. Since he has no other real family and is also highly dissatisfied with his job, should Susan leave he feels he has no reason to go on living. He also has two guns and a storehouse of medications amassed from his many hospitalizations for war injuries.

Susan decided to stay with her husband until he sought help. When she suggested therapy, she expected him to resist the idea. But he did not. Like many suicidal persons, her husband was ambivalent about whether to live or die and was looking for someone else to save him. After he made noticeable progress in therapy and began to develop a support system, Susan left, confident that should her husband become suicidal again he would have a therapist and friends to lean on.

In my experience, however, Susan is an exception. Usually a dissatisfied partner does not feel she can end her relationship with a veteran if there is a suicide threat. As miserable as she may be, she does not want her departure to be the proverbial "straw that broke the camel's back" and bear the guilt of her vet's death on her conscience.

If children are involved and the veteran has stated to her, in front of the children, "If you leave me, I'll kill myself," or has made an overt suicide attempt, the pressure on the woman to stay can be enormous. "If you divorce Dad, he'll die," or "Don't let my dad die," children have told their already guilt-ridden mothers. Some partners have heard the same guilt-evoking message from family members, friends, or their vet's war buddies: "If you leave and he kills himself, it'll be all your fault."

As children grow older, their arguments against separation may become more elaborate and may become confused with their own life issues. Some children, however, may argue for separation rather than against it. "Go ahead. Leave him and let him kill himself like he says he will. He's so miserable, he's better off dead. He wants to die anyway," a teenager told her mother. The family stayed intact, but her father attempted suicide anyway. He was half-dead when he was found, but he managed to survive. Years later the daughter, now a young mother, attempted suicide in the exact same manner on the exact same date in the exact same location as her father's unsuccessful suicide attempt.

Suicide is one of the top ten causes of death in the United States among the general population, with about ten to twelve suicides per one hundred thousand Americans per year. Large-scale studies of the general population, including both veterans and nonveterans, have found higher rates of suicidal thoughts and behavior among people who suffer from PTSD than among those who suffer from other anxiety disorders, such as generalized anxiety disorder or panic disorder. Yet another community study found that 20 percent of persons diagnosed with PTSD reported suicide attempts. The rates for persons diagnosed with another disorder was 4 percent and for persons without any psychiatric diagnosis 1 percent. There are no specific statistics on suicide among partners and children of veterans, and the few available suicide statistics for combat veterans are highly controversial.[5]

Even if researchers agreed on a specific number, this number may not be an accurate reflection of the actual suicide rate. In some instances, the suicide is masked: sometimes certain poisonings, drug overdoses, one-car collisions, and other vehicular accidents are viewed as suicidal. However, it is impossible to interview the victim to determine whether the cause of death was a lethal mistake or a sincere wish to die. Along these lines, alcohol and drug abuse, obesity, noncompliance with medical directives, and other kinds of self harm can be seen as forms of slow suicides. Yet when these self-destructive behaviors result in premature deaths, these deaths are not included in suicide statistics.

Furthermore, it is not uncommon to find veterans working in the police force, firefighting, or rescue operations; working on dangerous construction sites; volunteering to handle radioactive or other dangerous materials; or performing some of the most risky tasks in their particular field. The question arises as to what degree, if any, a veteran's decision to participate in these or other types of dangerous activities is motivated by a suicide wish. Perhaps some veterans chose these vocations because they acquired training and experience in these areas during their military career. Another possibility is that vocations such as police, firefighting, or rescue operations reflect an individual's willingness to put his life on the line for the welfare of others. Or perhaps these choices reflect sensation-seeking or a way to recapture the excitement and adrenaline highs that might have been part of that veteran's combat experience.

Similar questions regarding possible suicidal motivation can also arise when a veteran has hobbies such as skydiving; high-speed motorcycle racing; boating (when he cannot swim); or winetasting, gourmet cooking, or cake baking (when he is diabetic). If part of a veteran's motivation for pursuing a life-threatening hobby or avocation truly does stem from a conscious or unconscious death wish, should he die as the result of his lifestyle, his death will not be ruled as suicide.

Similarly, if a vet provokes another person—his partner, the police, a drunken or armed stranger or attacker, or a violent known enemy—into killing him, his death will probably be listed as murder, not suicide. According to a study of spouse murders, some murders are "victim-precipitated in that the victim is a 'direct positive precipitator in the crime.'"[6] This does not mean that the victim merely quarreled with or insulted the offender. It means that the victim was the first to use physical force, to show and use a weapon, or to strike a blow.

"Ted was begging to die," explains Elaine. "Yet he always laughed at men, especially vets, who killed themselves. Just to prove he wasn't a 'wimp' like they were, he'd drive fast down icy hills and eat wild mushrooms without checking to see if they were poisonous. Once Ted and I were cornered by two muggers. I gave them my purse immediately, but Ted refused to give up his wallet. When they pounced on him, I was certain it was the end."

Luckily a police car passed by just at the right moment. But there was no police car in Elaine's kitchen when Ted threatened to scald her with boiling water. This threat climaxed a Memorial Day weekend of physical abuse and threats on the life of Elaine's mother, whom Ted was certain was trying to convince Elaine to leave him.

The more Elaine tried to calm down Ted, the harder he punched her. Then he began boiling water and shouted: "You ungrateful bitch! I'll scar your face so that nobody else will ever want you. That way, you'll never leave me." At this point Ted handed Elaine a loaded rifle and dared her to shoot him. As he came at her with the pot of boiling water, Elaine shot him. Was his death homicide, suicide, or both?

Elaine's story illustrates researchers' conclusions on mate slayings: a "higher proportion of husbands than wives provoked their mates into killing them, that is, first struck their mates and changed the level of social interaction from that of verbalizing to assaulting."[7] One study theorizes that men who view suicide as unmasculine or passive, but who nevertheless harbor serious suicidal wishes, may achieve their death wish not by killing themselves directly, but by placing themselves in dangerous situations where they invite another person's attack.[8]

Characteristics of Suicidal Veterans

There is no one type of suicidal veteran or suicidal partner or child. However, the following characteristics have been found to correlate with suicide:[9]

- Presence of a major psychiatric disorder, such as PTSD, depression, manic-depressive illness, alcohol or drug abuse, schizophrenia, paranoid personality disorder, or another psychosis.

- The lack of strong affiliative bonds to another person or group of persons; feelings of not belonging to anyone or to any human group.

- Social isolation: lack of a support system, an inability to use available supports; or a major loss within the veteran's support system (e.g., loss of a special friend, close family member, or doctor).

- Familiarity with or possession of firearms or other weapons.

- Feelings of helplessness, hopelessness, worthlessness, or humiliation.

- Unresolved guilt over participation in or witnessing of killing, atrocities, crimes, or other immoral or illegal acts.

- Feeling responsible, to one extent or another, for the death or injury of another person, especially of a child, family member, or close friend.

- Feelings of being trapped, stuck, or sinful.

- Sudden, nonmedically monitored stopping of taking medications for depression, anxiety, or any other psychiatric disorder.

- Significant increases in physical pain, especially when combined with little hope of relief or cure, or chronic, unremitting physical pain due to war injuries or to newly developed physical problems.

- A family history of suicide or depression, or a recent suicide of a friend, relative, or war buddy.

- Death of a parent or caretaker prior to the age of twelve.

- Prior suicide attempts or reckless behavior.

- Untreated medical problems.

- Conflicts with authority (employers, the law, or government agencies).

- Suppressed rage or free-floating hostility.

- Negative view of past, present, and future.
- A mind-set that views violence, even violence toward oneself, as a viable solution to life's problems.

Warning Signs of Impending Suicide

A partner must be alert to signals, not only from her vet but also from her children, that suicide is on their minds. She must also take seriously any wishes on her part to end her own life. Signals that suicide may be imminent include the following:

- Announcements of suicidal thoughts or intentions, such as, "I'm going to kill myself," "I won't be here for Christmas," "You won't have to worry about me anymore," "This might be the last time you see me," or "This is my last day."
- Suicidal writings or drawings, notes written as if already dead.
- Termination behaviors: giving away prized possessions, writing a will, cleaning up unfinished business, saying good-bye to friends and relatives, purchasing a burial plot, writing one's own eulogy, designing one's tombstone, purchasing a one-way ticket to a potential suicide location.
- Noticeable withdrawal from family or friends or from previously attended therapy.
- Any dramatic change in mood or emotional state.
- Changes in eating habits (that result in significant weight gain or weight loss).
- Changes in sleeping habits (increased sleeping, fitful sleep, insomnia).
- Loss of interest in friends and formerly pleasurable activities, like sex, music, or sports.
- Difficulties with concentration.
- Excessive or inappropriate guilt.
- Increased alcohol or drug usage.
- Decreased functioning at work (or in school).
- Preoccupation with fanatical or cult material.

- Outbursts of violent or rebellious behavior (especially if out of character).

- Psychomotor retardation: slumped posture, slow movements, repetitious behavior and statements.

- Any evidence of loss of touch with reality.[10]

Most suicides do not happen without warning. The suicidal veteran, like other suicidal persons, will often give clues regarding his intentions. Do not think, "No, it could never happen in my family," as if suicide was a moral disgrace or a phenomenon limited to the mentally deranged or the lower socioeconomic classes. In the United States suicide occurs proportionally among all levels of society, among the well educated as well as the uneducated, and among mentally healthy persons who are, nevertheless, extremely unhappy.[11]

While you should not try to assess your veteran's suicidal potential on your own, you need both to be aware of the factors that increase the likelihood of suicide and to share information about your veteran's suicidal intentions with an appropriate mental health professional, clergyperson, or other authority like the police. Upon the mere mention of the word "suicide" or upon the emergence of any of the suicidal indicators listed above, you should encourage your vet to seek professional help. Even if he is only thinking suicidal thoughts and has no definite plan, his suicidal thoughts need to be openly discussed. If the vet is already in treatment, encourage him to share his suicidal thoughts with his therapist. Left unaired, the negative thoughts can feed upon themselves and develop into a full-blown suicide crisis.

In general, the probability of suicide is increased if the veteran has a well-thought-out, definite plan for killing himself rather than a vague wish to die. For example, the veteran who says he is planning to kill himself with an overdose of pills, but does not know what pills he would take (or in what quantities) and does not have a specific date established for his suicide, is probably less likely to kill himself than the veteran who has spent two weeks in the library researching various types of medications, has already purchased the pills, and has a definite date in mind. Similarly, the veteran who says he will shoot himself, but does not own a gun and has no plans to purchase a gun, is less likely to kill himself than the veteran who has one or more guns at his immediate disposal and who spends much of his spare time at rifle ranges. This does not mean that the vet who talks about suicide but does not have a plan is not capable of suicide. He is, and his suicidal wishes need to be acknowledged and openly discussed.

Another sign of imminent suicide is if the vet feels compelled to act on his impulse to self-destruct.[12] Statements such as "I'm afraid to be alone," "I don't know if I can stop myself," "There's a voice in my head that says, 'Do it! Do it, now!'" or "Hide the rat poison. I'm afraid I'll take some," warrant an immediate response. Even if the veteran has several powerful deterrents to his suicidal plans, such as a strong commitment to his job, family, or certain friends, or strong religious beliefs against suicide, if he is evidencing any signs that he is unable to control his impulses, he should not be left alone. He may need hospitalization, or at least the intervention of a therapist or clergyperson. If the veteran states that God, voices, or some force outside himself is "ordering him" to kill himself, psychiatric hospitalization is almost always needed.

Yet another sign is if the veteran, after having communicated in some way that he is planning to kill himself, is unable to talk to anyone about his suicidal wishes or plans. As long as he can talk about his suicidal feelings and maintain an emotional connection with at least one person, whether it be his partner, a relative, a friend, or a therapist, there is hope.

If you think your vet may be considering suicide, ask him the following questions:

- Do you want to kill yourself?

- Do you have a plan?

- What is your plan?

- On a scale of 1 to 20, what is the probability you will put your plan into effect? Or, how much do you want to die? How much do you want to live?

- Do you have a particular date in mind?

- Do you feel you must kill yourself?

- Do you feel there is someone trying to kill you? (This question is for vets with paranoid tendencies.)

- Is there someone, or something, telling you to kill yourself? (This is for vets with histories of psychoses or paranoia.)

- Are you willing to give me the pills, the gun, the keys to the car (or whatever is the designated means of suicide)?

- Can you promise me you won't kill yourself until you talk to a therapist (the family doctor, a clergyperson, or some other trained professional)?[13]

The veteran's responses to these questions can help a partner identify the possibility that her veteran might hurt himself. If he has a plan and a date, is unwilling to relinquish the means of self-destruction, or is unable to commit to not killing himself for a short period of time, you must not hesitate to act. In addition to any observable signs or disturbing answers to the above questions, you must also trust your own gut reaction.

If for any reason you feel that your vet might possibly hurt himself or is not in control of himself, seek outside help immediately by calling his physician or therapist; a local Vet Center or Veterans Affairs medical center; the local police, rescue service, or social services department; or any local hospital, mental health clinic, or suicide crisis hotline for help. If necessary, take the vet to a hospital emergency room. You should also attempt to get control over any guns, knives, pills, or other means of self-destruction.

If there are signs of impending suicide and you cannot stay with the vet, a relative, family friend, or neighbor should be called to be home with the veteran. While some vets have welcomed the protective presence of another human being, others have yelled at their partners that they don't need "babysitters." Similarly, in situations where suicide seems imminent and the partner insists on finding help, sometimes the vet resists her efforts. In response, she can firmly say: "I am afraid. You just indicated to me that you are thinking about killing yourself. I care about you too much to take the chance that you might act on your impulse. Even if the chances of you killing yourself are one in a million, you mean too much for me to give you the opportunity to end your life. I would rather be safe than sorry."

Sometimes a partner's firmness has resulted in the veteran consenting to go for help or allowing a relative or friend to stay with him. Other times, however, the vet has become more resistant, if not hostile, toward the partner. Yet, it is not uncommon for some suicidal persons (whether they are veterans or not) to become angry or abusive at the very persons from whom they are seeking help. Many times, this hostility reflects the anger the vet harbors toward some other person.

Partners should not take a vet's resistance and anger personally, nor allow it to deter them from protecting their vet from his own impulses. However, if your vet begins to threaten violence—whether toward himself, toward you, or toward someone else—then you must reconsider your strategy.

In several instances vets have threatened to jump into their cars and speed to certain death or otherwise harm themselves, or their partner, if she so much as touches the phone. In a few dramatic cases, vets have barricaded themselves in their homes with their wives and children and sometimes weapons as well. "If you call the police, I'll kill myself first," "If the police come, I'll fire at them and let them kill me," or "Anyone you call near this house, even if it's my sister, is history! I don't care if I go to jail. There's no reason to live anymore anyway." In other instances, the partner is cowed into not calling for outside assistance by his threats to divorce or leave her.

Although it is not generally advisable for a partner to try to handle her suicidal vet on her own, in some instances you may be forced to do so. Even though you are not a trained therapist, there may be times you need to act like one. Through your talking, you might buy time and convince your vet to seek help and give life a chance.

Discuss the subject of suicide with your vet directly. Many partners are afraid to mention the subject, thinking that this might precipitate a suicide attempt. However, generally, suicidal persons experience great relief when afforded the opportunity to talk openly about their suicidal thoughts. Often they have not shared their suicidal feelings with others for fear of disapproval and rejection.

The suicidal veteran needs to be told, "When you say you want to kill yourself, I believe you," not "Oh, you can't mean it," "You'll get over it soon enough," or "Nothing is that bad." The latter responses can convey to the veteran one or more of the following messages:

1. Suicide is so socially unacceptable or morally repugnant to me, I don't want to discuss it.

2. There's something wrong with you if you are talking that way.

3. You aren't entitled to feel that bad.

4. I'm sick and tired of hearing you complain.

5. I don't care enough about you to listen.

Some partners assume that once their vet is in treatment, he is not at risk for suicide unless they hear otherwise from the veteran's counselor, physician, or other helping professional. This is not necessarily the case. Some medical and mental health professionals overlook or discount obvious warning signs of suicide. Perhaps some of them are uncomfortable with the subject of death or suicide, or perhaps they have had so much success with certain treatment methods or medications that they have trouble recognizing instances where their methods, however excellent, simply aren't working. Yet even the most sensitive and competent helping professionals may find it hard to predict suicide because high-risk individuals often do not share the true extent of their misery. For example, a suicidal vet may not want to disappoint or displease his doctors or other helpers and therefore pretends to be improving when, in fact, he is deteriorating. Or perhaps he had planned to share his suicidal thoughts in group, but time ran out before he had the opportunity to speak or another vet's crisis monopolized the session.

While the problem of suicide may be discussed in therapy, in some cases it is to his partner or another family member, rather than to a helping professional, that a vet may first reveal his suicidal desires or the true extent of his wish to die. Furthermore, even after a vet has received help with and successfully overcome an acute suicidal crisis or protracted suicidal period, suicidal thoughts can return. If his response to life's many dilemmas was to become suicidal at one point in time, he may respond in like manner at some future time, for therapy does not spare the veteran (or anyone else) from life's agonies.[14]

When a vet is suicidal, his partner may find herself wondering how she will handle life without him—for example, how she will handle shouldering total responsibility for herself, her family, and her home. Yet she may be afraid to begin making concrete preparations, such as pursuing a higher-paying job or a training program, lest she aggravate the situation. "If only I knew when he was going to do it, I could make plans," one wife explains half-jokingly. At the same time, she, like other partners of suicidal vets, feels trapped inside her home. She's afraid to leave her husband alone, with good reason. The last time she left him alone, she came home to find him online searching for suicide sites. Even if he insists that she go out alone, she stays home—just in case. Her children's social lives are also restricted. In essence, the family's entire life has slowly become tied up with the veteran's problems.

Living with a suicidal or potentially suicidal vet can emotionally deplete, alienate, and anger his partner. Yet there may be times when she is called upon to ignore her anger and help pull her vet through suicide crises. For example, after Linda managed to shove Jesse back into therapy, she thought she was finished acting as his counselor. Yet there were still many times when she had to help him deal with his suicidal feelings. In these discussions, she used the same approach and many of the same arguments against suicide as she did the first time Jesse was close to death.

Linda's first step was to ask Jesse, "Why do you want to kill yourself?" or "What has changed in your life that you now want to die?"

While a suicidal condition is the result of many factors, not just one incident, there may be a single incident or a future imagined negative event that precipitates a suicidal crisis. It is not the incident itself, but the meaning of the incident that creates the overwhelming pain. In talking to a suicidal veteran, or to any other suicidal person, it is important not to mock that person's reasons for wanting to commit suicide, regardless of how insignificant those reasons might seem. It is also important to probe beneath the specific incident to discover its meaning to that person.

For example, Jesse's suicidal crisis was precipitated by his chief at work calling him "stupid" and making derogatory statements about his work performance. Instead of saying, "There you go again, overreacting to everything as usual" or "That's a dumb reason for wanting to commit suicide," Linda empathized: "For someone like you, Jesse, whose identity is so wrapped up in his work and in being intelligent, being called stupid must have been absolutely devastating."

Linda then tried to move Jesse away from the specific incident to the general issues that the incident symbolized. For Jesse, his chief's remarks had highlighted the fact that ever since the war, Jesse had begun to lose confidence in his own professional abilities. All of his life, being called "stupid" was one of his greatest fears. Now he had been called that by a man whom he respected.

Jesse also felt like a failure as a husband and father. He knew he was not meeting his family's emotional needs and felt guilty that because of his change in job status (from a practicing surgeon to a medical-report writer), his wife had to work outside the home. He was certain that Linda greatly resented him and was staying with him only out of duty, not out of love, and that his inadequacies as a father were the cause of his daughter Joleen's depression and his son's rebelliousness and defiance. Caught in the negative all-or-nothing thinking that often characterizes depressed persons, Jesse was also positive that Joleen would never improve, that he would never again be close to Jesse Jr., and that he and Linda could never recapture their old romance.

Last but not least, the derogatory comments made by Jesse's superior at work had reminded Jesse of all the times he had failed to save lives or felt incompetent as a combat medic.

"But killing yourself now won't bring back the dead!" Linda shouted. "And would the dead men and women whose deaths you want to honor want you to kill yourself or would they want you to use your talents and skills to do something positive in this world? Can you go on living—for them?"

"I'm crazy, I'm crazy, I don't deserve to live," Jesse replied.

"You're not crazy! You weren't on a dream vacation—you were in a war. Stop beating yourself up! You can't blame yourself for everything bad that happened over there. Is it your fault there weren't always enough medical supplies and personnel?"

If the veteran believes in God or has a religious or spiritual value system that includes a reverence for life, his partner can use all the theological and religious arguments against suicide that are part of his understanding of the universe. Jesse, however, hated God. Yet Linda was still able to tell him that his life had a purpose.

"The reasons for your existence may not be clear to you at the moment, Jesse," she said. "And they may not become apparent to you for quite some time, but you are here on this earth for a reason. In the past, you've helped a lot of people as a surgeon. Although you focus on the people who died on your operating table, you did save a lot of lives. Also, even if you never perform another operation, just writing those medical reports serves a purpose. I know you wanted to be a famous doctor, Jesse, but you don't have to be famous to matter to me or the kids. We love you. If you kill yourself, we'll be devastated."

"I'm a mess, Linda, and frankly, those kids would be better off without me. Jesse Jr. wishes me dead all the time!"

"He doesn't mean it, Jesse, and even a messed-up father is better than no father at all. If you think you're a bad father now, I say that if you kill yourself, you really will be a bad father. Even if you have the most legitimate reasons in the world for ending your life, our kids won't understand. All they'll know is that Daddy didn't care enough about them to stay alive. If you kill yourself, their emotional problems won't get better, they'll only get worse because they'll feel abandoned and betrayed by you."

Linda then began to list Jesse's various strengths and talents, in a sincere, not superficial, manner. At first, Jesse did not want to listen, for he did not quite believe that there was much positive about him. Yet, it did him good to hear Linda enumerate specific instances where he had shown integrity on the job, kindness and love to her and to others, and other admirable qualities.

"You're so down on yourself, you feel worthless," Linda continued. "But you're important to lots of people besides me and the kids." Linda then listed these people one by one.

In his depressed state, Jesse needed to be reminded that he mattered to others, that if he died he would be missed. Linda also emphasized that if he committed suicide he would be teaching his children that life was not worth living.

"Well, that's the truth. Life isn't worth living," Jesse insisted.

It would have made no sense for Linda to argue with Jesse that life could be joyous, unless she also empathized with his pain and depression.

"I know life seems black to you now, Jesse, and with good reason. I wish I could say that I truly understand, but I can't. I never was in a war and I've never had nightmares. I've never been demoted on my job or had many of the problems that have led you to feel so terrible. Maybe if I were you right now, I'd want to kill myself too. But I also know that feelings aren't facts and that very few situations are utterly hopeless. This is not to say that what you went through overseas wasn't horrible, horrible beyond belief. Some of your suicidal feelings have to do with your rage and sense of powerlessness over those events. But some of them have to do with the ways you feel powerless in your life today."

With a good therapist, Linda suggested, Jesse could make some changes that would make his life today more fulfilling and bearable.

"No situation is hopeless," Linda kept repeating, "not even your PTSD. You could get more therapy, get a different therapist, try out a war recovery inpatient program, or see if there's any medication that might help. If you don't want to talk to anyone or take pills, there's acupuncture and other kinds of help that don't involve talking or pills. There's no reason for you to feel so bad all the time."

"Nothing can help," Jesse insisted.

"That's your depression talking, not you! How do you know nothing can help unless you try? You walked out of therapy before you ever dealt with the hard stuff—your feelings. Give therapy another try. If it doesn't help after a few weeks or months, you can always kill yourself later."

"We can't afford any more help for me," Jesse replied.

"What's cheaper, therapy bills or funeral expenses?" A year of private counseling or medical attention, Linda estimated, was cheaper than a funeral. Furthermore, if Jesse killed himself, Linda was certain she would get so depressed she would have to go to therapy at least twice a week, for at least ten years, and the children would probably have to go to therapy for years, too, which could cost over $200,000. "So you see," Linda concluded, "it's really cheaper for you to get help. Besides, the VA and the Vet Centers are free or don't cost much."

Linda then pointed out that Jesse was evaluating everything in terms of mistakes made in the past and problems coming up in the future. Also, as part of his depression, he was negatively projecting into the future. "How do you know Joleen isn't going to get better? She's already made progress. And how do you know that a year from now Jesse Jr. and you won't be closer than you are today? Who knows, down the line you might even be doing surgery again. Who do you think you are, Jesse, to predict the future, some kind of god?"

Despite Linda's eloquence, Jesse kept insisting that life was hopeless and not worth living. Furthermore, he said, he would greatly appreciate it if Linda would keep her Pollyanna logic to herself. His feelings were not a matter of logic, life was not a matter of logic. No words could talk him out of his misery.

"Even the Jews in the Nazi concentration camps and prisoners of war in Vietnam, Korea, and World War II wanted to live," Linda said. "Sure, some of them died from giving up, but some of them carried on, hoping against hope that they would survive."

"Fools! They should have all committed suicide," Jesse retorted.

"Life is hard," Linda replied. "No one is happy all the time. Most of us live for moments, a few brief moments when we feel at peace with ourselves, when we see something beautiful, or when we feel close to someone. Some of those prisoners kept on living just to see a bird or the sun in the morning, or to show a small kindness to a fellow prisoner.

"I'm not bringing up the concentration camp victims to make you feel guilty, Jesse, or to make you feel like you have no right to feel miserable. But your situation, as terrible as it is, isn't as hopeless as theirs."

Linda then brought in examples of some of the persecutions experienced by immigrant friends of theirs from Lithuania. "They could have given up, many times, but they didn't. We all have an urge to live. So do you, Jesse, even though it's buried under your depression right now. A part of you wants to die, but another part of you wants to live, or else you would have already killed yourself."

Linda then also drew examples from some of Jesse's veteran friends who were missing arms and legs. "Would you tell your quadriplegic friend to go die because he lost the use of all his limbs?"

Just as Linda repeatedly needed to address Jesse's hopelessness, she needed to address his black-and-white thinking and irrational beliefs repeatedly. For example, just because Jesse and Jesse Jr. were arguing did not mean that they were enemies or that Jesse Jr. didn't love him anymore. Jesse Jr. was going through the typical adolescent process of separation from the parents. His rebelliousness would not last forever. Also, just because she and Jesse were having marital problems didn't mean *she* didn't love him.

"Are you angry at me, Jesse?" Linda asked. "They say that sometimes people kill themselves out of suppressed rage, as a form of vengeance on others. If you're angry at me, say so. I'd rather you yell at me and throw things all around the house than kill yourself."

Yes, Jesse was angry at Linda, but he was even angrier at one of his colleagues, in whom he had confided about his postwar problems. Jesse was certain that this colleague had shared this information with the chief of the department, which resulted in the chief's derogatory comments. Furthermore, this colleague's betrayal had activated all of Jesse's feelings of betrayal surrounding his war experience.

"Maybe you think that if you kill yourself, you'll be punishing this so-called friend of yours," Linda said. "Do you picture him at your funeral, overcome with remorse for how he mistreated you? Maybe he will drip with guilt, but I guarantee you, a week later, he'll be at a party having a wonderful time, and not think about you at all.

"Do you think that if you kill yourself you'll be getting back at me and the kids for the ways we've let you down? If you kill yourself, we certainly will be sorry for all the times we hurt your feelings or were mad at you. We'll miss you a lot, too.

"But we will go on to enjoy whatever there is that's enjoyable in this life. If you kill yourself, the main person you'll be hurting is yourself."

If the veteran is seeking vengeance on "the system" through his suicide, he needs to be reminded that the "system" will not be harmed one bit by his death. In fact, if he kills himself, he is letting the "system" win. While his death might create some commotion and perhaps even some guilt on the part of officials, these effects will be temporary. Most likely his death will confirm the officials' view that their treatment of him was right because, as proven by the fact that he killed himself, he was "just another crazy vet." If the vet truly wants revenge on "the system," he's better off learning how to channel that rage into positive action than in destroying himself.

The suicidal veteran can also be asked to identify his reasons for living. These deterrents to suicide can be mentioned to him as often as needed. He can also be asked to go back in time and remember when he felt loved, competent, successful, and needed. However, the severely depressed veteran may have great difficulty remembering this. He may become even more depressed realizing that he can't even remember what happiness and self-satisfaction ever felt like. At this point, it is important to assure him that, although it may be a struggle, he can and will get better.

If he fears he is "insane" or "crazy" because he has suicidal thoughts, he needs to be assured that many people have suicidal thoughts, even allegedly "normal" people. In time, and with help, the suicidal thoughts can lessen in frequency and intensity, as can other symptoms. He needs to view his despair and the symptoms that concern him as part of his combat trauma or other adverse experiences, not as permanent features of his personality. He can also be helped to look forward to a future where he has a greater sense of mastery over himself and his environment, and where life will not be as painful.

In talking to your suicidal vet, do not limit yourself to the suggestions presented in this chapter. Do not hesitate to use whatever arguments you feel would be encouraging to your vet and ask those who know and love him for help. Even if your vet is in treatment, do not hesitate to speak up. Our culture tends to over-rely on professionals, and women often feel inadequate in approaching their suicidal vet. Yet a woman may have much wisdom and can support her mate on a day-to-day basis with a depth of heart and commitment that far exceeds what may be found in a therapist's office. Furthermore, discard any ideas presented in this chapter that you feel would not be effective with your particular veteran.

Suicidal Thoughts in Children

Not only the veteran but also his partner or child can become suicidal. A number of children have not only talked about suicide, they have made suicide attempts, usually requiring subsequent hospitalization. In each case so far, the child gave one or more clear warning signs.

If you recognize one or more of the suicide warning signs listed in this chapter, in either yourself or your child, seek professional help as soon as possible. Young children are in special danger because they are not always aware of how final their actions can be. Also, they, like teenagers, tend to be more impulsive than adults, hence even more attention needs to be given to any indication that suicide is on their minds. Children and teens are also more likely to view life's problems as permanent rather than temporary. They may react intensely to events that to adults may seem "trivial." For instance, a teenage boy may want to kill himself because his girlfriend began to date another boy, or a teenage girl might consider suicide because she binged and gained three pounds.

Nevertheless, a child's or an adolescent's concerns, regardless of how insignificant they may seem, should never be dismissed as "trivial." They must be talked about. Just as partners hope that their veteran's suicidal intentions will disappear if they are not talked about, they also hope that their children's talk of suicide will magically go away if left undiscussed. This is not the case. A mother needs to address the subject of suicide as openly with her child or teen as she would with her vet. Some of the suggestions offered in this chapter for questioning and talking to the suicidal vet can also be used with appropriate modifications in approaching the suicidal young person.

In asking your child questions about his or her plans to commit suicide, you need not fear that you will spark a suicide attempt. In fact, your inquiry and concern may save your child's life, especially if you can convince him or her to talk to someone: the family physician, a therapist, a religious leader, or a trusted family friend. Do not allow your fears of not saying or doing the "right thing" or your guilt about the fact that your child has expressed suicidal wishes paralyze you from speaking from your heart.

Even if your child is in therapy, you cannot necessarily rely on the therapist to detect all the signs and to provide all the support and action your child needs. In a few instances, mothers did inform therapists or school officials about their child's suicidal intentions, and these authorities either did nothing, played down the risk of suicide, or indicated that the child's suicidal state was not their responsibility, but the responsibility of some other professional or authority.

Ultimately, it is up to the parents to provide proper care for their suicidal child and to support that child in the absence of responsible outside help and when the child is in therapy. After all, no professional cares as much about a child as do his parents. You must communicate your love in as many ways as you know how and let your child know that you are behind him or her 100 percent—for example, by being available to listen any time of the day or night. You can also tell your child that even more help is available: inpatient hospitalization, intensive outpatient psychotherapy, medication.

If your family has financial difficulties and your child might feel guilty about the cost of therapy or other such help, stress that such help is a necessity, not a luxury. "You don't know how sad it makes me to see you so unhappy that you want to die. No amount of money is important compared to having you safe and happy," a mother told a suicidal daughter who was greatly concerned about the cost of her therapy.

In addition, compile a list of the phone numbers of the local suicide crisis center or hotline, concerned relatives and friends, or other resources. Post these numbers near every phone in the house or program them into your child's cell phone and urge him or her to use these resources in case of an emergency. Remove firearms or dangerous medications from the home, or keep them under lock and key. Children who become overtly suicidal can be hospitalized involuntarily.

Suicide and Partners

Partners must also attend to their own suicidal impulses. If your thoughts begin to shift from simply thinking about suicide to planning the date and fantasizing about the funeral, run for help. Even if you are not serious about committing suicide, recurring or persistent suicidal thoughts betray a profound despair or sorrow or a suppressed rage, all of which merit professional consultation. If you become too afraid of yourself, hospitalization may be necessary.

Most of the partners I've worked with who seriously contemplated suicide were usually deterred by their dedication to their children or to other persons whom they loved, or by their realization that if they killed themselves, their veteran might feel so guilty he might commit suicide, too. Those partners who actually attempted suicide were primarily women who had a history of child abuse or of abusive relationships with men and who were also currently involved with a physically abusive veteran who was not in treatment or who dropped in and out of treatment as he desired.

These observations are consistent with the research results indicating that female incest survivors and battered and formerly battered women are at high risk for suicide.[15] Among all the suicidal women, three dynamics were present: active self-hate; suppressed or only partially recognized anger toward at least one, usually more than one, abusive male; and feelings of psychological or financial bondage to an emotionally and physically abusive vet.

Summary

A partner whose vet is at a high risk for suicide is living under immense pressure. On some level she may feel that she is both the source of and the solution to her vet's suicidal wishes. Her children may feel likewise. Even if she knows she is blameless, she may still feel responsible for preventing him from actually killing himself. Typically, once her vet has talked of suicide, she begins to carefully watch her speech and behavior so as to be as supportive as possible and may train her children to do the same. She (and perhaps the children as well) may take on additional responsibilities to try to make things as easy for the vet as possible.

In some cases, a partner may wonder if her vet's suicide threats are manipulative. Yet she may hesitate to confront him or to leave him for fear that he will actually carry out his threat. Perhaps she fears her children will condemn her if she leaves their obviously suffering father or perhaps one of her children or she herself is depressed and suicidal as well. Under such circumstances, it is difficult to think about the future.

All threats of suicide, even those made by a five-year-old child, need to be taken seriously. Whenever a veteran home is blighted with the possibility of suicide of one of its members, immediate action needs to be taken to help the hurting family member. Any means of self-destruction needs to be removed and the suicidal member must be provided with as much emotional support and professional attention as possible.

My husband was a P.O.W. During his nine months of captivity, he saw every horror imaginable and later inflicted those same horrors on as many V.C. as he could find. He has a special hatred for the South Vietnamese, whom he felt had abandoned him and allowed him to be captured.

When Bob came home with two b.k. [below knee] amputations, he proceeded to fry his brains with every kind of drug imaginable. For seven years, there wasn't a TV set in the family. He was so heavily into drugs, he'd steal from anyone, until, on the verge of insanity, he committed himself to a VA hospital. There he experienced a religious conversion and received the help that got him drug-free.

But some of the drugs he took had half lives. For years, residues from these drugs trickled down from his brain into his system. At such times, he'd leave home to avoid possibly hurting me or the kids. Sometimes he'd be gone for days at a time. I'd never know where he was or when he'd be coming home. Frankly, after several years of this, I got tired of making excuses for him and of shouldering the load alone and I told him so. Sometimes he apologized. Other times he just ignored me.

What Bob was like before 'Nam, I don't know. I met him afterward, while he was recuperating in an Army hospital. He seemed kind and generous and was making jokes about winning dance contests with his new prostheses. I felt sorry for him because he had lost his legs, but mainly because his family wasn't talking to him.

The whole family had marched against the war. Bob's father believed that God had punished Bob for killing people in Vietnam by taking away his legs. One of Bob's cousins had fled to Canada and another had preferred to cut off either a hand or a foot to avoid the draft.

The only one who forgave Bob was his mother. My mother felt the same way. Many times when I thought about leaving Bob, my mother and mother-in-law kept pointing out that Bob was a religious man who worked hard for his family and was not cruel in any way. Yet they didn't know the pain of liv-

ing with a man who was half-dead and who had lost all passion. I could go anywhere I wanted, see my friends as often as I pleased, but Bob never went anywhere with me or the kids except church—sometimes. He couldn't take crowds or noise.

I almost enjoyed it when Bob exploded. At least I knew he was there.

But his rage reactions were few. When the kids were growing up, Bob was like a stranger to us. His war medals sat in the middle of the living room and pictures of Vietnam decorated every wall. But neither I nor my children could ever mention the word "Vietnam." Newspapers, news magazines, and rice were forbidden, too, as were most feelings. Bob just couldn't take anger or tears. They gave him headaches and made his legs hurt.

The worse part for me was that my son interpreted his father's need for quiet and solitude as meaning that his father didn't love him, which was not the case. However, as a result of my husband's distancing, I think my son developed an inferiority complex, which was why he achieved below his potential at school and didn't socialize much.

But everything changed after our son joined the Army and had a taste of combat. Suddenly he understood his father and they e-mailed each other all the time. When he came home from combat duty, the first words out of his mouth were "I love you, Dad," and, miracle of miracles, for the first time ever Bob said, "I love you" to him and wept for hours.

Now they're almost inseparable, and with our grandchildren, Bob is the father he couldn't be when our kids were young. He's the husband I never had, too. He makes me breakfast every morning, leaves me little love notes, and wants to hold hands with me while we watch TV. If only he could have been one-tenth this loving when we were young!

I wish I didn't have resentments about the past, but I still do, especially about having to be both mother and father to our children when they were young. Sometimes I still hear them saying that if only I didn't nag Dad so much, he'd be okay. But life is sweet now, sweeter than I could have ever imagined, and I can feel the resentments slowly fading away. I used to get down on myself for staying in a marriage where my dreams of romance and shared parenting were constantly being disappointed. But today I'm proud that, in my woman's way, I sacrificed for my country by loving a combat vet whose spirit had suffered as much as his body. Without my dedication to him, none of us—not me or Bob or the kids and their kids—would have the loving family life we have today.

13

"I believe in love"

The Hope of Therapy

Before my husband began therapy, he blamed society for all his prob-
lems and I blamed him for all of mine. It took a year of individual and
group therapy for him to unload his war stories and to begin to accept
himself for what he did or didn't do overseas. Then came the even big-
ger job of trying to live life with all its ups and downs.

When we were having our rough times, some of my friends urged
me to leave him. But I had faith in him and felt that counseling could
help. And it has. We still have problems, though. Counseling hasn't
given me back the years I spent emotionally supporting a man whose
inner life was one raging storm after another. Counseling hasn't even
gotten rid of all Stu's symptoms. But it has made them much more
manageable.

Stu still gets depressed and angry, but not as often and not for so
long. His nightmares are almost gone and so is all that hate he was
carrying around. We even talk now. Before all we did was yell at each
other. Believe it or not, now we make "appointments" to talk about
things. If we find we can't communicate at home, we set aside time for
a "marriage tune-up" session with a marriage counselor.

By talking to my counselor and the partners of other vets, I've learned not to take it personally when Stu goes off. I just go and do something else. I've also learned not to blame him for all my problems. I have issues with my parents and things in my past that have nothing to do with him, and I have to work them out myself. But Stu had to get help and get on his feet before I felt free to take a look at myself. When he was into his depressions and his drinking, I didn't have that luxury. He's much better now, but that doesn't mean I am. After all those years of doing everything for everybody else, it's hard to shift gears.

Because of all his therapy, Stu doesn't need me as much as he used to. He's calmer, too. I'm glad, but it leaves me at a loss. Frankly, I'm so used to one crisis after another that sometimes I don't know how to handle all this peace. I also don't know what to do with all the resentments I've built up over the years. Maybe if I just told Stu about them, I'd get them off my chest and be rid of them. Yet I don't want to ruin the progress Stu and I have made or set back Stu in his recovery by making a big deal about things that happened years ago.

The miracle is that, despite everything, the love we had long ago isn't all gone. Don't ask me why or how, but it survived. There must be something strong between us, otherwise we would have been history a long time ago.

—RITA, WIFE OF A COMBAT VET

Today popular songs often call love an illusion and many books and media talk shows are devoted to finding pathologies in love relationships. Often a woman's dedication to her man is described as a "love addiction" or "codependency," or as an expression of one or more of her neurotic needs. Nevertheless, somehow, somewhere, despite all the disappointments and strains, many veterans and their partners still believe in love. Rita, whose story began this chapter, explains: "Why would I put up with him if I didn't love him? I know he has a bad case of combat trauma, but how often do you fall in love?"

When Rita first came to group, she was looking for ways to get Stu into counseling. On some level, however, she also hoped to heal him herself. Weren't her love and understanding enough? Hadn't she read numerous books on combat trauma? And, as the adult child of an alcoholic, wasn't she an expert caretaker? Yet Stu would not open up to her. In his view, Rita's desire to be helpful was intrusive. "You can't understand. You weren't there," was his standard reply to her carefully worded questions.

Medication

Can It Help?

Rita's next hope was medication. In recent years, a number of psychiatric drugs have proven effective in alleviating sleeping difficulties, depression, rage, and anxiety reactions and other symptoms. Since each symptom may express itself differently in each vet, and a vet may suffer from more than one mental or physical disorder, there is no one drug that has been used for any PTSD or any other combat-related disorder.[1] Ideally, medication is aimed at the symptoms that are most disabling to the vet.

While drugs are useful, they do not treat combat trauma, only the symptoms associated with it.[2] By reducing the severity of the symptoms, however, medication can increase the veteran's ability to function and his ability to deal with the roots of his symptoms—his combat-related issues—if he needs to or chooses to do so. If a veteran is in an extreme state of depression, anxiety, or hyperalertness, he may need medication to help reduce these symptoms so that he can concentrate in therapy or in other areas of his life. Similarly, if he is having so many flashbacks and intrusive thoughts that he can't concentrate on his job, he may need medication in order to function.

Sometimes veterans, like many other persons, prefer to obtain psychiatric medications from a general practitioner or a physician not associated with mental health. Perhaps they wish to avoid the stigma of "seeing a shrink." However, the vet's best bet for obtaining the right dose of the right medication (or combination of medications) is to consult a psychiatrist with expertise in trauma. If this is not feasible for economic or other reasons, a one-time consultation with a psychiatrist who can provide a second opinion or offer recommendations regarding medication is highly recommended. It may also be beneficial for this psychiatrist or other trauma expert to consult with the physician who is dispensing the medication.

In order to be effective, medication must be taken as prescribed (not only when one "feels bad") and must be monitored often. A medication that helps one vet may not help another. Some people find that none of the medications they try are useful or free of intolerable side effects. For other persons, however, medication provides almost immediate improvements in their mood, sleep, appetite, sex drive, and ability to tolerate stress. Still others undergo the often-frustrating and time-consuming process of experimenting with different dosages or different medications before they experience any significant relief.

If a person has a problem with alcohol, drugs, or food, or a medical condition requiring medications that might interact with psychiatric medications, the process of finding the right dose of the right medication to alleviate a certain symptom can become even more complicated. In addition, some psychiatric medications vary in their effectiveness from one racial or ethnic group to the next. Given that most of the research on psychiatric drugs is based on Caucasians, African American veterans and veterans from other ethnic groups may encounter even more difficulties establishing a helpful medication regime.[3]

Alternatives

Because of possible problems associated with medication, as well as the determination of many vets (as well as other people) not to become dependent on a pill, alternatives to medication may be sought. Among the existing alternatives are biofeedback, acupuncture, massage, meditation, muscle relaxation, breathing techniques, and any number of other coping techniques for managing symptoms and reducing stress, such as visualization or creating a safe place in one's mind which can provide comfort and strength during stressful moments.* In order to be effective, however, many of these coping methods, such as muscle relaxation, breathing techniques, and visualization, need to be practiced repeatedly until they are mastered. Using these techniques only during emergencies will not permanently lower body tension, and using them frantically can even increase anxiety levels.

See appendix B for helpful books on these and other coping methods.

Some people find it helpful to combine medication with one of these alternative methods. Medical supervision is required, however. Combining certain psychiatric drugs with other types of medication or with some of these alternative methods can lead to certain harmful physiological changes or psychological symptoms.

When It's Not Enough

In some cases, medication or an alternative treatment (or some combination of the two) is so helpful in helping a vet manage his most disruptive or distressing symptoms that he may not need, or desire, in-depth counseling. After all, it is not necessary for every veteran, or for any other trauma survivor, to undergo an archaeological expedition aimed at uncovering, and subsequently reliving, some of the most horrible moments of their lives. Yet for some vets, medication and other methods aimed at reducing their symptoms, although helpful, still leave them feeling uncomfortably empty, angry, sad, anxious, or feeling as if they are only surviving life rather than living it as they would wish. When this is the case, veterans may need to seek a form of individual or group therapy focused on reviewing their combat experiences and embracing the roots of their symptoms.

For most trauma survivors, especially those who, like combat vets, have undergone multiple traumas, medication alone is seldom the answer. While a useful adjunct to therapy, medication should never be used as a substitute for therapy. Indeed, the available research indicates that therapy is more effective in reducing symptoms of depression and PTSD than medication and that individuals who avail themselves of both psychotherapy and medication fare better than individuals who receive no type of help at all.[4]

The Healing Process

Carl Jung, a student of Freud and a famous psychologist in his own right, used the analogy of a growing tree to describe the client in therapy. The client, he said, is like a tree, naturally growing taller and fuller while its roots spread out wider and deeper into the ground.[5]

When the roots of a tree hit a large stone or other obstacle, do they try to shove the stone away or crack it? No. The roots just grow around the obstacle and then keep going. The stone may have interrupted or slowed the tree's growth for a while, but no stone, no matter how large, can stop the tree from growing.

In Jung's view, the stones in the way of the tree roots symbolize obstacles to personal growth. These obstacles can include an internal emotional conflict (for instance, loving and hating the same person or organization) or an external stressor (e.g., combat). In Jung's view, certain emotional conflicts are never totally eliminated; they are simply outgrown. They stay a permanent part of the person, just as the stones surrounded by tree roots become "part of" the tree. In the same way that roots can move far past the stones in their path to new territory, so can combat vets—or their partners—integrate and grow beyond their traumas and struggles.

Perhaps, today, your veteran's trauma is, to one degree or another, frozen in time, far away from the rest of him. However, once he has integrated the combat experience into his life, he can use some of the powerful energy generated by his military experiences to benefit himself, his family, and his community. Hence combat trauma can become a vital part of his life—just as the stones support and strengthen the root structure of the tree.

The struggles and burdens of his partner can follow a similar path. It is a truism that spiritual love is born of sorrow. In going through difficult times together and in facing the sorrows inherent to warfare, you and your vet can know a closeness that transcends relationships based on superficialities. Your commitment to each other will be real and substantial. Not only in your relationship with each other but also in all the parts of your life, you and your vet will have acquired an invaluable ability. You will have learned how to make positive uses out of your frustrations, fears, anger, pain, and any guilt either of you may be carrying. In this and in many other ways, you and your vet will be able to consider yourselves truly victorious.

Therapy as a Growth Experience

Both you and your vet need to rid yourselves of the idea that because of your problems, you are diseased or deficient. Such thinking harks back to what is known as a negative or "deficit" model of therapy, which assumes that the client, whether you, your vet or your child, is "sick," "wrong," or "inadequate" in some way. The therapist's role in this model is to help a client discover and purge his or her deficiencies.

In contrast, in a "growth" model of therapy (which has been my approach), the therapist's role is to help clients discover and develop their strengths. A growth model assumes that neither you nor your vet is deficient or abnormal; instead it was the events the vet experienced and the stresses you have endured that were highly abnormal. As a result, your vet may have developed certain defenses, certain ways of thinking, and other patterns that may have served him well during combat, but do not do so now. Similarly, you may have developed certain behaviors and attitudes that helped you cope but now have found that some of them are counterproductive.

As you and your vet grow and heal, many of these negative patterns will naturally fall by the wayside, because you won't need them anymore. In addition, the more your vet is able to look at his combat experience directly, and the more realistically and honestly you (or your child) can look at your feelings and needs, the less need any of you will have for defenses that limit your lives and your ability to establish a supportive relationship. In essence, healing means confronting what hasn't been confronted, integrating what hasn't yet been integrated, and binding up emotional wounds. Neither you nor your vet needs to be "fixed." You simply need support and help in identifying and beginning to resolve (or act in spite of) some of your inner conflicts as well as help in mobilizing your inner healing and creative powers.

Healing as a Nonlinear Process

Healing doesn't run in a straight path; it inevitably involves setbacks. For example, in recovering from the flu you may have several days of improved health, followed by a temporary relapse. This setback doesn't mean you won't recover from the flu; all it signifies is that the human body is not an inanimate object. It can't simply be repaired and then be expected to stay that way once and for all. Rather, it is delicate and complex. Yet it has great ability to withstand stress.

Like the body, the human psyche is also not inanimate. Either you or your vet may find yourselves taking three steps forward in the healing process, and then two steps back. That is fine; you are still making progress. Sometimes you or your vet goes backwards because you need to go backwards—if, for example, you have taken on more emotional material at a particular time. At that point you may have to retreat so that you can absorb the emotional shock and otherwise make sense of the material.

Accurate Diagnosis

Another prerequisite for the healing process is an accurate diagnosis. In the not-so-distant past, PTSD was largely unrecognized by the mental health community. Even today, some mental health professionals still doubt the validity of combat-related PTSD or have personal reasons for denying the existence of trauma and its aftereffects. Some minimize, if not almost totally ignore, the trauma of war and look for other reasons for the veteran's problems. As a result, many vets with PTSD were, and in some instances, still are, misdiagnosed as being neurotic or psychotic, or having various character disorders. Or, if they are diagnosed with PTSD or another combat-related condition, the PTSD or other combat-related condition is viewed as secondary to a childhood or other problem the veteran allegedly or actually had prior to his military service.[6]

Today, however, opposite dangers may also exist. As two veteran therapists point out, with increased recognition of PTSD, it is possible that therapists, especially veteran therapists, "see PTSD in every veteran . . . and . . . elevate the importance of that disorder and minimize or neglect additional psychopathology."[7] Perhaps in the past many veterans with PTSD were misdiagnosed as being character disordered or psychotic. However, there are veterans with PTSD who are also character disordered, schizophrenic, paranoid, or who have personality problems beyond PTSD.[8] For some veterans, the scars of previous traumas or difficult life circumstances may have only served to complicate and intensify their reactions to combat.

Similarly, in the past, veterans who did not develop PTSD, but another form of combat trauma, such as depression, may have received counseling that did not adequately address the role of combat in creating their particular traumatic reaction. Today, however, a veteran's struggle with depression or another type of combat reaction may be seen as being purely war related. For some veterans, this oversimplified view of their problems omits consideration of other forces which have shaped their psychological well-being.

Veterans can be helped. However, the full range of their problems must be acknowledged.

Cultural and Racial Factors

Another prerequisite for effective therapy is sensitivity to the veteran's socioeconomic background, gender, sexual orientation, and cultural background. Historically, ethnic and racial minorities in the United States have often been misdiagnosed as having more serious forms of mental illness.[9] Recent research completed on VA mental-health clients reveals that race continues to be a critical factor in such misdiagnosis, often outweighing other factors, such as differences in socioeconomic-status. For example, although the rates of schizophrenia tend to be consistent across cultures, the VA research study found that African American vets were four times more likely and Hispanic vets three times more likely to be diagnosed with schizophrenia than whites.[10]

Since most of our current therapeutic methods are based on white male, middle- or upper-class northern European models of mental health, the findings of the VA research study may reflect ignorance of and perhaps bias toward certain cultural or racial groups. Even some of our diagnostic codes have a cultural bias in that what is considered "normal" in one culture is viewed as "abnormal" in another. For example, there are variations from one culture to the next regarding what is viewed as an acceptable period of mourning or degree of emotional expressiveness, as a healthy degree of family closeness, as valid religious or spiritual experiences, or as the proper or respectful way of interacting with family members or handling interpersonal problems. Since few mental health professionals receive any significant training in cultural difference, sometimes they misinterpret certain cultural patterns and traditions as signs of mental illness.[11]

Cautions: When the Healing Process Is Not Advisable

If a veteran has been severely traumatized or is currently coping with a great deal of stress, the healing process described in this section and certain forms of counseling may not be advisable—for example, those that ask the vet to imagine, write about, or describe his traumas. While counseling may be helpful for some people, for others it has been shown to increase symptoms and depression. For example, some Nazi concentration camp survivors have fared much better by keeping their memories in denial than some who remember the horror. Similarly, preliminary studies of torture survivors from Cambodia and other Southeast Asian countries and from various military prison camps indicate that counseling that focused on their traumas made many of these people feel worse, not better. For these people, counseling that openly dealt with their traumas only deepened their sense of loss and helplessness. For them, supportive counseling for present-day concerns seemed to be more beneficial than delving into the past.[12]

If your veteran falls into one of these categories, or if he feels that he is better off not remembering his combat experiences, then he needs to focus on improving his coping skills rather than on gaining insight. Reviewing combat experiences should also be avoided if:

1. A vet has so much stress in the present that looking at combat experiences or other traumas is best saved for a later point in life.

2. A vet needs some other form of counseling (such as alcohol or drug rehabilitation, communication skills training, anger management, or assertiveness training) before tackling combat memories.

3. A vet needs medical attention, especially for chronic pain, hypertension, diabetes, or a heart condition.

4. A vet develops any of the alarming signs listed in the "Cautions" section of the introduction to this book (suicidal or homicidal thoughts, disorientation, hyperventilation, shaking, irregular heartbeat, and so on).

For example, Manny was the sole survivor of his squad, not just once, but twice. He also developed dozens of open sores from exposure to various toxic biochemical agents. His symptoms of PTSD and depression were so severe and his physical condition so painful that he could not work, and his wife had to assume a full-time job as well as a part-time job, while also taking care of the housework, the children, the finances, the car, and all of her husband's medical needs single-handedly. Manny's guilt about the stress his limitations imposed on his wife only worsened his PTSD and depression. He sought help at a Vet Center more out of concern for his wife than for himself. His goal was to be able to get back to work and help around the house more, not to get rid of his emotional pain.

However, individual therapy where the therapist urged him to talk about his war experiences and group therapy where other veterans shared war traumas only served to retraumatize Manny. Although it is normal for vets to experience some distress after talking about or hearing about war experiences, Manny experienced such severe negative reactions almost every time he went for counseling that the therapist advised him to discontinue treatment. Months later, Manny began bio-feedback therapy and mastered certain muscle-relaxation skills.

Today Manny works part-time and takes an active role in child care and other aspects of home life. His body sores and nightmares continue to plague him. There are still days he's so depressed, he can't get out of bed. But on most days Manny can smile, take pride in himself, and enjoy his children. To suggest or insist to Manny that he needs to revisit his military experience in therapy so he can stop having nightmares or ever getting depressed again would be both unrealistic and inadvisable, if not detrimental to the progress he has made.

The same cautions apply to partners who are trauma survivors.

The Stages of Healing from Trauma

In her landmark book, *Trauma and Recovery,* Dr. Judith Herman describes healing from trauma as a three-stage process involving the following:[13]

  1. Creating safety (making one's world as safe as possible);
  2. Uncovering the trauma and feeling the feelings; and
  3. Reconnecting (with one's self and others).

Stage 1: Creating Safety

External safety. One aspect of safety is external: A vet cannot begin to heal from his psychic or spiritual wounds if he is still being wounded. If he is in an abusive or exploitative living or work situation or is otherwise living in danger, he will need to take steps to create a safe living environment. The same holds true for you, his partner. For example, if you are expressing your frustrations by driving an unsafe car or by engaging in other risky behaviors, then you need to take corrective action.

Internal safety. Another aspect of safety is internal. A vet needs to feel safe with his thoughts, feelings, and behaviors before he can contemplate his war experiences. When the symptoms of PTSD, depression, or some other traumatic reactions make a veteran feel out of control, those symptoms need to be his primary area of concentration. In stage 2, the focus of the therapy is helping the veteran feel safe within himself by getting control over nightmares, intrusive thoughts, flashbacks, insomnia, depression, or any addiction, such as alcohol or drug abuse, gambling, or an eating disorder. It is not wise to begin the unsettling process of reexamining war experiences and the other stages of the healing process unless the vet feels he can exert at least some control over the symptoms that are creating the most havoc in his life.

Similarly, if, as the result of your own traumas from the past or the stresses in your current life, you are struggling with an addiction, symptoms of depression, states of high anxiety, or some other symptom that interferes with your life, managing that symptom is essential for your sense of internal safety. For both you and your vet, feeling safe within also means learning to tolerate strong feelings, such as rage, grief, and anxiety, without being destructive toward yourself or others.

As described above, under professional supervision—in addition to "talk therapy" with a competent therapist—medication, an alternative treatment, or learning and mastering some of the available coping techniques are often helpful. However, coping techniques, such as muscle relaxation or visualization, must be practiced and mastered.

Stage 2: Uncovering the Trauma and Feeling the Feelings

Only when a vet has established a certain degree of internal and external safety can he then safely proceed to the second stage of healing, which involves remembering the trauma and feeling the feelings associated with the trauma. The major feelings that need to be dealt with are anger, guilt, and grief.

For some vets, war experiences are quite vivid; for others, only partially remembered; for still others, almost totally repressed. The veteran's traumatic memories are not repressed because he is, or was, neurotic, but because by definition a trauma is an event that so overwhelms an individual that he cannot accept it as happening to him. Even if he remembers many of his experiences, it is the specific events that were especially traumatic or life changing which need to be brought into conscious awareness, then shared in group or individual therapy. The veteran does not need to remember all of his traumas. However, he needs to remember enough of his war experiences so that he can make sense of his symptoms and understand his emotional and other reactions to current reminders of the war and other aspects of his life today.

It can be extremely therapeutic for some vets to recall previously forgotten or dimly remembered traumatic experiences and share them with others. However, it is also necessary for a vet to rethink or re-evaluate his combat experiences and to understand the meaning of these events in his life. He especially needs to re-evaluate incidents about which he feels guilt or shame regarding a particular feeling, thought, action or inaction, or error in judgment. In many cases, the veteran fails to acknowledge how the complex and ambiguous nature of combat may have contributed to his behavior. A therapist or members of a veterans group can help the vet evaluate these and other critical incidents more objectively.

As a result, a vet may come to realize that perhaps he was not such a coward after all or perhaps his friends would have been killed anyway. If indeed his cowardice or viciousness resulted in an irreversible tragedy, the vet must feel the pain of his guilt directly rather than run from it. With the help and support of a therapist or a veterans group, he can try to learn to forgive himself. "The message is . . ." that many veterans ". . . did the best job in the situation that could have been done considering the circumstances and the resources available in the situation."[14]

In addition to reformulating his war experiences mentally, the veteran needs to take steps toward feeling the feelings associated with these experiences, feelings that were not felt at the time these particular events occurred. Repressed grief and repressed anger are usually the two major emotions that emerge. As these and other emotions rise to the surface, a vet can be helped in learning how to direct the powerful energy contained in some of his emotions into constructive, rather than destructive, channels. Often at this point, the veteran may begin to make associations between past and present and see how his war experiences and his reactions to them have impacted his life, positively as well as negatively.

Stage 3: Reconnecting with Self and Others

The third stage in healing involves re-establishing human ties. When a vet's life was dominated by combat memories or by an addiction or lifestyle that helped numb him to the effects of combat, most likely he did not have much time or energy to devote to relationships. Yet problems with his family, friendships, or love life may have caused him to withdraw or contributed to his turning to alcohol, drugs, food, gambling, or sex as a substitute for meaningful human contact. Once he has some understanding of his trauma and some control over his symptoms, including any addiction he may have had, he may be ready to begin to reestablish some old relationships and even consider building new ones.

The third stage also involves reconnecting with some of his former goals and values and having increased energy for present-day life and future plans. For some vets, healing involves a spiritual or moral dimension, as well as an emotional one. For these veterans, stage 3 may involve an attempt to re-evaluate or perhaps even reconnect with their former faith or with their spirituality. Spiritually, some vets seek absolution for their actions. For some vets, group therapy is the route to self-forgiveness. For others, the assistance of a rabbi, priest, minister, or other clergyperson or spiritual leader is needed. The need for absolution may also result in the veteran becoming involved in various "survivor missions" (such as helping other veterans or war refugees) or in other charitable works.[15]

Partners vary in their response to their veteran's survivor mission. Some partners join or even assume leadership roles in the humanitarian or service effort to which their veteran is committed. Others may not participate in their veteran's survivor mission, yet they are extremely tolerant of the time, energy, and money their vet devotes to helping fellow veterans or other persons in need. As they see their vet break out of his isolation, they rejoice. However, some partners also become resentful when their husband or boyfriend seems to be giving more time and love to others than to their relationship and children.

Healing Takes Time

Partners are often disappointed when therapy doesn't "fix" their veteran as rapidly as they desire. Women who have waited for many months (or even years) for their veteran to finally seek help often are dismayed to discover that the healing process can be painfully slow. Children, too, may be anxious for their father to improve. Recovery takes a long time—at least a year, usually two or three years. Depending on the individual, the severity of his traumatization, and the impact of any previous problems or traumas, it may take even longer. Often it is a lifelong process, as the vet continues to put together the pieces of himself shattered by the war and continues to make connections between combat experiences and his current outlook on and reactions to life. For example, some of a veteran's triggers may not be readily apparent. If a veteran was shot on September 11, for example, the veteran will probably be aware of this trigger. However, there may be other triggers of which he is unaware and which can only be revealed over time. Hence he might be feeling more depressed or more "hyper" in a situation that neither he, nor his partner, nor even his therapist realizes is a trigger until months or years later.

This lack of awareness should not be the cause of self-berating. For people who have been multiply traumatized, such as combat vets, uncovering triggers can take many years, if not a lifetime. This is absolutely normal and not a sign of "not trying hard enough" in therapy or lack of recovery.

The sooner the vet receives help after symptoms arise, the easier it will be for him to recover. If a veteran has been using negative ways of coping with his combat trauma for many years, these negative coping mechanisms may be firmly entrenched. Considerable time may be needed for healing to occur. Keep in mind also that healing requires that the veteran attend sessions regularly, not sporadically or only when in crisis. It also requires a positive recovery environment. Healing does not take place in isolation. If a veteran is not receiving sufficient emotional support from others, is struggling with serious economic, medical, family or other problems, or was retraumatized since the war, his ability to benefit from counseling will be significantly hindered.

The Meaning of "Healing" or "Recovery"

Family members sometimes hope that after their veteran undergoes therapy they will never hear the word "war" again or that they will no longer have to be distressed by the veteran's sadness, by his emotional or social withdrawal, or by any negativity or bitterness he may be carrying. However, just as rape victims cannot "forget" the rape, or battered women their abuse, some war experiences will remain with veterans until the day they die.

Counseling can help reduce the intensity and frequency of a veteran's symptoms and improve his ability to manage them. But therapy is not a surgical procedure that promises to permanently remove traumatic memories and their impact from the human mind, body, or soul. The veteran's sadness, anger, or other feelings about the war are bound to return. Being well, for the combat veteran, lies not in "feeling better all the time" or in "never thinking or hurting about the war again," but rather in being reintegrated into society and in being able to function in a family or career.[16] For the veteran, as for any human being, therapy has definite limits: it cannot promise the absence of pain, anger, disappointment, or injustice in life, only a closer emotional connectedness to one's self and others and an improved ability to take positive action toward solving problems.

Two Flawed Ideas about the Nature of Recovery

As psychologist Mary Harvey points out, in today's society there are two popular ideas of what it means to be "healed" or "recovered" from trauma.[17] These ideas are widely held not only by the general public but also by mental health and other professionals and by trauma survivors themselves. The first of these highly flawed ideas is that recovery is a global, all-encompassing state of positive thinking and action achieved through years and years and years and even more years of counseling. If a person isn't always (or almost always) full of optimism and self-confidence, then he or she is considered to be full of self-pity, "dwelling in the past," or "resistant" to therapy.

The second erroneous popular idea is that recovery involves eliminating any and all of one's post-traumatic symptoms. According to this idea, we can view ourselves as having "let go" or "overcome" our trauma only when we no longer think about it, no longer have feelings about it, or no longer have any symptoms as a result of it.

If these two ideas are the standards of recovery, then no combat veteran, not even one who has spent forty hours a week in therapy for ten years, could ever consider himself on the road to wellness. Why? Because, no matter how strong and determined you may be, you can't fight biology and expect to win.

Some post-traumatic responses, such as the startle response, sleeping problems, numbing, and intense emotional or physiological distress upon exposure to a reminder of the trauma, are survival responses hardwired into the body. Often they involve involuntary biochemical processes that no amount of "will power" or "determination" can eliminate. Since veterans are constantly being triggered by anniversary dates and other reminders of combat, as well as by current losses, disappointments, or major stresses (such as job or family problems), having post-traumatic symptoms is almost inescapable.

Furthermore, our world is still full of wars, crimes, vehicular accidents, and family violence. Hence veterans can be retraumatized not only by their own personal triggers but also by the traumas going on all around them. At the hands of a therapist with little training in combat trauma, who is unsympathetic toward traumatized people, who has simple solutions for the complicated problems presented by someone who has gone through a war, or who is in denial about their own life problems or traumatic experiences, therapy can also be so retraumatizing that many vets feel more disempowered than before they sought help.

Realistic Standards of Recovery

Since having symptoms (or being triggered) is almost inescapable, a veteran's progress cannot be measured by never again feeling empty, sad, anxious, enraged, hopeless, or helpless. Instead, consider the following criteria suggested by Harvey:[18]

1. *"Increased power or authority over memories."* If a vet had total or absolute power over his memories, he would be able to turn them on and off at will; that is, if thoughts of the war entered his mind, he could order them to go away and they would—in a snap. Having power over his memories would also mean that he could remember as many aspects of his war experiences when he wanted to remember. However, one of the most troubling aspects of combat trauma is the loss (or diminishment) of authority or power over one's memories. Some veterans wish they could forget or turn off certain memories, while others anguish because they can't remember certain memories. "If only I could forget," some wish; "If only I could remember," wish others.

Traumatic memory is not like other kinds of memory. Once traumatized, it is just as normal to remember graphic details of one's trauma (or traumas), or to remember some details or traumas but not others, or to have only a vague memory of them or no recall at all. There may even be a time a traumatic event (or detail about one) can be remembered, but the very next day or some other time, it cannot be recalled. This doesn't mean that a person is losing his mind, making up stories, or suffering from brain damage. Such is the nature of traumatic memories.

Given the nature of traumatic memory, progress can be measured as follows:

a. Suppose a vet remembers a combat experience when he doesn't want to be thinking about it and can't stop thinking about it, no matter how hard he tries. Progress doesn't mean that the vet can stop thinking about it automatically and forever, but that the time spent thinking about it decreases over time. For example, if it used to take a vet two hours to stop thinking about being attacked and now it takes the vet one hour, then the vet is successful.

b. If a vet can't recall a particular traumatic event or can recall only parts of it, but over time is able to remember more of the details and the correct sequence of events, the vet is successful.

Veterans I have worked with often compare themselves to other vets: "How come _____ remembers the full name, rank, and birthplace of all the guys in his unit and where they were born and raised and I can't even remember what anyone looked like?" or "How come _____ can talk about the war, then put it out of his mind and go on with his life? But whenever I talk about it, I have to take the next day off from work to recover?" Veterans should not compare themselves, or be compared by others, to other veterans! There is no hierarchy of suffering or recovery. Even though there are theories about why some people can remember more than others, no one really knows why. No one (including a therapist) has any scientific basis for upbraiding a vet for "not remembering" or for "remembering too much."

2. *"Memory with manageable emotion."* What usually happens when veterans remember the hell they've been through is that they remember with little or no emotion at all (numbing) or with overwhelming emotions that feel almost unmanageable in their intensity (hyperarousal or overstimulation). For example, remembering can flatten their emotions so much they feel numb or "dead inside," or bring forth so much emotion that they feel "blown away," as if the feelings associated with war—anger, fear, grief, self-hate, confusion—just jumbled themselves into one big ball that has the potential to propel them into the realm of insanity.

"Recovery" doesn't mean remembering without a strong emotional reaction (whether numbing or hyperarousal). Rather, recovery means that a vet can remember the war without the numbing or hyperarousal becoming debilitating or incapacitating to him. Remember that "feelings aren't facts" and that feelings are different from behaviors or actions (what one actually does or says).

3. *"Efforts to manage overwhelming emotions or post-traumatic reactions."* Recovery means being able to regulate or manage the anger, fear, numbing, or other responses one has to triggers. If not having symptoms is a measure of recovery, then a vet can't get any credit for being able to manage symptoms that are inescapable. Some credit needs to

be given to vets who try to manage their symptoms. It doesn't matter what that way is, whether it is medication, listening to music, massage, looking at a tree, or praying, as long as it is a way that does not harm the vet or any other living being.

The fact that a veteran can manage or at least makes an honest effort to manage his or her intense trigger reactions or other symptoms needs to be honored. Even if he just thinks about doing something positive as a way of managing a difficult moment but cannot follow through with the idea, he still deserves to congratulate himself. Thinking is an action and thinking about doing something to help one's self is the first step toward actually doing it.

4. "*Improved self-care.*" Recovery means the vet is increasingly willing or able to take care of himself physically, emotionally, and, if he has a spiritual side, spiritually. Is he able to do things which he feels are good for him even when he doesn't feel he is worth the trouble? Does he ask others for help to help himself grow stronger?

5. "*Increased self-respect.*" Is the vet growing in self-respect? Is more and more of his life free from self-doubt, irrational guilt, unnecessary secrecy, and other effects of war? Is he becoming increasingly consistent across various areas of his life?

6. "*Safe human relationships.*" Can the vet select friends and intimates who don't hurt him or cause him to hurt himself? Can he stay away from destructive people and substances even when he feels like ending it all? Can he renegotiate in a relationship to have his needs met? Can he compromise with others in a way that doesn't make it impossible for him to survive in a relationship?

7. "*Finding meaning.*" Recovery can also be measured by the degree to which the vet begins to make some meaning out of his combat experience. Often this becomes part of a larger process: that of making some meaning out of his life. This means coming to some decision about what matters in life and what to do with one's time on earth. A vet's therapist, doctor, parent, war buddy, or other friend cannot make these kinds of decisions for him. Others can help, however, by believing that, given enough time and support, a vet will be able to find meaning in the past and in the present and by being willing to support the vet as he himself figures out what combat meant to him and if any good can be wrestled out from all the bad. Even if a vet thinks that the war "meant nothing," or that it "made no sense," there may still be

some meaning in his combat experiences for him. Once he begins trying to salvage some meaning out of his painful past, he is on the road to recovery.

8. *"Recognizing personal growth and wisdom stemming from the trauma."* In recent years it's becoming increasingly recognized that combat veterans, like other survivors of extreme traumas, have the potential to experience certain positive benefits from their ordeals. Some of these potential benefits include: the ability to reevaluate their lives and reorder their priorities; increased self-reliance; increased awareness of the brevity and fragility of life; greater appreciation for loving relationships; increased compassion for others; spiritual development; and stronger partnerships and marriages.[19]

While time does not heal all wounds, and certain scars can remain for a lifetime, the realization that one has grown in some ways or developed a greater appreciation for life—one's own life and the lives of others—is another sign of recovery.

When Patient Partners Lose Their Patience

Even partners who understand why war recovery can take time may find it difficult to wait for signs of their vet's recovery to manifest themselves. Some partners are more patient than others. Those who are able to restrain themselves from asking more from their veteran in terms of their relationship, child care, or certain financial or household matters usually do so for fear of overloading their vet and impeding his recovery. "He can't deal with me [or the children, the bills, my parents, insurance companies, etc.]," they often say. Sometimes partners are advised by a therapist or well-meaning friend not to bring up major relationship or other problems until the vet has resolved many of his war-related issues.

In cases where the veteran's traumatic reactions are so severe that the veteran is severely regressed, almost totally noncommunicative, or extremely rigid or violent, a partner's decision to refrain from voicing her various concerns may be prudent. However, even the most saintly partner cannot be silent forever, nor can she always wait until her vet is substantially healed before she discusses certain matters with him. Some issues, especially regarding children, may need immediate attention. Furthermore, an improved relationship with his significant other and family and an increased capacity to deal with present realities are a part of the veteran's recovery. The veteran cannot be protected forever from knowledge about how his behavior is stressing his family.

For example, Rita needed her husband's written consent to place their son in a program for gifted children. However, this opportunity would require that their son be bused to a school that was not only miles from home but also located near a high-crime area.

Rita knew that when her husband Stu was seven, he had been in a school-bus accident. Furthermore, soon after he returned from combat duty, he had had a flashback while driving and nearly plowed into a school bus. Stu was preoccupied with his family's safety. Protecting them from every possible danger to their emotional or physical well-being was one of his paramount concerns.

Usually Rita avoided raising any issue that had the potential to make Stu "hyper," but if the necessary papers were not signed by a certain date, the placement would be given to another student. When she raised the issue with Stu, the following dialogue ensued:

"Don't pressure me. You know I can't take pressure. Let me get more counseling under my belt before bringing up things like that."

"But if we don't make up our minds soon, our son is going to lose his chance."

"It'll have to wait."

"But we can't wait."

"I said, 'It'll have to wait.'"

A day or two later, Rita raised the issue again and, once again, Stu insisted that he had to "get himself together" first. As the deadline approached and Rita pressed the issue again, Stu began accusing her of being willing to endanger their son's life. Rita, in turn, began accusing Stu of letting his "irrational fears" stunt their child's development. Then Stu started on Rita's weight and Rita let loose on the subject of how Stu and his "stupid war" had not only made her fat but also a nervous wreck.

As the argument escalated, the original subject of discussion was lost. Rita forgot about her own fears about busing and Stu about his pride in his son's abilities and deep desire to promote his son's education.

Meanwhile, the son, who was supposed to be sleeping, tried to stop the fight. "Don't fight because of me. I don't want to go to that new school anyhow. All I want to do is grow up and be a soldier like Daddy and get wounded in a war," he said.

"See what you've done! You've warped his mind," shrieked Rita.

Stu yelled back and the argument finally ended when Stu withdrew into a state of extreme numbing. At a total loss, Rita sought out Stu's counselor who suggested an emergency session limited to the school issue only. During the session, Stu and Rita were able to stop attacking one another and review the school problem objectively. Much to their surprise, they discovered that they basically agreed: both of them wanted every advantage for their son, yet were afraid of the busing and the poor neighborhood. They were then able to brainstorm alternatives, such as looking at programs in other counties, making arrangements to drive their son to school themselves or hiring someone to do so, or even relocating to an area with a gifted program nearer to their home or in a safer area.

As Rita's dilemma illustrates, a consultation with the veteran's therapist may be needed to help a woman decide whether or not to confront her vet (and on what issues) and to assist her in resolving certain issues that cannot wait. In this regard, couples counseling may also be helpful. When vets are in treatment, their partners can benefit from getting support for themselves. Either in individual or group therapy or a woman's support group, they can air concerns which they sometimes feel they must keep to themselves at home.

Unfortunately, sometimes women who decide to remain relatively silent until their veteran has achieved a certain level of recovery are accused of being "doormats" or "weaklings" or acting like "little girls." However, a woman's decision on this or any other matter (with the exception of abuse issues) needs to be respected. If therapists or other partners wish to be supportive, they can help the woman explore her fears and other reasons for not speaking up; help her identify the conditions under which she would feel it productive to raise certain issues; and help brainstorm alternative ways to manage the current situation and to approach her vet in the future.* *See appendix C for guidelines for effective communication.

On the other hand, women who speak up are sometimes accused of being "selfish" or "aggressive" or of undercutting or "sabotaging" their veteran's therapy because they are threatened by the vet's recovery or because they wish to dominate the vet. In my experience, such accusations are usually unfounded. Nevertheless, if a woman raises too many issues at the same time, the vet may feel "ambushed" and become so overwhelmed that productive dialogue on the issues may be impossible. It is also helpful for a partner to prioritize her concerns and to give some thought as to the most effective way to present her concerns. Although triggering the vet in some way may be unavoidable, problems can be presented in a manner that takes into account the veteran's specific triggers, traumatic mind-sets, and other aspects of his combat trauma.

"It gets worse before it gets better"

Partners, like veterans themselves, are surprised to find that often in the therapeutic process "it gets worse before it gets better." As Rita explains to newcomers:

> When your vet goes into therapy, you think, "Hurrah! The problems are finally over with." Well, guess what? There are more nightmares, more holes in the wall, more anger at you.
>
> In therapy all the feelings your vet bottled up for years start coming out, in his individual or group sessions, of course, but on you too. Stu even started drinking more—blaming it all on me, as usual. It got so bad, I started wondering why I ever begged Stu to go for help in the first place.
>
> Then, when the group started teaching him how to be assertive, rather than passive or aggressive, which were his usual styles, I got mad. Here I was, holding in everything for years and not being assertive so he wouldn't get upset and quit therapy, and here he was, practicing his group's assertiveness training on me. Then, when I objected, he accused me of undercutting his therapy.
>
> Now things have evened out between us. Thanks to the other partners I've talked to, I've learned how to be more assertive, too, and thanks to the men's group, Stu can take it. But it took us three years of counseling, not to mention a lot of yelling and a lot of tears and heartache on my part.
>
> But it was worth it. At least I have a marriage now. Before I had nothing.

Increased thinking about combat, as well as more emotionality, are expected parts of the healing process.[20] If the therapy is working, many of the veteran's long-buried emotions and memories will begin to surface. As they surface, the veteran will experience more inner turmoil, more restlessness, and more pain. Experiencing these feelings may make him temporarily inefficient in terms of work, more vulnerable psychologically, more withdrawn, and less emotionally available to his partner and others. Sometimes, as a defense against increased feelings of personal vulnerability, the veteran may become more hostile, or domineering, toward his partner and others.

Violence and verbal abuse are unacceptable and should not be tolerated. However, a partner can expect her vet to be not only angrier, but sadder, and perhaps more openly afraid. She may need to assure him frequently that he is not falling apart and that the feelings, although intense, will not destroy him. Neither will they last forever. The vet may also need to be reminded that although feeling his feelings can be a very painful and disorienting process, in the long run he will only be strengthened by facing his feelings rather running from them.

Rita's husband Stu, for example, sat in group for six months before he shared any of his combat experiences. "That night," Rita says, "he went out drinking. The next night, he cried on my lap all night long, just like a baby. Then he cried for almost a whole week afterward, too. He couldn't even go to work.

"'Am I going crazy?' he'd ask me.

"No, honey, you're just feeling your pain."

Starting Over Again

While Rita was overjoyed at Stu's progress, at first she didn't know how to act around him. "I'm not used to him being normal." It was also a new feeling for her not to have to think four times before she said anything to him. As Stu began to participate more and more in family life, Rita felt her prayers had been answered. Yet giving up her old role of managing almost everything all by herself was somewhat disorienting. Also, she was somewhat frightened of the demands her husband might make of her emotionally and sexually.

When Stu finished therapy, it was like starting all over again, not only in terms of renegotiating who was going to do what, but in terms of our entire relationship. After he came home from the war, Stu and I got into this pattern where he shut me out and I, in my own way, shut him out, too. I learned to not expect much from him emotionally, and sometimes even when he did want to be close, I rejected him. I guess I was angry at having to be the stable one while he was allowed to be moody and unpredictable.

Our entire relationship became centered around money and the children. We stopped going out and having fun together, like we used to before he went overseas. We even forgot how to talk to each other like man and wife, or even like friends. All our talk was about the house and the kids, me complaining about him, or him about me.

Now he wants to have a "real" relationship with me. But I've forgotten how to be relaxed around him. I'm a whiz at anticipating his moods and appeasing him, but now he wants to know me as an individual.

What a joke! After all these years of functioning, functioning, functioning, am I still an individual? Somewhere, in the midst of trying to survive and keep the family, and myself, from going under, I lost myself.

It's been months since I've read a book. I haven't done anything else interesting either. Is my husband now going to find me boring? Now that he's better, will he still want me?

Like Rita, other partners have voiced feelings of personal insecurity as they watch their vet become stronger. If a partner's previous relationship with her vet was based on being his caretaker, once she is not needed as intensely, she may fear the vet will abandon her. In my experience, however, very few veterans have left their partners following a positive therapeutic experience for combat trauma. More typically, it is the partners of vets who did not seek help or who attended therapy intermittently who were abandoned.

After a veteran has made strides in stage 1 and stage 2, he can begin to reconnect with himself, his goals for his life, his family and other loved ones, his community and other groups. In both large ways and small, he is "starting over." His partner may be "starting over," too. In some cases, the veteran's recovery can pose an identity crisis for his partner, who must now deal with herself and her own life, which in the past, to one degree or another, were put on hold because of her veteran's unmanageable traumatic reactions. Partners often state that prior to their veteran's progress in therapy, they felt that in constantly responding to the veteran's needs and the many family crises, they were losing their personal identity. Rita is typical of partners who face this kind of identity crisis.

I was a girl when I married. Now I sometimes feel like I'm an old lady, even though I'm not. My vet is fine, or almost fine, but I'm not, even though everybody expects me to be. Worse, I expect me to be. But just because he's got his combat trauma under fair control doesn't mean that I'm over my pain and anger.

Nowadays I even get hugs without asking for them. You'd think I'd be overjoyed. But I keep remembering all the times I was dying for a little love and never got a crumb.

Sometimes I think about telling my husband how I feel, but I don't want to ruin the progress he's made by bring up all my past resentments. Yet he senses my feelings and asks me why I'm so cold.

I never know what to say.

"Don't dare look back," I tell myself. "If you start thinking about all you sacrificed for him, you'll start putting holes in the wall and tearing up the furniture like he used to." Usually I try to cast out my resentments as soon as they crop up, but it doesn't always work. I guess all those years of supporting him before therapy and then during the stress of therapy have drained me. Sometimes I feel a great emptiness and hollowness inside, as if I've lost all my blood and have no more strength or love to give.

I want to get back to who I was before war came into my life. In my head, I know there's a wonderful future out there for me, but there's this bitter, angry woman standing in my way. That's me. She's tired, too, and part of it's her own fault for spoiling not only her husband but her children and her in-laws, too.

I'm in a rut and I know it, but I can't seem to get out of it. My husband isn't stopping me as much as he used to, although he still gets in my way. My main problem is that I don't know where to begin. There's got to be more to life than working and having a family. But what?

Sometimes Rita thinks about taking a course or pursuing a hobby, but it seems like too much effort. In her words, she suffers from "PTSD burnout." The cumulative effects of years of emotional and physical exhaustion have eroded her self-confidence to such a degree that she now doubts she will be able to complete any project she starts. It proved helpful to Rita to begin where she left off—to recall the experiences and activities that had sparked her interest prior to meeting Stu, especially prior to his combat duty, and see if any of them still offered her any joy or fulfillment. If she could just do something small for herself, just for herself, that could be the first step toward getting more satisfaction out of life.

Rita vaguely remembered that she had enjoyed painting before her marriage. Afterwards she took an art course and is now planning to start a small hand-painted card business which she could operate out of her home and promote with the help of the Internet. It all began, however, with her signing up for an afternoon art workshop which she almost didn't attend because her son needed a last-minute ride to a party. Gathering together all her assertive skills, she told him that in the future he would have to give her advance notice about his activities or find his own ride. She also insisted that this time his father do the chauffeuring. After years of feeling as if she were living in Stu's shadow, and the shadow of the war in which he fought, it was now time for her. What's more, she felt she had earned it.

Getting Help

Today both Vet Centers and Veterans Affairs medical centers offer counseling and other help for veterans. Often individual, group, and marriage counseling can be obtained through the psychiatric, psychological, or social-work services, or through the medical center's outpatient mental-hygiene clinic. In addition, several VA hospitals sponsor PTSD or war-recovery inpatient units. Inquiry about these PTSD or war-recovery units, as well as about help in the private sector, can be made at Vet Centers or at VA medical centers. All branches of the military offer counseling and other help for active-duty veterans.

A veteran may be reluctant to seek help because it violates his sense of masculinity; because he fears he will be misdiagnosed or misunderstood; because he fears that his mental-health appointments will be made known and negatively influence his career or social standing; or because he came to mistrust mental-health or other helping professionals due to negative experiences with such persons during his war experience. A veteran may also feel embarrassed to admit to still being bothered by events that occurred some months or years ago. Perhaps he feels he should be over his combat experiences by now and wonders if he is abnormal for still thinking or dreaming about the war. Or perhaps he envisions therapy as a form of entrapment.

Some vets do seek help on their own, but others are shoved into treatment by partners, children, other family members, or by employers.

Perhaps the most frequently asked question by partners is, "How do I get my vet into treatment?" The following section provides some suggestions to help you develop some ways of encouraging your vet to seek help that are suited for him as a unique individual. However, do not follow these suggestions blindly. As you read through them, think hard about your vet's personality, his interests, his military experiences, and his work situation. You, not this author or others, are the expert on your own vet. Often you, more than anyone else, know which approach will be most effective with him. In general, scolding him, telling him that he is "crazy," or listing his character defects will not motivate him to seek help. It's also important not to approach him during the anniversary date of an important combat-related event; when he's tired, upset, restless, or preoccupied with other matters; or while you are quarreling (or immediately afterwards). Likewise, it's important to avoid using words or terms that he might find upsetting; to follow the guidelines in appendix C; and to avoid repeating the same message of concern to him over and over again, for he will eventually grow immune to it. Consider the following ideas:

1. Use—don't attack—his values.

a. What qualities does your vet value in himself, in his war buddies, or in others' job?

Before you answer this question, take a few minutes to recall instances where he expressed admiration for someone who displayed a certain quality, such as competence, quick thinking, dedication to the job and family, or team spirit.

b. How might your vet's stress reactions or other psychological symptoms interfere with his desire to live up to those values? Are there instances where his symptoms (or the similar symptoms of a family member, war buddy, or coworker) already have interfered with work performance, family life, or some other area of life that matters to him?

c. Ask yourself: How can I express my concern that these symptoms could potentially harm another person (especially a family member) in a way that won't alienate him? Which words or phrases should I use? Which ones should I avoid?

You may wish to point out the danger his symptoms pose to himself; however, he may have been trained to ignore or minimize these dangers. Therefore it's important to emphasize instead the goal of being a loving family member or contributing citizen or of getting his work or another project done with as few problems as possible and any specific ways his symptoms interfere with meeting any of his goals. How would he feel if someone else was psychologically affected in a negative way or even physically injured because he couldn't think clearly, overreacted, or underreacted in a situation that required a clear-headed response, or made a mistake due to being triggered by a reminder of the war and not knowing how to manage his reaction? It is his duty to his family and others who care about him, to people who work with him, and to other people or organizations that he values and that are part of his identity to maintain his emotional health.

2. Address any fears your vet may have about seeking help which are based in myths: for example, that seeking mental-health help means that he is weak, unmanly, crazy, "psycho," or incompetent (as a person, family member, worker, or individual of faith).

a. Do you have reason to believe your vet has any of these fears? If so, which ones?

b. Do you have reason to believe that his war buddies, co-workers, family, and others who matter to him believe in any of these myths? How is he affected by their views of seeking help?

c. Does your vet know of people who sought help and afterwards were either ridiculed, deemed unfit for duty, or even declared legally insane? What are the similarities between your vet's problems and overall life situation and those of these other individuals? What are the differences? If your vet's symptoms are less severe than those of these other individuals, or if your vet's work, family, or financial situations are more favorable than those of these other individuals, would it be helpful to point out some of these differences to him?

d. Do you think it would be helpful to share any of the following information with your vet which might help dispel these myths?

- Mental health problems are not all the same. While some people seek help for severe psychiatric illnesses, many seek help for specific problems that affect only part—not all—of their lives or for problems that arise due to stressful situations rather than due to their personality. If your vet truly had a severe psychiatric problem, then he probably wouldn't be able to work or to have a rational conversation with you. Unless he is out of touch with reality or totally out of control in some way, he can't legitimately be considered "crazy" or "psycho."

- Mental health problems are often medical problems as well. Since the mind, the body, and the emotions are closely interrelated, many psychological disorders can involve various physiological abnormalities. Just as your vet probably would not feel ashamed of having leukemia or diabetes, he need not be ashamed of having a psychological disorder, for in truth, many psychological disorders have a physiological component. For example, alcoholism involves a biochemical addiction, and PTSD involves involuntary adrenaline, and other physiological reactions. Similarly, depression can be caused by medical problems such as migraine headaches; low-grade neck, shoulder, or back pain; heart disease; diabetes; hypertension; chronic pain; cancer; and other long-term or life-threatening illnesses. Furthermore, some physical illnesses have symptoms that appear to be psychological in nature, but are symptoms of a bodily illness. Hence your vet may not have a psychological problem at all, but rather an illness that needs medical attention.

- Seeking help is a sign of intelligence, not weakness. If your vet had a work tool that needed some repairs, he'd probably be quick to fix the problem. He needs to view his reactions to combat reactions and other symptoms in a similar fashion. As an intelligent man who cares about doing his job well, he would be foolish to ignore any symptoms or pretend that they magically would go away. The sooner he acknowledges his symptoms and finds ways to manage them, the sooner he will be able to function at his maximum potential.

- Having combat-related psychological problems is not a sign of incompetence. In fact, it is often the sign of the opposite. Quite often it is the most competent, conscientious, and dedicated people who suffer from stress symptoms because they hold themselves to such high standards or because they give so much of themselves to their work and families.

- He is not alone. Many veterans develop combat trauma symptoms, and today there are many books and articles that *You might* describe the effects of war on mental health.* Furthermore, *want to have* even people who don't see combat or live in war zones can *some of these* suffer from clinical depression, anxiety disorders, and other *books or articles* problems. For example, according to a recent U.S. survey, *on hand. See* between 1990 and 2000 approximately one out of every *appendix B,* eight adults utilized antidepressant medication.[21] As of the *"Suggested* writing of this book, the number of persons who seek *Readings."* antianxiety and antidepressant medication continues to grow.

3. Address any fears your vet may have that seeking help means he could lose control over his life. For example, he may fear that he will be forced to comply with whatever is recommended by a mental-health professional; that he will have to attend months or even years of sessions; that he will have to be hospitalized in an inpatient psychiatric clinic or sent away to a rehabilitation center; or that he will be given psychiatric medications that turn him into a "vegetable" or "zombie."

a. Does your vet have any of the fears listed above? If so, which ones?

b. Do you think your vet would benefit from your sharing any of the following perspectives with him? If so, which ones?

- Seeking help isn't a lifetime commitment. You aren't asking him to commit to decades of counseling. You are asking him to take two hours out of his life for an initial consultation with a trained mental-health professional who may or may not recommend treatment. If treatment is recommended, many short-term treatments may be available. Suppose he's encouraged to attend twelve two-hour sessions. You could say, "You owe yourself twenty-four hours of help—that's one day out of your life. Is that too much to ask for all the suffering you've been through?"

- Unless he is suicidal or homicidal or out of control in some manner, he can't be forced to do anything against his will, much less be hospitalized or institutionalized without his consent.

- Your vet has choices. Often there are several different treatments available for a specific problem. He may be able to select the type of treatment he feels would be best suited to him. If he is not provided with a choice, he can inquire about options or seek a second opinion. Also, instead of seeing a mental-health professional, he could read self-help and other books on specific problems; attend relevant educational seminars or classes; or speak with a member of the clergy or a medical doctor (other than a psychiatrist) about his concerns.

- Should psychiatric medication be recommended, he can choose not to take it or may only need to take it for a short while. Many people use psychiatric medication on a temporary, not a life-long, basis to help them get through a particularly rough period and never use it again.

- If your vet does take the medication and suffers unpleasant side effects, he can talk to his doctor about alternatives. Furthermore, in some instances psychiatrists recommend relaxation techniques, energy therapies, therapeutic massage, acupuncture, improved nutrition, an exercise program, or other alternatives to psychiatric medications.

4. Address any fears your vet may have that therapy is a waste of time. If your vet believes that mental health treatment is useless, which, if any, of the following points of view and information might help persuade him otherwise?

- There is hope. Today there are many effective treatments available, especially for depression, anxiety disorders, and addictions. Some of these treatments are short-term and do not require in-depth analysis of personality. Many veterans have sought help and benefited.

- Self-control, discipline, and personal power are important values in the military and important values for anyone who wants to make a contribution to his family, job, and community. Treatment will not weaken but strengthen him. Therapy is not a cure-all, but it can teach him how to manage his emotions so they don't run his life. He can also learn more effective ways of dealing with people and with problem situations—all of which can boost his personal power.

- You could also say, "Haven't you suffered enough? Don't you deserve a little help?" or "How do you know it won't help until you've tried?"

5. Address any fears your vet has about his confidentiality being violated or any other fears about speaking freely to counselors being paid by his employer or by the military.

Unfortunately there are instances where confidentiality has been violated, with negative consequences for the vet. If your vet fears that his confidentiality may be violated, or if for any other reason he feels he can't speak freely to counselors being paid by his employer or provided by the military, he can seek help outside the system.

6. Consider which, if any, of the following additional suggestions might be helpful. Be sure to present these suggestions in your own words in a way that would best suit your vet.

- If he's entitled to mental health services as part of his military benefits or his current job, you could say, "You're always complaining about how much was asked of you in the military (or on this job). Well, here's a way the military (or your job) can give something to you," or "You paid for these services by putting your life on the line, so you might as well use them."

- If your vet refuses to seek help, ask him at what point he would decide he needed help. In his opinion (not your opinion or a doctor's opinion), what thoughts or behaviors on his part would indicate to him beyond a doubt that it was time to see a mental-health specialist? If he cannot answer this question for himself, ask him to answer this question in terms of yourself or someone else he loves: "What would you have to observe in me (or someone else) in order for you to decide that treatment was needed?"

- You can let your vet know that help is available by giving him the phone numbers of mental-health services available through the military, his job, and outside of his job. You can also give him pamphlets or educational materials about his condition and available services.

- You may fear, and justifiably so, that if you push too hard, your vet will become even more resistant to the idea of seeking help.

Perhaps you know better than to even mention the idea to him, knowing that the idea will be immediately rejected if it comes from you. If so, perhaps a respected coworker, family member, friend, war buddy, or member of the clergy may be more effective than you in convincing your vet that seeking help is an act of courage and honesty, not a sign of weakness.

Mental Health Emergencies

In some circumstances, you may not have the luxury of waiting for your vet to seek treatment. If he becomes so childlike, so violent, or so self-destructive or so disoriented that he cannot take care of himself or becomes a danger to himself or others, you may need to consider the possibility of urging him to seek help and, in extreme cases, of calling your local mental-health department or emergency services for assistance.

You may feel guilty about calling in rescue squads or literally driving your vet to a military, VA, or private hospital, or an alcohol- or drug-treatment center for help. However, if he's having so much trouble functioning, you are not hurting or betraying him. You may be saving his life by forcing him to seek help. If he can't think or act rationally, you need to treat him as a family member who needs help and take control of the situation.

Help for Partners

Perhaps you, or people important to you, share some of the same reservations about seeking professional help that hold back your veteran. Military wives or women whose fathers, siblings, or other relatives hold or held careers in the military or in other dangerous occupations, such as police work, firefighting, or rescue operations, may be especially hesitant to seek help. On a theoretical level, they may believe in the value of getting help; on an emotional level, however, they may feel ashamed of needing assistance.

Studies of military and police wives and girlfriends have found that they pride themselves on being self-reliant and supportive partners and on keeping their family together. Yet these women also report that, at times, they feel helpless, depressed, and alone. Many also suffer from stress-related medical conditions like headaches.[22] Practically no studies have been completed on the husbands and boyfriends of women veterans or on military couples. In my counseling experience, however, I have found the same patterns. There is no shame in having such reactions. Hundreds of research studies indicate such reactions are to be expected in situations of emotional or physical overload or in situations where one has little or no control over an important aspect of one's life.[23]

Although in our society stress symptoms, whether emotional like anxiety attacks or physical like shoulder pain, are increasingly seen as normal, often the partners of soldiers feel ashamed of experiencing them, and with good reason. Just as your mate was expected to be a hero or heroine, you may be expected to be a hero or heroine, too. For example, your partner was expected to persevere in the face of fear, fatigue, or other human limitations, and to put the mission and the needs of the group ahead of any personal needs and goals. On the front line, complaining about hardships or being concerned about personal desires may be viewed as dishonorable, if not disloyal.

Those same standards also may apply to you and other partners of combat veterans. You may be expected to fulfill your duties and support your partner, enduring all strains and sacrifices without complaint or any outward sign of distress. Living with the impossible expectation that you will be a hero or heroine all the time is a tremendous burden for both of you.

Even if you don't hold yourself to such standards, others might, and they may criticize you when you fail to live up to them. You need not discard these standards; however, in order to live up to them more fully, you may need some type of assistance. Needing help doesn't mean you are weak. If you were truly "weak," you would not be able to endure the stresses of living with a man or woman who is suffering. If you seek help, then you are behaving just like presidents who consult with cabinet members and dozens of aides; like generals who turn for guidance to experts in military strategy and technical operations; or like business executives who hire a consultant to help them meet their objectives. Like your veteran, you can use medication, coping skills, or counseling to help you grow stronger than you already are.

Summary

First and foremost, war recovery involves helping the vet come to understand and manage his traumatic reactions so that they no longer dominate his life. If needed, the veteran can then go on to examine and uncover the specific events in the war that he has been attempting to deny or that he has been unable to accept; feel some of the feelings associated with these traumatic events; and, ultimately, find constructive uses for his combat experiences.

Healing is not an absolute. It does not mean a total disappearance of symptoms, but rather a reduction in their frequency and intensity. Once the symptoms are under control, the veteran will be able to enjoy a more satisfying life. Most likely he will think about combat experiences many times, but they will no longer paralyze him or be the focus of his mental and emotional life. As he puts the war in perspective, he learns that he is not alone in his feelings. He will move from hopelessness and helplessness toward an attitude of gratitude that he is alive and can be useful to his family and society.

Healing is a lifelong process. Some time may pass before any gains are evident. During those initial months, therapy can create its own stresses on the veteran and his family. He may be retraumatized by what he remembers, by the intensity of his own emotions, or, if he is in a group setting, by the stories and emotions of other veterans.

This disruption affects not only the veteran but also his partner, who can expect to witness or to be impacted by some of the veteran's previously suppressed emotions. Furthermore, counseling for combat trauma does not necessarily solve all of the veteran's problems, his partner's problems, or all their relationship problems. Both the veteran and his partner need to take responsibility for their own lives and not fall prey to scapegoating one another. Couples counseling is often useful to help them develop effective communication skills and address problems left unresolved due to the veteran's combat trauma, such as parenting, division of labor in the home, and other such concerns for which nonveteran couples often seek help.

Partners who have nursed a vet first through his combat trauma, then through his war-recovery efforts, often complain of burnout. Once the vet is finally on the path to recovery, his partner may find herself carrying many months, if not years, of stored-up anger and resentment. She must then deal with the dilemma of what to do with this pile of grievances. While she may want to confront her vet directly, she may also want to enjoy the vet's improved emotional state and to keep the family peace.

Theoretically, the vet's progress in therapy can free his partner to focus on her own needs and goals. However, if the vet still adheres to traditional views of the woman's role or is unwilling to consistently assume various child-care or housekeeping functions, he may continue to pose an obstacle to her personal development. Even when the vet is supportive, his partner may experience difficulties grappling with the challenge of reestablishing or further developing her own identity and interests. In some instances, emotional and physical fatigue, as well as years of focusing on the veteran rather than herself, have depleted the woman's emotional, intellectual, and creative resources. Often a recuperation period is necessary before the woman can begin working on her own issues.

As a result of counseling, many couples have renewed their commitment to one another and can relate to each other on a deep and meaningful level. Not only in their relationship but also in their personal lives, they are able to make positive use of the frustrations, pain, and anger they experienced in the past.

Resources

Department of Veterans Affairs Medical Centers (VAMCs) and Veterans Outreach Centers (Vet Centers)

Every state has Veterans Administration medical centers (VAMCs) and Veterans Outreach Centers (Vet Centers). The VAMCs, formerly known as VA hospitals, offer both medical and psychiatric care. There are also specialized teams, called PTSD teams or, in some places, war-recovery teams, designed to assist veterans with combat stress on an outpatient basis. Some VAMCs offer specialized inpatient programs for veterans with combat trauma or addiction problems. Each VAMC has a Woman Veterans Coordinator, and some VAMCs have specialized services and programs for women, such as sexual-trauma recovery programs. The Vet Centers also have a sexual trauma program.

You can find the phone number of the VAMC nearest you by consulting the blue pages of your local telephone directory, your library, or your local hospital. To locate the Vet Center nearest you, either look for a listing in the local telephone directory or contact the VAMC nearest you. Sometimes Vet Centers are called outreach centers or readjustment counseling centers rather than Vet Centers. The following Web page provides contact and other information for VAMCs and Vet Centers nationwide: www.va.gov. (Toll-free phone numbers for the VA are listed in the section on page 414 titled "Help for Active-Duty Military and Their Families.")

If you want to find out about help for combat stress, sexual assault, or another military-related mental-health problem, call the VAMC nearest you. Ask the hospital operator for this information or ask to speak to an official in the outpatient mental health clinic or in the hospital's psychology, psychiatry, or social work service. Such persons can also provide you with information about alcohol- or drug-rehabilitation programs, war-recovery and sexual assault recovery programs, and other programs within the VA and in the community. Women veterans can ask to speak to the Woman Veterans Coordinator. Vet Centers can also provide information about VA programs and offer mental health services.

Perhaps you have a military-related problem for which the VA or Vet Center program does not have the appropriate specialist, or perhaps the nearest VA or Vet Center professional qualified to help you is located a considerable distance from your residence. If so, inquire if the VA will pay for the services of a non-VA professional who is qualified to assist you with your particular concern or who is located closer to your residence.

For information on compensation, housing, job training, educational benefits, and medical benefits, contact the VAMC, Vet Center, or a veterans service organization, such as the DAV (Disabled American Veterans). (See "Help for Veterans and Their Families" on pages 414–16.)

Information on the Center for Women Veterans, created to assist women veterans in accessing VA benefits and services, can be obtained at www.va.gov/womenvet.

See also militarywomen.org for the Military Woman's Homepage: Active Duty and Veteran Information; www1.va.gov/centerforminorityveterans for the Center for Minority Veterans; and www.dtic.mil/dacowits for the Defense Advisory Committee on Women in the Services.

Help for Addictions: Alcohol and Drug Abuse, Eating Disorders, Gambling, and Overspending

Names of treatment centers specific to a particular addiction or eating disorder can be obtained from the phonebook, hospitals, city or county mental health or social service agencies, your (or your partner's) employee and family support programs, a VAMC or Vet Center, a mental health or social service office in any of the various branches of the military (the Army, Navy, Marine Corps, Air Force, National Guard, Reserves, etc.), the National Council on Alcoholism and Drug Dependence (www.ncadd.org; 1-800-622-2255) or from twelve-step programs such as:

> Adult Children of Alcoholics; www.adultchildren.org; 310-534-1815
> Al-Anon and Ala-Teen; www.al-anon-alateen.org; 888-425-2666
> Alcoholics Anonymous; www.alcoholics-anonymous.org; 212-870-3400
> Debtors Anonymous; www.debtorsanonymous.org; 781-453-2743
> Gamblers Anonymous; www.gamblersanonymous.org; 213-386-8789
> Nar-Anon; alcoholism.about.com/od/naranonresources; 800-477-6291
> Narcotics Anonymous; www.na.org; 818-773-9999
> Overeaters Anonymous; www.overeatersanonymous.org; 505-891-2664

Resources for professionals include:

Addiction Technology Transfer Center; www.nattc.org/links.html;
    816-235-6888
Association for Addiction Professionals; www.naadac.org; 800-548-0497
Co-Occurring Center for Excellence; www.coce.samhsa.gov;
    301-951-3369
Eating Disorder Referral and Information Center; www.EDReferral
    .com (no phone)

Information about these and other twelve-step programs can also be obtained from your telephone directory or local library or from the National Help Line (1-800-662-HELP). Some branches of the military and some VAMCs offer specialized outpatient programs or inpatient units that treat substance abuse. Some Vet Centers conduct substance-abuse recovery groups or permit AA, NA, or other twelve-step programs to meet at their facilities.

Help for Disabilities

Information on disability benefits and services can be obtained from physicians, medical insurance representatives, personnel or benefits officers; your local, county, and state social service and disability offices; disability or injury lawyers; the Department of Veterans Affairs (see "Help for Active-Duty Military and Their Families" on page 414 for toll-free numbers) or a Vet Center, or any of the following organizations:

American Pain Foundation; www.painfoundation.org; 888-615-7246
American Pain Society; www.ampainsoc.org; 847-375-4715
Center for Research on Women with Disabilities (CROWD); www
    .bcm.edu/crowd; 800-442-7693
Consortium for Citizens with Disabilities; www.c-c-d.org; 202-783-
    2229
Military Severely Injured Center; www.MilitaryHomefront.dod.mil
    /troops/injuredsupport; 877-774-1361
National Amputation Foundation; www.nationalamputation.org; 516-
    887-3600
National Brain Injury Association; www.biausa.org; 800-444-6443
National Federation of the Blind; www.nfb.org; 410-659-9314
National Foundation for the Treatment of Pain; www.paincare.org;
    713-862-9332
National Organization on Disability; www.nod.org; 202-293-5960

You can also consult your local telephone directory or library for contact information on these and similar organizations, such as the National Head Injury Foundation or the National Burn Victim Foundation. There are also numerous books on disability and the family. Ask your local librarian for assistance.

Disabled American Veterans (www.dav.org; 877-426-2838) had a network of service officers to help with claims before the government did and continues to offer claims services to veterans. Over thirty other veterans service organizations are chartered by Congress and/or recognized by the VA for claim representation. The following Web page provides a listing and contact information for chartered veterans service organizations: www.va.gov/vso. (See also "Help for Veterans and Their Families" on pages 414–16.)

Help for Partner Abuse

In the Military

Family Advocacy officers or representatives exist on every Army, Navy, Air Force, Marine Corps, and Coast Guard installation. They can usually be contacted directly or through a family service or family support center. Abused partners or wives may also contact the clergy service, the medical department, the staff judge advocate, any mental health or medical professional, the nearest Women's Advocacy office (if available), the abuser's commanding officer, or anyone in his or her chain of command.

Help can also be obtained from the Military Family Resource Center (www.MilitaryHomefront.dod.mil; 703-696-9053) as well as from any of the civilian sources listed in the following section, such as courts, social service agencies, churches, libraries, hospitals, and battered women's shelters. Even partners living on bases under exclusive federal jurisdiction may seek help from civilian resources.

Civilian Partners

You can get help from the courts, from the police, and through local organizations such as battered women's shelters, city or county social-service agencies, churches, or community hotlines. Local universities, colleges, and junior colleges also have hotlines and women's associations that may be of assistance. Check your Yellow Pages in the telephone book or call your local police station, library, or hospital for direct assistance or for the location of helping agencies and groups. Vet Centers (sometimes called outreach or readjustment counseling centers) or the psychology service, social work service, psychiatry service, or mental health clinic of your nearest Veterans Administration medical center may also have listings for local abused persons programs and agencies.

The National Domestic Violence Hotline (www.ndvh.org; 800-799-7233) provides twenty-four-hour multilingual assistance to victims of family violence. The National Center for Victims of Crime (www.ncvc.org; 800-FYI-CALL) provides assistance to victims of domestic violence (and other violent crimes). The Web site Stop Abuse for All (www.safe4all.org) has a member-contributed resource list for the abused.

Help for Child Abuse

Due to child-abuse reporting laws, most mental health and other health care professionals—both within the military and in the community—have listings of resources for both abusing parents and abused children. State or county social service offices, local police stations, courthouses, hospitals, as well as private physicians and mental health professionals will also have listings for local helping agencies for both abusive parents and abused children.

Any of the resources listed in "Help for Partner Abuse" (above) can provide assistance or referral for child abuse. Help is also available through:

Child Welfare Information Gateway; www.childwelfare.gov;
    800-394-3366
National Child Abuse Hotline; www.childhelpusa.org; 800-422-4453

Help for Sexual Assault

Women subjected to military sexual assault can seek help at the nearest VAMC or Vet Center as described above or from community sources listed in the following section.

Community Help for Combat Trauma, Sexual Assault, and Other Concerns

You may choose to seek help outside of the military or outside of the Veterans Administration's medical centers or Vet Centers. If so, remember that you have the right to shop around for a therapist or a treatment program and to ask questions. To begin the selection process, compile a list of names. Get recommendations from friends, doctors, and people who report having had positive therapeutic experiences; from hospitals with specialized treatment programs for survivors of trauma (especially for the trauma of concern to you and your family); the police; university health or counseling centers (if you are a student); and local mental health and social services agencies, which are usually run by either the city or county.

VAMCs, Vet Centers, local addiction and eating-disorder treatment programs, local battered women's and sexual assault centers and hotlines, local women's health centers, and other local women's organizations usually have referral lists of trauma specialists. Either the national headquarters or the state or local chapters of the following organizations may also have lists of qualified professionals:

> American Association for Marriage and Family Therapy; www.aamft .org; 703-838-9808
> American Association of Pastoral Counselors; www.aapc.org; 703-385-6967
> American Dance Therapy Association; www.adta.org; 410-997-4040
> American Music Therapy Association; www.musictherapy.org; 301-589-3300
> American Nurses Association; www.nursingworld.org; 301-628-5000
> American Psychiatric Association; www.psych.org; 703-907-7300
> American Psychological Association; www.apa.org; 800-374-2721
> Anxiety Disorders Association of America; www.adaa.org; 240-485-1001
> Association for the Advancement of Behavior Therapy; www.aabt.org; 212-647-1890
> Association for Play Therapy; www.a4pt.org; 559-252-2278
> International Society for Traumatic Stress Studies; www.istss.org; 847-480-9028
> National Association for Poetry Therapy; www.poetrytherapy.org; 866-844-6278
> National Association of Social Workers; www.socialworkers.org; 202-408-8600
> National Board of Certified Counselors; www.nbcc.org; 336-547-0607
> National Mental Health Association; www.nmha.org; 800-969-6642
> National Organization for Women (NOW); www.now.org; 202-628-8669

Sexual assault survivors can also call the Rape, Abuse and Incest National Network (www.rainn.org) at 800-656-HOPE.

Your telephone directory, local library, or social service agency can provide you with the phone numbers of any local chapters of the organizations listed above. If you contact any of these organizations, be sure to inquire if the therapist and programs are identified by specialty, such as combat trauma, sexual trauma, or depression. Contact only those therapists whose specialty area(s) match your needs.

The following organizations may also be helpful in locating a therapist and providing information:

Anxiety Disorders Association of America; www.adaa.org;
 240-485-1001
Association of Traumatic Stress Specialists; www.atss.info; 800-991-2877
Depression and Bipolar-Support Alliance; www.dbsalliance.org
Give an Hour; www.giveanhour.org; (no phone)
International Foundation for Research and Education on Depression;
 www.depression.org; 410-268-0044
International Society for the Study of Dissociation; www.issd.org;
 703-610-9037
National Anxiety Foundation; www.lexington-on-line.com/naf.html;
 (no phone)
National Center for Post-Traumatic Stress Disorder; www.ncptsd.org;
 802-296-6300
National Institutes of Mental Health; www.nimh.hin.gov/publica
 /depression.crm; 800 826-3632
PTSD Alliance; www.PTSDAlliance.com
The Sidran Institute and Press; www.sidran.org; 410-825-8888
Survivors Art Foundation; www.survivorsartfoundation.org; (no phone)

Help for Sexual Difficulties

Few states issue a sex therapy license per se, so most who specialize in this field are licensed in something else, commonly psychology or social work, then seek certification from professional organizations. Long-distance sex therapy by phone or online is not recommended. There are no federal or state regulations on distance therapy of any type; no studies have been completed on its effectiveness; and there is no accountability for clients or therapists.

Organizations and Web sites that may be of some help include the American Association of Sexuality Educators, Counselors, and Therapists (AASECT) (www.aasect.org); the Sexual Health Network (www.SexualHealth .com), which addresses variety of sexual issues, including comprehensive information on sexuality and disability; "1001 Ways to Be Romantic" (www .1001waystoberomantic.com), which gives romance tips from the author of *1001 Ways to Be Romantic* and *Bring Food, Arrive Naked;* AfraidtoAsk.com, for advice on sexually transmitted diseases (www.afraidtoask.com/std.html); and www.healthysex.com, the Web site for author and sex therapist Wendy Maltz, MSW.

Help for Active-Duty Military and Their Families

Air Force: www.af.mil; www.tricare.osd.mil; USAF Combat Support
    and Family Service, deploymentlink.osd.mil/deploy/family/family_
    support.shtml
Air National Guard: www.ang.af.mil
Army: Army Family Team Building (www.myarmylifetoo.com)
Coast Guard: www.uscg.mil
Marines: www.usmc.mil, then click on *Family*; Marine Corps
    Community Service (www.usmc-mccs.org)
National Guard: www.arng.army.mil
Navy: Fleet and Family Support Division (www.lifelines.navy.mil)

Two Web sites listing help for both veterans and active-duty military
(including the National Guard and the Reserves) are www.MilitaryMental-
Health.org and www.veteransandfamilies.org.

Toll-free numbers for contacting the VA:

Education (GI Bill): 1-888-442-4551
Health Care Benefits: 1-877-222-8387
Income Verification and Means Testing: 1-800-929-8387
Life Insurance: 1-800-669-8477
Mammography Helpline: 1-888-492-7844
Special Issues-Gulf War/Agent Orange/Project Shad/Mustard Agents
    and Lewisite/Ionizing Radiation: 1-800-749-8387
Status of Headstones and Markers: 1-800-697-6947
Telecommunications Device for the Deaf (TDD): 1-800-829-4833
VA Benefits: 1-800-827-1000

Help for Veterans and Their Families

Numerous veterans service organizations offer assistance to veterans and
their families. Among them are the following:

African-American Post Traumatic Stress Disorder Association;
    www.aaptsdassn.com; 866-322-0766
Air Force Sergeants Association; www.afsahq.org; 800-638-0594
American Ex-Prisoners of War Service Foundation;
    www.powfoundation.org; 914-528-7147
American GI Forum of the United States; www.agif.us; 303-458-1700
American Legion; www.legion.org; 202-861-2700
American Veterans of World War II, Korea, and Vietnam (AMVETS);
    www.amvets.org; 877-726-8387

American War Mothers; www.americanwarmoms.org; 202-362-0090

Army and Navy Union, USA; www.armynavy.net; (no phone)

Blinded Veterans Association; www.bva.org; 800-669-7079

Blue Star Mothers of America; www.bluestarmothers.org; (no phone)

Catholic War Veterans, USA; cwv.org; 703-549-3622

Jewish War Veterans of the USA; www.jwv.org; 202-265-6280

Italian American War Veterans of the USA; www.itamvets.org;
     800-462-3292

Marine Corps League; www.mcleague.com; 800-625-1775

Military Order of the Purple Heart of the USA; www.purpleheart.org;
     (no phone)

National Association for Black Veterans; www.nabvets.com;
     877.622.8387

National Association of County Veterans Service Officers; www.nacvso
     .org; (no phone)

Navy Club of the United States of America; www.navyclubusa.org;
     800-628-7265

Paralyzed Veterans of America; www.pva.org; 800-424-8200

Retired Enlisted Association; www.trea.org; 800-338-9337

United Spinal Association; www.unitedspinal.org; 718-803-3782

Veterans Assistance Foundation; www.veteransassistance.org;
     877-823-9433

Veterans of Foreign Wars; www.vfw.org; 800-839-1899

Vietnam Veterans of America; www.vva.org; 800-882-1316

Women Air Force Service Pilots of World War II; www.wasp-wwii.org;
     (no phone)

Women's Army Corps Veterans Association; www.armywomen.org;
     (no phone)

Swords for Plowshares: Veterans Rights Organization; www.swords-to-
     plowshares.org; 415-252-4788

Veterans service organizations vary greatly in the types of services offered. However, in general, the services range from claims assistance and information and referrals for health, education, tutoring, jobs, and legal assistance, to help in obtaining medical care or discharge review.

A directory of veterans service organizations can be found at www .va.gov/vso. For a current listing of the address and phone number of these organizations, you can also consult your local telephone directory. If the organization you are interested in does not have a chapter in your area or is not listed in your local telephone directory, contact information for the nearest office of the organization can possibly be obtained from another local veterans organization or from the VAMC or Vet Center nearest you.

Your local library should have a listing of veterans organizations, as well as the address and phone number of the national headquarters of various veterans organizations.

The U.S. Office of Personnel Management (Federal Job Information Center National Office, Washington, D.C.) offers federal job information to vets, including information on veterans preference in appointments, credit for military service, jobs for preference eligibles only, special appointing authorities for disabled veterans, as well as other services.

In some areas the American Red Cross offers limited financial (and other) services to veterans. Check with the local office of the American Red Cross for further information.

Local universities and colleges and local and state or country employment commissions, personnel departments, or labor departments sometimes have special offers for veterans. Check in a local directory or call the nearest Vet Center for more information.

APPENDIX B

Suggested Readings

Within each category below is a section called "Technical but Still Helpful," which contains books for professionals and well-read nonprofessionals.

Addictions: Alcohol, Drug and Food Abuse, Gambling and
    Overspending
Combat Trauma and Trauma in General
Children and Parenting
Depression
Family Violence
Physical Injury and Pain
Relationships
Sex
Sexual Trauma
Trauma Recovery

Addictions: Alcohol, Drug, and Food Abuse, Gambling and Overspending

Books and other materials on various forms of addiction are available through the twelve-step programs listed in appendix A under "Help for Addictions" and through Hazelden Educational Materials (www.hazelden.org).

Federman, Edward J., and Charles E. Drebing. *Don't Leave It to Chance: A Guide for Families of Problem Gamblers.* Oakland, Calif.: New Harbinger Publications, 2000.

Greenfield, David N. *Virtual Addiction.* Oakland, Calif.: New Harbinger Publications, 1999.

Potter-Efron, Ronald T. *Angry All the Time.* Oakland, Calif.: New Harbinger Publications, 2005.

Sbraga, Tamara Penix, and William T. O'Donohue. *The Sex Addiction Workbook: Proven Strategies to Help You Regain Control of Your Life.* Oakland, Calif.: New Harbinger Publications, 2004.

Technical but Still Helpful

Abbot, Ann A., ed. *Alcohol, Tobacco, and Other Drugs: Challenging Myths, Assessing Theories, Individualizing Interventions.* Washington, D.C.: National Association of Social Workers, 2000.

Connors, Gerard J., Dennis M. Donovan, and Carlo C. DiClemente. *Substance Abuse Treatment and the Stages of Change: Selecting and Planning Interventions.* New York: Guilford Press, 2004.

DiClemente, Carlo C. *Addiction and Change: How Addictions Develop and Addicted People Recover.* New York: Guilford Press, 2003.

Najavits, Lisa. *Seeking Safety: A Treatment Manual for PTSD and Substance Abuse.* New York: Guilford Publications, 2005.

Ouimette, Paige, and Pamela J. Brown, eds. *Trauma and Substance Abuse: Causes, Consequences, and Treatment of Comorbid Disorders.* Washington, D.C.: American Psychological Association, 2003.

Petry, Nancy. *Pathological Gambling: Etiology, Comorbidity, and Treatment.* Washington, D.C.: American Psychological Association, 2005.

Striegel-Moor, Ruth, and Linda Smolak, eds. *Eating Disorders: Innovative Directions in Research and Practice.* Washington, D.C.: American Psychological Association, 2001.

Thombs, Dennis L., Ph.D. *Introduction to Addictive Behaviors.* 3rd ed. New York: Guilford Press, 2006.

Combat Trauma and Trauma in General

In addition to the sources listed here, see "Community Help for Combat Trauma, Sexual Assault, and Other Concerns" in appendix A for Web sites.

Armstrong, Keith, and Suzanne Best. *Courage after Fire: A Readjustment Guide for Military Personnel Returning from Iraq and Afghanistan and Their Families.* Berkeley, Calif.: Ulysses Press, 2005.

Broyles, William. *Brothers in Arms.* New York: Knopf, 1986.

Cockburn, Alexander, and Jeffrey St. Clair. *Imperial Crusades: Iraq, Afghanistan and Yugoslavia.* New York: Verso, 2004.

Danelo, David J., and Steven Pressfield. *Blood Stripes: The Grunt's View of the War in Iraq.* Mechanicsburg, Pa.: Stackpole Books, 2006.

Donelly, Michael, and Denise Donelly. *Falcon's Cry: A Desert Storm Memoir.* Westport, Conn.: Praeger, 1998.

Durrant, Michael. *In the Company of Heroes.* Toronto: Putnam, 2003.

Fanning, Patrick, and Matthew McKay. *Being a Man.* Oakland, Calif.: New Harbinger Publications, 1993.

Foster, Douglas. *Braving the Fear.* Frederick, Md.: PublishAmerica, 2006.

Grossman, D. *On Killing: The Psychological Cost of Learning to Kill in War and Society.* New York: Little Brown, 1995.

Hansel, Sarah, Ann Steidle, Grace Zaczek, and Ron Zaczek. *Soldier's Heart: Survivors' Views of Combat Trauma.* Baltimore: Sidran Press, 1995.

Ignatieff, Michael. *Virtual War: Kosovo and Beyond.* New York: Picador USA, 2001.

Jones, Lynne. *Then They Started Shooting: Growing Up in Wartime.* Cambridge: Harvard University Press, 2005.

Judah, Tim. *Kosovo: A War and Revenge.* New Haven: Yale University Press, 2002.

Latty, Yvonne, and Max Cleland. *In Conflict: Iraq War Veterans Speak Out on Duty, Loss, and the Fight to Stay Alive.* Sausalito, Calif.: PoliPointPress, 2006.

Margolis, Eric. *War at the Top of the World: The Struggle for Afghanistan, Kashmir and Tibet.* Oxford: Routledge, 2002.

McAllister, Matthew. *Beyond the Mountains of the Damned: The War Inside Kosovo.* Ottawa: Esprit de Corps Books, 2002.

Nivat, Anne. *The Wake of War: Encounters in Iraq and Afghanistan.* Boston: Beacon Press, 2005.

Scruggs, Jan, and Joel Swerdlow. *To Heal a Nation.* New York: Harper and Row, 1985.

Scurfield, Raymond. *A Vietnam Trilogy: Veterans and Post Traumatic Stress: 1968, 1989, 2000.* New York: Algora Publishing, 2004.

Shay, Jonathan. *Achilles in Vietnam.* New York: Atheneum Press, 1994.

———. *Odysseus in America: Combat Trauma and the Trials of Homecoming.* New York: Scribner's, 2002.

Shepard, Ben. *A War of Nerves: Soldiers and Psychiatrists in the 20th Century.* Cambridge: Harvard University Press, 2001.

Stewart, Roy. *Prince of the Marshes and Other Occupational Hazards of a Year in Iraq.* New York: Harcourt Press, 2006.

Swofford, Anthony. *Jarhead: A Marine's Chronicle of the Gulf War and Other Battles.* New York: Scribner's, 2003.

Taylor, Scott. *Diary of an Uncivil War: The Violent Aftermath of the Kosovo Conflict and Beyond.* New York: New York University Press, 2004.

Tick, Edward. *War and the Soul: Healing Our Nation's Veterans from Posttraumatic Stress Disorder.* Wheaton, Ill.: Quest Books, 2005.

Williams, Kayla. *Love My Rifle More than You*. New York: W.W. Norton, 2005.

Technical but Still Helpful

Audiocassettes taped live during the sessions of annual meetings of the International Society for Traumatic Stress (www.istss.org) can be ordered from Professional Programs, Inc., P.O. Box 221466, Santa Clarita, CA 93122-1466, or by phone (661-255-7444).

Beckham, J. C., B. L. Lytle, and M. E. Feldman. "Caregiver Burden in Partners of Vietnam Veterans with Posttraumatic Stress Disorder." *Journal of Consulting and Clinical Psychology* 64 (1996): 1068-72.

Brewin, C., B. Andrews, and J. Valetine. "Metal Analysis of Risk Factors for Posttraumatic Stress Disorder in Trauma-Exposed Adults." *Journal of Consulting and Clinical Psychology* 68 (2000): 748-66.

Figley, Charles. *Trauma and Its Wake*. Vol. 1: *The Study and Treatment of Post-Traumatic Stress Disorder*. New York: Brunner/Mazel, 1985–86.

———. Vol. 2: *Traumatic Stress Theory, Research, and Intervention*. New York: Brunner/Mazel, 1986.

Herman, Judith. *Trauma and Recovery*. New York: Basic Books, 1992.

Hotope, M., A. S. David, L. Hull, V. Nikalou, C. Unwin, and S. C. Wessely. "Gulf War Illness—Better, Worse, or Just the Same? A Cohort Study." *British Medical Journal* 327 (2003): 1370-72.

Kelley, William E., ed. *Post-Traumatic Stress Disorder and the War Veteran Patient*. New York: Brunner/Mazel, 1985.

Peterson, Christopher, and Martin E. Seligman, eds. *Character Strength and Virtues: A Handbook and Classification*. Washington, D.C.: American Psychological Association, 2004.

Rosenheck R. A., H. Bucknell, A. S. Blank, F. Farley, A. L. Fontana, M. J. Friedman, et al. *War Zone Stress among Returning Persian Gulf Troops: A Preliminary Report*. West Haven, Conn.: New England Program Evaluation Center, 1991.

———., and A. Fontana. *The Long Journey Home: Treatment of PTSD in the Department of Veterans Affairs: Fiscal Year 2001 Service Delivery and Performance*. West Haven, Conn.: Northeast Program Evaluation Center, 2002.

Sonnenberg, S., A. Blank, and J. Talbott, eds. *The Trauma of War: Stress and Recovery in Vietnam Veterans*. Washington, D.C.: American Psychiatric Press, 2005.

van der Kolk, B. A., A. McFarlane, and L. Weisaeth. *Traumatic Stress: The Effects of Overwhelming Experience on Mind, Body, and Society*. New York: Guilford Press, 1996.

Children and Parenting (See also reading list for Family Violence.)

Magination Press: Self-Help Books for Kids and the Adults in Their Lives, sponsored by the American Psychological Association, offers books on helping children understand their emotions, cope with separation from a parent, and other issues.

Books, CDs, and other resources for parents, teachers, and youth workers on parenting and helping children cope with a wide range of behavioral problems and growth issues (such as separation, peer pressure, vocational planning, money management) are available from Resources for Youth Work (www.independentlivingresrouces.com or www.ilrinc.com), at 800-821-0001.

Barnard, Martha Underwood. *Helping Your Depressed Child: A Step-by-Step Guide for Parents.* Oakland, Calif.: New Harbinger Publications, 2003.

Brown, Stephanie, and Virginia M. Lewis, with Andrew Liotta. *The Family Recovery Guide: A Map for Healthy Growth.* Oakland, Calif.: New Harbinger Publications, 2000.

Faber, Adele, and Elaine Mazlish. *Siblings without Rivalry: How to Help Your Children Live Together So You Can Live Too.* New York: Quill, 2002.

————. *What Every Parent and Teacher Needs to Know: How to Talk So Kids Can Learn at Home and in School.* New York: Rawson Associates, 1995.

Fanning, Patrick, and Matthew McKay, eds. *Family Guide to Emotional Wellness.* Oakland, Calif.: New Harbinger Publications, 2000.

Gottman, John, and Joan De Claire. *The Heart of Parenting: Raising an Emotionally Intelligent Child.* New York: Simon and Schuster, 1997.

McDermott, Diane, and C. R. Snyder. *The Great Big Book of Hope: Help Your Children Achieve Their Dreams.* Oakland, Calif.: New Harbinger Publications, 2000.

Nemeth, D., K. Ray, and M. Schexnayder. *Helping Your Angry Child: A Workbook for You and Your Family.* Oakland, Calif.: New Harbinger Publications, 2003.

Nicholson, Joanne, Alexis D. Henry, Jonathan C. Clayfield, and Susan M. Phillips. *Parenting Well When You're Depressed: A Complete Resource for Maintaining a Healthy Family.* Oakland, Calif.: New Harbinger Publications, 2001.

Polce-Lynch, Mary. *Boy Talk: How You Can Help Your Son Express His Emotions.* Oakland, Calif.: New Harbinger Publications, 2002.

Rapee, R., S. Spence, V. Cobham, and A. Wingnall. *Helping Your Anxious Child: A Step-by-Step Guide for Parents.* Oakland, Calif.: New Harbinger Publications, 2000.

Rogers, Peter D., and Lea Goldstein. *Drugs and Your Kid: How To Tell if Your*

Child Has a Drug/Alcohol Problem and What to Do about It. Oakland, Calif.: New Harbinger Publications, 2002.

Sherman, Michelle D., and De Anne Sherman. *Finding My Way: A Teen's Guide to Living with a Parent Who Has Experienced Trauma.* Edina, Minn.: Seed of Hope Books, Beavers Pond Press, 2005. (This can only be ordered from www.seedsofhopebooks.com.)

Technical but Still Helpful

Christophersen, E., and S. Mortweet. *Treatments that Work with Children: Empirically Supported Strategies for Managing Childhood Problems.* Washington, D.C.: American Psychological Association, 2001.

Fraser, Mark W., ed. *Risk and Resilience in Childhood: An Ecological Perspective.* 2nd ed. Washington, D.C.: National Association of Social Workers, 2004.

Hibbs, Euthtymia D., and Peter S. Jensen, eds. *Psychosocial Treatments for Child and Adolescent Disorders: Empirically Based Strategies for Clinical Practice.* 2nd ed. Washington, D.C.: American Psychological Association, 2005.

Pennel, Joan, and Gary R. Anderson, eds. *Widening the Circle: The Practice and Evaluation of Family Group Conferencing with Children, Youths, and Their Families.* Washington, D.C.: National Association of Social Workers, 2005.

Depression

In addition to the sources listed here, see "Community Help for Combat Trauma, Sexual Assault, and Other Concerns" in appendix A for Web sites.

Bieling, Peter J., and Martin M. Antony. *Ending the Depression Cycle: A Step-by-Step Guide for Preventing Relapse.* Oakland, Calif.: New Harbinger Publications, 2003.

Burns, David D. *Feeling Good: The New Mood Therapy.* New York: Signet Books, New American Collection, 1980.

Copeland, Mary Ellen. *The Depression Workbook.* Oakland, Calif.: New Harbinger Publications, 1992.

DePaulo, J. R., and L. Horvitz. *Understanding Depression: What We Know and What You Can Do about It.* New York: John Wiley and Sons, 2002.

Dockett, Lauren. *The Deepest Blue.* Oakland, Calif.: New Harbinger Publications, 2001.

Hardin, Kimeron, and Marny Hall. *Queer Blues: The Lesbian and Gay Guide to Overcoming Depression.* Oakland, Calif.: New Harbinger Publications, 2001.

Heckler, Richard. *Waking Up Alive: The Descent, the Suicide Attempt, and the Return to Life.* New York: Grosset Books, 1994.

Honos-Webb, Lara. *Listening to Depression: How Understanding Your Pain Can Heal Your Life.* Oakland, Calif.: New Harbinger Publications, 2006.

Martell, Christopher R., and Michael E. Addis. *Overcoming Depression One Step at a Time: The New Behavioral Activation Approach to Getting Your Life Back.* Oakland, Calif.: New Harbinger Publications, 2004.

Paterson, R. *Your Depression Map: Finding the Sources of Your Depression and Chart Your Own Recovery.* Oakland, Calif.: New Harbinger Publications, 2002.

Technical but Still Helpful

Bongar, Bruce. *The Suicidal Patient: Clinical and Legal Standards of Care.* 2nd ed. Washington, D.C.: American Psychological Association, 2002.

Goldson, David B. *Measuring Suicidal Behavior and Risk in Children and Adolescents.* Washington, D.C.: American Psychological Association, 2003.

Maximin, Anita, and Lori Stevic-Rust. *Treating Depression in the Medically Ill: A Clinician's Guide.* Oakland, Calif.: New Harbinger Publications, 2000.

Mazure, Carolyn, and Gwendolyn P. Keita. *Understanding Depression in Women: Applying Empirical Practice.* Washington, D.C.: American Psychological Association, 2006.

Rudd, M. David, Thomas Joiner, and M. Hasan Rajab. *Treating Suicidal Behavior: An Effective, Time-Limited Approach.* New York: Guilford Press, 2001.

Shneidman, Edwin. *Comprehending Suicide Landmarks in 20th Century Suicidology.* Washington, D.C.: American Psychological Association, 2001.

Weissman, Myrna M., John C. Markowitz, and Gerald L. Klerman. *Comprehensive Guide to Interpersonal Psychotherapy.* New York: Basic Books, 2000.

Yapko, Michael D. *Hand-Me-Down Blues: How to Stop Depression from Spreading in Families.* New York: Golden Books, 1999.

Family Violence

Berry, Dawn Bradley. *The Domestic Violence Sourcebook.* 3rd ed. Lincolnwood, Ill.: Lowell House, 2000.

Cavacuiti, Susan. *Someone Hurt Me.* Bloomington, Ill.: Enhancement Books, 2001.

Copeland, Mary Ellen, and Maxine Harris. *Healing the Trauma of Abuse: A Woman's Workbook.* Oakland, Calif.: New Harbinger Publications, 2000.

Holmes, Margaret. *A Terrible Thing Happened.* Washington, D.C.: Magination Press, 2001.

Martin, Del. *Battered Wives*. New York: Pocket Books, 1976.

Walker, Lenore. *The Battered Woman*. New York: Harper and Row, 1979.

Technical but Still Helpful

Barnett, Ola W. *It Could Happen to Anyone: Why Battered Women Stay*. Thousand Oaks, Calif.: Sage Publications, 1993.

Borland, Marie, ed. *Violence in the Family*. Atlantic Highlands: Manchester University Press, 1976.

Byrne, C.A., and D. S. Riggs. "The Cycle of Trauma: Relationship Aggression in Male Vietnam Veterans with Symptoms of Posttraumatic Stress Disorder." *Violence and Victims* 11 (1996): 213-25.

Cavell, Timothy A. *Working with Parents of Aggressive Children: A Practitioner's Guide*. Washington, D.C.: American Psychological Association, 2003.

Dutton, D. G. *The Batterer: A Psychological Profile*. New York: Basic Books, 1995.

Dutton, Donald. *The Abusive Personality: Violence and Control in Intimate Relationships*. New York: Guilford Publications, 1998.

Fontes, Lissa. *Child Abuse and Culture: Working with Diverse Families*. New York: Guilford Publications, 2005.

Gelles, R. *The Violent Home*. London: Sage Publications, 1972.

Madanes, Cloe. *Sex, Love, and Violence: Strategies for Transformation*. New York: W. W. Norton, 1990.

Murphy, Christopher M., and Christopher I. Eckhardt. *Treating the Abusive Partner: An Individualized Cognitive-Behavioral Approach*. New York: Guilford Publications, 2005.

Rathus, Jill, and Eva Feindler. *Assessment of Partner Violence: A Handbook for Researchers and Practitioners*. Washington, D.C.: American Psychological Association, 2004.

Silva, Raul, ed. *Posttraumatic Stress Disorders in Children and Adolescents: A Handbook*. New York: W. W. Norton, 2004.

Walker, Lenore E. A. *Abused Women and Survivor Therapy: A Practical Guide for the Psychotherapist*. Washington, D.C.: American Psychological Association, 1994.

Physical Injury and Pain

Johnson, Jim, and Scott D. Boden. *The Multifidus Back Pain Solution: Simple Exercises that Target the Muscles that Count*. Oakland, Calif.: New Harbinger Publications, 2002.

Lewandowski, Michael. *The Chronic Pain Care Workbook: A Self-Treatment Approach to Pain Relief Using the Behavioral Assessment of Pain Questionnaire*. Oakland, Calif.: New Harbinger Publications, 2006.

Mason, D. *The Mild Traumatic Brain Injury Workbook*. Oakland, Calif.: New Harbinger Publications, 2004.

Roth, George. *The Matrix Repatterning Program for Pain Relief*. Oakland, Calif.: New Harbinger Publications, 2005.

Technical but Still Helpful

Eimer, Bruce N., and Arthur Freeman. *Pain Management Psychotherapy: A Practical Guide*. New York: John Wiley and Sons, 1998.

Miller, Laurence. *Shocks to the System: Psychotherapy of Traumatic Disability Syndromes*. New York: W. W. Norton, 1998.

Relationships

See also Patience Press (www.patiencepress.com) for copies of "Post-Traumatic Gazette" and www.matsakis.com for articles on trauma, guilt, depression, and related issues.

Black, Jan, and Greg Enns. *Better Boundaries: Owning and Treasuring Your Life*. Oakland, Calif.: New Harbinger Publications, 1998.

Brill, Stephanie. *The Queer Parent's Primer: A Lesbian and Gay Families Guide to Navigating the Straight World*. Oakland, Calif.: New Harbinger Publications, 2001.

Byron, Katie, with Stephen Mitchell. *Loving Is What Matters*. New York: Three Rivers Press, 2002.

Catherall, Don R . *Back from the Brink: A Family Guide to Overcoming Traumatic Stress*. New York: Brunner/Mazel, 1991.

Childre, Doc, and Deborah Rozman. *The Anger Workbook for Women: How to Keep Your Anger from Undermining Your Self-Esteem, Your Emotional Balance, and Your Relationships*. Oakland, Calif.: New Harbinger Publications, 2004.

Fruzzetti, Alan. *The High-Conflict Couple: A Dialectical Behavioral Therapy Guide to Finding Peace, Intimacy and Validation*. Oakland, Calif.: New Harbinger Publications, 2006.

Gottman, John M., and Joan De Claire. *The Relationship Cure*. New York: Crown Publishers, 2001.

———, and Nan Silver. *The Seven Principles for Making Marriage Work*. New York: Three Rivers Press, 1999.

———, and Julie Schwartz. *Ten Lessons to Transform Your Marriage*. New York: Crown, 2006.

Hanson, P. *Survivors and Partners: Healing the Relationships of the Sexual Abuse Survivor*. Longmont, Colo.: Heron Hill Publishing, 1991.

Henderson, Kristin. *While They're at War: The True Story of American Families on the Homefront*. New York: Houghton Mifflin, 2006.

Mason, Patience. *Recovering from the War: A Guide for All Veterans, Family Members, Friends and Therapists.* High Springs, Fla.: Patience Press, 1990 (formerly *Recovering from the War: A Woman's Guide to Helping Your Vietnam Vet, Your Family and Yourself* [New York: Viking Penguin, 1990]).

Matsakis, Aphrodite. *Trust After Trauma: A Guide to Relationships for Trauma Survivors and Those Who Love Them.* Oakland, Calif.: New Harbinger Publications, 1996.

————. *Vietnam Wives: Facing the Challenges of Veterans Suffering from Post Traumatic Stress Disorder.* 2nd ed. Baltimore: Sidran Institute Press, 1996.

McKay, Matthew, and Kim Paleg. *When Anger Hurts Your Relationship: Ten Simple Solutions for Couples Who Fight.* Oakland, Calif.: New Harbinger Publications, 2001.

Wall L., Cynthia. *The Courage to Trust: A Guide to Building Deep and Lasting Relationships.* Oakland, Calif.: New Harbinger Publications, 2005.

Technical but Still Helpful

Catherall, Don, ed. *Handbook of Stress, Trauma and the Family.* New York: Brunner-Routledge, 2004.

Cohen, S., L. G. Underwood, and B. H. Gottlieb, eds. *Social Support Measurement and Intervention: A Guide for Health and Social Scientists.* New York: Oxford University Press, 2000.

Gergen, K. J. *Realities and Relationships.* Cambridge: Harvard University Press, 1994.

Gurman, A. "Brief Therapy and Family and Couple Therapy: An Essential Redundancy." *Clinical Psychology: Science and Practice* 8 (2001): 51–65.

Johnson, Susan. *Emotionally Focused Couple Therapy with Trauma Survivors.* New York: Guilford Publications, 2005.

Prager, Karen J. *The Psychology of Intimacy.* New York: Guilford Press, 1995.

Rabin, C., and C. Nardi. "Treating Post-Traumatic Stress Disorder Couples: A Psychoeducational Program." *Community Mental Health Journal* 27 (1991): 209–24.

Ragsdale, Katherine Hancock, ed. *Boundary Wars: Intimacy and Distance in Healing Relationships.* New York: Pilgrim Press, 1996.

Revenson, T., K. Kayser, and Guy Bodenmann. *Couples Coping with Stress: Emerging Perspectives on Dyadic Coping.* Washington, D.C.: American Psychological Association, 2005.

Riggs, D. S. "Marital and Family Therapy." In *Effective Treatments for PTSD,* eds. E. B. Foa, T. M. Keane, and M. J. Friedman. New York: Guilford Press, 2000, 280–301.

Wachtel, Ellen F., Ph.D. *Treating Troubled Children and Their Families.* New York: Guilford Press, 2004.

Sex

Cervenka, Kathleen. *In the Mood Again: A Couple's Guide to Reawakening Sexual Desire.* Oakland, Calif.: New Harbinger Publications, 2003.

Ellison, Carol R. *Women's Sexualities: Generations of Women Share Intimate Secrets of Sexual Self-Acceptance.* Oakland, Calif.: New Harbinger Publications, 2000.

Herman, J. R., and J. Lo Piccolo. *Becoming Orgasmic. A Sexual and Personal Growth Program for Women.* London: Patches, 1996.

Masters, W., and V. Johnson. *The Pleasure Bond: A New Look at Sexuality and Commitment.* Boston: Little Brown and Company, 1970.

Metz, Michael E., and Barry W. McCarthy. *Coping with Erectile Dysfunction: How to Regain Confidence and Enjoy Great Sex.* Oakland, Calif.: New Harbinger Publications, 2004.

———. *Coping with Premature Ejaculation: How to Overcome PE, Please Your Partner, and Have Great Sex.* Oakland, Calif.: New Harbinger Publications, 2003.

Northrup, Christine, M.D. *The Wisdom of Menopause: Creating Physical and Emotional Health and Healing During the Change.* New York: Bantam Books, 2001.

Steven, D. Solomon, and Lorie Teagno. *Intimacy After Infidelity: How to Rebuild and Affair-Proof Your Marriage.* Oakland, Calif.: New Harbinger Publications, 2006.

Westheimer, Dr. Ruth. *Dr. Ruth's Guide to Good Sex.* New York: Warner Books, 1984.

Technical but Still Helpful

Firestone, Robert W., and Joyce Catlett. *Fear of Intimacy.* Washington, D.C.: American Psychological Association, 1999.

Leiblum, S., and L. Pervin. *Principles and Practice of Sex Therapy.* New York: Guilford Press, 1980.

Lo Piccolo, J. *Handbook of Sex Therapy.* New York: Plenum, 1978.

Masters, W., and V. Johnson. *Human Sexual Inadequacy.* Boston: Little, Brown, 1970.

Sexual Trauma

Davis, Laura, and Ellen Bass. *The Courage to Heal: A Guide for Women Survivors of Child Sexual Abuse.* New York: Perennial (Harper Collins), 1988. Also available on audiocassette.

Lauer, Teresa. *The Truth about Rape: Emotional, Spiritual, Physical and Sexual Recovery.* Gold River, Calif.: RapeRecovery.com., 2001. This book lists more than 600 associations, Web sites, books, videos, and other resources on a wide range of topics, including campus rape, the criminal justice system, sexually transmitted diseases, scar therapy, chronic pain, art therapy, rape-related pregnancy, self-defense, sexuality, and symptoms commonly associated with rape trauma, such as panic disorder, addiction, anger, and guilt.

Matsakis, Aphrodite. *The Rape Recovery Handbook: Step-by-Step Help for Survivors of Sexual Assault.* Oakland, Calif.: New Harbinger Publications, 2003.

Technical but Still Helpful

Foa, E. B., and B. O. Rothbaum. *Treating the Trauma of Rape: Cognitive Behavioral Therapy for PTSD.* New York: Guilford Press, 1998.

Koss, M., and M. Harvey. *The Rape Victim: Clinical and Community Interventions.* Newbury Park, Calif.: Sage Publications, 1991.

Petrak, Jenny, and Barbara Hedge. *The Trauma of Sexual Assault: Treatment, Prevention and Practice.* West Sussex, England: John Wiley and Sons, Ltd., 2002.

Resick, P. A. "Cognitive Processing Therapy (CPT) for Rape-Related PTSD and Depression." *Clinical Quarterly* 4, nos. 3/4 (Summer/Fall): 3-4.

Ullman, S. E., and H. Filipas. "Predictors of PTSD Symptoms Severity and Social Reactions in Sexual Assault Victims." *Journal of Traumatic Stress* 14 (2001): 369-89.

Trauma Recovery

Adams, Kathleen. *The Way of the Journal.* Baltimore: Sidran Institute Press, 1998.

Allen, Jon G. *Coping with Trauma: Healing Through Understanding.* Washington, D.C.: American Psychiatric Publishing, 2005.

Bourne, Edmund. *The Anxiety and Phobia Workbook.* 3rd ed. Oakland, Calif.: New Harbinger Publications, 2001.

————. *Beyond Anxiety and Phobia: A Step-by-Step Guide to Lifetime Recovery.* Oakland, Calif.: New Harbinger Publications, 2001.

————, and Lorna Garano. *Coping with Anxiety: Ten Simple Ways to Relieve Anxiety, Fear, and Worry.* Oakland, Calif.: New Harbinger Publications, 2003.

Brantley, Jeffrey. *Calming Your Anxious Mind: How Mindfulness and Compassion Can Free You of Anxiety, Fear, and Panic.* Oakland, Calif.: New Harbinger Publications, 2003.

Burns, George W. *101 Healing Stories: Using Metaphors in Therapy.* New York: John Wiley and Sons, 2001.

Childre, Doc, and Deborah Rozman. *Transforming Stress: The HeartMath Solution for Relieving Worry, Fatigue and Tension.* Oakland, Calif.: New Harbinger Publications, 2005.

Gallo, Fred, and Harry Vincenzi. *Energy Tapping: How to Rapidly Eliminate Anxiety, Depression, Cravings and More Using Energy Psychology.* Oakland, Calif.: New Harbinger Publications, 2000.

Kabat-Zinn, Jon. *Coming to Our Senses: Healing Ourselves and the World through Mindfulness.* New York: Hyperion Books, 2005.

Kübler-Ross, Elisabeth, and David Kessler. *Life Lessons: Two Experts on Death and Dying Teach Us About the Mysteries of Life and Living.* New York: Scribner's, 2003.

————. *On Grief and Grieving: Finding Meaning in Grief.* New York: Scribner's, 2006.

Lynch, John R. *When Anger Scares You: How to Overcome Your Fear of Conflict and Learn to Express Your Anger in Healthy Ways.* Oakland, Calif.: New Harbinger Publications, 2004.

Matsakis, Aphrodite. *I Can't Get Over It: A Handbook for Trauma Survivors.* 2nd ed. Oakland, Calif.: New Harbinger Publications, 1996.

————. *Survivor Guilt: A Self-Help Guide.* Oakland, Calif.: New Harbinger Publications, 1999.

Mayo, Peg Elliot. *The Healing Sorrow Workbook: Rituals for Transforming Grief and Loss.* Oakland, Calif.: New Harbinger Publications, 2001.

McKay, Matthew, and Patrick Fanning. *Self-Esteem.* 3rd ed. Oakland, Calif.: New Harbinger Publications, 2000.

————, and Peter Rogers. *The Anger Control Workbook.* Oakland, Calif.: New Harbinger Publications, 2000.

Miller, Dusty. *Your Surviving Spirit.* Oakland, Calif.: New Harbinger Publications, 2003.

Potter-Efron, Ronald T. *Stop the Anger Now: A Workbook for the Prevention, Containment, and Resolution of Anger.* Oakland, Calif.: New Harbinger Publications, 2001.

Schiraldi, Glenn. *The Post-Traumatic Stress Disorder Sourcebook: A Guide to Healing, Recovery and Growth.* New York: McGraw-Hill, 2000.

Trudeau, G. *The War Within: One More Step at a Time (A Doonesbury Book).* Kansas City, Mo.: Andrews McNeel, 2006.

Williams, Mary Beth, and Soili Poijula. *The PTSD Workbook: Simple, Effective Techniques for Overcoming Traumatic Stress Symptoms.* Oakland, Calif.: New Harbinger Publications, 2002.

Technical but Still Helpful

Bakal, Donald. *Minding the Body: Clinical Uses of Somatic Awareness.* New York: Guilford Press, 2001.

Barlow, David H. *Anxiety and Its Disorders: The Nature and Treatment of Anxiety and Panic.* 2nd ed. New York: Guilford Publications, 2002.

Foa, E., T. Keane, and M. Friedman, eds. *Effective Treatments for PTSD: Practice Guidelines from the International Society for Traumatic Stress Studies.* New York: Guilford Publications, 2000.

Foy, David W., ed. *Treating PTSD: Cognitive-Behavioral Strategies.* New York: Guilford Press, 1992.

Leary, Mark, and Robin M. Kawolski. *Social Anxiety.* New York: Guilford Press, 1995.

Machiodi, Cathy A. *Expressive Therapies.* New York: Guilford Press, 2005.

Matsakis, Aphrodite. *Post-Traumatic Stress Disorder: Complete Treatment Guide.* Oakland, Calif.: New Harbinger Publications, Inc., 1994.

Miller, Geri. *Incorporating Spirituality in Counseling and Psychotherapy: Theory and Technique.* New York: John Wiley and Sons, 2003.

Rabinowitz, Frederic E., and Sam Cochran. *Deepening Psychotherapy with Men.* Washington, D.C.: American Psychological Association, 2002.

Schacter, Daniel L. *The Seven Sins of Memory: How the Mind Forgets and Remembers.* New York: Houghton Mifflin, 2001.

Schwarz, Robert. *Tools for Transforming Trauma.* New York: Brunner-Routledge, 2002.

Shapiro, Ester R. *Grief as a Family Process: A Developmental Approach to Clinical Practice.* New York: Guilford Publications, 1995.

Smyth, Larry. *Overcoming Post-Traumatic Stress Disorder.* Oakland, Calif.: New Harbinger Publications, 1998.

Stamm, B. Hudnall, ed. *Secondary Traumatic Stess: Self-Care Issues for Clinicians, Researchers and Educators.* Baltimore: Sidran Press, 1999.

Williams, T., ed. *Post Traumatic Stress Disorders: A Handbook for Clinicians.* Cincinnati, Ohio: Disabled American Veterans, 1987.

Wilson, J., M. Friedman, and J. Lindy, eds. *Treating Psychological Trauma and PTSD.* New York: Guilford Publications, 2001.

Wilson, John, and Terence Keane, eds. *Assessing Psychological Trauma and PTSD.* 2nd ed. New York: Guilford Publications, 2004.

Worell, Judith, and Pamela Reme. *Feminist Perspectives in Therapy: Empowering Diverse Women.* 2nd ed. New York: John Wiley and Sons, 2003.

Guidelines for Effective Communication

Talking about Difficult Issues

The following suggestions are designed to help you and your partner communicate clearly and respectfully, so that talking about your problems doesn't create more frustrations or hurt. However, the guidelines presented here, especially those on talking about stressful events or sexual problems, may only begin to address the many challenges involved in effective communication. Individual or couples counseling may also be needed. (See appendix A, "Resources," for guidance in finding counseling, and appendix B, "Suggested Readings," for helpful books.)

1. *Do not wait until a crisis to communicate.* Nip problems in the bud by setting aside time to talk at the first sign of a problem and by checking in with each other regularly.

2. *Find an appropriate time and place to talk.* Don't try to problem solve when one of you is hungry, tired, or distracted. Find a private place that is relatively free of distractions.

3. *Set time limits* on your discussion.

4. *Don't blame* most of your problems on one another's work or interests.

5. *Don't ridicule* each other or each other's friends or family members.

6. *Separate the past from the present.* Don't blast each other with feelings that belong to someone else or to some other situation.

7. *Sort out which problems belong to you, which to him, and which to forces beyond your control.* Before you share your negative reactions to something he did or said, own up to your contribution to the problem and point out the role of outside factors.

8. *Be clear about the kinds of changes you want in your relationship.* Make sure you specify what you're willing and not willing to do to help effect these changes.

9. *Establish ground rules.* Agree that certain behaviors are unacceptable, such as name-calling, threats, shouting, or physical violence, including self-injury, throwing things, or breaking objects.

10. *Think about what brings you together.* Before you begin your discussion, talk about what attracted you to one another in the first place and what keeps you together today.

11. *Draw upon past successes.* Talk about how you coped as a couple when you faced problems in the past. What worked and what didn't work? Can any of the ways that proved successful in the past help you with the problems you are facing today?

12. *Practice active listening and paraphrase.* Before you respond to something that he has said, put what you heard him say in your own words and ask him if you heard him correctly. He should do likewise.

13. *Empathize, don't moralize.* Even if you don't like the way he feels, don't tell him he "should" have reacted differently. Try to put yourself in his position. If he's just experienced a particularly stressful event, don't tell him to "stop thinking about it," "let go," "get over it," or "get a life." Never call him a crybaby, a whiner, or a sissy. He should do likewise and not call you names either.

14. *Use "I" statements.* An "I" message is a statement about how you feel or think, about what you want or need, or about what you will or will not do. In contrast, a "you" message blames another person or situation for how you feel. For example, "You're driving dangerously" is a "you" message; "I'm frightened when you drive this fast. If you don't slow down, I will need to find another way home," is an "I" message. Even though you may feel the other person is wrong and your anger at that person is completely legitimate, it's important to focus on what you want or need. If there is danger, however, your first priority is to protect yourself and make yourself safe.

15. *Use time-outs.* When someone's temper begins to flare, it's time to take a break.

16. *Don't take anger at face value.* As human beings we are wired to view anger coming at us as a sign of danger or at least an attack on our worth. However, anger can also be a mask for other feelings, such as sadness or confusion. It can also reflect a problem with depression, addiction, diabetes, or any number of other medical or psychological problems.

17. *Stay focused.* Although many of your problems are probably interrelated, you will get nowhere jumping from one to the other. Focus on one issue at a time.

18. *Know that some problems have no solution.* Decide which problems are solvable and which are not and work only with the solvable ones.

19. *Build the positives.* What experiences usually bring you closer? Are you willing or able to set aside time for more of such experiences? Pull out your calendars and get started!

20. *Monitor yourselves.* If one of you develops any of the symptoms listed in the "Cautions" section in the introduction to this book, stop your discussion and follow the directions provided.

21. *Let other family members know when it's not their fault.* The presence of combat trauma and other stresses in a family can make every family member more sensitive than usual to any signs of rejection or disapproval. With emotions at such a high pitch, it's easy for every family member's irritability, anger, numbness, or sadness to be taken personally by others. For example, if your partner sees you frowning, he may assume you're upset with him even if you aren't; if he doesn't want to cuddle with you, you may assume he doesn't find you desirable even when he does. The hurt feelings that usually result from misreading one another's moods or actions as personal rejections or criticisms can easily lead to unnecessary quarrels, stony silences, or feelings of alienation.

Some of these needless conflicts can be avoided by simply letting the other person know when your bad mood or unavailability to them isn't their fault. If that person has indeed offended or disappointed you, but their behavior is not the main reason for the way you feel, this also needs to be stated. If you usually try to hide your negative feelings from others, you may feel you don't need to make these kinds of announcements. Yet your true feelings may reveal themselves in your posture, facial expression, tone of voice, or some other subtle way. People who live together can be amazingly adept at picking up on one another's feelings no matter how artful the disguise.

Letting others know when they aren't to blame does not mean apologizing for yourself or giving long complicated explanations about why you are feeling or acting a certain way. All that's needed are a few sentences such as: "You matter a lot to me. I'm concerned that I might be acting as if I'm criticizing or rejecting you (or am annoyed, angry, or impatient with you). But I'm not. The way I'm feeling right now is not about you. You haven't said or done anything wrong."

You don't need to make these announcements all the time lest they become burdensome or so ordinary that they aren't even heard. Be selective, but do not ignore a sigh, a downcast look, or other signs that your mood or behavior has been misinterpreted as some kind of rejection.

Because children tend to think they cause most of the events in their lives, it's especially important to help prevent them from jumping to such conclusions. Use concrete examples, preferably drawn from their own lives, to help them better understand. For example, ask them to recall a time when they didn't want to talk or play with anyone, even their best friend. Or remind them of a time when they couldn't do something they wanted to do, couldn't have something they wanted, or were looking forward to something and plans were canceled. Remind them of a time when a pet or relative died, a friend moved away, or when they were ill.

After they identify such a time, ask questions like, "Was it your friend's fault you were in a bad mood and didn't feel like talking or playing?" and "After that happened and you didn't want to talk to or be with your friend, did that mean you didn't like your friend anymore or wanted your friend to go away?" Then you can draw parallels between the situation they described and the one they are experiencing now, stressing that a parent's temporary bad mood or unavailability isn't necessarily their fault and doesn't mean the parent thinks poorly of them.

22. *Use reality checks.* Reality checks involve asking someone if he or she is thinking or feeling what you think that person is thinking or feeling. For example, suppose your partner is late and you conclude that he's late because he's upset with you over a particular matter or because he's experiencing more symptoms of depression, PTSD, or anxiety than usual. You may be right, but the only facts you have are his tardiness and your reactions to it. Reality checks such as the following might help clarify matters: "Maybe I'm off base, but I'm wondering if you are sore at me about _____ (or if something triggered you, or if you're feeling more depressed than usual)? I'm not trying to start a long discussion about one of our issues (or about your depression/PTSD/the war, and so forth). All I want to know is if I'm reading you right or not"; or "I need to check something out. Are you upset with me about something?" (or, "Are you more depressed than usual?" and so forth).

Reality checks do not obligate either of you to discuss the issue at hand. If you would like to talk about this issue at some mutually agreed upon time in the future, you can certainly say so. However, you need to make it clear that your sole purpose is to determine whether your interpretation of his behavior is accurate. Do not imply or, worse, insist that he discuss a possibly sensitive topic right then and there. This could create friction and make reality checks unwelcome. Reality checks, like any other communication skill, should not be overused.

23. *Find nonthreatening ways to handle missteps.* Because of the stresses in the home, you and your partner may make a few foolish mistakes. If one or both of you have been in counseling or have been able to communicate about your problems on your own and have agreed to handle certain

situations in better ways than in the past, there may be times when one or both of you revert to old ways rather than to any understandings you have reached as the result of counseling or improved communication. These missteps need to be accepted for what they are—missteps—not personal attacks or signs of a character flaw.

Accepting missteps doesn't mean ignoring them. Although it is not advisable to call each other on every misstep, it may be useful to point out those that occur repeatedly. A friendly reminder that you have agreed to do things differently now that you are together again may not only be necessary, but welcome. Such reminders need to be previously agreed on and worded in nonthreatening ways. If you and your partner agree that you will remind him when he starts acting like a commanding officer, your first impulse might be to say: "There you go, ordering me around again. Stop treating me like a child!" Here's a more loving alternative, "I love hearing your voice in this again even when you sound like there's an emergency when there isn't one."

By the same token, you would probably feel offended if he pointed out your failure to coordinate with him by saying: "And you say I act like a general, but just look at you. Ha! You're as bad as I am." Here's a more loving alternative: "Look at me. I'm home and glad to be with you again (or, Look at me. I'm not as depressed/confused/'out of it'/haunted by the war as I was in the past, leaving you to shoulder so many of the responsibilities at home). How about next time you consult with me before you make a decision like that?"

Some behaviors that are currently causing tensions may have served a useful purpose originally. For example, being prompt and giving firm orders were all essential parts of his recent work experience, just as acting independently was a requirement while you were managing on your own. Reminders that acknowledge any positive features of the problem behavior can be especially effective. Here are some examples: "I bet some of your orders saved many lives"; "It's amazing how disciplined one has to be in your kind of work. That takes a lot of dedication"; "This family is so lucky to have someone who knows how to get things done."

Although you can suggest reminders, he needs to make the final decision about how he wants to be approached. The same holds true for you. However, sometimes even the most carefully chosen words can trigger the other person's defensiveness or retaliatory anger. Using a nonverbal way of communicating, such as a certain hand signal, may be a better idea.

Talking about Traumatic or Stressful Events

Not sharing difficult experiences or pretending that sufferings have been forgotten can lead to feelings of alienation between you and your partner. On the other hand, if you speak freely with one another, he may overwhelm you with accounts of horrific incidents and you may overwhelm him with accounts of your agony. You may have felt shut out when he wasn't sharing, but now that he is, you may feel drained, frightened, or sad. He may have similar reactions after learning about your pain.

Since there seem to be as many pitfalls to sharing on a deep level as there are to acting as if they didn't matter that much anyway, you may not know what's best: to talk about stressful events or to remain silent. There are no clear-cut answers. Furthermore, there is no way to share "perfectly," that is, sharing just enough to better understand each other but not so much as to cause undue distress or open the door to certain misunderstandings. The following suggestions can help minimize the possibility of a negative outcome.

1. *Don't push him to talk.* When he doesn't want to talk about his traumas, do not assume that he is rejecting you. He may simply not want to relive experiences he would rather forget. Someday he may need to tell someone about all the awful things that he experienced, but it is not your role to be his healer or therapist. You can support him without assuming that responsibility, for which you are not trained.

2. *Don't push yourself to talk or to listen.* There may be times you don't want to hear about your partner's traumatic experiences. This is normal and doesn't mean you don't want to support him. There may also be times you don't want to talk about your difficult moments. This is also normal and doesn't mean you don't want to be close to him. Like him, you are entitled to your limits. There is no rule that people who love each other have to tell each other everything.

3. *Avoid extremes.* In general, extremes, such as saying practically nothing about one's struggles or true feelings or the opposite, sharing every detail and every feeling, are to be avoided. Also, try not to share everything at once, but in little bits, with breaks in between so you have time to digest what you've heard or shared and recuperate from any strong emotions you may have experienced.

4. *Let your "guts" be your guide.* If you feel you've said enough or heard enough, say so, but in a gentle caring manner. Encourage him to do the same. If you aren't sure about whether or not to share a personal matter with him or hear about one of his traumatic experiences, wait until you are sure. At the very least, give yourself a few days to mull it over. It's possible

you may decide to share some, but not all, aspects of your personal pain or to listen to some, but not all, of his experiences.

5. *Ask each other how to be supportive.* If he does open up to you, you may wonder what to say or if you should say anything at all. Ask him how you can best be supportive of him. If he doesn't know, you can figure it out together as you go along. Similarly, he can ask you how best to support you should you chose to tell him about some of your most trying moments. When you feel "stuck" about how to be supportive to one another, a good question to ask may be, "How can I help?"

Talking about Sexual Disinterest

Each man and woman is unique in his or her sexuality. In sexual matters especially, there is wide variability in strength of desire. However, sexual desire also is influenced by the quality of the nonsexual aspects of a couple's relationship with one another.

Exposure to death and dying can dampen the sexual interest of even the most virile man (or the most sexually alive woman). The psychic numbing that often develops under conditions of extreme stress may have left your partner feeling not only emotionally "empty" but sexually inert as well. You may be similarly troubled if you are coping with the communication and other issues presented by your partner's combat trauma or by your own experience with trauma or other stresses. Under such conditions, it's hard to feel sexy.

When either you or your partner shuts down sexually, the first step is to be honest about it. In a sex-obsessed culture where sexual disinterest is often seen as a sign of failure, admitting to sexual disinterest may not be easy. But keeping it a secret or making excuses, such as having a headache, solves nothing. In contrast, a clear statement, such as, "My feelings for you haven't changed, but I'm not feeling sexual right now (or lately)," can be freeing.

If you wish, you can refer to the specific incident that has affected you. Both you and your partner, however, need to refrain from graphic descriptions of human suffering that could retraumatize one or both of you, leading to even more sexual shutdown, or the opposite, agitation. Follow the Communication Guidelines in this appendix regarding talking about painful topics. For example, don't say, "When you kiss me, I see the blood gushing out of your buddy's head." All you need to say is, "War is so depressing, it's hard to feel sexual." If you need to talk about a horrible event which your partner has shared with you or which you have experienced yourself in any detail, do so with a trained therapist, not your partner.

In addition, be sure to mention the positives: that you cherish being with your partner; that feelings don't last forever; that sharing a sad moment can bring you closer. For example, you could say: "I want to be close to you, but at this moment I'm thinking about some unhappy things you saw while you were away. When the sadness lifts, I know I'll want to be with you more fully." If you wish, you can suggest a nonsexual form of touching such as "I'd like it if you'd hold my hand" (or "put your arms around me" or "lie quietly next to me").

Encourage your partner to be honest also, emphasizing that this doesn't mean that he has to explain himself or describe a horrible event in detail. Neither do you have to explain your disinterest in great detail (unless you need to for other reasons). A simple statement such as, "I'm not up for it to-night," or "I feel bad because something bad happened today," is enough. In general, it's best to reserve the bedroom for sleep, lovemaking, and other pleasant activities.

To Significant Others

Some Do's and Don'ts

> Your heart is empty
> But you won't let me in.
> Your dreams are lost
> But you won't let me in.
>
> I want to help you carry the pain
> But you won't let me in.
> No matter how much I love you
> You won't let me in.
> —AN OLD GREEK FOLK SONG

To be the partner of a combat veteran who is still suffering from a severely life-limiting form of combat trauma requires an enormous amount of patience and sensitivity. It is quite easy to feel discouraged (and angry) when he does not seem to respond to your efforts to be supportive of him and to create the kind of emotional and sexual partnership you desire.

At times your vet may ignore your efforts to be helpful and perhaps even interpret them in a negative way. Unless you have emotionally or physically attacked him or unless you unintentionally triggered him by doing or saying something that, unbeknownst to you, reminded him of his combat days, any mistrustful or cynical response on his part may reflect his devastating war experiences rather than your actions or intentions.

Perhaps your veteran withdraws from you at the very moment you are trying to be close by sharing your feelings. The more intense the feelings you are sharing, the more threatening they may be to your vet. As a result, he may avoid you or, alternatively, respond with sarcasm and other forms of anger. Because you have just taken the risk of making yourself emotionally vulnerable to your partner, such responses can leave you feeling quite alone and abandoned. The assurance and affirmation you need from him may not be forthcoming, but not because you don't deserve an attentive response or because you necessarily "said something wrong." Rather the reason may lie in the possibility that emotional interactions and deep feelings can trigger some combat veterans and diminish their ability to respond appropriately. Furthermore, the more your veteran is aware of having disappointed or hurt you or of not having responded "normally," the more inadequate, guilty, and ashamed he may feel. These painful feelings create even more stress, which further increases the vet's difficulty in responding to you in a caring way.

Your vet's ability to listen to your emotions, or the emotions of others, and to respond on an emotional level is influenced greatly by the level of anxiety, depression, or stress he is experiencing at that moment. In general, as people become less depressed and anxious and more self-accepting (as the result of progress in the healing process or some other type of success or positive experiences), they are more receptive to the love and support others have to offer and more able to take the risk of sharing on an emotional level.

However, it is your responsibility (as well as his) to learn to communicate effectively and be sensitive to the impact of combat trauma on your veteran's ability to be close to you. Perhaps you have tried very hard to follow the Guidelines for Effective Communication in appendix C or the communication suggestions provided by a therapist, member of the clergy, other knowledgeable professional, or a credible self-help book. Yet if your veteran hasn't tried to learn better communication skills and is still experiencing severe episodes of depression, PTSD, or some other traumatic reaction, you may still be frustrated in achieving emotional closeness in your relationship.

Having been exposed to many traumatic war experiences may have left your veteran with less energy available for relating (see chapter 4). More so than people who have never been traumatized, those who have known repeated or severe trauma spend a significant portion of their psychic energy trying to stay safe: that is, being vigilant about their environment and in relationships; trying to manage their anxiety, depression, and emotional pain; and trying to sort out present from past realities. This means they have less time and energy available for relationships and other activities.

For some combat veterans, relationships with anything more than minimal emotional content can sometimes feel more like threats than sources of comfort. If this is the case, your vet might be reacting to you the same way he reacts to others in relationships involving some degree of emotional sharing. On the other hand, if you are critical and rejecting of your vet and pressing your vet to relate in ways that you know can trigger him, then you may be contributing to your veteran's distress. For these reasons, it is important that—at some point—you become part of your veteran's recovery or therapy efforts, so that the ways you might unintentionally be triggering him can be identified and dealt with and so that the problems that originated as the result of combat trauma can be identified and not blamed on you.

Your veteran is important, but so are you. His feelings matter, but so do yours. Just because you were not in a war doesn't mean you are less important than the veteran. (Similarly, just because he has or had symptoms of combat trauma doesn't mean he is inferior or less important than you.) You are entitled to some happiness, pleasure, and power, despite the enormity of your veteran's pain.

1. *Do not tolerate abuse of any kind.* Under no circumstances should your veteran's difficulties be used as an excuse for emotional, physical, sexual, or economic abuse of you or anyone else. Neither you, nor any other person or living being, needs to tolerate any form of exploitation in the name of being supportive. Abuse of any kind helps no one, not you, nor the vet, nor any children involved. If you are being told (either by the vet, a counselor, relatives, or friends) to accept certain kinds of pain and deprivation in the name of combat experiences, this is a misuse of the veteran's war history. Emotional, physical, economic, and sexual abuse, lying, stealing, or destroying other people's property are not symptoms of PTSD, depression, or any other traumatic reaction. Although isolated instances of abuse can occur when a veteran is dissociated or in a hyperalert state, there are important differences between trauma-related aggressive outbursts and full-blown battering relationships.*   *See chapter 8.*

You need to be safe. If you feel you are in danger, you need to seek professional medical, psychiatric, legal, or police services to ensure your safety. You cannot help your veteran heal from his traumatic experiences by allowing him to brutalize you or any other living being.

2. *Educate yourself.* Knowledge is power. Learn all you can about PTSD, clinical depression, dissociation, addiction, or whatever type of traumatic reaction and symptoms your loved one is experiencing. You will also want to learn about any stress-related or other emotional or physical problems you may be having. There are now many excellent books on the trauma of war and on women and stress. Information is your first line of defense against assuming you are responsible for most of your loved one's distress, in understanding his behavior and emotions, and against not taking action to help yourself with your own problems.

If, after you have made some attempt to learn about combat trauma, you still blame your vet for his symptoms, you may need to do more reading and learning about combat and trauma. You may also need talk to someone about your blaming feelings. If to any significant degree you still disbelieve or condemn your vet for some of his symptoms or for some of his behavior during combat, your attitude will eventually reveal itself. When it does, the veteran may experience renewed or increased feelings of guilt, shame, inadequacy, or anger, which can lead to an increase in symptoms or even some form of relapse.

Your acceptance of the veteran's pain is critical. The criticism and rejection of family members have been found to be a major cause of relapse among individuals suffering from a variety of psychiatric problems, including schizophrenia, depression, and post-traumatic stress disorder.

It can be argued that those who were criticized by their families enough to cause a relapse may have brought the criticism on themselves by their difficult behavior and attitudes. However, family interactions are complex and each family situation is different. Gross generalities cannot be made about what came first: the criticism or the behavior that evokes the criticism. What is clear, however, is that there is an interactive effect. Negative family reactions can make a veteran's condition worse. The veteran's worsened condition, however, creates stress on the family, which can lead to more hostility or rejection of the veteran, which, in turn, can lead to increased negative symptoms in the veteran, which further stress the veteran's family members, and so forth.

Once a negative cycle is begun, it tends to reinforce and repeat itself. For example, suppose your vet forgets an important appointment and says that he forgot because of his depression, anxiety, PTSD, or other war-related problem. You may have learned that memory problems are a frequent post-trauma symptom yet also wonder if he forgot because he doesn't value his promises to you, is angry at you about some other matter, or is using his combat trauma as an "excuse" for being irresponsible. If you then begin criticizing him, he may retaliate by criticizing you or withdrawing from you. The end result is that you both end up feeling alone, abandoned, and unloved. Neither you nor he is getting your needs met, and the resulting sense of deprivation can make both of you more irritable and hostile toward one another, which sets the stage for more criticism, rejection, and withdrawal.

Such a negative interactional pattern can take on a life of its own. Action is needed to stop the vicious cycle. It doesn't matter who started the negative pattern—you or the veteran. Once it begins, it has the potential to harm both of you (as well as your children). The veteran's combat-related symptoms are aggravated by the tension in your relationship, and you run the risk for developing or worsening any existing stress symptoms or other psychological problems. In such situations, action, such as professional assistance, is needed to help break the cycle.

3. *Develop a support system for yourself.* There will be times when your vet will not be emotionally or physically available to you. Hence you cannot make him the only source of affection, companionship, or affirmation in your life. Even if you had a partner who was free of combat trauma, he would not be available every time you needed him. Nobody can be available all the time. Are you?

Therefore, you need to have other people to talk to and relax and have fun with. Just because your vet doesn't want to socialize or become involved in certain activities outside the home doesn't mean that you have to remain isolated—or give up exercising, going to class, or participating in some type of social, educational, religious, or other group. While there may be times when you may need to postpone some of your plans in order to be supportive of your vet, you cannot sacrifice your life for him.

Our society tends to emphasize putting one's self first and focusing on one's individual needs. Yet the hard truth is that all relationships, whether at home or at work, require some kind of compromise. The issue is not whether or not you will have to compromise, but how much to compromise and on what issues. Neither one of you can be sustained on a steady diet of self-sacrifice. While you need to consider your partner's needs, you also need to take care of yourself by maintaining some friendships and pursuing some of your own interests or there will be no self to help support the vet. It bears repeating that taking care of yourself is just as important as helping to take care of the vet.

Balancing your needs with the needs of your vet may sound easy in theory, but difficult in practice. Yet it is possible. The first step is to have an open discussion about your needs and to work out a plan with your loved one to help meet each other's needs. If your vet needs time alone due to an anniversary, a depressive episode, or an emotional shutdown, you and your vet can brainstorm ways of meeting some of your needs for companionship.

Many unfounded jealousies and unnecessary misunderstandings can be avoided if relevant issues are discussed before a crisis, not during one. For example, in the midst of the confusion, terror, and emotional pain of a trigger reaction or anniversary reaction, your vet may have mixed feelings toward you. On the one hand, he may want to cling to you like a terrified child clings to its mother. On the other hand, he may want you to leave him alone. If he doesn't know how to ask you for some space, he may yell at you or criticize you in order to make you go away. This is probably the worst time to announce to him that you are going to make your needs (not his) a priority and that no matter how he is feeling, you are going to do what you need to do for yourself.

You may be in the right in feeling that you are entitled to bring up past issues and the issue of the importance of your needs and desires; however, bringing up such concerns when your vet is struggling to hold on to his sanity may not be productive. Due to his emotional state, your vet may not be receptive to listening or to giving. If he does hear you, he may feel guilty about not being able to meet your needs and want you to do what you need to do to be happy. On the other hand, he may be jealous and resentful that you are capable of socializing or of wanting to do something positive for yourself while he is trapped in the emotions and physical states of the past. At such times, the vet's awareness of the toll his symptoms are taking on his life is made vivid by the contrast between where he is at and where you are at. To him, it may seem as though you have a life, and he does not.

You, on the other hand, may feel that enough of your life has been taken up by the veteran's combat trauma. If the vet is aware of the sacrifices and efforts you have made for him, he might feel guilty at having "been a burden" and fear that you will leave him if he has yet another panic attack, dissociative episode, bout of depression, or flashback.

You don't have to wait until your vet is "all better" to enjoy your life, talk about yourself, or build a support system. You need a support system now, independent of your loved one's situation. Your support system can include members of your nuclear and extended family, neighbors, members of an organization of your choice, or your own therapist or therapy group. Just as the vet can't do it alone, neither can you. You need supportive others to help you cope with the crises imposed by the impact of war on your family, as well as to give you support when your vet is not available to you emotionally.

Just as you cannot be your vet's sole support, he cannot be your sole support either. Building and then maintaining a network of friends takes time, effort, and commitment. If you are working and have many responsibilities, it may be difficult to make the effort, but it is critical that you make some attempt to connect with others. Similarly, if you have children, it is important that they, too, develop and maintain friendships and pursue their own interests.

You or your children sacrificing your other relationships, your social and leisure time involvements, and your sources of emotional, intellectual, athletic, and spiritual growth and satisfaction is not going to help your veteran. The better you take care of yourselves, the more you will have to give him on a daily basis, especially during times of stress.

3. *Know and anticipate triggers and anniversary reactions.* Ask your vet to write a list of his triggers and anniversary dates. Next to each one, he should write down ways that others might be able to help him during such difficult moments. Over time, he may recall additional triggers and these can be

added to the list. He may also find that some situations that used to trigger him no longer do so, and these situations can be removed from the list.

After you review his list, decide if you are willing or able to be supportive in any of the ways he has indicated would be helpful. Just because your vet wishes someone would be helpful in certain ways doesn't mean you have to be or are the only person who can do so. If you can, terrific. For those items you can't help with, try to find other people who can or find other ways for the vet to meet his needs.

Remember, you are not a saint, and it is not the sole purpose of your life to be there 100 percent of the time in every way possible for the veteran. You may or may not be able to go along with what he feels would be the most desirable response or assistance on your part. You may only be able to help out in part of what he wishes. If he knows this in advance, he can seek out others to provide the additional support needed.

Once again, it is more productive to discuss how to handle triggers and anniversary times when neither of you is stressed or when you are feeling good about one another, rather than after or during an argument about other matters.

You can help your vet make this list by asking him what he would like or how you could help when he is experiencing an emotional shutdown, an anniversary or trigger time, a hyperalert stage, or a time of depression. Does he want you around? If so, how much? Is it necessary for you to be there the entire time?

Quite possibly, he may be uncertain about how you could help him. A part of him may want to be left alone; another part may want you nearby. Perhaps he wants you home with him but does not necessarily want to communicate or do something with you. Yet you are a person, too, with needs of your own. As you ask your vet for clarification on how you can best be supportive, you also need to talk about what you need to do to take care of yourself. While you might be able to put some of your personal plans or needs aside some of the time, you cannot always do so.

The more you can talk about what your respective needs are before you are in the crisis situation of a trigger or anniversary reaction, the easier it will be to negotiate and make plans. After you make a plan and try it out, evaluate it afterwards. What helped? What didn't help? Is there anything either of you would like to do different next time?

While you need to have a plan, the plan needs to be flexible. Trigger events, anniversaries, emotional shutdowns, and depressions vary in intensity. Sometimes the veteran may need you more than at other times. Would your vet be able to state that to you? Similarly, perhaps you agreed to stay with the vet on a particular evening, but when that evening came, you were beset with a pressing need of your own. Would you be able to state that to him?

Given that life is full of the unexpected and that neither you nor the vet can predict the intensity of your emotions and your needs of one another at some future point in time, it is good if both you and the vet have a supportive network of friends, relatives, and professionals to whom you can turn (if you cannot turn to one another).

No matter how much you love your vet, you cannot make him your life. To the extent that your vet is embroiled in the past or immersed in his recovery program, you may have a relatively lonely life if you restrict your life according to his needs. If your vet makes progress in recovery, he may have more to give you emotionally down the line. But this may or may not occur and the speed of this kind of progress is unpredictable.

You may also have triggers and anniversaries which need to be listed and discussed. Even if they aren't related to traumatic events, they may cause you tremendous emotional distress. Your partner needs to be aware of these emotional facts about you, just as you are aware of his emotional realities. Your triggers need to be respected and taken care of, and part of your planning may include how your vet can help you through your difficult times. If, in addition, certain words and actions of the vet survivor trigger you, this also needs to be discussed. However, if you cannot talk about triggers without the discussion becoming a hostile exchange or an otherwise unproductive endeavor, you may want to seek the help of a professional counselor or clergyperson.

4. *Know the importance, and limits, of being supportive.* Respecting trigger and anniversary times, going to therapy with your vet, respecting his need to disclose or not disclose aspects of his war experiences to you, and realizing that he may not always be as available to you as you or he would like, are all ways of being supportive. Not tolerating abuse of yourself or self-abuse on the vet are also ways of being supportive. While you may want to be supportive, you cannot be all things to your loved one. No matter how much you love him, your love cannot "fix" the past or "make right" all the hardships and any injustices he has experienced. If you exhaust yourself trying to nurture your loved one, you may end up resentful when he does not heal as rapidly or thoroughly as you had hoped.

An Al-Anon slogan is applicable here: "C-C-C" stands for Cause, Control, and Cure. You didn't cause the vet's related problems. You can't control him and you can't cure him either. While you can definitely worsen the situation and while your support is invaluable, you can't undo the past, no matter how much he might like you to and how much you might wish to do so. If you refrain from criticizing the vet for his symptoms; if you don't blame all the family's problems on his war experiences and reactions to them; if you respect his need to withdraw or be alone; and if you make an effort not to needlessly trigger him, you are being wonderfully supportive.

5. *Back off when necessary.* If the vet says, "Back off! I can't deal with this now," you might want to consider dropping the subject. Backing off in this way will not "cure" him, but pressing forward has the potential of triggering him into a deeper depression, rage reaction, or dissociated state. At such times, his ability to think rationally and to attend to you are impaired. Consider bringing up the subject at a later point in time, for to force discussion when the vet is having a traumatic reaction generally is not productive.

However, if the matter is urgent and the vet does not wish to discuss it, you may need to take action and make a decision on your own. If your vet asks you to back off almost all the time, rather than just on occasion, then you have a problem of a more serious nature. At this point, you may need to seek professional consultation.

Despite the many difficulties described in this book, if you are committed to your relationship with your veteran, the rewards can be enormous. At the end of all the struggles to understand each other, you and your veteran will be closely bonded, like comrades in arms. Indeed, you have fought in a kind of war together: a war against the ghosts of the past; a war against ignorance, misperceptions, selfishness, and selflessness (which can be a "psychological enemy" in its own right); and a war against the capacity of combat trauma to destroy human connections.

Some Do's and Don'ts

1. Don't tell the vet to "let go" or "forget the past," to "get a life" or "get over it."

2. Don't call the vet a "crybaby," a "psycho case," "a sicko," or a "whiner."

3. Don't blame all your relationship problems on the war or the veteran's reactions to it. For example, don't say, "We can't have a good relationship because you have all these triggers," or "You and your darn war," or "I can never have fun with you because you freak out all the time."

4. Don't automatically assume the veteran's emotional coolness is a sign of rejection or disinterest. Do a reality check first.* *See appendix C for guidelines for effective communication.

5. Do not expect the vet to respond to a death or illness in the family or another important loss as others do.

6. Don't press the vet for details of the war or of his therapy or recovery efforts. Respect his need not to disclose certain aspects of his past or his treatment. He, in turn, needs to respect your need to not disclose certain aspects of your life.

7. Don't press the vet to solve a problem or do something if he clearly

indicates that he has reached his limit and feels like exploding or is starting to shut down. In emergency situations, make the best decision you can, consulting with others, if possible, and take constructive action.

8. Don't tolerate emotional, physical, or sexual abuse of yourself, others, or any living being.

9. Don't try to be your vet's therapist or magic rescuer. You can be supportive without making him your "project" or your entire life.

10. Do expect there to be times the vet doesn't trust you and needs to be distant from you.

11. Don't mock him for his symptoms.

12. Do develop a support system for yourself.

13. Do work together with the vet on a plan to handle predictable difficult times, such as anniversary dates of an important battle or of the death of a comrade, so as to meet some of your needs as well as his.

14. Do work together with your vet to create an "emergency plan" for the unpredictable times he begins to feel out of control, extremely depressed, or about to relapse into addiction. This emergency plan should include the name of doctors, therapists, hospitals, friends, and family members.

15. Do know the signs of impending suicide and take action immediately. (See chapter 12.)

16. Do try to find some kind of balance between taking care of yourself and the needs of your vet.

17. Do be honest with yourself, and your vet.

Notes

Introduction

1. Jonathan Shay, *Odysseus in America: Combat Trauma and the Trials of Homecoming* (New York: Scribner's, 2002).

2. Nelly Tucker, "For Wounded Vets; Airborne Backup," *Washington Post,* Aug. 21, 2005, D1, D2.

3. Shay, *Odysseus in America.*

4. J. Holloway, "Army Uncovers Mental Health Service Gap," *Monitor on Psychology* (July/August 2004): 35–37.

5. C. W. Hoge, C.A. Castro, S. C. Messer, D. McGurk, D. Cotting, and R. L. Koffman, "Combat Duty in Iraq and Afghanistan: Mental Health Problems and Barriers to Care," *New England Journal of Medicine* 351 (2004): 13–22.

6. Gaitbri Fernando, "Finding Meaning After the Tsunami Disaster: Recovery and Resilience in Sri Lanka." *Traumatic Stress Points* 19, no. 1 (Winter 2005): 1, 12.

7. R. Kishon-Barash, E. Midlarsky, and D. R. Johnson, "Altruism and the Vietnam War Veteran: The Relationship of Helping to Symptomatology," *Journal of Traumatic Stress* 12, no. 4 (Oct. 1999): 655–62.

8. Barbara Wilson, "Women in the Military: Facts and Figures about Women's Role in the Armed Forces" (1996), http://womensissues.about.com/library/weekly/aa092801a.html.

Chapter 1. The Reality of Combat Trauma

1. Gregg Zoroya, "1 in 4 Iraq Vets Ailing on Return," *USA Today,* Oct. 18, 2005, www.usatoday.com/news/world/iraq/2005-10-18-troops-side_x.htm.

2. J. Shay, *Achilles in Vietnam: Combat Trauma and the Undoing of Character* (New York: Macmillan, 1994), 83.

3. *Diagnostic and Statistical Manual of Mental Disorders,* 4th ed. (DSM-IV-TR) (Washington, D.C.: American Psychiatric Association, 2000).

4. Kitty K. Wu, Sumee K. Chan, and Tracy M. Ma, "Posttraumatic Stress, Anxiety, and Depression in Survivors of Severe Acute Respiratory Syndrome (SARS)," *Journal of Traumatic Stress* 18, no. 1 (Feb. 2005): 39–42.

5. Aphrodite Matsakis, *I Can't Get Over It—A Handbook for Trauma Survivors* (Oakland, Calif.: New Harbinger Publications, 1994).

6. DSM IV; Matsakis, *I Can't Get Over It.*

7. Andrew J. McClurg, "Dead Sorrow: A Story about Loss and a New Theory of Wrongful Death Damages," *Boston University Law Review* 85 (Feb. 2005): 1–51.

8. "A Short History of PTSD: From Thermopylae to Hue Soldiers Have Always Had a Disturbing Reaction to War," *The VVA Veteran* 25, no. 2 (March/April 2005): 27–30.

9. J. Ikin, D. McKenzie, M. Creamer, A. McFarlane, H. Kelsall, D. Glass, A. Forbes, K. Horsley, W. Harrex, and M. Sim, "War Zone Stress Without Direct Combat: The Australian Naval Experience of the Gulf War," *Journal of Traumatic Stress* 18, no. 3 (2005): 193–204.

10. Sarah Haley, "The Vietnam Veteran and His Preschool Child: Child Rearing as a Delayed Stress in Combat Vets," *Journal of Contemporary Psychotherapy* 14, no. 1 (1984): 114–21.

11. Dave Grossman, *On Killing: The Psychological Cost of Learning to Kill in War and Society* (New York: Little, Brown, 1995), 92.

12. Ibid.; Shay, *Achilles in Vietnam*.

13. R. Janoff-Bulman, *Shattered Assumptions: Towards a New Psychology of Trauma* (New York: Free Press, 1992).

14. Shay, *Achilles in Vietnam;* J. Shay, *Odysseus in America: Combat Trauma and the Trials of Homecoming* (New York: Scribner's, 2002); A. Fontana and R. Rosenheck, "Trauma, Change in Strength of Religious Faith and Mental Health Services Used Among Veterans Treated for PTSD," *Journal of Nervous and Mental Disease* 192 (2004): 579–84; A. Fontana and R. Rosenheck, "The Role of Loss of Meaning in the Pursuit of Treatment for Posttraumatic Stress Disorder," *Journal of Traumatic Stress* 18, no. 2 (2005): 133–36.

15. Thomas Ricks, "Army Spouses Expect Reenlistment Problems," *Washington Post,* March 28, 2004, A1, A16–17.

16. Ibid., A16.

Chapter 2. Frequently Asked Questions about Combat Trauma

1. Stephen Cozza, "Combat Exposure and PTSD," *PTSD Research Quarterly: The National Center for Post-Traumatic Stress Disorder* 16, no. 1 (2005): 1–3; Iowa Persian Gulf Study Group, "Self-Reported Illness and Health Status Among Gulf War Veterans: A Population-Based Study," *Journal of the American Medical Association* 277 (1997): 238–45; C. W. Hoge, C. A. Castro, S. C. Messer, D. McGurk, D. Cotting, and R. L. Koffman. "Combat Duty in Iraq and Afghanistan, Mental Health Problems and Barriers to Care," *New England Journal of Medicine* 351 (2004): 13–22; N. J. Stimpson, H. V. Thomas, A. L. Weightman, F. Dunstan, and G. Lewis, "Psychiatric Disorder in Veterans of the Persian Gulf War of 1991: Systematic Review," *British Journal of Psychiatry* 182 (2003): 391–403; P. B. Sutker, M. Uddo, K. Brailey, and A. N. Allain, "War-Zone Trauma and Stress-Related Symptoms in Operation Desert Shield/Storm (ODS) Returnees," *Journal of Social Issues* 49 (1993): 33–50.

2. Hoge et al., "Combat Duty in Iraq and Afghanistan"; Cozza, "Combat Exposure and PTSD."

3. Cozza, "Combat Exposure and PTSD."

4. Ibid.

5. Carol Vercozzi, "The War That Refused to Die: Vietnam Again," unpublished paper, Department of Communications, Hartford, Mass., 1963; R. P. Grinker and J. P. Spiegel, *Men Under Stress* (New York: McGraw-Hill, 1945).

6. Jim Goodwin, Psy.D., *Continuing Readjustment Problems Among Vietnam Veterans: The Etiology of Combat Related Post-Traumatic Stress Disorders* (Cincinnati, Ohio: Disabled American Veterans National Headquarters, 1986); Grinker and Spiegel, *Men Under Stress;* Merrill Lipton and W. Shaffer, "PTSD in the Older Veteran," *Military Medicine* 151 (1986): 522–26; A. J. Glass, introduction to *The Psychology and Physiology of Stress,* ed. P. G. Bourne (New York: Academic Press, 1969), xiv–xxx.

7. P. G. Bourne, *Men, Stress, and Vietnam* (Boston: Little, Brown, 1970).

8. Hoge et al., "Combat Duty in Iraq and Afghanistan"; Cozza, "Combat Exposure and PTSD"; J. Shay, *Achilles in Vietnam: Combat Trauma and the Undoing of Character* (New York: Macmillan, 1994); P. Thienes-Hontos, C. Watson, and T. Kucala, "Stress Disorder Symptoms in

Vietnam and Korean War Veterans," *Journal of Consulting and Clinical Psychology* 50 (1982): 558–61; Edward Caroll, "Stress Disorder Symptoms in Vietnam and Korean War Veterans: A Commentary on Thienes-Hontos, Watson, and Kucala," *Journal of Consulting and Clinical Psychology* 51, no. 4 (1983): 616–18; P. Thienes-Hontos, "Stress-Disorder Symptoms in Vietnam and Korean War Veterans: Still No Difference," *Journal of Consulting and Clinical Psychology* 51, no. 4 (1983): 619–20.

9. Cozza, "Combat Exposure and PTSD"; J. H. Streimer, "The Psychosocial Adjustment of Australian Vietnam Veterans," *American Journal of Psychiatry* 142, no. 5 (May 1985): 616–18; Bruce Bowman et al., "Psychiatric Disturbances Among Australian Vietnam Veterans," *Military Medicine* 150, no. 2 (1985): 77–79; Bruce Bowman, "Post-traumatic Stress Disorder (Traumatic War Neurosis) and Concurrent Psychiatric Illness Among Australian Vietnam Veterans: A Controlled Study," *T.R. Army Medical Corps* 131 (1985): 128–38; T. Dwyer, L. Blizzard, K. R. Delaney, K. W. Horsley, W. Harrex, and H. Schwarz, "War-Related Psychological Stressors and Risk of Psychological Disorders in Australian Veterans of the 1991 Gulf War," *British Journal of Psychiatry* 185 (2004): 116–26; Zahava Solomon et al., "The 'Koach' Project for Treatment of Combat-Related PTSD: Rationale, Aims, and Methodology," *Journal of Traumatic Stress* 5, no. 2 (1992): 175–94.

10. Houston Vietnam Veteran Leadership Program, "Vietnam Veteran Fact Sheet," compiled by Richard K. Kolb, Houston, Texas, March 20, 1985, 4 (data taken from "Veterans in the U.S.: A Statistical Portrait," 1980 U.S. Census); Kulka et al., *Trauma and the Vietnam War Generation*; J. Wolf, T. Keane, D. Kaloupek, C. Mora, and P. Wine, "Patterns of Positive Readjustment in Vietnam Combat Veterans," *Journal of Traumatic Stress* 6, no. 2 (1993): 179–94.

11. Kulka et al., *Trauma and the Vietnam War Generation*; Richard D. Lyons, "Vietnam Veterans Turn to Therapy," *New York Times*, Nov. 13, 1984, 3.

12. Hoge et al., "Combat Duty in Iraq and Afghanistan"; Iowa Persian Gulf Study Group, "Self-Reported Illness and Health Status"; R. H. Stretch, D. H. Marlowe, K. M. Wright, P. D. Bliese, K. H. Knudson, and C. H. Hoover, "Posttraumatic Stress Disorder Symptoms among Gulf War Veterans," *Military Medicine* 161 (1996): 407–10; Sutker et al., "War-Zone Trauma and Stress-Related Symptoms," 33–50; Dwyer et al., "War-Related Psychological Stressors."

13. Hoge et al., "Combat Duty in Iraq and Afghanistan."

14. Arthur S. Blank Jr., "The Unconscious Flashback to the War in Vietnam Veterans: Clinical Mystery, Legal Defense and Community Problem," in *The Trauma of War: Stress and Recovery in Vietnam Veterans*, ed. S. Sonnenberg, A. Blank, and A. Talbott (Washington, D.C.: American Psychiatric Press, 1985).

15. Charles Figley, ed., *Stress Disorders Among Vietnam Veterans* (New York: Brunner/Mazel, 1978); Jerome Yesavage, "Dangerous Behavior by Vietnam Veterans with Schizophrenia," *American Journal of Psychiatry* 140, no. 9 (Sept., 1983): 1180–83.

16. Shay, *Achilles in Vietnam*.

17. Hoge et al., "Combat Duty in Iraq and Afghanistan."

18. Cozza, "Combat Exposure and PTSD"; Thomas Dikel, Brian Engdahl, and R. Eberly, "PTSD in Former Prisoners of War: Prewar, Wartime, and Post-war Factors," *Journal of Traumatic Stress* 18, no. 1 (Feb. 2005): 69–77.

19. Cozza, "Combat Exposure and PTSD"; Sutker et al., "War-Zone Trauma and Stress-Related Symptoms."

20. Shay, *Achilles in Vietnam*.

21. W. B. Gault, "Some Remarks on Slaughter," *American Journal of Psychiatry* 128, no. 4 (Oct. 1971): 82–86.

22. Lars Mehlum and Lars Weisaeth, "Predictors of Posttraumatic Stress Reactions in Norwegian UN Peacekeepers 7 Years after Service," *Journal of Traumatic Stress* 15, no. 1 (2002): 17–26; Ben Shephard, *A War of Nerves: Soldiers and Psychiatrists in the Twentieth Century* (Cambridge: Harvard University Press, 2001).

23. S. Futterman and E. Pumpian-Midlin, "Traumatic War Neuroses Five Years Later," *American Journal of Psychiatry* 108, no. 6 (1950): 401-8.

24. Vercozzi, "The War That Refused to Die"; Blank, "Unconscious Flashback"; D. Johnson, H. Lubin, R. Rosenheck, S. Fontana, S. Southwick, and D. Charney, "The Impact of the Homecoming Reception on the Development of Posttraumatic Stress Disorder: The West Haven Homecoming Stress Scale (WHHSS)," *Journal of Traumatic Stress* 10, no. 2 (April 1997): 259-78; P. Schnurr, C. Lunney, and A. Sengupta, "Risk Factors for the Development versus Maintenance of Posttraumatic Stress Disorder," *Journal of Traumatic Stress Studies* 17, no. 2 (April 2004): 85-96.

25. Shay, *Achilles in Vietnam*.

26. As cited on p. 405 in Bruce Pentland and James Dwyer, "Incarcerated Vietnam Veterans," in *The Trauma of War: Stress and Recovery in Vietnam Veterans,* ed. S. Sonnenberg, A. Blank, and A. Talbott (Washington, D.C.: American Psychiatric Press, 1985), 405-16.

27. Shay, *Achilles in Vietnam;* Dave Grossman, *On Killing: The Psychological Cost of Learning to Kill in War and Society* (New York: Little, Brown, 1995); Peter Marin, "Moral Pain," *Psychology Today* (Nov. 1981): 68-80; A. Fontana and R. Rosenheck, "Trauma, Change in Strength of Religious Faith and Mental Health Services Used Among Veterans Treated for PTSD," *Journal of Nervous and Mental Disease* 192 (2004): 579-84; A. Fontana and R. Rosenheck, "The Role of Loss of Meaning in the Pursuit of Treatment for Posttraumatic Stress Disorder," *Journal of Traumatic Stress* 18, no. 2 (2005): 133-36.

28. Gary Sorenson, "Veterans Struggle to Integrate War and Values," *Vet Center Voice* 6, no. 11 (Dec. 1985): 5-6; Fr. Patrick Devine, "PTSD Shadows Moral/Spiritual Dimension," *Vet Center Voice* 6, no. 6 (July 1985): 1, 9.

29. Harry C. Holloway and Robert J. Ursano, "Vietnam Veterans on Active Duty: Adjustment in a Supportive Environment," in *The Trauma of War,* ed. Sonnenberg et al., 323-38.

30. Shay, *Achilles in Vietnam;* Schnurr, Lunney, and Sengupta, "Risk Factors"; K. Kaniasty, "Social Support and Traumatic Stress," *PTSD Research Quarterly: The National Center for Post-Traumatic Stress Disorder* 16, no. 2 (2005); R. J. Turner, "Direct, Indirect and Moderating Effects of Social Support Upon Psychological Distress and Associated Conditions," in *Psychosocial Stress: Trends in Theory and Research,* ed. H. B. Kaplan (New York: Academic Press, 1983).

31. B. A. Van der Kolk, A. McFarlane, and L. Weisaeth, eds., *Traumatic Stress: The Effects of Overwhelming Experience on Mind, Body, and Society* (New York: Guilford Press, 1996).

32. Blank, "Unconscious Flashback," 293-320.

33. John Wilson, as cited in Lyons, "Vietnam Veterans Turn to Therapy," 5.

34. Eric Gerdemen, "PTSD and the Vietnam Veteran," unpublished paper, Vet Center Program, Region II, Baltimore, Md., 194.

35. A. B. Adler, M. A. Vaitkus, and J. A. Martin. "Combat Exposure and Posttraumatic Stress Symptomatology among U.S. Soldiers Deployed to the Gulf War," *Military Psychology* 8 (1996): 1-14; H. Orcutt, D. Erickson, and J. Wolfe, "The Course of PTSD Symptoms Among Gulf War Veterans: A Growth Mixture Modeling Approach," *Journal of Traumatic Stress Studies* 17, no. 3 (June 2004): 195-202; D. J. Erickson, J. Wolfe, D. W. King, L. A. King, and E. J. Sharkansky, "Posttraumatic Stress Disorder and Depression Symptomatology in a Sample of Gulf War Veterans: A Prospective Analysis," *Journal of Consulting and Clinical Psychology* 69 (2001): 41-49.

36. J. Ikin, D. McKenzie, M. Creamer, A. McFarlane, H. Kelsall, D. Glass, A. Forbes, K. Horsley, W. Harrex, and M. Sim, "War Zone Stress Without Direct Combat: The Australian Naval Experience of the Gulf War," *Journal of Traumatic Stress* 18, no. 3 (2005): 193-204.

37. Ibid.

38. Stretch et al., "Posttraumatic Stress Disorder Symptoms"; Orcutt et al., "The Course of PTSD Symptoms."

39. Kulka et al., *Trauma and the Vietnam War Generation;* Orcutt et al., "The Course of PTSD Symptoms"; A. Y. Shalev, S. Freedman, T. Peri, D. Brandes, R. Sahar, S. P. Orr et al.,

"Prospective Study of Posttraumatic Stress and Depression Following Trauma," *American Journal of Psychiatry* 155 (1988): 630–37; R. C. Kessler, A. Sonnega, E. Bromet, M. Hughes, C. B. Nelson, and N. B. Breslau, "Epidemiological Risk Factors for Trauma and PTSD," in *Risk Factors for Posttraumatic Stress Disorder,* ed. R. Yehuda (Washington, D.C.: American Psychiatric Press, 1999), 23–60; Erickson et al., "Posttraumatic Stress Disorder"; M. Crawford and R. Unger, *Women and Gender: A Feminist Psychology,* 3rd ed. (Boston: McGraw-Hill, 2000).

40. Orcutt et al., "The Course of PTSD Symptoms"; A. Bloom and R. Lyle, "Vicariously Traumatized: Male Partners of Sex Abuse Survivors," in *The Abuse of Men: Trauma Begets Trauma,* ed. Barbara Jo Brothers (New York: Haworth Press, 2001), 9–28.

41. Kulka et al., *Trauma and the Vietnam War Generation;* Dikel et al., "PTSD in Former Prisoners of War."

42. Kaniasty, "Social Support and Traumatic Stress"; Johnson et al., "Impact of the Homecoming Reception," 259–78; J. Shay, *Odysseus in America: Combat Trauma and the Trials of Homecoming* (New York: Scribner's, 2002).

43. Aphrodite Matsakis, "Trauma and Its Impact on Families," in *Handbook of Stress, Trauma, and the Family,* ed. D. Catherall (New York: Bruner Routledge, 2004), 15–32.

44. L. Irving, L. Telfer, and D. Blake, "Hope, Coping and Social Support in Combat-Related Posttraumatic Stress Disorder," *Journal of Traumatic Stress* 10, no. 3 (July 1997): 465–80.

45. Aphrodite Matsakis, *I Can't Get Over It—A Handbook for Trauma Survivors* (Oakland, Calif.: New Harbinger Publications, 1994).

46. A. Kardiner, *The Traumatic Neuroses of War* (New York: Hoeber, 1941).

47. B. A. van der Kolk, "The Trauma Spectrum: The Interaction of Biological and Social Events in the Genesis of the Trauma Response," *Journal of Traumatic Stress* 1 (1988): 273–90.

48. R. R. Wilson, *Breaking the Panic Cycle: For People with Phobias* (Rockville, Md.: Phobia Society of America, 1987).

49. R. Kishon-Barash, E. Midlarsky, and D. R. Johnson, "Altruism and the Vietnam War Veteran: The Relationship of Helping to Symptomatology," *Journal of Traumatic Stress* 12, no. 4 (Oct. 1999): 655–62.

50. S. Falsetti, P. Resick, and J. Davis, "Changes in Religious Beliefs Following Trauma," *Journal of Traumatic Stress* 16, no. 4 (Aug. 2003): 391–98; P. Linley and S. Joseph, "Positive Change Following Trauma and Adversity: A Review," *Journal of Traumatic Stress* 17, no. 1 (Feb. 2004): 11–22; P. Linley, "Positive Adaptation to Trauma: Wisdom as Both Process and Outcome," *Journal of Traumatic Stress* 16, no. 6 (Dec. 2003): 601–10; Kishon-Barash et al., "Altruism and the Vietnam War Veteran"; S. Joseph, R. Williams, and W. Yule, "Changes in Outlook Following Disaster: The Preliminary Development of a Measure to Assess Positive and Negative Responses," *Journal of Traumatic Stress* 6, no. 2 (April 1993): 271–80.

51. S. Falsetti, Resick, and Davis, "Changes in Religious Beliefs Following Trauma"; A. Matsakis, *Trust After Trauma* (Oakland, Calif.: New Harbinger Publications, 1998); Joseph et al., "Changes in Outlook Following Disaster"; Linley, "Positive Adaptation to Trauma"; Linley and Joseph, "Positive Change Following Trauma"; Kishon-Barash et al., "Altruism and the Vietnam War Veteran."

52. Linley, "Positive Adaptation to Trauma," 602.

53. Ibid.; Linley and Joseph, "Positive Change Following Trauma."

54. Kishon-Barash et al., "Altruism and the Vietnam War Veteran"; Joseph, Williams, and Yule, "Changes in Outlook Following Disaster"; Linley, "Positive Adaptation to Trauma"; and Linley and Joseph, "Positive Change Following Trauma."

55. Kishon-Barash et al., "Altruism and the Vietnam War Veteran."

56. Linley and Joseph, "Positive Change Following Trauma," 16.

57. Lars Weisaeth, "The European History of Psychotraumatology," *Journal of Traumatic Stress* 15, no. 6 (Dec. 2002): 443–52.

58. Linley and Joseph, "Positive Change Following Trauma," 16.

59. Viktor Frankl, *Man's Search for Meaning* (New York: Simon and Schuster, 1959).

60. Colman McCarthy, "Welcome Soldiers to the Peace Corps," *Washington Post*, Aug. 21, 2005, Outlook B7.

Chapter 3. Common Traumatic Reactions

1. Ben Shephard, *A War of Nerves: Soldiers and Psychiatrists in the Twentieth Century* (Cambridge: Harvard University Press, 2001).

2. S. R. Thorp and M. B. Stein, "Posttraumatic Stress Disorder and Functioning," *PTSD Research Quarterly, The National Center for Post-Traumatic Stress Disorder* 16, no. 3 (2005): 1–3.

3. H. Orcutt, D. Erickson, and J. Wolfe, "The Course of PTSD Symptoms Among Gulf War Veterans: A Growth Mixture Modeling Approach," *Journal of Traumatic Stress* 17, no. 3 (2004): 195–202.

4. B. Kaplan, ed., *Psychosocial Stress: Trends in Theory and Research* (New York: Academic Press, 1983); B. A. Van der Kolk, A. McFarlane, and L. Weisaeth, eds., *Traumatic Stress: The Effects of Overwhelming Experience on Mind, Body, and Society* (New York: Guilford Press, 1996).

5. M. Creamer, P. Morris, D. Biddle, and P. Elliott, "Treatment Outcome in Australian Veterans with Combat-Related Posttraumatic Stress Disorder: A Cause for Cautious Optimism?" *Journal of Traumatic Stress* 12, no. 4 (Oct. 1999): 545–58.

6. Shephard, *War of Nerves;* van der Kolk et al., *Traumatic Stress.*

7. Thorp and Stein, "Posttraumatic Stress Disorder"; van der Kolk et al., *Traumatic Stress.*

8. Ibid.

9. Ibid.

10. R. Miranda, L. A. Meyerson, B. P. Marx, and P. M. Tucker, "Civilian-Based Posttraumatic Stress Disorder and Physical Complaints: Evaluation of Depression as a Mediator," *Journal of Traumatic Stress* 14 (Aug. 2002): 297–302; R. A. Fleet, N. Kazantzis, N. Long, C. MacDonald, and M. Millar, "Traumatic Events and Physical Health in a New Zealand Community Sample," *Journal of Traumatic Stress* 15, no. 4 (Aug. 2002): 303–12.

11. D. W. Black, C. Carney, V. L. Forman-Hoffman, E. Letucky, P. Peloso, R. F. Woolson, and B. N. Doebbeling. "Depression in Veterans of the First Gulf War and Comparable Military Controls," *Annals of Clinical Psychiatry* 16 (2001): 53–61.; A. Y. Shalev, S. Freedman, T. Peri, D. Brandes, R. Sahar, S. P. Orr, et al., "Prospective Study of Posttraumatic Stress and Depression Following Trauma," *American Journal of Psychiatry* 155 (1988): 630–37.

12. J. Vasterling, J. Constans, and B. Hanna-Pladdy, "Head Injury as a Predictor of Psychological Outcome in Combat Veterans," *Journal of Traumatic Stress* 13, no. 3 (July 2000): 441–52; J. Morrison, *When Psychological Problems Mask Medical Disorders: A Guide for Psychotherapists* (New York: Guilford, 1997).

13. "A Short History of PTSD: From Thermopylae to Hue Soldiers Have Always Had a Disturbing Reaction to War," *The VVA Veteran* 25, no. 2 (March/April 2005): 27–30.

14. Bonnie Green, M. Grace, and G. Glesser, "Identifying Survivors at Risk: Long-Term Impairment Following the Beverly Hills Supper Club Fire," *Journal of Consulting and Clinical Psychology* 53, no. 5 (1985): 672–78; J. Modlin, "PTSD: No Longer Just for War Veterans," *Post Graduate Medicine* 79, no. 3 (Feb. 15, 1986): 26–44; Alexander McFarlane, "Post Traumatic Morbidity of a Disaster," *Journal of Nervous and Mental Disease* 174, no. 1 (1986): 4–14.

15. Morton Bard, foreword to *PTSD: A Handbook for Clinicians,* ed. T. Williams (Cincinnati, Ohio: Disabled American Veterans, 1987), iii.

16. Arthur S. Blank Jr., "The Unconscious Flashback to the War in Vietnam Veterans: Clinical Mystery, Legal Defense and Community Problem," in *The Trauma of War: Stress and Recovery in Vietnam Veterans,* ed. S. Sonnenberg, A. Blank, and A. Talbott (Washington, D.C.: American Psychiatric Press, 1985), 297.

17. *Diagnostic and Statistical Manual of Mental Disorders,* 4th ed. (DSM-IV-TR) (Washington, D.C.: American Psychiatric Association, 2000), 393.

18. Ibid.

19. *Vietnam Veteran,* August 1980, as cited in Blank, "Unconscious Flashback," 293.

20. Aphrodite Matsakis, *Vietnam Wives: Facing the Challenges of Life with Veterans Suffering Post-Traumatic Stress,* 2nd ed. (Baltimore, Md.: Sidran Institute Press, 1996).

21. Gary Sorenson, "Hinterlands Are Home, Not a Hideaway, for Vietnam Veterans," *Vet Center Voice* 6, no. 9 (Oct. 1985): 1; Gregg Zoroya, "1 in 4 Iraq Vets Ailing on Return," *USA Today,* Oct. 18, 2005, www.usatoday.com/news/world/iraq/2005-10-18-troops-side_x.htm (retrieved Oct. 19, 2005).

22. B. A. van der Kolk, "The Body Keeps the Score: Approaches to the Psychobiology of PTSD," in *Traumatic Stress,* eds. van der Kolk et al.; B. A. van der Kolk, "The Biological Response to Psychic Trauma," in *Post Traumatic Therapy and Victims of Violence,* ed. Frank Ochberg (New York: Brunner/Mazel, 1988), 25–38.

23. Van der Kolk, "The Body Keeps the Score"; van der Kolk, "The Biological Response to Psychic Trauma."

24. Ibid.

25. R. Novaco and C. Chemtob, "Anger and Combat-Related Posttraumatic Stress Disorder," *Journal of Traumatic Stress* 15, no. 2. (April 2002): 123–32.

26. Ibid.

27. Aphrodite Matsakis, *I Can't Get Over It—A Handbook for Trauma Survivors* (Oakland, Calif.: New Harbinger Publications, 1994).

28. Matsakis, *Vietnam Wives;* Shephard, *War of Nerves;* Thomas Dikel, Brian Engdahl, and R. Eberly, "PTSD in Former Prisoners of War: Prewar, Wartime, and Post-war Factors," *Journal of Traumatic Stress* 18, no. 1 (Feb. 2005): 69–77.

29. Van der Kolk, "The Body Keeps the Score"; Van der Kolk, "The Biological Response to Psychic Trauma."; Matsakis, *I Can't Get Over It.*

30. Ibid.

31. Blank, "Unconscious Flashback," 297.

32. Peter A. Ziarowsky and Daniel C. Broida, "Therapeutic Implications of Nightmares of Vietnam Combat Veterans," *The V.A. Practitioner* 1, no. 7 (July 1984): 63, 67–68.

33. R. Jaffe, "Dissociative Phenomenon in Former Concentration Camp Inmates," *International Journal of Psychoanalysis* 49 (1968): 310–12.; W. G. Niederland, "Clinical Observations on the Survivor Syndrome," *International Journal of Psychoanalysis* 49 (1968): 313–15; Judith Herman, *Trauma and Recovery: The Aftermath of Violence—from Domestic Abuse to Political Terror* (New York: Basic Books, 1992).

34. Blank, "Unconscious Flashback," 297.

35. Ibid.

36. Christine Courtois, *Healing the Incest Wound: Adult Survivors in Therapy* (New York: W. W. Norton, 1988); Mike Lew, *Victims No Longer: Men Recovering from Incest and Other Sexual Child Abuse* (New York: Nevramont Publishing, 1988).

37. B. A. van der Kolk, D. Pelcovitz, S. Roth, F. Mandel, A. McFarlane, and J. Herman, "Dissociation, Somatization and Affect Dysregulation: The Complexity of Adaptation to Trauma," *American Journal of Psychiatry* 153, no. 7 (July 1996): 83–93.

38. A. T. Beck, *The Diagnosis and Management of Depression* (Philadelphia: University of Pennsylvania Press, 1973).

39. Shephard, *War of Nerves;* van der Kolk et al., eds., *Traumatic Stress.*

40. Herman, *Trauma and Recovery;* van der Kolk et al., eds., *Traumatic Stress.*

41. Shephard, *War of Nerves;* Herman, *Trauma and Recovery.*

42. D. Burns, *Feeling Good: The New Mood Therapy* (New York: Signet Books, 1980).

43. Herman, *Trauma and Recovery.*

44. Kasia Kozlowska, "Healing the Disembodied Mind: Contemporary Models of Conversion Disorder January," *Harvard Review of Psychiatry* 13, no. 1 (Feb. 2005): 1–13.

45. "A Short History of PTSD."

46. Ibid.; E. Jones, R. H. Hodgins-Vermaas, B. McCartney, C. Everitt, D. Beech, L. P. Poynter, K. C. Palmer, S. C. Hyams, and S. C. Wessely, "Post-Combat Syndrome from the Boer War to the Gulf War: A Cluster Analysis of Their Nature and Attribution," *British Medical Journal* (2002): 320–23.

47. Morrison, *When Psychological Problems Mask Medical Disorders;* Herman, *Trauma and Recovery.*

48. Jones et al., "Post-Combat Syndrome."

Chapter 4. Emotional Distancing

1. Aphrodite Matsakis, "Trauma and Its Impact on Families," in *Handbook of Stress, Trauma, and the Family,* ed. D. Catherall (New York: Bruner Routledge, 2004), 15–32; B. A. van der Kolk, A. McFarlane, and L. Weisaeth, eds., *Traumatic Stress: The Effects of Overwhelming Experience on Mind, Body, and Society* (New York: Guilford Press, 1996).

2. E. R. Nijenhuis, J. Vanderlinden, and P. Spinhoven, "Animal Defensive Reactions as a Model for Trauma-Induced Dissociative Reactions," *Journal of Traumatic Stress* 11, no. 2 (April 1998): 243–60.

3. Ibid.

4. A. Ruscio, F. Weathers, L. A. King, and D. W. King, "Male War-Zone Veterans' Perceived Relationships with Their Children: The Importance of Emotional Numbing," *Journal of Traumatic Stress* 15, no. 5 (Oct. 2002): 351–58.

5. *The Best Years of Our Lives* (Fort Wayne, Ind.: Vet Center, 1985).

6. Matsakis, "Trauma and Its Impact on Families"; van der Kolk et al., eds., *Traumatic Stress;* Catherall, ed., *Handbook of Stress, Trauma, and the Family.*

7. John Cruden, "Vet Center Staff Members Analyze Homeless Situation," *Vet Center Voice* 8, no. 2 (1987): 3–7.

8. Matsakis, "Trauma and Its Impact on Families"; van der Kolk et al., eds., *Traumatic Stress.*

9. Douglas Scaturo and Peter Hayman, "The Impact of Combat Trauma Across the Family Life Cycle: Clinical Considerations," *Journal of Traumatic Stress* 5, no. 2 (April 1990): 273–88.

10. Danieli Yael,. "As Survivors Age," *PTSD Quarterly: National Center for Posttraumatic Stress Disorder* 4, no. 1 (Winter 1994): 1–7.

11. As cited in John Lagone, "The War That Has No Ending," *Discover,* June 1985, 45–54.

12. J. Gallager, D. Riggs, C. Byrne, and F. Weathers, "Female Partners' Estimations of Male Veterans' Combat-Related PTSD Severity," *Journal of Traumatic Stress* 11, no. 2 (April 1998): 367–75.

13. Susan Orsillo, R. Heimberg, H. Juster, and J. Garrett, "Social Phobia and PTSD in Vietnam Veterans," *Journal of Traumatic Stress* 9, no. 2 (April 1996): 235–52.

14. Ibid.

Chapter 5. Combat Trauma and Sex

1. Mary Crawford and Rhoda Unger, *Women and Gender: A Feminist Psychology,* 3rd ed. (Boston: McGraw Hill, 2000); William Masters and Virginia Johnson, *The Pleasure Bond: A New Look at Sexuality and Commitment* (Boston: Little, Brown, 1970); Clark E. Moustakas, *Loneliness* (Detroit: Spectrum Books, Prentice-Hall, 1961).

2. Masters and Johnson, *The Pleasure Bond,* 29.

3. Crawford and Unger, *Women and Gender.*

4. Ibid.

5. Edward M, Carroll, Drue B. Rueger, David W. Foy, and Clyde P. Donahoe, "Vietnam Combat Veterans with Posttraumatic Stress Disorder: An Analysis of Marital and Cohabitation Adjustment," *Journal of Abnormal Psychology* 94, no. 3 (1985): 329–37.

6. E. Letourneau, P. Schewe, and B. C. Frueh, "Preliminary Evaluation of Sexual Problems in Combat Veterans with PTSD," *Journal of Traumatic Stress* 10, no. 1 (Jan. 1997): 125–40; D. Riggs, C. Byrne, F. Weathers, and B. T. Litz, "The Quality of the Intimate Relationships of Male Vietnam Veterans: Problems Associated with PTSD," *Journal of Traumatic Stress* 11, no. 1 (Jan. 1998): 87–102; A. Egendorf, C. Kadushin, R. Laufer, G. Rothbard, and L. Sloan, *Legacies of Vietnam: Comparative Adjustment of Veterans and Their Peers,* vol. 3 (New York: New York Center for Policy Research, March 1981); T. Yaeger, R. Laufer, and M. Gallops. "Some Problems Associated with War Experience in Men of the Vietnam Generation," *Archives of General Psychiatry* 41 (1984): 327–33.

7. Carroll et al., "Vietnam Combat Veterans"; Letourneau et al., "Preliminary Evaluation of Sexual Problems."

8. Ben Shephard, *A War of Nerves: Soldiers and Psychiatrists in the Twentieth Century* (Cambridge: Harvard University Press, 2001).

9. Crawford and Unger, *Women and Gender;* Masters and Johnson, *The Pleasure Bond;* Sandra R. Leiblum and Lawrence A. Pervin, eds., *Principles and Practice of Sex Therapy* (New York: Guilford Press, 1980).

10. Wilhelm Reich, *The Function of the Orgasm: The Discovery of the Orgone* (New York: World Publishing, 1971), 138, 240.

11. Carol Vercozzi, "The War That Refused to Die: Vietnam Again," unpublished paper, Department of Communications, Hartford, Mass., 8.

12. Reich, *Function of the Orgasm,* 82, 298–99.

13. Ibid.

14. Masters and Johnson, *The Pleasure Bond;* W. H. Masters and V. E. Johnson, *Human Sexual Inadequacy* (Boston: Little, Brown, 1970); J. F. O'Connor, "Sexual Problems, Therapy and Prognostic Factors," in *Clinical Management of Sexual Disorders,* ed. J. K. Meyer (Baltimore: Williams and Wilkins, 1976); Leiblum and Pervin, *Principles and Practice of Sex Therapy;* Joel Fischer and Harvey Gochros, *Handbook of Behavior Therapy with Sexual Problems,* 2 vols. (New York: Pergamon Press, 1977).

15. Crawford and Unger, *Women and Gender;* Masters and Johnson, *Human Sexual Inadequacy.*

16. Lenore Walker, *The Battered Woman* (New York: Harper and Row, 1979).

Chapter 6. Anger, Grief, and Guilt

1. Jean Beckman, Allison Roodman, J. Barefoot, T. Haney, M. Helms, J. Fairbank, M. Hertzberg, and Harold Kudler, "Interpersonal and Self-Reported Hostility Among Combat Vets with and without PTSD," *Journal of Traumatic Stress* 9, no. 2 (1996): 123–32; R. Novaco and R. Chemtob, "Anger and Combat Related Posttraumatic Stress Disorder," *Journal of Traumatic Stress* 15, no. 2 (2002): 123–32; P. Calhoun, J. Beckham, M. Feldman, J. Barefoot, T. Haney, and H. Bosworth, "Partners' Ratings of Combat Veterans' Anger," *Journal of Traumatic Stress* 15, no. 2 (2002): 113–36.

2. Ibid.

3. E. Kübler-Ross, *On Death and Dying* (New York: Knopf, 1981).

4. E. Kubany, "A Cognitive Model of Guilt Typology in Combat-Related PTSD," *Journal of Traumatic Stress* 7, no. 31 (1994): 10–19.

5. Adapted from A. Matsakis, *Survivor Guilt: A Self-Help Guide* (Oakland, Calif.: New Harbinger Publications, 1999).

6. Kubany, "Cognitive Model of Guilt Typology."

7. A. Freud, *The Ego and the Mechanisms of Defense* (New York: International Universities Press, 1996).

8. S. Freud, 1961. "The Ego and the Id," in *The Standard Edition of the Complete Psychological Works of Sigmund Freud,* vol. 19, ed. and trans. J. Strachey (London: Hogarth, 1961).

9. Freud, *The Ego and the Mechanisms of Defense.*

10. P. Tournier, *The Best of Tournier* (New York: Harper and Row, 1977).

11. E. Kubany, "Thinking Errors, Faulty Conclusions, and Cognitive Therapy for Trauma-Related Guilt," *National Center for Post Traumatic Stress Disorder Quarterly* 7 (1997): 6–8.

12. H. Krystal, "Trauma: Consideration of Its Intensity and Chronicity," in *Psychic Traumatization,* ed. H. Krystal and W. Neiderland (Boston: Little, Brown, 1971), 11–28.

13. Kubany, "Cognitive Model of Guilt Typology."

14. Ibid.

15. Kubany, "Thinking Errors, Faulty Conclusions, and Cognitive Therapy."

16. Tournier, *The Best of Tournier.*

17. Ibid.

18. Ibid.

19. Ibid., 48.

20. R. Morin, "Hail to the Philanderers-in-Chief, Unconventional Wisdom," *Washington Post,* July 26, 1998, C5.

21. Tournier, *The Best of Tournier,* 47–48.

22. Kubany, "Thinking Errors, Faulty Conclusions, and Cognitive Therapy."

23. Kubany, "Cognitive Model of Guilt Typology"; Krystal, "Trauma"; L. C. Terr, "Time Sense Following Psychic Trauma: A Clinical Study of Ten Adults and Twenty Children," *American Journal of Orthopsychiatry* 53 (1983): 244–61.

24. Kubany, "Cognitive Model of Guilt Typology."

25. Kubany, "Thinking Errors, Faulty Conclusions, and Cognitive Therapy," 7.

26. Ibid.

27. Ibid., 6.

28. Tournier, *The Best of Tournier,* 69.

29. Ibid., 55.

30. B. A. van der Kolk, "The Body Keeps the Score: Approaches to the Psychobiology of PTSD," in *Traumatic Stress: The Effects of Overwhelming Experience on Mind, Body, and Society,* ed. B. A. van der Kolk, Alexander McFarlane, and Lars Weisaeth (New York: Guilford Press, 1996).

31. L. P. Solursh, "Combat Addiction: Overview of Implications in Symptoms Maintenance and Treatment Planning," *Journal of Traumatic Stress* 4, no. 2 (1989).

32. Ibid.; J. Shay, *Achilles in Vietnam: Combat Trauma and the Undoing of Character* (New York: Macmillan, 1994).

33. Shay, *Achilles in Vietnam.*

34. Ibid.

Chapter 7. Multiple Roles

1. A. Matsakis and B. Sigall, "Multiple-Role Women," *The Counseling Psychologist: Counseling Women III* 8 (1979): 26–27.

2. P. Calhoun, J. Beckman, and H. Bosworth, "Caregiver Burden and Psychological Distress in Partners of Veterans with Chronic Posttraumatic Stress Disorder," *Journal of Traumatic Stress* 15, no. 3 (2002): 205–12.

3. Matsakis and Sigall, "Multiple-Role Women," 26–27; Mary Crawford and Rhoda Unger, *Women and Gender: A Feminist Psychology,* 3rd ed. (Boston: McGraw Hill, 2000).

4. Matsakis and Sigall, "Multiple-Role Women," 26–27; Crawford and Unger, *Women and Gender.*

5. Crawford and Unger, *Women and Gender.*

Chapter 8. Battered Women

1. Lenore Walker, *The Battered Woman* (New York: Harper and Row, 1979).

2. H. Orcutt, L. King, and D. King, "Male-Perpetrated Violence among Vietnam Veteran Couples: Relationship with Veteran's Early Life Characteristics, Trauma History, and PTSD Symptomatology," *Journal of Traumatic Stress* 16, no. 4 (2003): 381–90; J. Schafer, R. Caetano, and C. L. Clark, "Rates of Intimate Partner Violence in the United States," *American Journal of Public Health* 88 (1998): 1702–4; Miki Paul, "Clinical Implications in Healing from Domestic Violence: A Case Study," *American Psychologist* 56, no. 8 (2004): 807–17; Murray A. Strauss, Richard J. Gelles, and Suzanne K. Steinmetz, *Behind Closed Doors: Violence in the American Family* (New York: Anchor Books, 1970); Roger Langely and Richard Levy, *Wife Beating: The Silent Crisis* (New York: E. P. Dutton, 1977); Murray Strauss, "Wife Beating: How Common and Why?" *Victimology* 2, nos. 3–4 (1978): 443–58; Margaret Jensvold, "The Female Brain: The Intersection of Traumatic Experience and Hormonal Events in the Lives of Women," presentation, Trauma, Loss and Dissociation: The Foundation of 21st-Century Traumatology meeting, Alexandria, Va., 1995.

3. Evan Stark and Anne Flitcraft, "Medical Therapy as Repression: The Case of the Battered Woman," *Health and Medicine* (Summer/Fall 1979); Programs for Battered Women: Data Summary Report, Minnesota Dept. of Corrections, St. Paul, Minn., 1982; Evan Stark, Anne Flitcraft, and William Frazier, "Medicine and Patriarchal Violence: The Social Construction of a 'Private' Event," *International Journal of Health Services* 9, no. 3 (1979).

4. Walker, *Battered Woman;* Marie Borland, ed., *Violence in the Family* (Atlantic Highlands: Manchester University Press, 1976); Richard T. Gelles, *The Violent Home* (London: Sage Publications, 1972); Del Martin, *Battered Wives* (New York: Pocket Books, 1976).

5. Paul, "Clinical Indications"; Strauss et al., *Behind Closed Doors;* Strauss, "Wife Beating"; Walker, *Battered Woman;* Langely and Levy, *Wife Beating;* Gelles, *Violent Home;* Martin, *Battered Wives;* "Analysis of Official Army Reports of Spouse Abuse: 1982," Army Family Advocacy Program, U.S. Army Community and Family Support Center, Alexandria, Va.; Beryce W. MacLennan, U.S. General Accounting Office, "Problems in Estimating the Nature and Extent of Family Violence in the Armed Forces," *Research Report: National Security Management,* National Defense University, Washington, D.C., April 1985.

6. L. Vogel and L. Marshall, "PTSD Symptoms and Partner Abuse: Low Income Women at Risk," *Journal of Traumatic Stress* 14, no. 3 (July 2001): 569–84.

7. Ibid.

8. Ibid.

9. C. A. Byrne and D. S. Riggs, "The Cycle of Trauma: Relationship Aggression in Vietnam Veterans with Symptoms of Posttraumatic Stress Disorder," *Violence and Victims* 11 (1996): 213–25; E. M. Carroll, D. B. Rueger, D. W. Foy, and C. O. Donahoe, "Vietnam Combat Veterans with Posttraumatic Stress Disorder: Analysis of Marital and Cohabiting Adjustment," *Journal of Abnormal Psychology* 94 (1985): 329–37.

10. Walker, *Battered Woman.*

11. David France, "A Nation's Shame: Domestic Violence and Older Adults," *AARP* (Jan./Feb. 2005): 72–77.

12. R. Novaco and C. Chemtob, "Anger and Combat-Related Posttraumatic Stress Dis-

order," *Journal of Traumatic Stress* 15, no. 2 (April 2002): 123–32; V. Savarese, M. Suvak, L. A. King, and D. W. King, "Relationships Among Alcohol Use, Hyperarousal, and Marital Abuse and Violence in Vietnam Veterans," *Journal of Traumatic Stress* 14, no. 4 (Oct. 2001): 717–32.

13. Novaco and Chemtob, "Anger and Combat-Related Posttraumatic Stress Disorder."

14. Savarese et al., "Relationships among Alcohol Use"; L. A. King and D. W. King, "Male-Perpetrated Domestic Violence: Testing a Series of Multifactorial Family Models," Final Report to the National Institute of Justice, Grant 98-WT-VX-OC31 (2000).

15. K. Leonard and H. Blane, "Alcohol and Marital Aggression in a National Sample of Young Men," *Journal of Interpersonal Violence* 7 (1992): 19–30; D. Murdoch, R. Pihl, and D. Ross, "Alcohol and Crimes of Violence: Present Issues, *The International Journal of the Addictions* 25 (1990): 1065–81.

16. Murdoch et al., "Alcohol and Crimes of Violence"; Savarese et al., "Relationships among Alcohol Use"; King and King, "Male-Perpetrated Domestic Violence."

17. Savarese et al., "Relationships among Alcohol Use."

18. Walker, *Battered Woman;* W. Arkin and L. Dobrosfsky, "Military Socialization and Masculinity," *Journal of Social Issues* 34 (1978): 150–67; Rick Ritter and Bobbie De Pew, "Masculinity and the Vietnam Vet," Fort Wayne Vet Center, Fort Wayne, Ind.

19. C. Courtois, *Healing the Incest Wound: Adult Survivors in Therapy* (New York: Norton, 1988); Orcutt et al., "Male-Perpetrated Violence"; King and King, "Male-Perpetrated Domestic Violence."

20. D. Wolfe, P. Jaffe, S. Wilson, and L. Zak, "Children of Battered Women: The Relation of Child Behavior to Family Violence and Maternal Stress," *Journal of Consulting and Clinical Psychology* 53, no. 5 (1985): 657–65.

21. Mark Kaufki, as cited in John Cruden, "Anger Dominates Hostile, Inappropriate Social Responses," *Vet Center Voice* 7, no. 10 (1986); J. Shay, *Achilles in Vietnam: Combat Trauma and the Undoing of Character* (New York: Macmillan, 1994); Aphrodite Matsakis, *I Can't Get Over It—A Handbook for Trauma Survivors* (Oakland, Calif.: New Harbinger Publications, 1994).

Chapter 9. Women Veterans

1. Barbara Wilson, "Women in the Military: Facts and Figures about Women's Role in the Armed Forces" (1996), http://womensissues.about.com/library/weekly/aa092801a.html; \Barbara Wilson, "Women in Combat—21st Century" (1996), http://userpages.aug.com/captbarb/combat21.html.

2. See Barbara Wilson's articles at http://userpages.aug.com/captbarb, including "Myths, Fallacies, Falderol and Idiotic Rumors about Military Women: Debunking Rumors, Fallacies, Legends, Gossip, Fables, Nonsense," "Women Soldiers in the American Revolutionary War: Amazing Women in War and Peace," "Women Were There: The Wars of 1912 and 1846 and the Spanish American War," "Women Were There: Women in the Civil War," "WWI: Thirty Thousand Women Were There," "Women in the Korean Conflict," "Vietnam—Southeast Asia, 1964–1973," "Operation Urgent Fury and Operation Just Cause," "Operations Desert Shield/ Desert Storm," and "Women in Combat—21st Century."

3. Wilson, "Women in the Military: Facts and Figures," 1.

4. Ibid.

5. Ibid.; Wilson, "Operation Urgent Fury and Operation Just Cause"; Barbara Wilson, "Women in the National Guard" and "Operations Desert Shield/Desert Storm," both at http://userpages.aug.com/captbarb.

6. Barbara Wilson, "The Military Service Academies" (1996), http://userpages.aug.com/captbarb/academies.html.

7. Wilson, "Women in Combat: Why Not?" (1996), http://userpages.aug.com/captbarb/

combat.html; Wilson, "Women in the Military: Facts and Figures," and "Operation Urgent Fury and Operation Just Cause"; http://www.census.gov/compendia/statab/national_security_veterans_affairs.

8. Wilson, "Women in the National Guard" and "Operations Desert Shield/Desert Storm."

9. Wilson, "Women in Combat—21st Century."

10. Ibid..

11. Wilson, "Women Soldiers in the American Revolutionary War," "Women in the Korean Conflict," and "Women Were There: Women in the Civil War."

12. Wilson, "Vietnam—Southeast Asia, 1964–1973."

13. Barbara Wilson, "Women in World War II—They Also Served—WASP" (1996), http://userpages.aug.com/captbarb/femvetsalso.html.

14. S. Freedman, N. Gluck, R. Tuval-Mashiach, D. Brandes, T. Peri, and A. Shalev, "Gender Differences in Response to Traumatic Events: A Prospective Study," *Journal of Traumatic Stress* 15, no. 5 (2002): 407–13.

15. Susan Faludi, *Backlash: The Undeclared War Against American Women* (New York: Doubleday/Anchor Books, 1991); M. Crawford and R. Unger, *Women and Gender: A Feminist Psychology*, 3rd ed. (New York: McGraw Hill, 2000); R. Sandecki, "Women Veterans," in *Post-Traumatic Stress Disorders: A Handbook for Clinicians*, ed. T. Williams (Cincinnati, Ohio: Disabled American Veterans, 1987), 160–61.

16. P. Chesler, "The Amazon Legacy," in *The Politics of Women's Spirituality*, ed. C. Spretnak (New York: Doubleday/Anchor Books, 1982), 103.

17. Crawford and Unger, *Women and Gender*.

18. Ibid.

19. Sandecki, "Women Veterans," 161.

20. Crawford and Unger, *Women and Gender*; Wilson, "Myths, Fallacies, Falderol and Idiotic Rumors."

21. Crawford and Unger, *Women and Gender*; Wilson, "Women in the Military: Facts and Figures."

22. H. Orcutt, D. Erickson, and J. Wolfe, "The Course of PTSD Symptoms Among Gulf War Veterans: A Growth Mixture Modeling Approach," *Journal of Traumatic Stress Studies* 17, no. 3 (June 2004): 195–202; R. H. Stretch, D. H. Marlowe, K. M. Wright, P. D. Bliese, K. H. Knudson, and C. H. Hoover, "Posttraumatic Stress Disorder Symptoms among Gulf War Veterans," *Military Medicine* 161 (1996): 407–10.

23. Crawford and Unger, *Women and Gender*.

24. Ibid.

25. Ibid.

26. Sandecki, "Women Veterans," 162.

27. Crawford and Unger, *Women and Gender*.

28. Sandecki, "Women Veterans."

29. Wilson, "Myths, Fallacies, Falderol and Idiotic Rumors."

30. Ibid., 2.

31. Crawford and Unger, *Women and Gender*; J. Shay, *Odysseus in America: Combat Trauma and the Trials of Homecoming* (New York: Scribner's, 2002); Wilson, "Myths, Fallacies, Falderol and Idiotic Rumors."

32. Wilson, "Myths, Fallacies, Falderol and Idiotic Rumors."

33. Freedman et al., "Gender Differences in Response to Traumatic Events," 407–13; Orcutt et al., "The Course of PTSD Symptoms," 195–202; R. Kimberling, G. Clum, and J. Wolfe, "Relationship among Trauma Exposure, Chronic Posttraumatic Stress Disorder Symptoms, and Self-Reported Health in Women: Replication and Extension," *Journal of Traumatic Stress* 13, no. 1 (2000): 115–28; A. Wagner, J. Wolfe, A. Rotnitsky, S. Proctor, and E. Erickson, "An In-

vestigation of the Impact of Posttraumatic Stress Disorder on Physical Health," *Journal of Traumatic Stress* 13, no. 1 (2002): 41–55.

34. Freedman et al., "Gender Differences in Response to Traumatic Events."

35. Crawford and Unger, *Women and Gender.*

36. Sandecki, "Women Veterans."

37. "Examining Trauma in Relation to Health, Healthcare, and Gender," recording of Thirteenth Annual Meeting, International Society for Traumatic Stress Studies, Montreal, 1997, tape 2; B. A. van der Kolk, S. Roth, D. Pelcovitz, and S. Sunday, "Disorders of Extreme Stress: The Empirical Foundation of a Complex Adaptation to Trauma," *Journal of Traumatic Stress Studies* 18, no. 5 (Oct. 2005): 389–99; L. L. Merrill, C. E. Newell, M. P. Milner, M. P. Koss, L. K. Hervig, S. R. Gold et al., "Prevalence of Paramilitary Adult Sexual Victimization and Aggression in a Navy Recruit Sample," *Military Medicine* 163 (1998): 209–12; S. M. Frayne, K. M. Skinner, L. M. Sullivan, T. O. Tripp, C. S. Hankin, N. R. Kressin, et al., "Medical Profile of Women Veteran's Administration Outpatient Who Report a History of Sexual Assault Occurring While in the Military," *Journal of Women's Health and Gender Based Medicine* 8 (1999): 835–45.

38. Wilson, "Myths, Fallacies, Falderol and Idiotic Rumors."

39. "Examining Trauma in Relation to Health, Healthcare and Gender."

40. Veterans Health Programs Extension Act of 1994 H.R. 3313 (House Resolution), http://www.congress.gov/cgi-lis/bdquery/D?d103:1:./temp/~bdybzM:@@@SD&summ2=m&: dbs . . . ; Department of Veterans Affairs Real Property and Facilities Management Improvement Act of 2004, H.R. (House Resolution) 3936.

41. "Sexual Trauma: Diagnosis, Treatment and Related Issues," videotape, Department of Veterans Affairs National Training Program, produced by the National Media Development Center for Office of Public Health and Environmental Hazards (Washington, D.C.: VA Headquarters, 1993).

42. P. Palmieri and L. Fitzgerald, "Confirmatory Factor Analysis of Posttraumatic Stress Symptoms in Sexually Harassed Women," *Journal of Traumatic Stress* 18, no. 6 (2005): 657–66.

43. V. Magley, C. Waldo, F. Drasgow, and L. Fitzgerald, "The Impact of Sexual Harassment on Military Personnel: Is It the Same for Men and Women?" www.questia.com/PM.qst?a=o&d=77001841; Herman, *Trauma and Recovery.*

44. C. Hankin, K. Skinner, L. Sullivan, D. Miller, S. Frayne, and T. Tripp, "Prevalence of Depressive and Alcohol Abuse Symptoms Among Women VA Outpatients Who Report Experiencing Sexual Assault While in the Military," *Journal of Traumatic Stress* 12, no. 4 (1999): 601–12; Merrill et al., "Prevalence of Paramilitary Adult Sexual Victimization."

45. Hankin et al., "Prevalence of Depressive and Alcohol Abuse Symptoms"; B. S. Coyle, D. L. Woman, and A. S. Van Horn, "The Prevalence of Physical and Sexual Abuse in Women Veterans Seeking Care at a Veterans Administration Medical Center," *Military Medicine* 161 (1996): 588–93; M. Murdoch and K. L. Nichol, "Women Veterans' Experiences with Domestic Violence and with Sexual Harassment While in the Military," *Archives of Family Medicine* 4 (1995): 411–18; "Sexual Trauma: Diagnosis, Treatment and Related Issues"; "Examining Trauma in Relation to Health, Healthcare and Gender."

46. "Sexual Trauma: Diagnosis, Treatment and Related Issues"; Aphrodite Matsakis, *Rape Recovery Handbook* (Oakland, Calif.: New Harbinger Publications, 2003).

47. Matsakis, *Rape Recovery Handbook.*

48. Ibid.

49. Ibid.

50. "Sexual Trauma: Diagnosis, Treatment and Related Issues"; D. G. Kilpatrick, C. N. Edmunds, and A. K. Seymour, *Rape in America: A Report to the Nation* (Arlington, Va.: National Victim Center, 1992).

51. Ibid.; Matsakis, *Rape Recovery Handbook.*

52. Sarah Ullman and Henrietta H. Filipas, "Predictors of PTSD Symptom Severity and Social Reactions in Sexual Assault Victims," *Journal of Traumatic Stress* 14, no. 2 (2001): 369–89.

53. Matsakis, *Rape Recovery Handbook*.

54. "Sexual Trauma: Diagnosis, Treatment and Related Issues"; Kilpatrick, Edmunds, and Seymour, *Rape in America*.

55. Matsakis, *Rape Recovery Handbook*.

56. Herman, *Trauma and Recovery;* Matsakis, *Rape Recovery Handbook*.

57. L. A. King and D. W. King, "Traumatic Stress in Female Veterans: A National Center for PTSD Fact Sheet, U.S. Department of Veterans Affairs" (2005), http://www.neptsd.va.gov/facts/veterans/fs_women/vets.html.

58. Sandecki, "Women Veterans," 159–69.

59. Ibid., 159, 161; Barbara Wilson, "Vietnam—Southeast Asia, 1964–1973" (1996), http://userpages.aug.com/captbarb/femvetsnam.html.

Chapter 10. Military Couples

1. "Married to the Military—Dual Military Couples," U.S. military blog from Rod Powers, Your Guide to the U.S. Military, Aug. 30, 2004, http://usmilitary.about.com/b/a/108960.htm.

2. Aphrodite Matsakis, *Vietnam Wives: Facing the Challenges of Life with Veterans Suffering Post Traumatic Stress,* 2nd ed. (Baltimore, Md.: Sidran Institute Press, 1996).

3. Barbara Wilson, "Women in the Military: Facts and Figures about Women's Role in the Armed Forces" (1996), http://womensissues.about.com/library/weekly/aa092801a.htm.

4. A. Witchel, "Confessions of a Military Wife," *New York Times Magazine* 6 (2005): 62–67.

5. J. Morris, "Dual Military Couples," *NCO Journal* (2006), http://usmilitary.about.com/od/army/a/dualmilitary.htm.

6. Aphrodite Matsakis, "Counseling Dual Trauma Couples," in *Handbook of Post-Traumatic Therapy,* ed. M. B. Williams and J. Somner (Westport, Conn.: Greenwood Publishing, 1994); C. Courtois, *Healing the Incest Wound: Adult Survivors in Therapy* (New York: Norton, 1988).

7. Courtois, *Healing the Incest Wound*.

Chapter 11. Children in Veteran Families

1. Anonymous, "Kid of a Vet," Handout #17, Vet Center, Fort Wayne, Ind., 1986, 1–2.

2. J. Albeck, M. Armsworth, N. Auerhaln, C. Figley, H. Kudler, D. Lamb, K. Nader, L. Pearlman, K. James, and L. Fitzgerald, "The Intergenerational Effects of Trauma," Trauma, Memory and Dissociation, International Society for Traumatic Stress Studies, Annual Convention, Chicago, November 1994, audiotapes 12, 13, 14, and 15.

3. Ibid.

4. Joseph Albeck, "Intergenerational Consequences of Trauma: Reframing Traps in Treatment Theory—A Second Generation Perspective," *Handbook of Post-Traumatic Therapy,* ed. Mary Beth Williams and John F. Summer Jr. (Westport, Conn.: Greenwood Press, 1994): 106–28.

5. Phil G. Shovar, "Medical Professionals," in *Post-Traumatic Stress Disorders: A Handbook for Clinicians,* ed. T. M. Williams (Cincinnati, Ohio: Disabled American Veterans, 1987), 145–59.

6. Ibid., 145, 146.

7. Candice Williams and T. Williams, "Family Therapy for Vietnam Veterans," in *The Trauma of War: Stress and Recovery in Vietnam Veterans,* ed. S. Sonnenberg, S. Blank, and J. Talbott (Washington, D.C.: American Psychiatric Press, 1985), 195–209.

8. Christine Reppucci and Thomas James, *Intervention with Children of Vietnam Veterans* (Charlottesville,Va.: Community Outreach to Vietnam Era Returnees [COVER], 1988), 1.

9. R. Rosenheck and P. Nathan, "Secondary Traumatization in the Children of Vietnam Veterans with Posttraumatic Stress Disorder," *Hospital and Community Psychiatry* 36, no. 5 (May 1985): 538–39.

10. Ellen Salom,Vet Center North, personal communication, May 15, 1987.

11. Melanie Suhr, "Trauma in Pediatric Populations," *Advanced Psychosomatic Medicine* 16 (1986): 31–47; S. Paulauska, C. Ottaviano, and S. Campbell, "Children of Divorce: Some Clinical Issues," Department of Psychology, Clinical Psychology Center, University of Pittsburgh, Pittsburgh, Pa.: Symposium presented at the Fifth Annual National Conference on Feminist Psychology, Pittsburgh, March 2–5, 1978.

12. Albeck et al., "Intergenerational Effects of Trauma"; D. Catherall, ed., *Handbook of Stress, Trauma, and the Family* (New York: Brunner-Routledge, 2004).

13. B. A. van der Kolk, "Post-Traumatic Stress Disorder," in *Post-Traumatic Stress Disorder: Psychological and Biological Sequelae* (Washington, D.C.: American Psychiatric Press, 1984); Joel L. Silverman, "Post-Traumatic Stress Disorder," *Advanced Psychosomatic Medicine* 16 (1986): 115–40; Robert Rosenheck, "Impact of Posttraumatic Stress Disorder of World War II on the Next Generation," *Journal of Nervous and Mental Disease* 174, no. 6 (June 1986): 319–27; John J. Sigal, "Effects of Paternal Exposure to Prolonged Stress on the Mental Health of the Spouse and Children," *Canadian Psychiatric Association Journal* 21 (1976): 169–72; Harvey Barocas and Carol Barocas, "Manifestations of Concentration Camp Effects on the Second Generation," *American Journal of Psychiatry* 130, no. 7 (July 1973): 820–21; John Sigal and Vivian Rakoff, "Concentration Camp Survival, A Pilot Study of Effects on the Second Generation," *Canadian Psychiatric Association Journal* 16 (1971): 393–97; J. T. Freyberg, "Difficulties in Separation and Individuation as Experienced by Offspring of Nazi Holocaust Survivors," *American Journal of Orthopsychiatry* 50 (1980): 87–95.

14. Sarah Haley, "The Vietnam Veteran and His Preschool Child: Child Rearing as a Delayed Stress in Combat Vets," *Journal of Contemporary Psychotherapy* 14, no. 1 (Spring/Summer 1984): 114–21.

15. Sigal and Rakoff, "Concentration Camp Survival," 395.

16. Sarah Haley, "Treatment Implications of Post-Combat Stress Response Syndrome for Mental Health Professionals," in *Stress Disorders Among Vietnam Veterans: Theory, Research and Treatment,* ed. Charles Figley (New York: Brunner-Mazel, 1978), 254–64.

17. B. A. van der Kolk, H. Boyd, J. Krystal, et al., "PTSD as a Biologically Based Disorder: Implications of the Animal Model of Inescapable Stress," 123–34, in I. Liberzon, J. L. Abelson, S. B. Flagel, J. Raz, and E. A. Young, "Neuroendocrine and Psychophysiological Responses in PTSD: A Symptom Provocation Study," *Neuropsychopharmacology* 2 (1990): 40–50.

18. Shovar, "Medical Professionals," 153.

19. T. Williams, "Therapeutic Alliance and Goal Setting in the Treatment of the Vietnam Veteran," in *Post-Traumatic Stress Disorders of the Vietnam Veteran* (Cincinnati, Ohio: Disabled American Veterans, 1980), 25–34.

20. D. Harrington and J. Jay, "Beyond the Family: Value Issues in the Treatment of Vietnam Veterans," *Family Therapy Networker* 6, no. 3 (May/June 1982): 13–15, 44–45.

21. Haley, "The Vietnam Veteran and His Preschool Child," 115.

22. Ibid.

23. H. Glover, "Guilt and Aggression in Vietnam Veterans," *American Journal of Social Psychiatry* 1 (Winter 1985): 15–18.

24. Haley, "The Vietnam Veteran and His Preschool Child," 116.

25. Salom, personal communication, May 15, 1987.

26. Rosenheck and Nathan, "Secondary Traumatization in the Children of Vietnam Veterans"; Rosenheck, "Impact of Posttraumatic Stress Disorder"; Silverman, "Post-Traumatic

Stress Disorder"; Sigal, "Effects of Paternal Exposure to Prolonged Stress"; H. Epstein, *Children of the Holocaust* (New York: Putnam, 1979).

27. Rosenheck and Nathan, "Secondary Traumatization in the Children of Vietnam Veterans"; Rosenheck, "Impact of Posttraumatic Stress Disorder"; Silverman, "Post-Traumatic Stress Disorder"; Sigal, "Effects of Paternal Exposure to Prolonged Stress"; Epstein, *Children of the Holocaust*.

28. Rosenheck and Nathan, "Secondary Traumatization in the Children of Vietnam Veterans," 538.

29. Ibid.; Rosenheck, "Impact of Posttraumatic Stress Disorder."

30. Dani Rowland-Klein, "The Transmission of Trauma Across Generations: Identification with Parental Trauma in Children of Holocaust Survivors," in *Handbook of Stress, Trauma, and the Family,* ed. Catherall, 117–38; Silverman, "Post-Traumatic Stress Disorder"; Barocas and Barocas, "Manifestations of Concentration Camp Effects."

31. Alexandra Teguis, presentation at the Vietnam Experience, conference sponsored by the Springfield, Va., Vet Center, Disabled American Veterans, Washington, D.C., April 3–4, 1987; Robert Rosenheck, "The Role of Family Therapy in Treatment of PTSD," unpublished paper, presented at "Diagnosis and Management of Post-Traumatic Stress Disorders in the V.A.," V.A. Mid-Atlantic Regional Medical Education Center, Baltimore, Md., Aug. 21, 1985.

32. C. T. Wang and D. Dark, *Current Trends in Child Abuse Reporting and Fatalities: The Results of the 1997 Annual Fifty-State Survey* (Chicago: National Committee to Prevent Child Abuse, 1997), Catherall, ed., *Handbook of Stress, Trauma, and the Family,* Susan Limber, "Dante Cicchetti—An Odyssey of Discovery: Lessons Learned Through Three Decades of Research on Child Maltreatment," *Journal of the American Psychological Association* 59, no. 8 (Nov. 2004): 728–41; Murray Strauss, Richard Gelles, and Suzanne Steinmetz, *Behind Closed Doors: Violence in the American Family* (Garden City, N.Y.: Anchor Press, 1980).

33. Murray Strauss, "Ordinary Violence, Child Abuse, and Wife Beating: What Do They Have in Common?" in *The Dark Side of Families,* ed. David Finkelhor, R. J. Gelles, G. Hotaling, and M. Strauss (Beverly Hills, Calif.: Sage Publications, 1983); Lenore Walker, *The Battered Woman* (New York: Harper and Row, 1979).

34. Catherall, ed., *Handbook of Stress, Trauma, and the Family;* Limber, "Dante Cicchetti."

35. Walker, *Battered Woman.*

36. Ibid., 37; Liberzon et al., "Neuroendocrine and Psychophysiological Responses"; Silverman, "Post-Traumatic Stress Disorder"; Rosenheck, "Impact of Posttraumatic Stress Disorder"; Barocas and Barocas, "Manifestations of Concentration Camp Effects"; Sigal, "Effects of Paternal Exposure to Prolonged Stress"; Sigal and Rakoff, "Concentration Camp Survival."

37. Catherall, ed., *Handbook of Stress, Trauma, and the Family;* Limber, "Dante Cicchetti"; Lenore Walker, "Children as Victims: Prostitution and Pornography: Children as Victims of Violence," Battered Women's Research Center, Colorado Women's College, symposium presented at the American Psychological Association, New York City, September 1979.

38. Catherall, ed., *Handbook of Stress, Trauma, and the Family;* Limber, "Dante Cicchetti"; Walker, "Children as Victims."

39. Ibid.

40. J. Spinazzola, M. Blaustein, and B. A. van der Kolk, "Posttraumatic Stress Disorder Treatment Outcome Research: The Study of Unrepresentative Samples," *Journal of Traumatic Stress* 18, no. 5 (Oct. 2005): 425–36.

41. L. N. Robins, *The Vietnam Drug User Returns,* Special Action Office Monograph, Series A, no. 2 (Washington, D.C.: U S. Government Printing Office, 1974); L. N. Robins, "Veterans' Drug Use Three Years After Vietnam," Washington University School of Medicine, Department of Psychiatry, St. Louis, 1974; E. P. Nace, C. P. O'Brien, I. Mintz et al., "Adjustment among Vietnam Veteran Drug Users Two Years Post Service," in *Stress Disorders Among Vietnam Veterans: Theory, Research, and Treatment,* ed. C. R. Figley (New York: Brunner/Mazel, 1978),

71–128; J. A. O'Donnell, H. J. H.Voss, and R. R. Clayton. *Young Men and Drugs—A Nationwide Survey* (Washington, D.C.: U.S. Government Printing Office, 1976); M. B. Ray, "The Cycle of Abstinence and Relapse among Heroin Addicts," *Social Problems* (1961): 132–40; D. Waldorf, *Careers in Dope* (Englewood Cliffs, N.J.: Prentice-Hall, 1973).

42. Ann Corbett, "The Alcoholics' Legacy," *Washington Post,* April 6, 1987, C5.

43. Rosenheck, "Impact of Posttraumatic Stress Disorder," 322; Rosenheck, "The Role of Family Therapy in Treatment of PTSD."

44. Albeck et al., "Intergenerational Effects of Trauma."

45. Ibid.

46. Salom, personal communication, May 15, 1987.

Chapter 12. Suicide and the Veteran Family

1. Joel Paris, "Half in Love with Easeful Death: The Meaning of Chronic Suicidality in Borderline Personality Disorder," *Harvard Review of Psychiatry* 12, no. 1 (Jan./Feb. 2004): 42–48; C. Ernst and J. Goldberg, "Antisuicide Properties of Psychotropic Drugs: A Critical Review," *Harvard Review of Psychiatry* 12, no. 1 (Jan./Feb. 2004):14–40; D. Reynolds, R. Kalish, and N. Farberow, "A Cross Ethnic Study of Suicide Attitudes and Expectations in the U.S.," in *Suicide in Different Cultures,* ed. Norman Farberow (Baltimore: University Park Press, 1975), 35–50; V. M. Victoroff, *The Suicidal Patient: Recognition, Intervention, Management* (Oradell, N.J.: Medical Economics Books, 1983); A. L. Berman, "Suicide," Staff Development Seminar, Counseling Center, University of Maryland, College Park, Md., April 17, 1987.

2. D. K. Reynolds and N. L. Farberow, *Suicide Inside and Out* (Berkeley: University of California Press, 1976).

3. Victoroff, *Suicidal Patient.*

4. Paris, "Half in Love with Easeful Death"; C. W. Smith and E. T. Bope, "The Suicidal Patient: The Primary-Care Physician's Role in Evaluation and Treatment," *Postgraduate Medicine* 79, no. 8 (June 1986): 195–99, 202; D. K. Reynolds and N. L Farberow, *Endangered Hope—Experiences in Psychiatric Aftercare Facilities* (Berkeley: University of California Press, 1977); C. Carney and A. Salganik, "Teenage Suicide: The Despair, the Doubts, and the Haunting 'Why?'" *Washington Post,* March 24, 1982; Victoroff, *Suicidal Patient;* Ernst and Goldberg, "Antisuicide Properties of Psychotropic Drugs"; Berman, "Suicide."

5. S. Bhatia, M. Khan, and A. Sharma, "Suicide Risk: Evaluation and Management," *American Family Physician* 34, no. 3 (Sept. 1986): 167–74; J. C. Ballenger, J. R. T. Davidson, Y. Lecrubier, D. M. Nutt, E. B. Foa, R. C. Kessler et al., "Consensus Statement on Posttraumatic Stress Disorder from the International Consensus Group on Depression and Anxiety," *Journal of Clinical Psychiatry* 81 (2000): 60–66; J. Davidson, D. Hughes, D. Blazer, and L. George, "Posttraumatic Stress Disorder in the Community: An Epidemiological Study," *Psychological Medicine* 21 (1991): 713–21; Theola Labbe, "Suicides in Iraq, Questions at Home: Pentagon Tight-Lipped as Self-Inflicted Deaths Mount in Military," *Washington Post,* Feb. 19, 2004, A01; Vernon Loeb, "Military Cites Elevated Rate of Suicide," *World News,* Jan. 15, 2004, A14.; Centers for Disease Control and Prevention Weekly, "Suicide Prevention Among Active Duty Air Force Personnel – United States, 1990–1999," *Morbidity and Mortality Weekly Report (MMWR)* 48, no. 46 (Nov. 26, 1999): 1053–57; Jeffrey Stein, "Coming Home," *Progressive* 45, no. 10 (April 1981): 10–16; N. Hearst, T. Newman, and S. Hulley, "Delayed Effects of the Military Draft on Mortality," *New England Journal of Medicine* 314, no. 10 (March 1986): 620–24; Centers for Disease Control, "Vietnam Experience Study: Post-service Mortality Among Vietnam Veterans," *Journal of the American Medical Association* 257, no. 6 (Feb. 13, 1987): 790–95; Daniel A. Polluck, "PTSD and the Risk of Suicide," *American Journal of Psychiatry* 140, no. 1 (Jan. 1992): 142–43; Norman Farberow, Kang Han, and Tim Bullman, "Combat Experience and Post-Service Psychosocial Sta-

tus as Predictors of Suicide in Vietnam Veterans," *Journal of Nervous and Mental Disease* 178, no. 1 (Jan. 1990): 32–37; Daniel A. Polluck, Philip Rhodes, Coleen Boyle, Pierre Decoufle, et al., "Estimating the Number of Suicides among Vietnam Veterans," *American Journal of Psychiatry* 147, no. 6 (June 1990): 772–76.

6. Martin E. Wolfgang, "Husband-Wife Homicides," *Journal of Social Therapy* (1956): 263–71.

7. Ibid.

8. M. E. Wolfgang, "Who Kills Whom?" *Psychology Today* 3 (1969): 55, 56, 72, 74.

9. Berman, "Suicide"; Victoroff, *Suicidal Patient;* Smith and Bope, "Suicidal Patient"; Bhatia et al., "Suicide Risk"; M. Iga and K. Tatai, "Characteristics of Suicides and Attitudes toward Suicide in Japan," in *Suicide in Different Cultures,* ed. Farberow, 255–80; Herbert Hendlin and Anne Haas, "Suicide and Guilt as Manifestations of PTSD in Vietnam Combat Veterans," *American Journal of Psychiatry* 148, no. 5 (May 1991): 586–91; Herbert Hendlin, "PTSD and the Risk of Suicide: Reply," *American Journal of Psychiatry* 149, no. 1 (Jan. 1991): 143.

10. Eric Gerdemen, "PTSD and the Vietnam Veteran," unpublished paper, Vet Center Program, Region II, Baltimore, Md.

11. Berman, "Suicide"; Victoroff, *Suicidal Patient;* Bhatia et al., "Suicide Risk"; Smith and Bope, "Suicidal Patient"; Paris, "Half in Love with Easeful Death"; Ernst and Goldberg, "Antisuicide Properties of Psychotropic Drugs"; Ben Schutz, "The Suicidal Patient," Staff Development Seminar, Veterans Administration Medical Center, Washington, D.C., May 12, 1982.

12. Berman, "Suicide"; David D. Burns, *Feeling Good: The New Mood Therapy* (New York: New American Library, 1980); Schutz, "The Suicidal Patient."

13. Berman, "Suicide"; Schutz, "The Suicidal Patient."

14. Ibid.

15. Kathy Fisher, "Sexual Abuse Victims Suffer into Adulthood," *APA Monitor* 18, no. 6 (June 1987); Lydia Savina, *Help for the Battered Woman* (South Plainfield, N.J.: Bridge Publishing, 1987).

Chapter 13. The Hope of Therapy

1. John Yost, "The Psychopharmacologic Treatment of the Delayed Stress Syndrome in Vietnam Veterans," in *Post-Traumatic Stress Disorders of the Vietnam Veteran,* ed. T. Williams (Cincinnati, Ohio: Disabled American Veterans, 1980): 125–33; John Yost, "The Psychopharmacologic Management of Post-Traumatic Stress Disorder (PTSD) in Vietnam Veterans and in Civilian Situations," in *Post Traumatic Stress Disorders: A Handbook for Clinicians,* ed. T. Williams (Cincinnati, Ohio: Disabled American Veterans, 1987), 93–102; Merrill Lipton and W. Shaffer, "PTSD in the Older Veteran," *Military Medicine* 151 (1986): 522–24; Spencer Falcon, "Psychopharmacology and PTSD: Sharing a Perspective," presentation at Diagnosis and Management of Post-Traumatic Stress Disorders in the V.A., Baltimore, Aug. 21–23, 1985; Irvin Allen, "PTSD Among Black Vietnam Veterans," *Hospital and Community Psychiatry* 371 (Jan. 1986): 55–60.

2. Falcon, "Psychopharmacology and PTSD"; Yost, "The Psychopharmacologic Treatment of the Delayed Stress Syndrome"; Yost, "The Psychopharmacologic Management of Post-Traumatic Stress Disorder."

3. Falcon, "Psychopharmacology and PTSD"; Yost, "The Psychopharmacologic Treatment of the Delayed Stress Syndrome"; Yost, "The Psychopharmacologic Management of Post-Traumatic Stress Disorder"; Allen, "PTSD Among Black Vietnam Veterans"; Shankar Vedantam, "Mind and Culture: Psychiatry's Missing Diagnosis: Racial Disparities Found in Pinpointing Mental Illness," *Washington Post,* June 28, 2005, A1, 10, 11, 16; R. Guthrie, *Even the Rat Was White: A Historical View of Psychology* (New York: Harper and Row, 1976); D. Atkinson, G.

Morten, and D. Sue, *Counseling American Minorities: A Cross-Cultural Perspective* (Madison, Wis.: Brown and Benchmark, 1993).

4. R. L. Lindauer, R. L., Berthold Gersons, P. M. Els, K. Blom, I. Carlier, K. I. Vrijlanft and M. Olff, "Effects of Brief Eclectic Psychotherapy in Patients with Posttraumatic Stress Disorder: Randomized Clinical Trial," *Journal of Traumatic Stress* 18, no. 3 (June 2005): 205-12.

5. G. Corey, *Theory and Practice of Counseling and Psychotherapy,* 6th ed. (Belmont, Calif.: Wadsworth/Thomson Learning, 2001).

6. Jelinek and Williams, "Post-Traumatic Stress Disorders"; J. Jelinek and T. Williams, "PTSD and Substance Abuse in Vietnam Combat Veterans: Treatment Strategies and Recommendations," *Journal of Substance Abuse Treatment* 1 (1984): 87-97; J. Walker and J. Cavenar, "Vietnam Veterans: Their Problems Continue," *Journal of Nervous and Mental Disease* 170, no. 3 (1982): 174-80.

7. M. J. Jelinek and T. Williams, "Post-Traumatic Stress Disorders and Substance Abuse: Treatment Problems, Strategies and Recommendations," in *Post-Traumatic Stress Disorders: A Handbook for Clinicians,* ed. T. Williams (Cincinnati, Ohio: Disabled American Veterans, 1987), 103-18; Walker and Cavenar, "Vietnam Veterans."

8. Jelinek and Williams, "Post-Traumatic Stress Disorders"; Walker and Cavenar, "Vietnam Veterans."

9. Guthrie, *Even the Rat Was White;* Atkinson et al., *Counseling American Minorities.*

10. Vedantam, "Mind and Culture."

11. Guthrie, *Even the Rat Was White;* Atkinson et al., *Counseling American Minorities.*

12. F. Ochberg, "PTSD Therapy and Victims of Violence," in *Post-Traumatic Stress Disorders,* ed. Williams.

13. Judith Herman, *Trauma and Recovery: The Aftermath of Violence—from Domestic Abuse to Political Terror* (New York: Basic Books, 1992).

14. Tom Williams, "Diagnosis and Treatment of Survivor Guilt," in *Post-Traumatic Stress Disorders,* ed. Williams, 75-92.

15. Williams, ed., *Post Traumatic Stress Disorders.*

16. Candice Williams and Tom Williams, "Family Therapy for Vietnam Veterans," in *The Trauma of War,* ed. Sonnenberg et al., 195-209.

17. M. Harvey, "Stories of Resiliency in Trauma Survivors: The Treatment of Trauma: Advances and Challenges," audiotape from eleventh annual meeting of the International Society for Traumatic Stress, Boston, November 2-6, 1995.

18. Ibid.

19. E. Salter and P. Stallard, "Posttraumatic Growth in Child Survivors of a Road Traffic Accident," *Journal of Traumatic Stress* 178, no. 4 (2004): 335-40.

20. Herman, *Trauma and Recovery.*

21. G. Langer, "Use of Antidepressants in a Long-Term Practice," April 10, 2000, http://abcnews.go.com/onair/WorldNewstonight/poll1100410.htm.

22. Aphrodite Matsakis, *I Can't Get Over It—A Handbook for Trauma Survivors,* 2nd ed. (Oakland, Calif.: New Harbinger Publications, 1996).

23. B. A. van der Kolk, A. McFarlane, and L. Weisaeth, eds., *Traumatic Stress: The Effects of Overwhelming Experience on Mind, Body, and Society* (New York: Guilford Press, 1996).

Index

Italic page numbers refer to the personal stories interspersed throughout the text